THE FIGHTING 30TH DIVISION

THE **FIGHTING 30TH DIVISION**

They Called Them Roosevelt's SS

MARTIN KING, DAVID HILBORN,
AND MICHAEL COLLINS

CASEMATE
Philadelphia & Oxford

Published in the United States of America and Great Britain in 2015 by
CASEMATE PUBLISHERS
908 Darby Road, Havertown, PA 19083
and
10 Hythe Bridge Street, Oxford, OX1 2EW

Copyright 2015 © Martin King, David Hilborn, and Michael Collins

ISBN 978-1-61200-301-6
Digital Edition: ISBN 978-1-61200-302-3

Cataloging-in-publication data is available from the Library of Congress and
the British Library.

10 9 8 7 6 5 4 3 2 1

Printed and bound in the United States of America.

For a complete list of Casemate titles please contact:

CASEMATE PUBLISHERS (US)
Telephone (610) 853-9131, Fax (610) 853-9146
E-mail: casemate@casematepublishing.com

CASEMATE PUBLISHERS (UK)
Telephone (01865) 241249, Fax (01865) 794449
E-mail: casemate-uk@casematepublishing.co.uk

MIX
Paper from
responsible sources
FSC® C011935

CONTENTS

DEDICATION

This volume is dedicated to all the soldiers and surviving veterans of "Old Hickory," the indomitable 30th Infantry Division, and to all Allied military personnel who fought in World War II. Veterans are a finite resource. Honor their memory; take pride in their deeds; and most importantly never forget their sacrifices and their service. Remember! They owe us nothing; we owe them everything.

ACKNOWLEDGMENTS

First, I'd like to thank all the indomitable veterans who generously gave up their valuable time to participate in the writing of this book. Second, many thanks to my co-authors and dear friends, Mike Collins and David Hilborn, for contributing their expertise, knowledge, and frequently-needed moral support. Sincere thanks to Steve Smith, Tara Lichterman, and all at Casemate for taking this project on board. I've had the good fortune to work with some talented editors in the past, but Patti Bonn is by far the best to date. Many thanks to her for turning this manuscript into a book. Grateful thanks to my wife, Freya, for absolutely everything. I should also mention my unruly off-spring, Allycia and Ashley Rae, who sensibly kept well out of my way while I was writing this. My clan, Graham (Joe), Sandra, Debbie, Marc, Rachel, Ben, and Jake, without whom I would have written this anyway, but they're always very supportive. I would also like to thank the wonderful Mrs. Augusta Chiwy for teaching me to care about veterans. Sincere thanks to my dear friends in the US, Commander Jeffrey (Cheeser) Barta; Lt. Col. Jason Nulton; Col. Gregory Julian; Mike and Jim Edwards; Mike O'Niel; Jim Hilborn; and Jim Kraynak, for their continued support and encouragement. Not forgetting my dear friend, Mr. Roland Gaul, of the National Museum of Military History (Luxembourg) for the generous use of his tremendous archive of photographs. Warm thanks to Adjutant Eric "Rony" Lemoine and the men at the "Nuts" cellars in Bastogne who, for some inexplicable reason, always treat me like royalty. Thanks to 589th Field Artillery Battalion veteran John Schaffner; Dirk de Groof; his wife, Kristine; and their kids for occasional entertainment and excellent Single Malt. Many thanks to Volker Dederichs for his expertise

and advice. Last but not least, I'd like to thank Mr. Ed Slotwinski for providing the spark (I didn't forget); also many thanks to his lovely wife, Lisa; their daughter, Elizabeth; and her husband, Cody. Many blessings to you all.
—MARTIN KING

Foremost, I want to thank my co-authors and good friends, Martin King and Michael Collins. They are true gentlemen and I am forever grateful to both for giving me the opportunity to realize a lifelong dream. Thanks to the Casemate team, including Steve Smith, Tara Lichterman, and Libby Braden, as well as to our fantastic editor and partner, Patti Bonn. Special thanks to my wife, Andrea, and to my wonderful children, Matthew and Emma. The three of them are the greatest source of inspiration, pride, and joy in my life. Thanks also to my father, Jim, and to my sister, Jennifer, for their ongoing support and encouragement. I am also grateful to my late mother and "teacher," Mary Gretchen, who is dearly missed. She always said my best contributions would be made through writing. My heartfelt thanks to my Uncle Jim and Cousin Mike whose efforts to tell the story in film of Augusta Chiwy, the "Forgotten Angel of Bastogne," brought Martin King, Mike Collins, and me together. Thanks to my mother-in-law, Linda; father-in-law, Doug (Cdr. USNR Ret.); and the rest of my extended family for their love and support. Posthumous thanks to my wife's grandfather, Cdr. Ernest Graham, who fought the Japanese in the Pacific in WWII from the bridge of a destroyer; and my grandmother, CPO Katherine Hilborn, who served her country during the war and achieved, at the time, a rank held by few women in the US Navy. Both provided inspiration for this book. I am indebted to our friend and Old Hickory veteran, Frank Towers of The 30th Infantry Division Veterans of WWII. Without his active support for this project, and assistance locating living veterans, this book would not have been possible. In his late nineties, Frank still manages to serve as historian and editor of the 30thinfantry.org website which houses a treasure trove of information on the unit. I am also grateful to Warren Watson, who manages the 30th Infantry Division Old Hickory website, oldhickory30th.com, another excellent resource for those interested in the history of the division. Special thanks to Lt. Col. Wes Morrison of the 30th Armored Brigade Combat Team who, along with Frank Towers, kindly agreed to co-write the foreword to the book. Thanks to Jeff Rogers who allowed us to use accounts from his outstanding book, *Old Hickory Recon*, detailing the experiences of veteran Marion Sanford. The assistance provided

by Jim West of Indianamilitary.org; and Matt Rozell and the Teaching History Matters website, teachinghistorymatters.com, was appreciated. Thanks to all of the family members of the noble warriors of the 30th who helped to provide photographs, personal accounts, and memorabilia so that the war stories of their loved ones could be told. Finally, I want to pay homage to all Old Hickorymen, past and present, especially to those who fought and died in WWII. In particular, I owe a debt of gratitude to veterans Francis Currey, Frank Deegan (who passed away before the publication of this book), Frank Denius, Bill Gast, John O'Hare, King Kenny, Richard Lacey, Ed Middleton, Victor Neiland, John Nolan, Marion Sanford, Hank Stairs, and Harold Williams. These men are true American heroes and it has been an honor to tell their stories.
   —DAVID HILBORN

Thank you first off to my two co-authors and great friends, Martin King and David Hilborn. To share in the excitement of finding new bits of information or locating another veteran to interview with you both has been great. Also, thank you both for your patience and support during this project. A big thank you goes out to my lovely wife, Lisa, for her love, encouragement, and understanding during the writing of this book. A special thanks to my mother, Joanne, and father, John, and the rest of the Collins clan: brothers, John and Chris, and their lovely wives, Melissa and Maria, and all of my Collins nieces Morgan, Katie, Keira, Margo, and nephew Henry. Thank you also to the Biros family: my mother-in-law, Sue, and father-in-law, Jim, my sister-in-law, Sarah, and brother-in-law, Tim, and nephew Will. A special thanks goes to the staff at the Siena College Library, especially Gary Thompson, Sean Conley, and John Vallely, who supported me during the writing of this book. Also thank you to Dr. Amy Gelinas and the staff at St. Joseph Central High School for your continued support. Thank you to Chris Begley and Lindsay Silverblatt for letting me stay with you during my trips down to the Archives. Thank you to the 10th Armored Division Veterans Western Association for your support. Thank you Howard Liddic for helping with any problems I had while researching at the Archives. Thank you to Warren Watson of the Old Hickory website for your support, knowledge, and help with photographs for this book. Thank you to Frank Towers for continuing to preserve the 30th Division's history and for co-writing the foreword. Thank you to Lt. Col. Wes Morrison who co-writing the foreword so we will not forget the legacy of the 30th Infantry in today's conflicts. Finally, thank you to the 30th Infantry veterans who shared their story with us, especially my good friend Francis Currey. I hope this book will help memorialize the soldiers who did not return home, but whose sacrifice helped Old Hickory succeed during World War II.

—MICHAEL COLLINS

FOREWORDS

A very thorough research, by the authors, has given credit to the true *heroes* of the battles of Normandy, Aachen, the Bulge, and the Rhine in World War II, the officers and men, at and below the combat battalion level. The generals—like Simpson, Bradley, and Patton—were the planners and leaders, but were never engaged in actual combat. It was the *soldier* who won these battles.

The 30th Infantry Division, named "Old Hickory" and code-named "Custom," was called by historian S. L. A. Marshall the "most outstanding infantry division in the European Theater of Operations (ETO)" during the entire war.

The officers and men of Old Hickory were the product of a civilian army, well trained by competent officers into a cohesive fighting machine that outsmarted the best of the German Army's elite divisions. Although a National Guard unit, it never received the credit to which it was due all through the war; it was always relegated to the bottom of the publicity lists of accomplishments that gave more credit than was due to the Regular Army divisions in the ETO.

A majority of the officers and men of the 30th were from farms and small towns throughout the country, although at the beginning, they were predominantly from North and South Carolina and Tennessee. Consequently they brought with them considerable knowledge of tractors, trucks, and other farm-related vehicles, which gave them enhanced knowledge of military vehicles. Most had a basic knowledge of guns from their experiences in hunting deer, squirrels, and rabbits, making them excellent marksmen.

It is only fitting and proper that these "Old Hickorymen" be given the honor of being the best soldiers to fight against the best that the enemy—the Germans—had to offer.

This book, through its interviews with the heroes of Old Hickory, shows how a group of civilians can overcome the best-trained professional soldiers.

It was the officers and soldiers, the leaders of small combat units, who were the *real* heroes, as noted in this book, and the deeds of these men shall live on forever.

Heroism never goes out of date!

FRANK W. TOWERS
Executive Secretary–Treasurer
Historian and Editor
The 30th Infantry Division Veterans of WWII

———

In February 2004, hundreds of citizen soldiers with the 1st Battalion, 120th Infantry, 30th Brigade Combat Team, waited on a plane taking them to Iraq and Old Hickory's first combat deployment since World War II.

As a young 29-year-old company commander, I searched for something inspirational to say to my soldiers as they boarded to put them at ease. I reached back to the 30th Division's sterling record in World War II as that inspiration and said, "Remember those citizen soldiers of the 120th Infantry Regiment who came before you 60 years ago today. We wear their patch, and we cannot fail."

The combat record of the 30th Infantry Division in the ETO led it to being named the "outstanding infantry division of the ETO" by Colonel S. L. A. Marshall, the official US Army historian for the theater. The citizen soldiers of the 30th Division saved the Normandy breakout by standing firm at Mortain; later, they again stopped Hitler's vaunted *SS* panzer units in the Battle of the Bulge, halting the German advance and thus turning the tide of that pivotal engagement. They were so respected by their German opponents that Axis Sally referred to them as "Roosevelt's *SS*."

Despite such an incredible combat record, the Old Hickory story from World War II remains elusive and often overlooked. This book will help change that. It tells the story of this incredible group of citizen soldiers from the ground level, the soldier's personal view. The World War II veterans interviewed for this book are true citizen soldiers. Most of them served in the

30th for World War II only and then returned to their civilian lives and built the United States we know today. Their story is one that should never be forgotten.

By virtue of my service in the 30th and membership in the 30th Infantry Division Association, I have developed friendships with many of the veterans interviewed for this work. They are humble, accomplished people from all different backgrounds. They all have one thing in common, they love their country; and the 30th, Old Hickory, and all those associated with it.

In 2009, Hank Stairs, a World War II veteran of 1st Battalion, 117th Infantry Regiment, told several of us redeploying to Iraq in 2009, "When you see a long shadow trailing behind you in the desert of Iraq, know it is us; we will always be with you, marching along with Old Hickory." The incredible World War II veterans of the 30th Infantry Division have a story to tell that must not remain in the shadows and this book will help begin to shed light on their incredible experiences.

OLD HICKORY!

CHARLES W. MORRISON
Lieutenant Colonel, Infantry
30th Armored Brigade Combat Team
8 October 2014

INTRODUCTION

Why were they called "Roosevelt's *SS*"? It is, after all, a potentially nefarious reference. Surely this couldn't be regarded as a compliment? Considering the atrocities and infamy attached to this particular section of Adolf Hitler's armed forces, it may have even been considered a slight. It may be argued that it doesn't seem appropriate to compare a reputable US infantry division to the notorious Nazi *SS*. First and foremost it's important to state for the record that the name was not attributed by the Allies who knew them simply as "Old Hickory." That particular handle was first used for Andrew Jackson, who was born near the North/South Carolina border and had earned his reputation as a tenacious Indian fighter and backwoodsman. Jackson later earned great popularity among his fellow countrymen and women when, as a major general, his army defeated the British at the Battle of New Orleans. Jackson's fame increased considerably when he stormed Pensacola and drove the British away once and for all. In recognition of his service Jackson was appointed the first federal territorial governor of Florida and then went on to become a US senator in 1823 before becoming the seventh president of the United States in 1828. He was re-elected in 1832.

Soldiers who initially joined the 30th Infantry Division when it was activated in August 1917 at Camp Sevier, South Carolina, came from the National Guard units of North and South Carolina, Tennessee, and Georgia, the same area where Andrew Jackson grew up.

The original insignia was personally designed by Maj. Gen. George W. Read, who at the time commanded the division, and later commanded II Corps. The patch honors Old Hickory, reflected in the "O" and the "H" that appears on the division's shoulder patch with the Roman numeral "XXX"[30] centrally positioned in royal blue on a background of scarlet. The name was chosen because it was considered as best exemplifying the substantial fighting qualities of soldiers from the previously mentioned states.

After the Normandy campaign, the 30th was often referred to by the Allied army as the "Work Horse of the Western Front." Seasoned *Waffen-SS* commanders themselves initially attributed the *SS* reference to the 30th Division and it stuck for the duration. In a letter to Division Headquarters, Maj. E. L. Glaser of Palm Beach, Florida, suggested changes to the Old Hickory patch. It was reported to *Stars and Stripes* in the following way:

> WITH 30TH DIV. The Joes of the 30th Div. have thrown one of the "Sally's" sallies right back in the Nazi propaganda gal's face. Sally had been saying in her nightly English language broadcast that the 30th boys were "FDR's *SS* Troops." The boys rather fancied the idea. They pointed out they really were Elite Troops, a chosen few and top-notch fighters. Major E. L. Glaser of Palm Beach, Fla., decided to adopt the designation and make a new division patch to go with it. The result was a design, now under consideration at division head-quarters, which combines the O and the H of the 30th's Old Hick-ory with the two flashes of lightning which comprise the *SS* troopers' insignia, and to top it off the President's well-known initials.[1] [This change was never officially authorized, but some troops altered their patches and wore them while they could get away with it. *Au.*]

The "Sally" they referred to was more popularly known as "Axis Sally," Mildred Gillars (born November 29, 1900, Portland, Maine; died June 25, 1988, Columbus, Ohio), an American citizen who had moved to Berlin in 1934. There she became a notorious enemy radio broadcaster alongside peo-ple such as the British "Lord Haw Haw" whose famous introduction, "Ger-many calling, Germany calling," earned him a hangman's noose after WWII.

When they could, troops were entertained by Axis Sally broadcasting from Berlin. She had a very sexy voice and an excellent inventory of popular American music which was alternated with her intelligence reports. "Good morning, Yankees. This is Axis Sally with the tunes that you like to hear and a warm welcome from radio Berlin. I note that the 461st is en route this morning to Linz where you will receive a warm welcome. By the way, Ser-geant Robert Smith, you remember Bill Jones, the guy with the flashy convertible who always had an eye for your wife, Annabelle? Well, they have been seen together frequently over the past few months and last week he moved in with her. Let's take a break here and listen to some Glen Miller." It was not a morale builder for the GIs, even when she was wrong.

In 1949, Mildred Gillars was tried on eight counts of treasonable conduct, but convicted of just one, which was enough to get her locked up until 1961. She died of cancer in 1988. Her radio broadcasts were intended to spread discontent and disillusion among the ranks, but they were largely unsuccessful. And they didn't stop Old Hickory.

The Division was initially created on 18 July 1917, just three months after the United States entered World War I. Existing components of the Tennessee State Militia and National Guard were merged to become the 30th Infantry Division. The battle honors of these component units extended from the Revolutionary War engagement known as the Battle of King's Mountain right up to the Spanish-American battles of San Juan Hill and Santiago. Early in July 1918 they finally arrived at Le Havre, France, and immediately set about training with the British Army in Flanders and Picardy. On the 9th of July they were assigned to hold the line east of Poperinghe in the Dickebusch and Scherpenburg sector to become acquainted with the hell of Flanders fields. Later on they were called on to participate in the second Somme offensive that culminated in the breaking of the almost impenetrable Hindenburg Line. When the armistice arrived at the 11th hour of the 11th day in November 1918, the 30th Division had chalked up approximately half of the medals awarded by the British to US forces in WWI. There were also twelve Medals of Honor.

That was going to be a hard act to follow, but with a new theatre and a new world war to demonstrate their unique talents, the men of the 30th Infantry Division were going to attempt to rise to the challenge and forge an even greater reputation.

The 30th Division arrived in Normandy on 10 June, four days after D-Day. Their initial objective was to replace the battered 29th Division that had been decimated at Omaha Beach. They were put into action almost immediately and were soon being unanimously referred to as the "Work Horse of the Western Front" due to their tenacity in battle against seasoned SS units. They quickly gained the attention of the German commanders who praised their efforts and said that they were operating with the same discipline, intensity, and rigor as the real SS, hence Roosevelt's SS.

By the end of WWII, the 30th Infantry Division had accumulated a remarkable list of battle honors. It spent 282 days in combat earning five battle stars in the Normandy, Northern France, Rhineland, Ardennes-Alsace, and Central Europe campaigns. Ten Presidential Unit Citations were awarded to subordinate units within the division (including the 743rd Tank Battalion and 823rd Tank Destroyer Battalion, both attached to the 30th). Six Old Hickorymen earned Medals of Honor—three posthumously. More than eighty men earned Distinguished Service Crosses, the nation's second highest award for valor. Approximately 20,000 Purple Hearts were awarded to soldiers wounded or killed in action in the ETO. In addition, the division took approximately 53,000 prisoners over the course of its campaigns. At war's end, the entire division was placed fifth on a list of eight divisions up for consideration for the Presidential Unit Citation. It never received this recognition, however, to the intense disappointment of those who served in the unit.[2]

After the war, Colonel S. L. A. Marshall, the official US Army historian for the European Theater of Operations (ETO), reviewed combat records for all US Army infantry divisions serving in the theater and cited the 30th Division as, ". . . the outstanding infantry division in the ETO." This was remarkable because the 30th was a National Guard outfit, not a Regular Army unit. Initially, the Division was a formation comprised of ordinary men. Once in combat, however, the citizen soldiers of the Fighting 30th morphed into warriors. They accomplished truly extraordinary feats, never failing in their missions, and they did so with great gallantry and a degree of efficiency that was unmatched. Colonel Marshall wrote:

16 March 1946

Dear General Hobbs:
Now that I am leaving the service, I thought it might be well to give you the following information for whatever satisfaction you might derive therefrom.

I was historian of the ETO. Toward the end of last fall, for the purpose of breaking the log-jam of paper concerning division presidential unit citations, General Eisenhower instructed me to draw up a rating sheet on the divisions. This entailed in the actual processing that we had to go over the total work of all the more experienced divisions, infantry and armor, and report back to him which divisions we considered had performed the most efficient and consistent battle services.

We so did, and we named certain infantry divisions in the first category and same with armor, and we placed others in a second category, and yet others in a third. The 30th was among five divisions in the first category.

However, we picked the 30th Division No. 1 on the list of first category divisions. It was the combined judgment of the approximately 35 historical officers who had worked on the records and in the field that the 30th had merited this distinction. It was our finding that the 30th had been outstanding in three operations and that we could consistently recommend it for citation on any one of these three occasions. It was further found that it had in no single instance performed discreditably or weakly when considered against the averages of the Theater and that in no single operation had it carried less than its share of the burden or looked bad when compared with the forces on its flanks. We were especially impressed with the fact that it had consistently achieved results without undue wastage of its men.

I do not know whether further honors will come to the 30th. I hope they do. For we had to keep looking at the balance of things always and we felt that the 30th was the outstanding infantry division in the ETO.

Respectfully yours,
/s/ S. L. A. Marshall
Colonel S. L. A. Marshall, GSC
Historian of ETO[3]

PART ONE

NORMANDY AND NORTHERN FRANCE

NORMANDY CAMPAIGN
6 June–24 July 1944

NORTHERN FRANCE CAMPAIGN
25 July–14 September 1944

CHAPTER ONE
HELL IN *LE BOCAGE!*

By June 1944, the 30th Infantry Division had spent four years training intensively for this appointment to meet their battle-hardened German adversaries in France. Now, during that historic summer, while legends and reputations were being made, that training would be put to the ultimate test.

HAROLD WILLIAMS, 105TH ENGINEER COMBAT BATTALION

I was in the motor pool to start with. They put me in Water Purification at the beginning measuring streams, water supply, back flushing, and taking samples. There were three of these units in the 30th Division. One day, they wanted a volunteer to drive an amphibian. We were in Florida and we would practice bridge building. That kind of fascinated me. From then on I was assigned to a 2-1/2-ton truck. We traveled by train from Florida to Tennessee to Camp Forest. It was a tent city. Tullahoma was the name of the town. This was just prior to maneuvers. We had all kinds of training there. Eventually, we held maneuvers that went on for weeks. We were all over Tennessee and maybe even into parts of Kentucky. After finishing maneuvers the Division came out with high standards, really high. Then we were ordered to Indiana, to Camp Atterbury. It was fall and it was getting cold. We were placed in a two-story barracks. Every day we would get up at daybreak, have roll call, and then we would hike with combat bags and rifles. We would hike approximately four to five miles to a firing range. This went on all the time, rain or shine. Before we left we would take some bread, a piece of cheese, and an apple, and away we would go. We would get back from our hike in the evening before dark. This went on into January. We had to report to a set of buildings, where there were officers from Washington who interviewed us on our training and other things. Our ratings were pretty high so it was determined that we were ready to ship out. It leaked out that we were headed to the Pacific. I think it was a deliberate leak. We boarded the train and we started to travel east, so we knew damn well that we were not headed west. We ended up at Camp Myles Standish on the Cape near Boston. It was just a staging area. Some of us got new equipment and new rifles. I can remember going on KP duty and it went around the clock; that's how enormous the camp was.

We were in a state of high secrecy. Trucks took us to south Boston and we boarded ships that were waiting for us. I was on the USS John Ericsson and there were three ships, I believe, that transported the Division. From there we landed in Liverpool, another unit unloaded in Blackpool, and the third one, I believe, on the Clyde in Scotland. From there we moved by train east to London. The Division was broken up when we got there, meaning some were bivouacked in separate towns. We didn't operate as a whole. We went into London and there was an air raid going on. The city was being bombed and we spent the night there in the yards. We waited until it was over, then we proceeded to the town of Win- chester. We hadn't had a shower in two weeks, since we had gotten on the boat. We were packed in like sardines and we needed showers pretty badly. We were quartered in Quonset huts. We got our showers in the morning and went down to the chow line. A whistle blew shortly after and they called all drivers to fall out. The drivers fell out in an area in the front near the curb and the motor pool officer came by with a jeep. As our name was called from the roster each one of us got into the jeep and drove it a foot or two. We backed it up and then got out. This qualified us for driving in the U.K.![1]

KING KENNY, RECONNAISSANCE PLATOON, 823RD TANK DESTROYER BATTALION

I got a draft notice when I was 18, but before I was called up I went down to the enlistment center and enlisted in the Army on 13 January 1943. We went to Texas in a Pullman car with two guys to a bunk, upper and lower—you had never met the guy before in your life. We went to Brownwood, Texas; to Camp Bowie; and then on to Camp Hood (now Fort Hood) for advanced training. That went on through the summer and it was very hot. We then went down to Camp Claiborne, Louisiana, to go on maneuvers. When we finished, we were given ten days' leave. When we got back we went on to Boston and Camp Myles Standish which we left in April. If my memory is correct, we either landed or were at sea on Easter Sunday in 1943.

We landed in Liverpool north of London and got on trains headed to a town named Hereford. We unloaded and formed one whole battalion at the station. I remember some little kids coming by in their beanies, short pants, and jackets and one kid said, "Hey look they're Scots!" and another kid said, "They're Aussies!" and finally one kid said, "They're Yanks!" We stayed in civilian homes. Our officers came from Fort Riley, Kansas. Initially my unit was Headquarters Company and they formed a Reconnaissance Company. I was in the 2nd Platoon of Reconnaissance Company, 823rd Tank Destroyer Battalion. My rank at that time was private. Ultimately I was a buck sergeant and squad leader.

Initially, the 823rd used half-tracks towing the three-inch anti-tank gun. The towed guns were very effective at Mortain and did much damage. The battalion had 36 guns, each company had 12 three-inch guns. The difficulty in operating towed guns was digging in the trails so that they were anchored. They had tremendous recoil when firing. Later, and I don't know when, we got some M10s. I don't know how many M10s we had at the time, but I know that the M10s were as effective as the towed guns—it depended who was calling the shots.

Theoretically, Recon was the eyes and ears of the battalion. Normally, we had one jeep up front called "the point," another jeep behind it, then two M8s. The M8 had a 37mm cannon with a .50-caliber machine gun on the turret. It had a driver, a radioman, a gunner, and a commander. Two more jeeps would follow including what we called "getaway jeeps." That was our mobile recon platoon. As recon, however, we did some walking and we had to get out a good deal.[2]

ED MIDDLETON, 730TH ORDNANCE COMPANY

Based on training in several mechanical trades in the six years prior to Army induction in April 1941, I was transferred to Ordnance and reported to the 30th in December 1943 at Camp Attlebury, Indiana. There the unit was preparing for departure for Europe. We sailed out of Boston on Lincoln's Birthday, 12 February, and landed in Scotland on Washington's Birthday on 22 February. My ship was a South American cruise liner that was part of one of the largest convoys of ships to sail.

From there we went to the south of England, and we set up our operation. All of the troops going over in that convoy took only personal equipment, in other words, their weapons and their clothing and things like that. Our job when we got to England was to go to all the supply depots and pick up equipment to distribute to the division. My job was armament maintenance officer. I was a second lieutenant at the time, and I had just been commissioned and transferred to ordnance from anti-aircraft. We then moved up to Central England and continued drawing the organization's equipment, distributing it to the troops. Armament included weapons and instruments that the troops needed for their combat missions.[3]

FRANK DENIUS, BATTERY C, 230TH FIELD ARTILLERY BATTALION

After four years of Junior ROTC, I had Senior ROTC at the Citadel and was inducted for active duty when I was 18 on June 1, 1943. I was a forward observer. I went through instrument and survey training at Camp Roberts, California. I was also Chief of Detail in a field artillery battery and had additional responsibilities as a forward observer. I went to England with all kinds of engineers, infantry and every form of service. I was selected in England, along with about 30 others, to go through Ranger training. After Ranger training I was assigned to the 30th Infantry Division. I joined the 30th six weeks before the invasion.[4]

Men from the 743rd Tank Battalion who landed in support of the 116th Regimental Combat Team at Omaha Beach on D-Day were eventually transferred to the 30th Division after refitting, and fought alongside them during the Normandy campaign. On the 6th of June they were huddled together trying to remain vertical as relentless buffeting waves of the English Channel battered the sides of their LCTs (Landing Craft Tank) and caused many of them to wretch violently. Gradually the ominous sight of the approaching beach came into view. From this point the die had been cast and there was no turning back. From the night's assembly area where the invasion craft had gathered, then from a line of departure in the Bay of the Seine, the assault force of the 743rd Tank Battalion moved tenuously toward all-out combat.

WILLIAM GAST, COMPANY A, 743RD TANK BATTALION

A tank weighs approximately 35 tons. That's 70,000 lbs! Our first tanks had a cast hull with a 75mm main gun, a .30-caliber machine gun mounted beside it on the right, and another .30-caliber machine gun, known as a bow gun, which the assistant driver operated. There was also a .50-caliber machine gun mounted on top of the turret with a 360-degree traverse that the tank commander could use as direct fire or anti-aircraft. A little later we received a tank with a welded hull. It had more armor plate and a lower silhouette of the turret. Later this same tank came with a 76mm main gun. They all had two levers that came up from the floor that were used to steer and brake; a clutch; an accelerator petal; also a gear shift lever with five speeds forward and one reverse. By the way, the transmission was unsynchronized. Just to the left of the driver was the instrument panel. These tanks had four different engine configurations. First was five six-cylinder Chrysler Marine engines mounted in a series. Second was a diesel engine. Third was a nine-cylinder Wright Continental Whirlwind Radial engine. Fourth was a 500-horsepower Ford V/8. We had rubber-cleated tracks, also steel-cleated tracks. We were taught how to remove and replace a track and also a cleat when needed. The gas tank holds about 250 gallons. For my gas mileage, I got about two gallons per mile. Out on an open, level, hard-surfaced road I could get the tank up to about 35 miles per hour, top speed. Each tank has a crew of five men: driver, assistant driver, gunner, assistant gunner, and a tank commander. Our tank was a Sherman M4 Medium Tank.

The channel was very rough. It was cold, misty, and wet. We were getting nervous. Because the hours were dragging on, we threw a tarp under the tank to try to get some sleep. Too much tension!

Through the night we became friendly with the LCT captain. We got to talking about getting the LCT in close enough to the beach so when the ramp was lowered, and we drove our tanks off, they would not be submerged. He promised he would get us close enough.

Now it's just around 0600 hours in the morning and as we looked out over the side of our LCT there were boats and crafts as far as you could see. "Mount up and get your engines started." This is it! The Captain of the LCT did as he promised. The front ramp was lowered and the first tank drove off. Then I drove down the ramp and I could feel my tracks turning . . . then they took hold of the bottom of the channel and I was able to move forward. As I found out later, the water had all kinds of metal obstacles to prevent us from coming onto the beach. The beach was loaded with everything you could think of to keep us from advancing.

Now my hatch is closed and sealed. How can I see? In the middle of my hatch was a slit with a little hinged cover. I was able to push a periscope up through this slit by hand. Inside I had a little window about three inches high and about six inches wide for me to see outside. For me to be able to look around I had to manually push it forward and backward to see up and down. Turn it to left or right to see in those directions.

In the meantime I had to drive the tank. I had two levers that came up from the floor. I pulled on the right one to go right, pulled on the left one to go left and pulled on both together to stop the tank. Sometimes it took both hands just to pull one lever. In addition, I had to operate a clutch with my left foot, and an accelerator pedal with my right foot.

Then there was the gear shift lever. I had five speeds forward and one reverse, which also took both hands to operate. We had intercom radios in the tank that didn't work most of the time. So, the only one who could really see was the tank commander who would have to stick his head up out of the turret. He had a very dangerous job. He told me where to drive by kicking me on the right shoulder to go right or the left shoulder to go left. He would have to hang on to the turret rim with both hands and put both feet on my shoulders for me to back up. Plus he had to see from which direction the firing was coming to tell our gunner where to concentrate his firing. I could hear the machine-gun bullets hitting our tank, it sounded like throwing marbles at a car. I could feel the big shells exploding in front and beside us. It would make the tank shake.

By dusk we finally made it up to the wall. That's as far as we could go. Up against the wall we were protected from direct fire, and started to get a little organized. We learned that out of 15 tanks of A Company, five of us made it. I have something that bothers me to this day. The beach was covered with dead and wounded soldiers. There is no way of telling if I ran over any of them with my tank.

Pictures . . . video games . . . movies . . . words . . . they simply do not convey the feeling of fear . . . the shock . . . the stench . . . the noise, the horror and the tragedy . . . the injured . . . the suffering . . . the dying . . . the dead!

Sometime during the night the engineers were able to blast enough of the wall away, enabling us to exit the beach the next morning and get on top of the bluff.[5]

At this moment, the Shermans were still unavailable, immobilized within the steel sides of their Navy's LCTs. Two companies of tanks had been especially waterproofed, equipped with top-secret canvas sheathing and propeller drives which would allow them to "swim in" to the beach under their own power when the box-nosed ramps of the LCTs were dropped in deep water offshore. They were called Duplex Drive (DD) tanks. These had worked perfectly well on the lakes in northern England where there were no waves. The low free-board (height of deck above the water) meant that the tank needed relatively calm water to avoid being swamped. Emergency gear was given to the crew which included an amphibious tank escape apparatus as well as inflatable rafts, in case the tank began sinking. Crews also had been trained to escape from a submerged tank. The tanks maximum water speed was quite slow, only four knots, and the DDs had inherent difficulties with steering while afloat. In the entire D-Day operation, 290 DD tanks were used. Out of those, 120 were launched at sea and 42 of these floundered and sank as they failed to negotiate the churning seas of the English Channel. Approximately 140 DD tanks were launched in very shallow water or directly on the shore.

Now it was the turn of the 743rd Tank Battalion's LCTs to go. Each one was loaded to capacity. Each carrying four medium tanks and their crews, the amphibious vanguard tenuously approached the shore. Above their heads German artillery boomed and shells exploded in close proximity, causing the LCTs to pitch and dip violently and shower the GIs waiting to disembark with asphyxiating sea spray.

FRANK HARPER, COMPANY C, 743RD TANK BATTALION

When we landed on Omaha Beach we went in with the troops. The Channel was so rough . . . we were supposed to go in with the engineers. People were everywhere and a lot of our tanks never made it to the beach itself because of the water. A lot of them sank right before they hit the beach and a few of them got hit.

If I remember right, we got hit and it disabled the tank. Then we scrambled on foot. We all went together and got what tanks we could past the beach and up the hill. I went to work immediately on the gasoline engines that run the generator that kept the batteries up. There wasn't room for all of us to go in the good tanks that were still in action. So we filled in where we could until we got the tanks ready to go. Some the tanks just had tracks off of them and they had to be repaired but the service company didn't go in with us. They came in the next day, as I remember.[6]

Before they banged down their hatches, tankers of the 743rd on the invasion boats narrowed their eyes in an attempt to focus on the detail that was emerging on the indistinct horizon ahead of the plunging craft. From behind them they heard the boom of intense artillery barrages being delivered from the armada of warships. As they negotiated the buffeting waves it was possible to discern orange flashes from shells impacting against the Normandy beaches. The tankers anxiously pulled the brims of their helmets down over their faces and gritted their teeth. This was it, they were finally going ashore.

Within moments German coastal guns had elevated their firing angle and started to respond in earnest, the first salvos ripping into the surf at short range just off the beach. Other German gunners attempted to stem the first advance wave of combat engineers who were vainly attempting to tackle murderous underwater obstacles such as barbed wire; and anti-tank and anti-personnel mines. Sherman tanks, half-tracks, and trucks of the 743rd were the first armor to attempt that hellish strip of sand that would become known *ad infinitum* as Omaha Beach. This was just the beginning of a long and terrible fight for men of the 30th Division that would endure almost without pause until the end of the war in May 1945.

The first actual 30th Division unit to arrive at Omaha Beach on D-Day +4 was the 230th Field Artillery Battalion. They had been sent to replace an artillery battalion of the 29th Division that had lost most of its pieces in the choppy English Channel off the coast of Grandcamp-les-Bains. Other units from the 30th Division arrived in France during the night of 13/14 June. The first casualties in the 30th Division were incurred when a Landing Ship Tank (LST) carrying members of the 113th Field Artillery Battalion struck a German mine just off the Normandy coast. The final toll for that unfortunate incident was two killed, eight wounded, and 20 missing. It wouldn't be long, however, before the entire division was thrown into the fray.

ED MIDDLETON, 730TH ORDNANCE COMPANY

When the invasion of France began on 6 June, we were still in England. We sent a task force in behind the invasion as part of the 29th Infantry Division. In part of that task force was a field artillery battalion and one of their batteries discovered they had a weapon that was unsafe to fire, a 105mm howitzer. We were waiting in England for orders to come over, so they sent for me to bring my spare 105mm howitzers to replace the one that was out of action. We got priority to sail from Portsmouth across to the beach. We arrived late on D+1 and got priority to land. We landed and traveled overnight, under black-out conditions, until we got to our bivouac area. There we found out where the out-of-action howitzer was and went to fix it. It was damaged in the bore a third of the way up. On inspection I determined that it had been fired, since it carried away the prior material, so I asked them to pick a target to fire the weapon along with the other three to see how they fired together. After doing that we determined that the howitzer was still safe to fire. So instead of replacing it, I left it with them. From then on, I would take a group of small arms repairmen, along with parts and cleaning materials, and go up to the infantry squad in reserve and make sure that their weapons were in good order.

We also kept visiting the field artillery battalion to make sure the howitzers were firing correctly. At first there wasn't too much show of wear, however, it turned out that in the breach mechanism pieces kept chipping off and the battery's barrels had to be replaced. During the course of the war, I replaced all 48 of the battery's barrels. That was primarily my job when we got ashore.

We were also supposed to have extra weapons and supplies for the troops. We ran out very quickly, so we established battlefield recovery and I had all the frontline troops collect army ordnance—ours and the enemy's—and they let us know where it was. We picked it up and took care of it. By the time we got to the Ardennes and the Battle of the Bulge, I had a 2-1/2-ton-truckload of M1 rifles which I distributed to the backup troops who were coming up to help us. Basically, it was a routine operation. We would be close to the front lines and I was far enough forward that I did not have to wear a tie, but I was far enough back not to get shot at every day. When we got to a town, some of the locals would come as a group and ask us to go to different locations to find Germans that were still around.

After the invasion, St. Lô was the first major city that was liberated and the 30th was the lead division for that operation. As we went forward, however, there was a river on the left and another division on the right, so we were pinched out.[7]

FRANK DENIUS, BATTERY C, 230TH FIELD ARTILLERY BATTALION

Forward Observing: The forward observer accompanied leading infantry units to observe targets, in either an attacking or defensive mode, and to direct artillery fire in support of the infantry. In order to see targets, forward observers needed to advance with the infantry. If there was a church steeple, I would be in it observing the enemy targets and directing artillery fire onto those targets. Once a target was observed, whether it was German infantry or tanks, I would look at coordinates on my map and then relay them to the artillery Fire Direction Center that was seven or eight miles behind the front lines. I'd say, "Fire Mission," to my radio operator, Sergeant Sherman Goldstein, who communicated it to the Fire Direction Center. Then I would give them the coordinates for the target. The artillery would then fire a round and I would observe where it hit. Depending where it hit, I would adjust fire onto the target. When the round landed in the target area I would give another command, "Fire for Effect." That meant the target was sighted and the adjusted fire had landed on the target. When that command was given, the Fire Direction Center would call back, "On the Way" to let us know artillery fire was on its way to the target.

My unit, the 230th Field Artillery, was a 105mm howitzer battalion. There were three 105mm battalions in the 30th Infantry Division. Each one of the three supported an infantry regiment and there were three regiments in the 30th. The 230th supported the 120th Infantry Regiment, but that did not necessarily mean that we only fired for the 120th. We would fire for any regiment in the division that was in an attacking or defensive position. The 120th Infantry and the 230th Field Artillery were known as the 120th Regimental Combat Team. Ninety percent of time, as a forward observer, I was with the lead battalion and the lead company of that battalion in the attack.

We were not infantry. Rather, we were attached to them. Sometimes we had a lieutenant in charge of our party. We had a 100-pound radio with a 15-foot high antenna. Half of the 100 pounds was the radio and the other half was the battery. A telephone and microphone were attached to the radio. We had to attach the battery pack to it and then run up the antenna. It not only exposed us when we were in the open, but it was also difficult to get into position. The radio was pretty reliable, but the charge in the battery pack didn't last long, particularly in cold weather. To charge it, we would connect it to the electrical system of our jeep when possible.

I had a close connection with the infantry company commander. He was the guy I had to be close to because he knew from his scouts and leading infantry where the enemy was. I was with him both on the attack and on the defense, along with Sergeant Goldstein. Sometimes terrain would separate us and we couldn't gather together. One of the things that made the 30th so successful was that every time we went into defensive positions and dug in, I pre-adjusted artillery fire with the help of Sergeant Goldstein on likely counterattack locations in front of our infantry. In other words, if there were roads or trails that might lead tanks towards our position, I zeroed in those areas ahead of time. I referred to these pre-adjusted areas as something like "Emergency Barrage 1" or "Emergency Barrage 6." At night, if we heard noise in those areas, I would just call into the Fire Direction Center, "Fire Emergency Barrage 6," and I would have rounds on that target in two to three minutes. There was never a time when I didn't automatically pre-adjust protective emergency barrages, this was standard operating procedure. It was very difficult to adjust fire at night, particularly when we were under attack, so these emergency barrages worked well.

Landing in France on Omaha Beach: *The US 1st Infantry Division and the US 29th Infantry Division were the initial units that landed on Omaha Beach. My unit, the 30th Infantry Division, was in Corps Reserve. That meant that in the event the 1st or 29th suffered heavy casualties (which the 29th and 1st did) then we would have to be rushed in. This happened and the 230th Field Artillery Battalion was rushed in to support a regiment of the 29th Division, I believe it was the 115th Infantry Regiment. They suffered terrible casualties and lost their artillery while landing on Omaha.*

The 230th moved from Southampton to the Channel to Omaha Beach. My party went in on a British ship and then we transferred by rope ladders into LCIs (Landing Craft Infantry) for the trip to Omaha. I remember climbing down the ladder into the LCI. You had to know how to handle the weight of your equipment, your balance, and your footing. But most importantly, you had to grab hold of the vertical strands of the rope because if you had the parallel sides the guy above you would step on your hands. You had to be very careful. The sea was rough and the ladder swung out. I had to jump the last six to eight feet into the LCI, which was rolling and shaking. Then we all got seasick going in. The LCI had a ramp which lowered and we went out the front.

It was chaotic on the beach. I saw a lot of dead and wounded GIs. We were under artillery and mortar fire from the Germans. A few German aircraft came over but they weren't the problem. The real issue was that German artillery was still coming in. It was harassment fire because they didn't have observation on us. Scaling the cliff on Omaha Beach was one of those things I will always re-member. We climbed the cliffs and joined the 29th, which had moved inland by what I think was the second day. We moved in and provided artillery support for them for the next six days. We didn't know those guys so they had to get to know us and we had to get to know them under combat conditions. The 30th Division eventually started to land on the second and third days, and after the sixth day the 230th rejoined the 30th Division.[8]

MARION SANFORD, 30TH CAVALRY RECONNAISSANCE TROOP (MECHANIZED)

They had briefed us, but they didn't take us out on D-Day. On D+4 [10 June] we got on an LCT and started toward France. We got in sometime in the after-noon. The LCT that I was on lowered the front end of it and a jeep went off [the ramp]. That was the last time we saw that jeep; I don't know how deep the water was. Two British guys were operating the LCT. One of them said, "I think it's too deep, mate." We moved down [the beach] and we got in that time. We went up [toward the front]. There wasn't any small arms fire going on, but artillery and mortar were coming in real heavy as we were going off the beach. I rode the half-track, winding around that steep hill. When we got on top, we had to stop because of the traffic in front of us. My vehicle caught fire because of the way we'd water-proofed it. I used my fire extinguisher; a man from another vehicle threw me one and I used it, but there was still a little bit of fire. Where we [had] stopped, I looked over in a ditch and there was some water and mud. I thought I'd jump down there and get some water and mud and put it out. I jumped down there and I looked to my right and about two feet from me was a sign with a skull and crossed bones on it. It was a land-mine sign. I don't believe I touched the ground until I got back on that vehicle. I said, "Let it burn."[9]

KING KENNY, RECONNAISSANCE PLATOON, 823RD TANK DESTROYER BATTALION

We left Hereford on June 4th in the evening, went down the road quite a way and then bivouacked and pitched tents in a field. The next day we formed our battalion unit. Major General Hobbs, the CO of the 30th Infantry Division, made a speech that the 823rd was now part of the 30th Infantry Division and it would be the tank destroyer battalion for the division. We then went on into Portsmouth and I remember it raining like the dickens. It was fenced and once you went in there, you were locked in. We went into a tent and there was a map up. They said there were going to be friendly troops on your right and on your left and anything in front is fair game.

Recon went in first. We went over on LSTs. I looked back and I remember the number on ours was 357. We landed and somebody from the 29th Infantry Division took us up to a hill and said, "Wait here." Later, a jeep came up with a trailer with some hot food in it and they fed us. The same jeep and trailer that brought the food went back up the hill, and when it came back down it was loaded with bodies! So then we went up the hill and filled in for either L or K Company of the 116th Infantry Regiment (29th Division) which had been in the first wave of the invasion and had many KIA. We were with them for maybe two or three days. Then we came down to a marshaling area for our unit. That's where we took our first casualties. There was some artillery behind us and misfired and hit some trees. Everybody used to "poo-poo" the idea that our battalion doctor was an OB-GYN, but this guy came up and started treating the fellas who had been hit by shrapnel from the shells that had been hitting the trees. He really did a masterful job treating those guys. From that day forward the doctor was well received. But we never needed him for any GYN stuff![10]

FRANK TOWERS, COMPANY M, 120TH INFANTRY REGIMENT

As we approached the beach, we saw no cliffs or a wide beach. We were facing west when we were supposed to be facing south. We thought we were in the wrong place. The Service Company vehicles got off first, and then the 3rd Battalion troops unloaded. We were all on the beach. The beachmaster got together with our battalion commander and, looking at the chart, determined we were at the wrong beach. We were supposed to have landed on Omaha Beach.

There was a drop of about a foot from the ramp on the ship to the beach. The vehicles could get off the ship okay but they could not get back on; they were stranded. Our captain decided he would take Service Company down to where we were supposed to be while the rest of our battalion re-boarded ship for the trip over to Omaha Beach. We were about five or six hours late when we landed on Omaha. All of the rest of the regiments had cleared out and gone to their appointed bivouac areas, but we didn't know where they were. Being one of those spare wheels of the company, the battalion commander pointed to me to take his jeep and go up forward to find where the division was bivouacked and then to report back to him. I spoke with some of the guys along the road and I finally found the division's bivouac area. It was in the middle of hedgerow country.[11]

MARVIN SMITH, COMPANY K, 120TH INFANTRY REGIMENT

One stormy day, 6 June, we started to see hundreds and hundreds of US and British fighter and bomber planes, perhaps numbering into the thousands, fly over our location. Only days earlier, we had the great British general and hero, Monty Montgomery, and others came to speak to us. Montgomery ended his speech with the phrase "Good hunting!" We suspected that the invasion was at hand.

Then came that day, orders to entrain, and we were sent to the coast. There we were pledged to extreme secrecy and kept in tents and barracks which were highly camouflaged. We knew we were soon to enter into that great struggle on the continent of Europe. My first real fear came as we were briefed on a large-scale map showing our landing area, and that the enemy opposing us would likely be a panzer division. The very word "panzer" struck fear into our hearts—we knew what it meant.

Six days after D-Day, our turn came. We loaded on an LSI and headed for France! Our battalion commander had orders to go to Omaha Beach. The ship captain had conflicting orders to go to Utah Beach, 20 miles from Omaha Beach. Par for the course, SNAFU (Situation Normal All Fouled Up). In case of conflicting orders the ship captain's orders are superior, so we went to Utah Beach. We talked to the beachmaster while an enemy shell or two landed nearby. He told us to land here and walk to Omaha Beach, partly through enemy-held territory, or we could remain on ship and he would countermand the ship captain, to take us to Omaha Beach by sea. We chose the ship route.

As we neared Omaha Beach, we saw wrecked ships protruding out of the water, and low-flying blimps moored to ships to prevent low-flying enemy attacks. There was debris of all kinds from initial landings six days earlier. Most of the bodies had been removed by this time.

I noticed a large cliff on our right, overlooking Omaha Beach. An occasional enemy shell landed in the area. Then the large ramp was let down in the front. We stepped out into the water three or four feet deep, waded ashore, and started up the canyon road, marching inland. We stopped at the first town, Isigny, where there was a canteen. We loaded up on cigarettes and other supplies. There I was surprised to see my good friend, John Carbin, with Division Headquarters. There were hundreds of GIs' jeeps, trucks, tanks, etc. We were ordered to move forward on foot up a narrow blacktop road. It seemed to me Company K was all alone. Or perhaps we were leading the battalion up the road. I remember an eerie dark forest on my left for several miles.[12]

The 30th Division was promptly brought into the area between the Vire and Taute Rivers. As V Corps prepared to launch an attack toward St. Lô, General Omar Bradley unexpectedly ordered this to be brought to a halt. Despite having beaten off an attack by the *17th SS-Panzer-Grenadier Division,* the link between his two corps located between Carentan and Isigny was still scanty. There was still a distinct possibility, moreover, that the German forces would reassert themselves and launch a new assault on the US positions there. XIX Corps was just becoming operational in this area and it was necessary to adjust troop assignments between the corps. By 0100 hours on 15 June, a hastily-improvised combat team from the 120th Infantry Regiment was assembled and prepared. The freshly arrived 120th had occupied a 7,500-yard sector previously held by the airborne troops of the 501st. On two recent occasions the area had been the scene of some intense fighting. It was imperative to discern the size and composition of German forces in the vicinity, so at 0630 hours an artillery barrage was launched by the 230th and four other field artillery battalions, supported by the battleships of the Western Naval Task Force.

An hour later Allied fighter-bombers swooped on enemy positions in the path of advance and at 0800 hours, the infantry and tanks moved out. It was a slightly ignominious start to the 30th Division's combat because the convoy that transported the division commander, Major General Leland Hobbs, and his staff officers managed to get lost and inadvertently became the spearhead of the assault reaching the forward assembly area of the tanks before deducing that they'd taken the wrong road. At this time, Company D was attached to the 3rd Battalion because neither the latter's heavy weapons company nor the 1st Battalion's rifle company had arrived in time to join in the activities.

FRANK DEEGAN, COMPANY D, 119TH INFANTRY REGIMENT

We were sitting somewhere in Normandy for a week or two, I never knew where I was. When we shoved off through another outfit's lines, I don't know who they were, I remember seeing a young soldier who was dead. We passed his body. I was 19 at the time and this guy looked like he was my kid brother; he was so young. That was my first impression we were in a war (other than a sniper who took a shot at us when we moved out from our defensive position). I felt sorry for him. He looked younger than my brother, about 13 or 14. I have always remembered his face because he looked like he was smiling.[13]

As soon as the leading squads had surreptitiously inched past the railroad leading east from Carentan they ran into concerted German opposition. The village of Lenauderie, less than a mile south of the tracks, appeared to be the epicenter of German activity, but after a 40-minute battle this was effectively eradicated by 2nd Battalion, 119th Infantry Regiment; by midday the battalion had crept forward another quarter-mile to the outskirts of Montmartin en Graignes. The men from Old Hickory, supported by the 743rd Tank Battalion, headed towards a church steeple towering above the centuries-old farm buildings and immediately became engaged in some hard fighting. These village squares and churches were going to become very familiar sights to the US troops over the coming weeks and months. As the 2nd Battalion fought their way into the center of the village it took another hour before they were in possession of it.

After successfully occupying Montmartin en Graignes, the 2nd Battalion got to work securing the position before nightfall. Earlier on, sometime around mid-afternoon, the newly-arrived 1st Battalion, 119th, had worked its way down through sporadic artillery fire and passed through the 2nd Battalion's positions before pivoting southeast to force their way towards a small enclave of houses located close to the Vire River. Meanwhile, the 3rd Battalion of the 120th Infantry Regiment was having its own baptism of fire and discovering the bane of all the Allied divisions currently in Normandy, *"Le Bocage!"* This meant they were enduring the painstaking hedgerow to hedgerow fighting that came to epitomize the fighting in Normandy and was equally detrimental to all sides. The 3rd Battalion made slow but steady progress against stiff resistance until they reached the village of La Compte, which lay beside the highway a half-mile south of Montmartin. A wide sweep to the west by a platoon of tanks and a reinforced platoon of infantry brought pressure on the town from the flank and as the afternoon drew to a close, a mopping up operation got underway. At the end of the day the 120th had occupied Monmartin en Graignes and the high ground north of the Vire et Taute Canal.

When the 117th Infantry Regiment landed in France it was moved into an assembly area in the vicinity of Neuilly la Forêt. The 117th's 2nd Battalion organized a defensive position along the Vire River, extending from Neuilly la Perot approximately 2,000 yards south. Company G, 117th Infantry, was motorized and designated as Corps Reserve. On 16 June 1944, the regiment moved into an assembly area in the vicinity of Lison, France, with orders to prepare for an attack across the Vire River on the morning of 17 June. The attack order was initially postponed for 24 hours and then postponed indefinitely while the 3rd Battalion organized an active defensive position along the Vire River, extending from Airel north to Reuilly la Ferret. The 117th, minus its 3rd Battalion, was allocated as part of the Corps Reserve. For the remainder of the month the 1st and 3rd Battalions would be involved in some minor skirmishes, but on the whole their activities would be confined to rigorous patrolling and recon of the area.

The 30th Division was led by the 120th Infantry Regiment and during the following days the rest arrived in dribs and drabs until, by 17 June, the entire division was safely on land. One of the first German units they encountered was the *SS-Panzer-Grenadier Regiment 38* of the *17th SS-Panzergrenadier Division "Götz von Berlichingen."* This particular division had been formed in France from remnants of other divisions and consisted of mainly Rumanian and French volunteers. Collectively it was under the direct command of *LXXX Corps,* part of *Generalfeldmarschall* (general of the army) Gerd von Rundstedt's *Army Group D,* and it was going to be seriously decimated in the ensuing Normandy battles. This would be in no small part thanks to the 30th Division who quickly discovered that fighting between the centuries-old tight hedgerows of the Normandy countryside, *Le Bocage,* was going to demand an almost complete revision of tactics.

MARION SANFORD, 30TH CAVALRY RECONNAISSANCE TROOP (MECHANIZED)

We spent that first night, all night, without light, cleaning the waterproofing off that we'd put on. Every evening for the first 27 out of 30 days, the airplane came, which we called "Bed-Check Charlie." Of course, he had come that first night, too.

We were in the hedgerows of Normandy. We spent the first few days getting everything cleaned up to go. Then on a Sunday afternoon, several days after we'd gotten there, the Germans counterattacked at St. Jean de Daye. That was our first action. They tried to cut the beachhead in two, but they didn't get through. After that, we started attacking. We'd stay behind the hedgerows and the Germans were behind the next hedgerow. A lot of times the fenced-in land was not over half an acre; sometimes not that much. You could hear the Germans talking and I'm sure they heard us at times, too.[14]

FRANK DENIUS, BATTERY C, 230TH FIELD ARTILLERY BATTALION

Silver Star Action: The 120th Infantry Regiment moved inland behind the 29th Infantry Division. We made a midnight march around to the west of Omaha Beach and jumped off the next morning in a surprise attack. We were on the right flank, or west, of the 29th Division. Our objective was to capture a location along a highway that headed to Ste. Mère Église. We were successful in the attack, most likely because we surprised the Germans with the midnight march and went around their main defensive positions which were strung out to defend against the 29th.

We then found ourselves right out in the middle of hedgerow country. Those fields were 75–100 yards wide and square in shape. Apple trees, orchards, and cattle were in them. There were also dead cows everywhere from artillery fire. The Germans defended each hedgerow and each one made for a perfect defense. We would fight directly across the hedgerow from them and they would line up a machine gun and dig in a tank at the corners. You had to crawl over those hedgerows to advance. As you went over you faced crossfire from tanks, machine guns, and rifles. My job as an artillery forward observer was to try to detect the German defensive positions in the line of hedgerows and direct artillery fire into those areas, without causing damage or casualties among our troops.

On 17 July, I was with Lieutenant Miller, an artillery lieutenant serving, as his assistant forward observer, when he was killed by machine-gun fire right in front of me. He had peered over the hedgerow with his binoculars which reflected light and they detected him. Goldstein and I had half the radio each, carrying it forward and calling behind Lieutenant Miller. When he was killed by machine-gun fire I was able to get into position to direct artillery with the help of radio Sergeant Goldstein, and knocked out the German infantry and the tanks. We had to call out from the hedgerow to ask the infantry who were in the next hedgerow where the enemy tanks and infantry were dug in. Once they were knocked out, our troops were able to advance, and for that action I was awarded my first Silver Star.[15]

The 30th Division understood full well that they would have to establish new methods of fighting in this new checkerboard landscape crisscrossed by thick hedgerows and interspersed by small, age-old villages. They started by organizing a new, more-effective telecommunications network by mounting telephones on the outsides of their tanks so that supporting infantry could talk directly to the tank crews. Infantrymen strapped one phone onto the rear of a Sherman's back deck then connected it by wire to a second phone located inside the tank's turret. By using such back-deck telephones, soldiers could direct tankers against concealed German positions. This did have some drawbacks, however, because infantrymen were forced to expose themselves to enemy fire while talking on these back-deck telephones. Some units attempted to solve the problem by letting a long strand of communications wire trail behind the tanks. Infantrymen then connected a field telephone to the end of the trailing wires and talked with the tank's crews from a safer position. Dangling wires, though, often accidentally broke, pulled loose from the tanks, or got entangled in the tanks' treads. Infantrymen and tank crews discovered the best way to communicate was through the tanks interphone boxes, which were connected directly into the tanks' intercom systems, and were then mounted on each Sherman's back deck in empty ammunition containers. To talk with the tankers, infantrymen simply plugged a radio handset into the interphone boxes. The handsets' long cords permitted soldiers to lie down behind or underneath the tanks to protect themselves while talking to the tank crews. This capacity for innovation was ubiquitous in the Allied forces at the time and was a direct contradiction of the largely intransigent methods of combat employed by the Axis forces. As the months wore on, tanks would become an integral part of the 30th Divisions combat operations. The infantry became renowned for often jumping onto the hulls of these Shermans to get into the fight faster.

Many of the soldiers in the 30th Division had never been overseas before and were keen to get to know the locals in Normandy. Their first experience of combat did make them a little overcautious though.

GEORGE SCHNEIDER, HEADQUARTERS COMPANY, 120TH INFANTRY REGIMENT

We had landed in Normandy the first week of July and it was now 12 or 13 July. In the valley just beyond our tent there was a French farm that we had visited and met the farmer. He had a son named André with whom we quickly struck up a deal to get our canteens filled with cider in exchange for a few cigarettes. I was still carrying a pair of brown dress shoes that I had no use for and gave them to André. Why I was still lugging these around I have no idea. On 15 July, André's father was mowing some hay with a scythe until he struck an unexploded German artillery shell. This incident put an abrupt halt to the hay making. It seemed insignificant at the time, but was instrumental in creating panic throughout Normandy the night of 15 July. There was a small stream running through André's farm and an American engineering unit had set up a portable shower on the stream. Water from the stream was heated slightly and pumped into overhead tanks that provided showers by gravity feed. The night of 15 July was a clear night with fairly bright light provided from a partial moon. The Germans lobbed a large phosphorous artillery shell that landed near the shower unit and the engineer sentry on duty saw in the moonlight the white smoke from the shell and smelled the newly-mowed hay. His imagination prevailed over any analysis of the situation and immediately screamed "Gas!" and fired three shots. The signal for gas was to shout "Gas!" and fire three shots, ring a bell three times or create and sound in a series of three. The sentry's training to recognize either phosgene or chloropicrin as smelling like newly-mowed hay was too well embedded in his mind.

When my buddy, Tom Sneezak, a real nice guy from Amherst, Ohio, and I heard the alarm for gas, we quickly donned our gas masks and covered our uniforms with chemically-impregnated clothing. The clothing was very stiff and it was with much effort that we were able to cover ourselves. The impregnated clothes were discarded soon after this incident. We cleared our masks by pulling the mask slightly from the cheek and blowing out any gas that might have entered and then we went to normal breathing. Sneezak kept saying that he was going to die because his mask was leaking and he could smell the gas. He finally calmed down and we both fell asleep with our masks on. Hours later I was awakened by a chomping sound outside our tent. I pulled a flap back and in the moonlight I saw a horse eating grass. The horse appeared very much alive and he was not wearing a gas mask. We reasoned that the horse had lungs and a respiratory system similar to ours, so there must not be any gas in the air. Thanks to this profound scientific reasoning we removed our masks and concluded that the alarm had been false.

When we heard the alarm it quickly radiated from the sentry to all parts of Normandy. We could hear the three shots getting dimmer as the alarms penetrated into the countryside. Years later I mentioned this July incident to acquaintances that were in Normandy at the time and they recalled the event. It caused panic near the front where many had discarded their masks and as a substitute, were urinating in handkerchiefs and using that as a mask. For the remainder of the war I tried to keep my mask handy. The German soldiers we took prisoner were extra

*sensitive about their gas masks and always wanted to keep them. This was an item
a captured soldier was permitted to keep, according to the Geneva Convention.*

*Much of the other clothing and equipment I had were discarded. I cut off the
portion of the field pack that held any bulk like a shelter half and kept only the
canvass straps used as suspenders. The pouch holding the mess kit was retained on
the pack and held necessary items like toilet paper and extra socks. The suspenders
held the ammunition belt on which were attached a small first-aid kit of a bandage and a syringe of morphine; a canteen and canteen cup; the bayonet; and ammunition pouches. A lightweight raincoat was folded and held in place looped over
the back of the belt. An entrenching tool completed the equipment on the harness.
The gas mask was looped over the shoulder and carried on the side. The bag for
the mask was also good storage for other items. The breast pocket of the OD shirt
served as storage for a toothbrush and a spoon with a bent handle. Our underwear
was a two-piece long john and the outer uniform was the winter OD. A field
jacket sometimes was worn for additional cover. The M1 rifle and the steel helmet
completed the accoutrement of the well-dressed American soldier.[16]*

Even with the implementation of new tactics, fighting in the bocage was
dangerous and terrifying for everyone who participated. During the Normandy campaign the Germans were fully aware that they were vulnerable to
Allied air attacks so they actually used the terrain to their advantage by per-
fecting a method of fighting in and between the hedgerows to maximize their
use of camouflage and ambush tactics. By doing this they managed to almost
eradicate all traces of ground activity from the Allies. Consequently, this
method of concealed fighting exacerbated many Allied attempts to effectively
locate and destroy German positions. The 30th Division's first experience of
combat in the European theatre had been effective and intense, but they still
had to prove their metal as far as the other divisions were concerned. After
establishing positions along the Vire on 17 June, they became largely inert
for the ensuing three weeks while logistical and supply problems were dealt
with. This temporary hiatus would be seriously interrupted by the end of
June.

It became apparent just a few short weeks into the Normandy campaign
that the Allies were going to have to improvise and adapt some of their armor
to accommodate this new style of fighting, but therein lay their true strength.

One of the widely-used innovations was the "Culin Hedgrow Cutter."
The invention of this hedge-breaching device is generally credited to Sergeant Curtis G. Culin of the 2nd Armored Division's ("Hell on Wheels")

102nd Cavalry Reconnaissance Squadron. It should be acknowledged that Culin was initially inspired by a Tennessee "hillbilly" named Roberts, who during a discussion about how to overcome the bocage said, "Why don't we get some saw teeth and put them on the front of the tank and just cut through these hedges?" His suggestion wasn't treated seriously until huge saw teeth honed from scrap metal were fitted to the front of a Sherman tank. When General Omar Bradley attended a demonstration of the effectiveness of this device on 14 July 1944, he ordered the chief of First Army's Ordnance Section to supervise the construction and installation of as many of the "hedgerow cutters" as possible. The tanks to which they were fitted became known as "Rhinos." Roberts, the Tennessee man who actually proposed the original idea, was sadly never credited for this invention. The Allies were as resourceful as ever. They re-used steel acquired from German "tank traps" that covered the landing beaches in Normandy and within six weeks of the invention being introduced, virtually every Sherman tank there was fitted with a hedgerow cutter.

MARION SANFORD, 30TH CAVALRY RECONNAISSANCE TROOP (MECHANIZED)

Finally they put bulldozers on the front of the tanks, so they could knock a hole in the hedgerows to get through there. This was cattle country where we were. Dead cows, dead horses were everywhere, from artillery fire. This went on until 23 July. Normandy was a bad time in a lot of ways. They had a good bit of rain and mud. We had been eating K-rations, and the first piece of bread we got wasn't until about seven weeks after we got there. They came by and gave everybody a loaf of bread. I ate mine that night. We did not have a kitchen set up for our outfit. We had a little ol' gasoline Coleman stove in each vehicle, so that's what we cooked with. We made it through to the first of August. We had a few days' rest. [He told me in a phone conversation that his unit had a kitchen attached, but after they left, though, they did not see the kitchen until the war ended. Au.] My division of 16,000 men lost over 5,000 at that time. We were short, we needed replacements.

If you tried to get in there [the hedgerows] with a tank, the Germans had the only hole into it zeroed in with a tank gun and would knock it out. This fighting back and forth went on, and we weren't taking any ground at all. Some sergeant welded a piece of boiler metal on the front of a tank. He made it 15–18 feet long and cut some teeth in it. And the guy in the tank went up this hedgerow and wiggled around and got that tank through the hedgerow and then the tank carried bushes and trees with it. They started doing that with the tanks and they could get through. The infantry followed the tank and we advanced a little bit more that way.[17]

Necessity is the mother of invention and innovation born of necessity was always the pervading strength of the Allies, who maintained a consummate ability to adapt their tactics to suit the environment. It was this inventive capacity that proved to be a key ingredient that contributed to their eventual success in Normandy and throughout ensuing campaigns. In the seven weeks between D-Day and 31 July 1944, despite shortcomings in combat experience and the difficult Normandy terrain, the US First Army defeated the Germans in a series of battles that placed a premium on leadership and ingenuity at the small-unit level. Using new tactics and technical improvements allowed First Army units to home in, confront, and destroy a well-prepared defender.

HAROLD WILLIAMS, 105TH ENGINEER COMBAT BATTALION

Fear . . . it would get you briefly. I am talking about a period of 5–10 minutes. Then you picked up the pieces, so to speak. Bewildered is the best way I can describe it. You could only overcome your fear and move forward.

Hedgerows existed for centuries. Instead of fences they mounded dirt and then they planted bushes that grew to be 15–30 feet tall. You couldn't go from one field to another easily. The earth was 4–6 feet high and the hedges were formed in blocks. We were locked in them. We had bulldozers and later on tanks that could get through them.

We were attacking and I hadn't been there more than a few minutes. I broke down a bit and then I pulled myself together. Nobody was going to feel sorry for me. You're there for one purpose only, to do or die. We were herded into one of the openings into one of the fields. It might have been 2–3 acres. A bulldozer was near me punching holes in the hedgerow so we could move forward. The driver was shot—one...two...three! Then a buddy of mine, I don't know what his job was, he might have been a driver, took it upon himself to do what he could. He jumped on the dozer and that was the end of him. He was shot. There was mass confusion, nobody knew what was happening. More people were crowding behind us. We were told, in no uncertain terms, we had one direction to go. If we turned, people would shoot us. It sounds kind of harsh, but it made you consider things. We were there to go in one direction, forward. That's where we had to go. Our objective from that point was a little town called Isigny. It was right off the beach in hedgerow country. For 3–4 days we were locked in that area trying to gain ground.[18]

The 30th Division was reminded often during those summer months that the enemy knew their positions and was always peering at them from behind the bocage or from surrounding hills. They also knew only too well that the enemy was constantly in close proximity because he sniped with 88s and pounded at the 30th Division locations with mortars and heavy artillery. Under cover of night German machinegunners would move up into the swamp-lands while their patrols roamed menacingly in the murky darkness.

Intelligence and reconnaissance were equally important to the Allies and occasionally they managed to procure useful intelligence from unexpected sources. On one occasion two young students hiked all the way from the Sorbonne in Paris, and managed to find their way through the lines and pass on information regarding what they had observed en route. One audacious Frenchman from Graignes came surreptitiously by boat to inform the Allies that *SS* men were present in his town, and then he even went back to get more specific locations. For his efforts he insisted on, and was presented with, a certificate stating that he had personally helped in the task of liberating France.

There were also sporadic encounters with deserters, mostly Russians and Poles, who had been forcefully conscripted into the *Wehrmacht* while others were drawn from Nazi occupied territories. Some of these men were so insistent on the keenness of Germany's sorry foreign legions to desert, that propaganda shells and a public-address system were employed to incite further desertions, but with little success. Control by the German officers and non-commissioned officers was still too stringent to allow defectors. Other valuable information was collected by the 30th's artillery units and fragile observation planes that flew above the battlefield. The Germans responded to Allied air recon by redoubling their efforts to conceal their whereabouts during the long daylight hours.

German POWs later related horrific accounts of the losses they incurred during those early days of shelling. They told of whole companies afraid to leave their cover by daylight, of shell-ravaged kitchen wagons and endless long days of gnawing hunger. Due to Allied air superiority there were enough aerial photographs available at the time that provided even more information on the German positions. Despite all this valuable intelligence, Supreme Headquarters Allied Expeditionary Force (SHAEF) still considered it imperative to execute frequent foot patrols which went out night after night. It was still far too precarious to send out patrols in broad daylight due to the vast open spaces that had to be negotiated, and during the summer nighttime only lasted three or four hours so there was never any time to waste.

In the Normandy campaign the 30th Division more than adequately demonstrated its capability to engage the enemy in a hostile environment that distinctly favored the defender. They devised and employed tactics and combat procedures specifically designed to meet unexpected assignments. The Allies in general, furthermore, showed a remarkable capacity to learn from their mistakes and experiences. Leaders learned in combat how best to use their organic weapons and equipment. At the small-unit level, junior officers, sergeants, and enlisted men invented ways to solve tactical problems inherent in close combat in the bocage. Not only did the Army adapt, but it also applied a unique versatility that would ultimately work in their favor.

During those three weeks leading up to the end of June, the 30th Division was regarded by G-3 as providing "vigorous patrolling and active defense." G-3 was responsible for operations, including staff duties, exercise planning, training, operational requirements, combat development, and tactical doctrine.

FRANK TOWERS, COMPANY M, 120TH INFANTRY REGIMENT

Radio communication was not reliable. Telephone communication was also not reliable because tanks were running over the telephone lines and cutting them up. Artillery was also dropping in and cutting the lines. So we had to have a more dependable way to communicate between units. This was the reason my liaison position was created. I entered the Liaison Officer slot as the primary means of communication between battalion and regimental headquarters. I had a jeep, a driver, and two guards with me at all times. I would carry regimental orders down to battalion with instructions about the next objective; I would wait for battalion to devise a plan to take the objective; then I would carry that information back to regiment headquarters. With the telephones not being reliable, the Germans had the opportunity to tap into our lines to get information. The Germans could also intercept radio communications as well but there was no way for the Germans to get the information that I had. Later, at Mortain, I was transferred to be the division-to-regiment Liaison Officer.[19]

While the 30th Division awaited orders, the 743rd Tank Battalion was preoccupied with organizing repairs, assimilating replacements, and doing general maintenance. They had hit the beaches in Normandy hours before the infantry had arrived and had joined the 30th Division in time for their initial combat operations 15 June. They were to remain as part of the 30th Division for the duration of the war in Europe.

WILLIAM GAST, COMPANY A, 743RD TANK BATTALION

The hedgerow fighting began. Being inside the tank protected us from machine-gun and rifle fire, as well as fragments from artillery and mortar explosions. Being under constant fire, we would be buttoned up in our tanks sometimes for three or four days and nights at a time. Our steel helmets served many purposes. We would place them on a bunsen burner to heat some soup or coffee or whatever we had to eat. We used the same helmets for our elimination, then opened the hatch and quickly empty it out over the side.

Sometimes at night halts we would be able to get out of our tanks and dig a hole or trench large enough so we could lie down, make a dirt pile in front of the trench, then drive the tank over it. This would give some of us a chance to get some very much needed sleep. Of course, at least one would always stand guard in the tank. We alternated our turns.

This was also the time our supplies tried to catch up to us, primarily ammunition, rations, and fuel. Our gasoline was transported by 6 x 6 trucks in five-gallon cans known as Gerry cans. With artillery shells coming in, the driver would abandon his truck for a much safer place. You can imagine what would happen should a shell hit the truck. It would explode into a big ball of fire. The driver often did not return to his truck until it was emptied. Consequently, in order to get gas, we would have to sometimes walk half a mile or more and hand-carry two five-gallon cans at a time back to our tank, lift them up onto the deck, and the driver would pour it into the tank, which held about 250 gallons. Then, if we were still alive, we could try to get some sleep. We continued fighting through hedgerow after hedgerow, liberating town after town.[20]

The other tank unit synonymous with the 30th Division, the 823rd Tank Destroyer Battalion, arrived in Normandy 24 June and initially saw action with the 29th Division before being returned to the 30th. By the end of June the deep-water harbor of Cherbourg had been captured by US forces. After the D-Day landings the capture of this port was one of the most important early objectives for the Allies. It finally convinced most of the German high command that Normandy wasn't a precursor for an Allied invasion farther north at the ports of Calais and Boulogne. They had been reluctant to commit German divisions in the vicinity of these ports because of this, but now they realized that Normandy was going to be the main area of operations.

MARVIN SMITH, COMPANY K, 120TH INFANTRY REGIMENT

It soon grew dark. We could see to our front great fireworks lighting up the sky in places. We knew we were approaching the front lines. We moved into an assembly area, a place where troops are assembled to prepare for battle, to plan, or to get supplied with ammunition, a meal, or sleep, if possible. I hadn't slept much the last 48 hours, so I was dead tired and sleepy. I tried to bed down for a night's sleep.

I had just fallen soundly to sleep when my orderly was shaking my shoulder to get on the telephone as battalion headquarters was calling. Sound-powered telephones can be strung up in no time. We avoided our radio communication because the enemy might pick it up. Battalion headquarters informed me of a company commanders meeting immediately. We were to move out the companies immediately towards the front, only six to eight miles away. The next day we were to launch an attack with the line of departure to be a railroad track.

We were passing through elements of an airborne division (101st or 82nd). We walked along excited (frightened) as this was the real thing, and not just another training exercise. The darkness was eerie, but welcome protection from the eyes of the enemy. Even so, as we walked over a bridge an enemy sniper fired, adding to our fear. Nearing our destination, we heard the unmistakable sound of a German plane. The plane dropped a flare over our column of troops, which lit up and exposed us. In no time we heard the terrible whine of the enemy plane going into a nose dive down upon us. We automatically scattered unbelievably fast toward the ditches on either side of the road. A bomb screeched down toward us, but luckily, it hit just to the left of us. The concussion was terrific, and Sergeant Queen's helmet was blown off his head. Sergeant Queen was a completely bald man. What a laugh we had when morning came to see Sergeant Queen's bald head shining like a billiard ball without his helmet, but what an excellent target for the enemy!

As dawn arrived, our apprehension mounted. Several sniper bullets whined by. I thought how easy it would be to get picked off! Just as the attack started, large guns from the US Navy to our rear opened up on the enemy with extremely large shells that sounded like freight cars rumbling through the air. They seemed to be passing by just over our heads.

We were all tense and apprehensive. American airborne soldiers had been in this area before us, and had fought against strong resistance. The evidence of hard fighting was everywhere. A chill came over me when I saw the first dead Amer-

ican soldier (not from our outfit) with a bullet in his forehead. Death could come to any of us at any time. I remember thinking how different the dead looked compared to the dead seen at a funeral back home.

Ahead, sporadic firing broke out, and I knew L and I Companies had found the enemy and were engaged. I set up headquarters near a tree with my runner (messenger), the radio communication sergeant, and the executive officer (second in command of Company K). L Company was not moving forward, but was stopped in a fight with the enemy. It seemed in no time, perhaps only ten minutes of L Company fighting, until the Battalion Commander, Lieutenant Colonel McCollum, ordered K Company out of reserve by sending my 2nd Platoon (Lieutenant Pearsons) with an American tank to the right flank and rifle platoons into an assault on a group of old stone houses where the enemy appeared to be dug in around the houses.

One K Company rifle platoon became bogged down and did not move forward, but lay highly exposed in a small field approaching the enemy positions. Battalion Commander McCollum pointed out their vulnerable position of being seen easily and exposed to enemy fire with no walls or depressions in the land to protect them. I knew I had to get them on forward without delay to engage the enemy.

I ordered Sergeant Waker (machine-gun sergeant) to set up a machine gun in a corner of a field and fire constantly to the front into enemy positions to keep them pinned down. Then I ordered that he was to stop firing when I gave the hand signal, so that we would not be running into our own fire. I ran onto the field and ordered the men to run forward with me into the enemy lines. They really moved fast and in unison. We overran enemy foxholes and knocked down house doors to engage the enemy at short range. I jumped over an enemy foxhole, and uh-oh, there were those black boots and German helmet! He was lying face down in a foxhole. I fired into his leg, because I thought he was playing possum, and recoiled from firing a fatal bullet. This leg would put him out of action, and on I went!

Then came a decision I made which has haunted me ever since. One of the finest, most loyal, efficient sergeants I had ever worked with ran up to me and asked if he should search a German soldier just killed for any papers or letters that would reveal the name of the enemy outfit we were opposing. This information, when pieced together with other information back at Intelligence, would be vital in fighting the enemy. I said, "Yes, search him, but be careful." Within minutes the awful news came to me that this wonderful sergeant was KIA (Killed in Action). I was shocked. I walked forward and saw Sergeant Kaliff's body slumped over the dead German. What a terrible loss to me personally, and to the Company! I remember walking past him on forward expecting a shot or shots to hit me any second. This action caused Company K to be committed fully on the right of L Company – going forward in attack formation.

Rifle bullets began cracking over our heads, and I took cover behind a log. We couldn't see the enemy, but I detected the rifle fire was coming from our left. It is amazing how depressions in the ground and lying flat will protect you from bullets. Because of the loud crack I heard, I'm sure several bullets were only inches from my head.

I walked out near a narrow blacktop road and was amazed to see a French farmer wearing wooden shoes and leading a cow by a rope. He was coming from the direction of enemy lines through ours, but no one fire upon him. I recall wondering, why would he risk his life in full view of the enemy and all this shelling when he didn't have to? Now, I think he was probably getting his remaining livestock the heck out of there!

Another time two US Air Corps airmen showed up in our area. I asked them why they were up on the front. They said, "Oh, we just wanted some excitement and to be able to say we had been to the front lines." I wondered why anyone would risk his life if he didn't have to. Just one enemy mortar round could kill you. You can't hear them coming. They come in straight down from above and then burst into steel fragments and can take you straight into eternity.

We pushed onward toward the Vire River. During the march, two of our men had stepped on anti-personnel mines, severely wounding their legs and feet. With little further opposition, however, we finally reached our objective. I ordered K Company to dig in, they needed no prodding. We buttoned up for the night exhausted, and vowed to shoot anything that moved outside our foxholes. The company had accomplished their mission and our troops were now in position to deny the enemy any ground north of the river-canal toward the beaches.

A storm on the English Channel now was delaying the arrival of ships from England bringing essential ammunition, fuel, and supplies. As a result, the further attack across the river-canal was postponed as well.[21]

Now that the 30th were familiar with the enemy's tactics they were going to employ every available method to combat them. Up until this point the German high command had been reluctant to commit too many reserves to the fight for fear of weakening communication lines and rear guard defenses. They realized that the time had come to attempt some decisive action and redress the imbalance.

MANFRED TOON THORN, *1ST SS-PANZER DIVISION* "*LEIBSTANDARTE SS ADOLF HITLER*"

The next posting [of the division] was on 18 July to Normandy, to a little village of strategic importance, which we held for three weeks. Of all my war-time experiences, these three weeks were the most unforgettable, simply because this was another type of combat, and our enemy was not only on land, but also in the air and out at sea. In the early hours of the morning, under the commander, 1st Lt. Werner Wolff, 25 tanks left Bully, the town we were stationed in. I was driving tank number 734, one of the five tanks that made up the 3rd Platoon. At the age of 19 I was one of the older experienced men, and from the loophole of my tank this was something that I will never forget. With no idea what to expect we moved into a completely abandoned village. We stopped on the east side in an apple orchard with our tanks facing in a northerly direction. A kilometer away was Bourguebus where all the houses were intact, with green fields and meadows surrounding the village. Our platoon drove into the morning mist. I selected a spot for my tank about 30 yards away from the last house, and camouflaged it well. Far in the distance we could hear the sounds of battle, but in Tilly everything was quiet; Bourguebus was hidden by the mist. We knew that the enemy would be coming from that direction, and every now and again a stray shell whistled into the village, making us run for the cover of our tanks. With time the number of incoming shells increased and the accuracy improved! It improved so much that we asked permission to move closer to the houses to get some extra cover. This was granted, but not until the next day. Meanwhile, the orchard had become a graveyard of stumps and the blast from the shells had destroyed our camouflage. We had better protection from the houses where I managed to tear down some climbing ivy to cover my tank. Heinrich Theye, my friend, chose the house beside mine. He drove in at the "six o'clock" position and turned around to the "12 o'clock" in order to fire through the kitchen window. The rest of the platoon were scattered around. A centuries-old four-to-five-foot-high wall surrounded the house and had a blind corner, which practically hid me from view. We had slowly become aware of the difference between artillery fire coming from the destroyers off-shore and that coming from inland. Our infantry in front of us had little or no protection from this artillery fire and the long bombardments. On 22 July the bombardment only lasted for two hours, but that was just the beginning. The sun burned down outside and we burned inside because the temperature had reached 40 to 45 degrees [Centigrade, or 104 to 113 degrees Fahrenheit] in the tanks, nearly suffocating us due to the heat and the smoke. An oncoming smoke-screen always warned us of the approaching enemy, who attacked as soon as they had stopped firing.[22]

Despite the air of impending victory that permeated the Allied ranks, they were to discover all too soon that the German army was far from being a spent force and although some senior officers sensed that defeat could be imminent, they had no intention of surrendering. The joint coercion of strategic necessity combined with the terror of incurring the *Führer's* displeasure was sufficient impetus to induce German Commander-in-Chief West Field Marshal Günther von Kluge to hit back at the Allies as soon the opportunity presented itself. Von Kluge had been sent to replace von Rundstedt in late July, who then would be reinstated in September 1944. Such was the erratic and volatile nature of Hitler's mindset at the time.

During the Normandy campaign Rudolf von Ribbentrop was awarded the German Gold Cross and Panzer Assault Badge. Following the breakout from the Falaise Gap, he was promoted to Regimental Adjutant of *SS-Panzer Regiment 12, 12th SS-Panzer Division "Hitlerjugend" (Hitler youth)*. It was in this capacity that he saw action during the Battle of the Bulge. On 20 December 1944 he was wounded for the fifth time. He was awarded the Gold Wound Badge, and given command of *SS-Panzer Regiment 12, 12th SS-Panzer Division.* He commanded this unit until the Division surrendered to the Americans on 8 May 1945.

RUDOLF VON RIBBENTROP, 1ST SS-PANZER DIVISION "LEIBSTANDARTE SS ADOLF HITLER" AND 12TH SS-PANZER DIVISION "HITLERJUGEND"

My name is Rudolf von Ribbentrop. Hitler's Foreign Minister Joachim von Ribbentrop was my father. I commanded the 1st SS-Panzer Division "Leibstandarte SS Adolf Hitler" *while in Normandy so I experienced combat along the whole invasion front. I remember that on 4 June 1944, during the build up to the Normandy campaign, a messenger informed me that the invasion of the Allies would occur the following day. I vividly recall that 5 June came and went and nothing happened until that night when Allied parachute divisions began landing. Some weeks previous to this I had actually accompanied Field Marshall Erwin Rommel as he inspected the Atlantic Wall in Normandy. When the invasion occurred Rommel was in Germany with his family celebrating his birthday! It was no secret that Rommel wanted the armored divisions in the west to be moved to the coastal area, and he was right because, despite the absolute Allied air superiority, if we had been better prepared and had followed Rommel's advice, we would have driven the enemy back into the sea. On 1 August 1944 I was transferred from the* 1st SS-Panzer Division *to SS-Panzer Regiment 12, 12th SS-Panzer Division "Hitlerjugend."*[23]

230th Field Artillery Battalion, Action Against Enemy/ After Action Report, dated 21 July 1944

Unexpectedly, at 1600 hours 8 June 1944, the battalion received orders, to proceed immediately to a port of embarkation for the invasion front. (Rumor had it that the 230th had been especially chosen to replace an artillery battery of the 29th Infantry Division lost on the beachhead. This rumor was substantially correct) At 1645 hours the battalion was on the march; what was thought to be a "dry run" became literally a "wet run"—a cold drizzle continued to fall until embarkation at Southampton, England. (The battalion bypassed the ordinary marshalling area, going straight through to the docks.) General McLain saw the battalion off at St. Johns. By 0800 June 1944 this loading was completed. Headquarters Battery, A Battery, Service Battery, and Medical Detachment were loaded on LST 367 (British flag), and B Battery and C Battery on LST 261 (American flag). LST 367 was a veteran of the Mediterranean Theatre, having been at several ports in Sicily and at the Salerno and Anzio beachheads. On D-Day she carried British Royal Marines in France. The ships anchored in the bay until 2030 hours when they sailed in convoy. The crossing was uneventful and the ships anchored in the roadstead off Coleville, on the coast of Normandy 10 June 1944. Ships of all descriptions stretched as far as the eye could reach. Allied planes active. Because of beach congestion and unfavorable tide conditions disembarkation from the beached ships was not completed until 1530 hours. No incidents. Dewaterproofing was begun at a temporary transit area near Coleville. Coastal villages and towns in ruins. Battalion Commander's party went on reconnaissance; temporarily delayed by sniper in church tower. Around 0530 11 June, 1944 gun positions and bivouac areas were occupied neer Chantilly. Battallon in position to deliver reinforcing fires for 29th Division or direct support to 116th Infantry. Cpl. Hyder of A Battery captured first prisoner, a sniper, at 1015 hours, near headquarters area. Observation difficult because of terrain conditions. Lieutenant Jack Tafeen commenced registration from Air OP at 1131 hours. Order received to give general support to fires of 110th FA Bn. At 0500 12 June 1944 fires delivered in support of infantry attack. Lieutenant Vereen wounded in leg at forward. 459th AA attached to battalion. Mission changed to direct support of 116th Infantry. B and C Batteries displaced at 2330 hours. A Battery covered displacement. Sergeant Smith of C Battery reported missing in action at 1700 hours. He and Lieutenant Sayer met German patrol at roadblock. At 0115 hours 13 June 1944 A Battery displaced.

Lieutenant John R. Lloyd, Jr. was wounded in ankle. Four prisoners taken. Battery in position roughly north of St. Clair. Order received not to use artillery fire until all infantry weapons had been used.

Battalion was released at 0900 hours 14 June 1944 from attachment to 29th Division, and moved to new position southeast of Carantan (1 mile south of Catz), at 1505 hours. Naval liaison parties reported to CP. Battalion now in direct support of 120th Infantry, 30th Infantry Division. Liaison Officer from 58th FA Bn. reported to CP on 15 June 1944. Battalion supported 120th Infantry in its first attack on Mont Martin (reinforcing fires by A Battery, 197th FA Bn.); all objectives attained. 87th Armored in direct support of 119th Infantry on 120th's left. On 16 June, A Battery displaced to new position at request of Air Force Engineers to permit construction of airfield just south of and parallel to Carentan-Isigny highway. Battalion supported 120th Infantry advance south of Mont Martin to line just north of Vire Canal. LaRoy captured. (Impregnated clothing, worn since departure from St. John's, came off.) Mines and booby-traps (some under dead soldiers) reported. New positions to south were surveyed in 17 June 1944 for use in event of general advance. Battalion fired 1800 rounds at various targets and installations. Enemy reported to be *984th Infantry Division* and *37th* and *38th Regiments* of *17th SS-Division.* Enemy artillery seems to consist only of 88s. Enemy howitzers, however, reported registering. On 18 June 1944 battalion residue arrived. 531st AA attached to Battalion. Firing light—situation static. Patrols report enemy active laying mines. *2nd SS-Panzer Division "Das Reich"* reported in St. Lô. 120th Infantry in position to north of Vire et Taute Canal. There was little on 19 June 1944. Nineteen missions were fired. Liaison Officer from 101st Airborne arrived at CP. Enemy 88s (possibly higher caliber) reported. Enemy reported using hoot-owl call as signal. Intermittent mortar fire. Little activity on 20 June 1944. Fourteen missions—302 rounds fired. Units of enemy *17 SS-Division* in line. Enemy 105mm guns reported. Enemy units from Brittany may appear. Enemy ME 109 chased over area by our fighters; last seen smoking. No special occurrences on 21 June 1944. Eighteen missions—430 rounds fired. Movement of civilians through lines prohibited. Enemy artillery fire of harassing type. On 22 June 1944, 5 officers and 2 enlisted men replacements were received. Captain Baysinger was assigned to Battalion Staff. 2nd Lts. Dickerson and Swienty assigned to A Battery, 2nd Lt. Ward assigned to B Battery, and 2nd Lieutenant Arnold assigned to C Battery; 2 enlisted men assigned to A Battery. L 109 over Battalion area; foil near 58th FA Bn. B Battery strafed; no casualties. Battalion displaced to area north of Montmartin en Graignes. Enemy 105mm and mortar shells near area. On 23 June 1944 news of the death of S/Sgt Smith (reported missing in action on 13 June) was confirmed by Graves Registration Company. Reported that *Schnelle Brigade 30* in position. Enemy artillery fire more concentrated; 150mm howitzers being used. Sixteen missions—419 rounds were fired on 24 June 1944. On 25 June 1944 18 concentrations—408 rounds fired. 120th Infantry reports enemy unwilling to use artillery when air OP is up; also 2 out of 5 enemy shells are duds. On 26 June 1944 14 missions—384 rounds fired. No increase in enemy artillery strength noted; gun positions moved frequently. On 27 June 1944 Liaison Meer from 83rd Division reported to CP. Sixteen missions—229 rounds fired. On 28 June 1944—303 rounds fired. Wiretapping of our line continues. *Nebelwerfer,* suspected to be 105mm, heard. Prisoners from enemy *266th Infantry Division.* Enemy artillery using roving guns, harassing and interdiction fires. Propaganda shells and broadcast shells sent over enemy lines.[24]

CITATIONS FOR THE HEDGEROW FIGHTING IN FRANCE

Private First Class Theodore W. Beben, 120th Infantry Regiment, Silver Star citation:
For gallantry in action from 7 July 1944 to 8 July 1944, in France. During the hedgerow fighting in France, in order to employ tanks, it was necessary to blast paths through the hedgerows with dynamite as roads were not safe due to mines and enemy anti-tank guns. Private Beben and a comrade performed this dangerous task on ten different occasions although enemy fire was intense. On one occasion enemy fire was particularly heavy, but Private Beben courageously continued until he was wounded. Entered military service from Massachusetts.[25]

Private First Class Joseph Funk, Medical Detachment, 120th Infantry Regiment, Silver Star citation:
For gallantry in action on 10 July 1944, in France. Upon reaching the objective, Private Funk's company received a strong enemy counterattack and was forced to withdraw. Private Funk and a comrade refused to withdraw but remained to render medical care to the wounded. Despite the close proximity of the enemy, they adminis-

tered aid to a platoon leader who was severely wounded. Although they were captured by the enemy, their gallant and courageous actions were responsible for providing medical care despite extremely hazardous conditions. Entered military service from California.[26]

Major Joseph Funk, Medical Corps, Silver Star citation:
For gallantry in action on 28 July 1944, in France. Major Funk was assigned to duty as surgeon for an artillery unit. Enemy planes bombed the area, starting fires which were used as targets by succeeding waves of the hostile bombers. Major Funk was summoned to attend the wounded of the first attack, and was preparing to respond when the second wave came over. With utter disregard for his personal safety, and at the height of the second wave of bombings, Major Funk left the sanctuary of his shelter in response to the summons. In attempting to give succor to the wounded, Major Funk lost his life. The unselfish devotion to duty displayed by Major Funk reflects great credit on himself and is in keeping with the highest traditions of the Armed Forces. Entered military service from New Jersey.[27]

Captain Bliss H. Kelly, Corps of Engineers, 105th
Engineer Combat Battalion, Silver Star citation:
For gallantry in action on 21 June 1944, in France. Captain Kelly, with his patrol was investigating possible landing sites across a canal when they were suddenly subjected to heavy machine-gun and rifle fire, killing one member of his patrol and wounding Captain Kelly. Despite his painful wound, Captain Kelly courageously remained exposed to the enemy fire and provided covering fire for the withdrawal of the other members of the patrol. Only after they had reached safety did he withdraw from his position. Entered military service from Idaho.[28]

Captain Sidney Minkoff, Medical Corps,
120th Infantry Regiment, Silver Star citation:
For gallantry in action on 25 July 1944, in France. Captain Minkoff went forward of his aid station to reconnoiter routes for evacuation stations to be set up during intensive fighting. He personally evacuated the men from two burning tanks. He made six trips to the front

to supervise and assist in the evacuation of wounded men. His coolness under murderous fire and his complete disregard for personal safety; his courage; and most loyal devotion to duty reflect great credit upon himself. Entered military service from New York.[29]

CHAPTER TWO
THE "BREAKOUT"

Between D-Day and the Normandy breakout, numerous technical and tactical solutions had been meticulously rehearsed and
applied for use against this determined enemy. The 30th Infantry Division
had to address a shortfall in tactics suitable for fighting in this hedgerow-
covered countryside. They needed to innovate and adjust their combat procedures to compensate for this. An example of this capacity for innovation
occurred when the 30th Division had to prepare for a crossing at the 70-
foot-wide Vire River.

In the few weeks preceding the Vire attack, the 30th Division had
steadily moved inland and effectively succeeded in pushing the enemy back
behind the Vire et Taute Canal and the Vire River. Now the time was ripe
and for the first time the whole division had been assembled to work collectively on one objective. The Vire River courses 79.5 miles (128km) through
the towns of Vire, St. Lô, and Isigny-sur-Mer, before it reaches the English
Channel. Establishing this important bridgehead was going to prove an
arduous, but not insurmountable, obstacle to the division's progress. HQ had
already organized reconnaissance of this apparently vulnerable breach in the
German defenses. Field Marshal Erwin Rommel, fully aware of the situation,
suggested sending in the *Panzer Lehr Division* to confront the situation
because, in his opinion, they were the only available "battle ready" division at
the time.

Hitler, meanwhile, remained resolute in his opinion that an attack west
of the Vire River to save or possibly regain the harbour at Cherbourg was
imperative, despite von Rundstedt's insistence that the focal point should be

Caen. Hitler wasn't bothered if the reserves gathered near Caen were used for offensive or defensive purposes.

Moving the *Panzer Lehr* across the front from the vicinity of Caen to the area west of St. Lô would take, several days to accomplish nevertheless. It was imperative to the Germans, meanwhile, to muster enough force to

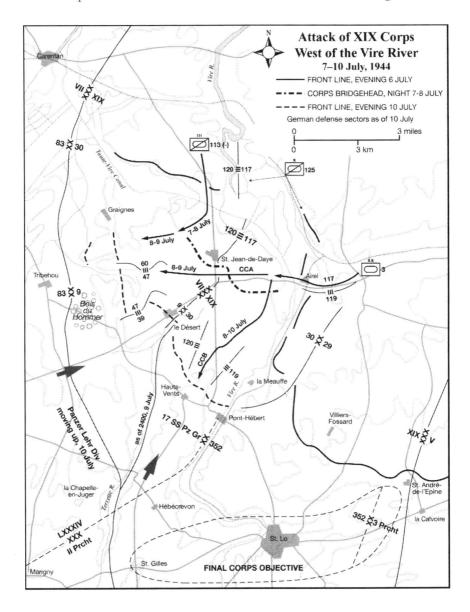

orchestrate an effective counterattack. They were compelled to find strong forces that were in closer proximity to the threatened area and available for immediate commitment. It was eventually decided to send in the *2nd SS-Panzer Division "Das Reich,"* most of which already was battling the VII and VIII Corps. Although von Kluge realized that drawing part of the *SS* armored division away from the *7th Army* could potentially weaken the west flank defenses, Rommel accurately pointed out that the Taute and Vire situation was much more critical and needed to be dealt with immediately.

A few weeks later, on the morning of 17 July, a Spitfire Mk. IX was making a sweep through the Normandy countryside when it noticed a solitary German staff car accompanied by a motorbike was driving along a small road in Normandy. Precisely who was flying the Spitfire is still hotly debated. The Spitfire immediately lined up his sights, went into a dive, and swooped low in the direction of the vehicle with his machine guns blazing. At that moment, Field Marshal Erwin Rommel was returning to his Headquarters at La Roche-Guyon after meeting with *I SS-Panzer Corps* commander, General Josef "Sepp" Dietrich, when the Spitfire struck. The rounds ripped through the car, killing the driver, and seriously wounding Rommel. He was dragged off the road and taken to a nearby hospital, whereupon the extent of his injuries was revealed. When Rommel regained consciousness the following day, he was told that he had suffered a quadruple skull fracture. Within a few days he was evacuated to a German military hospital, but for the duration of the actions in Normandy he would no longer be available. Sometime later he would be implicated in the assassination attempt on Hitler's life and coerced into taking his own life. At a time when Germany needed great generals, they were going to lose one of the best.

While assiduous preparations were initiated for this attack, no stone was left unturned. First, the 30th Division organized detailed reconnaissance of the area of the river that they had to cross; then they sent in the division's engineers who set about constructing makeshift ladders and footbridges in preparation for the eventual crossing. The ladders were intended to help them negotiate the steep banks on the far side of the river. This was going to be the 30th Division's trademark *modus operandi* for this and many future river and canal crossings. The plan was to initiate a two-pronged attack that would entail crossing both the Vire River and the Vire et Taute Canal. The 117th Infantry Regiment was designated to spearhead the crossing of the Vire at 0430, while the 120th Infantry Regiment was scheduled to drive across the canal at 1345.

The attack began in the time-honored fashion with an intense artillery barrage. On this particular occasion the barrage was provided by the three-inch guns of the 823rd Tank Destroyer Battalion, mortars from the 92nd Chemical Battalion, and additional artillery from the 203rd Field Artillery Battalion. This forced the Germans to keep their heads down while the 117th Infantry Regiment fixed bayonets and prepared to cross the river in something that was actually more reminiscent of a WWI battle. They stormed the German defenses with a rigorous zeal that was to become characteristic of this division and quickly overran these fixed positions. After achieving initial success with the assault, the drive south from this point became increasingly arduous. The Germans retaliated swiftly by bringing up two panzer divisions to help plug the gap inflicted by the 30th Division's attack.

MARVIN SMITH, COMPANY K, 120TH INFANTRY REGIMENT

All along the Vire River-Canal the "Krauts" (as we called them) were well hidden in the vines, trees, and bushes, and were well positioned to "defend unto death," as ordered by their Führer, *Adolf Hitler. A huge shell came into our location, sounding like a locomotive flying just overhead, and hit one of our jeep trailers full of ammunition, setting it on fire. It burned all night, but it was off to our left 200 yards or so. I was so very exhausted and could not get any undisturbed sleep, but alas, word came that K Company was to send two platoons to patrol forward after dark beyond our lines to a bridge on the Vire River. The mission: to see if the bridge was still intact. Two platoons of 50–60 men were needed because it was feared that there were many Germans between us and the canal, and we might have to fight our way through. I selected the platoons and gave my instructions. Our fear was great. To be ordered to patrol beyond enemy lines after dark was a devastating task. Regardless, we got started and I had the great Sergeant Dickens to assist me.*

I had not prayed to God before because, lacking in faith, I felt that it wasn't right to have nothing to do with God and then suddenly begin calling on Him in battle. I felt it was cowardly and that any real God would show little mercy toward anyone who had doubted Him. My fear won out, though, and I prayed, "Oh God, if there is a God, please protect us now as we go into the enemy area in this darkness. Help us now, oh God!" As we all moved forward together, I never heard a sound. We walked slowly with rifles and ammunition through fields and over hedgerows toward the canal about a mile to our front. How could 50–60 men advance in the dark so silently and undetected? Could it be that God had answered an agnostic's prayer?

As we continued onward, a German plane approached (I could tell by the sound) and a flare lit up the whole countryside. We froze in our positions, as we had been trained to do. The plane passed over us, flying low, but neither a bomb nor gunfire was released on us. The flare died away and on we went, carefully and silently. Sergeant Dickens was first to reach our mission objective and reported back that the bridge was destroyed and impassable. With this knowledge, we quietly crept back to our lines. We never once ran into any opposition that night. The vital information about the bridge was phoned back to Battalion headquarters, and another "Well done!" was chalked up for K Company. I slept a few short hours and then was awakened to hear orders from Battalion Headquarters that K Company would again be called upon to clear out any enemy to our front down to the canal. We were to "jump-off" within the hour. One of my sergeants came up and informed me that one of the men had shot himself in the foot and was recommending an investigation into the incident. There was little time for investigations. The motive for a self-inflicted wound was clear: fear of death in combat could drive a man to the brink of insanity.

More bad news followed: an artillery shell had hit, tearing the canteen and ammo belt of a K Company soldier off him. He somehow escaped harm, but it killed his buddy in the same foxhole. I felt a crushing sadness. I had lost, on our first day in combat, my best Sergeant, Kaliff, then this sad news of yet another of our own killed. With heavy hearts K Company assembled once more and started moving through deadly hedgerows, sunken roads, and swamps.

A sniper's shot rang out. Before I knew it, the whole company was blindly and wildly firing into a clump of trees—now everyone was wasting ammunition with no target to be found. This was an over-reaction, but every one of us had the jitters. Shortly thereafter, I saw one of our best soldiers pumping bullets into a ditch covered with grass and cursing wildly as he fired. He had found the sniper.

Along with advancing our lines, our task was to reconnoiter the whole canal area to our front, an area about two miles wide, and gather as much information as possible. I took my weapons platoon leader, Lieutenant Hansen; two platoons of men; and my runner, Private Raymond Boker; and moved toward the river. As we carefully felt our way through this area, I really didn't think any enemy troops would be observing us, as we were in a nearly impassable swamp. When we approached within 200 feet of the canal, however, we heard two or three rifle shots coming from across the water. I looked in the direction the sound came from and saw two figures just beside some bushes on the opposite side of the canal. They were barely discernible inside the thick foliage. Our mission was to gain intelligence and report back, so we were told to avoid a firefight, if possible. We retreated gradually and returned to our previous position, but upon seeing the enemy so close my hair stood on end! Being, often, only 50 feet or so from the Germans across the canal had kept everyone on edge for days. We could not talk out loud or move freely about. Our "essential to survival" foxholes were always cold, wet, and muddy. No showers or hot meals. Sleep was rationed in shifts, and we had to be constantly on guard against nighttime enemy incursions. After several days of close encounters along the line, I was most happy to receive orders that I Company would relieve K Company along the canal front.

When I Company relieved us, and as we were moving toward the rear, German 88s began firing on our positions. Apparently they had detected our movement, despite our efforts at concealment within the hedges. Each incoming shell with its screeching and screaming seemed as if it were destined to come right down my neck! Luckily, they hit to our left front and rear, and not a man in our company was hit. As we walked—crouching carefully, and spread out through a field one-quarter mile behind our former position (now held by I Company)—a previously-bypassed German machine gun opened up on us. I saw dirt flying up around me where bullets hit. Our training paid off because every man immediately hit the ground and then turned to return fire on the source. The enemy machine gun was silenced quickly and only one man was hit—wounded in the leg. It could have been worse, but we were spread out well and reacted rapidly.

Once relieved, our company rested in a reserve position to the rear about one mile. We were in the middle of a beautiful French orchard. I found a nice "home" under an apple tree, dug in, and set up camp. Now off the front, we were to get hot meals brought up in a company jeep trailer. Apparently a German observer had seen the jeep come over the high ground to our rear, though, and they shelled the area just as the cooks got the pots set out. Never before under fire, the cooks ran in all directions. The rest of us "hardened and experienced" combat veterans doubled up with laughter to see the cooks in their clean white uniforms making tracks, although it was really no laughing matter.

In my headquarters foxhole I propped a newly-arrived photo of my wife, Virginia, onto a dirt shelf. She was the girl I married and loved. I was filled with apprehension and dread now that we were in "reserve" and actually had time to ponder the days and weeks ahead of us. The picture had arrived just in time. I needed the assurance and comfort the little photograph provided me. I looked at and into her face. Out of the picture she spoke to me. She seemed to tell me she loved me, she trusted I would be okay, and she believed in me. She seemed to say, "You can do this! And remember our motto, 'We never miss!'" That was the personal slogan we had created together realizing each could rely on and depend on the other, absolutely and completely, to keep our word. We had never once failed, ever, to be at the appointed time and place we had said we would be; hence, we would often greet each other with, "We Never Miss!" This picture somehow gave me great comfort and solace at this crucial time, because with this leisure time to reflect, I had developed a somewhat fatalistic attitude about my survival. Her picture gave me great encouragement and finally I got much-needed sleep and rest.

The brief respite was good for all of us, but all too soon came the inevitable orders to press the attack forward, which for us meant returning to the front. The month of June was drawing to a close and each of General Bradley's divisions was clawing for ground on every front. The battle for control of the Carentan Peninsula was raging to the west of us, and the bloody days of stalemate at St. Lô still lay ahead. All this was unknown to us, however, as we were locked in our own "one little acre of hell at a time" in a horrid maze of endless hedgerows, and seemingly thousands of deadly fields to cross for miles upon miles ahead. How they all looked the same! And the endless rain! Always cold, and ever soaking wet and muddy. Would we ever survive to break out of this place? Germany seemed so far away—and home, even farther.

Everyone knew the attack across the Vire would be heavily defended. Our job now was to hold ground won and secure a route for the next push beyond the canal southward. We needed a better map of the terrain to find the best potential crossing point. With this objective in mind, I formed a small, lightly-armed reconnaissance party consisting of Lieutenant Hulbert, Lieutenant Nash, my runner Private Boker, and myself, to return again to the river bank and locate the best route around swamp land to the river shore. The four of us set out and carefully traversed around hedgerows between the swamp and the bridge, making our way south. Approaching with great care, we reached the canal safely and started walking parallel to the water's edge under cover, hidden by thick bushes. When we came upon an open gap about three or four feet wide, which would expose us, we paused. I was thinking, "Okay, each of us will run quickly across this opening one at a time." Just then, Private Boker said to me, "Wait, I'll cover you Captain," meaning, he would cross the gap first and then aim his rifle across the canal to cover us while we crossed. Just as he was saying this, he jumped out into the gap and raised his M1 into position. In that instant, a shot rang out from across the canal. Boker screamed once and slumped to the ground. I knew it was a fatal shot just by the way he fell. We were stunned.

Raymond J. Boker was posthumously promoted to sergeant and awarded the Purple Heart. In my mind, that could never be enough for what he did that day.

He is interred at the Normandy American Cemetery at Colleville-sur-Mer, France. I have visited his grave numerous times in the years since the war. When I remember Private Boker, I always think of the scripture verse, "Greater love hath no man than this: that he would lay down his life for his friends." Despite my shock and sadness, the fighting continued around me day and night.

We anxiously awaited the word to move out on the expected crossing attack, but were ordered to hold our positions and wait for a specifically timed, coordinated effort. As I visited K Company men and walked around their positions going through lonely fields and crossing hedgerows alone, I fully expected a sniper to strike me down.

When the 4th of July came and everyone was told to fire one shot simultaneously, everything from 155mm artillery to the smallest caliber rifle, all together at precisely 0100 hours. We did! Wow, I wonder what the enemy thought.

6 July. One month had passed since D-Day. My telephone rang and I was told to report to Battalion Headquarters for an extensive briefing regarding the next phase. The time had come, the attack was on! Nervously, I grabbed my .30-caliber carbine and trudged off to the HQ meeting. Tomorrow would be D-Day for us.

It was decided that our battalion was to attack across the Vire at a point to the right of the bridge, and to the left of the swampy area where we had encountered the enemy during that last reconnaissance. The 1st Battalion was to strike across the canal to our left with the main road between us. Battalion commander McCollum told me K Company was to lead the assault. I knew for sure the Germans would be in abundance in this area. We had encountered them daily since our arrival there. I was a bit more encouraged, though, when Colonel McCollum said in his deep southern draw, "See heah, Smith, I'll get any weapon you want up there for you. Ya'll just tell me what you want, because you and your company will be the assault company, I and L Companies will follow once you've secured the other side."

I replied, "That's good (referring to his offer), because I want M Company's heavy water-cooled machine guns there for us, plus we'll need some kind of footbridges or ladders to cross on, and the engineers will be needed to open gaps and move the ladders into place." The orders further specified that, following the crossing, the battalion objective was to take, secure, and hold the village of St. Jean de Daye, and there await further instruction.

Returning to the company, we held a briefing and steeled ourselves for what lay ahead. The road and bridge would be on K Company's left flank, with the 1st Battalion to the left of the road. This was the main road back to the beaches not so many miles behind us. We knew we could expect a major counterattack at any time, with a strong attempt to divide us, and push us back to the coast, only ten or twelve miles to the rear. Colonel McCollum made clear that failure was not an option.

By 7 July, we had been in a holding position, trading potshots with the enemy for approximately two weeks. All this time, they had been dug in just across from us, hidden by the thick foliage of trees and bushes, only a few yards away. We assumed they were waiting for us in force. The time of attack was set for 1300 hours, 7 July. As I had requested, Company M's heavy machine guns had been positioned under darkness the night before, as had the crossing ladders. The plan called for a feint by the regiment three mile to our right at another likely crossing point. American artillery and mortar fire would pound that area prior to our attack in an effort to cause the Germans to shift resources there, and thereby decrease enemy strength opposite our immediate front. Whether or not this feint had any of the desired effect, I may never know.

I set up my command post, radios, telephone, and runners about 100 feet behind the canal. At 1300 hours, the "commence attack" signal was given. I heard several loud explosions and soon received word from a platoon leader that the engineers had dynamited part of the hedgerow to make a place for the ladders, and that this blasting had stunned many of our men, and they were unable to proceed. Furthermore, the ladders, intended for use as footbridges across, were too short to complete the span. I told them we must cross anyway, and I turned to Lieutenant Hulbert, my executive officer, and told him, "Let's go. We must lead them across." We ran forward and found the far end of the ladders in the water. They were indeed too short! Across I went anyway, followed by Hulbert. We jumped into the water, and struggled on across. I remember I fired a round into the bank from my carbine (to assure myself it would still function when wet) and scrambled up the slippery enemy side. We emerged into a small field where we spotted an enemy machine gun firing towards us. I opened fire on it. At about the same time, I saw two German soldiers running to their rear. I opened fire on them, and they threw their rifles down and surrendered. I had wounded one by creasing his neck.

When I got near their machine gun, it was gone, but I saw Lieutenant Huffman, my platoon leader, lying on the ground. He was bandaging a wound himself. Medical aid men were following to assist. We progressed rapidly forward, being severely shelled by enemy artillery, or perhaps short American rounds, resulting in several of our fellows being wounded. I came upon them being attended by a German medic who wore a white sheet in front and back with a large red cross on it. By contrast, our medics wore only small *Red Cross* armbands which were soon covered with dirt and mud. Consequently, many medics must have been killed by the enemy, believing they were combat soldiers. This German medic spoke fluent English. One of my men brought him to me, and he said he had been on the Russian front also. He wanted to go back to his lines. I was very suspicious that he would give away our exact position to his soldiers, so I had him escorted to the rear Battalion Headquarters.

Then Sergeant Browning came to me, just as I saw several enemy soldiers running wildly around some long trenches to my front. Browning was asking what to do about them. I suggested capturing them if possible. If not, "Do what you must." We rushed on to the western edge of St. Jean de Daye. Resistance had crumbled, and we entered the western outskirts of the town, while the 1st Battalion attacked into the center. We claimed our objective and buttoned up (dug in) for the night. St. Jean de Daye was ours! We saw no French civilians in our zone. Apparently, they had left the battle area.[1]

KING KENNY, RECONNAISSANCE PLATOON, 823RD TANK DESTROYER BATTALION

As a GI you don't know what's going on. They said we were going to cross the Vire and I figured, boy, that's going to be something. How are we going to cross it? The Vire was not more than 20 yards wide and the bridge was still there. So it turned out we just went across it! Then, shortly after, darkness came on. There were a lot of troops around and somebody yelled, "Gas attack!" A couple of planes flew over and there was a tremendous amount of confusion. Everyone was fumbling around for their gas masks. Ultimately, there was no gas and I guess the only thing we learned from that was how to put our gas masks on quickly!

Next, we got into the hedgerow country and that was pretty static—a lot of firing and shooting over the hedgerows with rifles. Our basic weapon in Recon was an M1 rifle and for the TD (tank destroyer) crews, I think they had carbines. Our objective was not, "Let's make three miles!" It was more like, "Make 50 or 60 yards to the next hedgerow!" I saw a German running up towards us alone and I shot him. Later that afternoon as we moved through the hedgerows, the enemy was defending. I stopped and opened up that soldier's tunic thinking maybe he had some maps or something in it. I pulled out a picture of him along with what must have been his mother and father, just like any one of us would have. I will never forget that. If I had thought about it, I would have taken something that had his name so I could tell his folks that he had died bravely. I remember that distinctly.[2]

The 30th Division redressed the imbalance in troop strength by summoning the 117th Infantry Regiment, who planned to attack from south to west across the Vire River toward the small town of Vire. Two battalions of the 120th Infantry Regiment would attack the southern end with the 113th Cavalry Group (Mechanized) bringing up the rear to protect the right flank. The 119th Infantry Regiment would follow the Vire River along the southern route parallel to the 2nd Battalion, 120th Infantry that would advance from the west. Between these two regiments, the 743rd Tank Battalion was on hand to pivot in either direction as the situation demanded. A small party continued south to the main highway bridge over the Vire et Taute Canal, but discovered that it had been blown. The next day the 120th completed the grueling task of clearing the canal.

While the 1st Battalion, 120th Infantry advanced cautiously through the hedgerows downhill toward the exposed man-made swamplands of the Vire et Taute Canal–Vire River junction, Company F eliminated pockets of enemy resistance from the barnyards and ditches around the town of La Ray. The 3rd Battalion, 120th Infantry Regiment became engaged on the fringes of the western stretches of the sector as they worked on clearing out the Deville area. Then they sent a patrol to the bridge at Graignes, only to discover that it had been completely destroyed. That night the regiment was digging in along the gentle inclines that lead down to the dangerously exposed no-man's-land flanking the borders of the canal. The last serious action of the day occurred at around 1030 hours when a company of *SS-Panzer-Grenadier Regiment 38* made an impetuous but daring raid across the canal. The grenadiers were forced back by massed infantry and artillery fire. Interrogations of approximately 50 German prisoners who were taken during the previous two-days' fighting revealed that among the ranks of the Germans were elements of the *Grenadier Regiment 984*, who had been sighted as part of the *275th Infantry Division* in Brittany. There were also a few members of the seriously depleted *352nd Infantry Division.*

MARK SCHWENDIMAN, COMPANY I, 119TH INFANTRY REGIMENT

Putting finishing touches to combat training with the US First Army in England, the 30th launched its first attack in World War II in Normandy on 15 June 1944—D +9—after its first units had come ashore at Omaha Beach on D +4. In sniper-infested hedgerow country, the 30th's baptism of fire came in the Isigny area where it drove a stubborn German enemy beyond the Vire River and Vire et Taute Canal. Then in dangerous nightly patrols, it probed German positions in preparation for the assault crossing of the Vire River where, on 7 July, it started the push south out of the Cherbourg peninsula. Crossings of the Vire at dawn and the Vire et Taute Canal at 1300 the same day were masterfully executed. The preparatory artillery barrage left the Germans stunned in their foxholes and made the initial advance possible. Panzer troops were brought in to plug the gap thus created, however, and in the succeeding days other elite panzer and parachute troops counterattacked with the mission of seizing Isigny. Old Hickory nevertheless ground their way steadily ahead.[3]

The evidence of destroyed bridges and minefields along the stretches of the canal indicated that the Germans were planning to conduct mainly a defensive campaign. Sporadic bursts from 88s and other German artillery on the 30th Division's locations gave clear proof that the canal was going to be a particularly precarious obstacle that provided little cover. This was a further initiation for the division to the intricacies of hedgerow fighting as the other regiments of the Division began to take up position along the east bank of the Vire. On 15 June, the 117th Infantry Regiment was assigned to a position along the railroad tracks just east of the river and north of the town of Airel. There they encountered some opposition in their efforts to take a short concrete bridge over the Vire opposite Airel. They had discovered the bridge was completely intact, but withering machine-gun fire emanating from the opposite bank initially exacerbated attempts to secure the position. Only one battalion of the 117th was engaged in frontline combat at this time. The rest were bivouacked roughly a mile behind them. The 119th Infantry Regiment had been equally surreptitious in their dealings. They sent a platoon into the village of La Meauffe to supposedly take over guard duties from the unit there, but soon discovered that the town was still firmly in the hands of the Germans who were in no great hurry to abandon their positions. Intermittent fighting continued throughout the night of 18 June until Company B arrived at daylight to occupy the northeast section of the village.

The Germans asserted their desire to re-occupy this location by assuming static positions along a tree-covered low hill situated to the south of the village. From this position they poured fire into the village until finally on 19 June the battalion was pulled back to less exposed ground beyond the village perimeter. For the time being, the strategic importance of this place was considered negligible and definitely not important enough to expend valuable resources on its capture.

As the 120th Infantry Regiment's leading troops rambled to within sight of the canal, the opinion at Division Headquarters was that the attack should continue to the south, with an initial crossing that would effectively avoid the exposed waterlogged approaches to the canal. They would attack westward across the Vire River south of Airel. The artificial flooding effected by the Germans in this area prior to invasion had been less severe and the approaching troops were less likely to draw fire from German machinegunners and artillery observers in the vicinity. A warning order to that effect had already been issued and a swift reconnaissance of the proposed site by engineers had been completed before word came through from XIX Corps that all further advances were going to be postponed indefinitely pending the arrival of more men and equipment. This was the start of a three-week intermezzo while Corps HQ tackled the problems of logistics and supply for the steadily increasing number of men and machines that were arriving daily. This perpetual stream of US forces arriving at the beaches to facilitate further advances brought with it even more problems than had been expected.

During the ensuing three weeks, the division was not allowed to wallow in inertia, they occupied their time with what G-3 referred to as "vigorous patrolling and active defense." From 1 to 6 July, stringent training and simulated river crossings with assault boats were used in preparation for the eventual crossing. Practice in the construction and application of footbridges augmented these exercises. Satchel charges were prepared to be used for blowing gaps in the hedgerows.

On 7 July, a few hours before dawn, the Normandy skies above the Vire River were covered with pregnant, low-hanging clouds that intermittently obscured the full moon and managed to provide almost incessant drizzle. This drizzle soaked the hedges and rendered the smooth, clay, eight-foothigh banks of the river slippery. The 3rd Armored Division would be ready to cross as soon as it could be used. The 247th Engineer Combat Battalion and the 503rd Light Pontoon Company supported the Division's own 105th Engineer Battalion in bridging the river and canal while the 743rd Tank Battalion was divided into two assault regiments.

After a short night, at 0330 hours, Division Artillery began its preparatory artillery barrages on enemy positions. Half an hour previously 2nd Battalion, 117th Infantry Regiment, had started moving from its assembly area. Engineer guides met the assault companies at the last hedgerow on the near side of the river, 400 yards from the bank, and the engineers and infantry carried their rubber assault boats and scaling ladders down to the water's edge. Two battalions of the 117th, supported by a company from the 743rd Tank

Battalion, moved ahead on point. They crossed the Vire in flimsy assault boats that became waterlogged as soon as they were lowered. The 117th had initially encountered some problems while launching the boats from the steep banks due to the sharp angle at which they were launched. This caused the bows to dip and take on even more water. Some of them were so heavily weighed down by equipment that the men found it necessary to disembark and paddle across the river beside the craft to lessen the weight. As soon as the boatmen had crossed and discharged their loads, the engineer guides returned for the remainder of the troops. Enemy artillery fire, which until this time had been moderate, began to increase five minutes after the first crossing. At 0420 the first wave of 32 boats had navigated the 70-foot stream and the 2nd Battalion quickly established a bridgehead on the far riverbank. As a torrent of German artillery shells exploded dangerously close to them, the men of the 2nd Battalion hurriedly scrambled up the bank on the scaling ladders provided by the engineers and followed their instructions to move as fast as possible to the first hedgerow, which was roughly 400 yards beyond. As the engineers returned to reload the boats with GIs, lethal German 88mm guns opened fire again.

Despite incurring 40 percent casualties in those first assaults, the engineers still had to install the footbridge. The 3rd Platoon of Company B, 105th Engineer Battalion, began hauling the heavy preassembled footbridge down to the water's edge just as the first waves of men were moving out. As they lowered the first few sections German artillery began crashing down again. Some of the men actually swam out into the 14-foot-deep stream to secure the mooring on the far bank. It was a precarious and strenuous piece of work to get the footbridge assembled and working, but by 0530 repairs had been completed and it was ready to use.

The whole process demanded speed and precision. Almost a half an hour passed before the second wave began crossing the river. Enemy artillery and mortar fire intensified all around the river, making bow waves that rocked the boats and forcing the GIs to pull down their helmets as each deadly impact caused the water to flare up. The first three waves of infantry used assault boats and then, as soon as the footbridge was assembled and in place, they streamed over it. The engineer platoon had lost 17 men during the crossing and was later awarded the Distinguished Unit Citation for this action.

By early afternoon, the 120th Infantry Regiment was ready to attack due south with two battalions along the axis of the main highway leading south to Pont Hebert and St. Lô. The attached 113th Cavalry Group was to cross as soon as possible after the 120th to protect the Division's right flank. The 119th Infantry Regiment was designated to move along the Vire south of Airel, and the 2nd Battalion of the 120th on the west side opposite Graignes, would have to remain static until the opposing forces were driven back from other side of the canal.

What transpired the day after the attack went in was particularly detrimental to the progress of the advance. When Corps command sent up 3rd Armored Division's Combat Command B (CCB) to provide additional support, gridlocks began to accumulate on the approach roads. This made the US forces vulnerable and the situation was further exacerbated with the arrival of the German *2nd SS-Panzer Division "Das Reich,"* which was earmarked to participate in a concerted counterattack.

The following day, 9 July, the planned attack by the 119th Infantry Regiment failed to materialize on any significant scale. Rather than supporting the 119th's assault, the additional tanks on the roads and in open fields made the problems worse. The *2nd SS-Panzer*, meanwhile, brought up artillery from St. Lô and began slamming into forward elements of the 117th Infantry and 120th Infantry, causing them to fall back.

HAROLD WILLIAMS, 105TH ENGINEER COMBAT BATTALION

We were in the Pont Hebert area, which was wooded. We backed the truck and tanks underneath the trees for camouflage purposes, then I had one of the biggest scares during the whole war. All was quiet and there wasn't too much going on. All of the sudden, people started yelling, "Gas! Gas! Gas!" We dropped what we were doing and went for our gas masks. We all put them on as best we could. This was the only time in the war that I know this happened. In a few minutes word came up and down the lines, "All clear, false alarm." No gas was used but somebody somewhere thought it was. It was a pretty scary thing.

Later, two German planes came over. They were up a thousand feet or so and released cluster bombs. They drifted down by parachute until they were 200–300 feet off the ground. Then they exploded like firecrackers and released shrapnel everywhere. Well, everybody dove for cover. Quite a few men were wounded and a few were killed. I don't know the numbers. Then the planes were gone. My feeling was they'd be back. I don't think it had been 3–5 minutes and they came back at treetop level strafing our area. I was waiting for them when they came. I was able to knock down the one nearest me. Number one, I didn't fire at the plane, I gave it a lead. If you fired at it—a moving target, at any speed—you were not going to hit it. The plane flew maybe 1/3 to 1/2 mile trailing black smoke, then there was a ball of fire. A few guys around me witnessed it. I was firing the .50-caliber machine gun. My 2-1/2-ton truck had a ring mount on it for the .50-caliber. It had no top—it had been taken off when the machine gun was installed. I stood inside the ring on the passenger seat. That was my position.[4]

Panic was expertly avoided when 30th Division HQ responded quickly and decisively by reassigning 18 artillery battalions and initiating an intense barrage that was implemented with such accuracy and ferocity that it fell almost directly on to the heads of approaching Germans. It was this consummate display of cool, clear thinking by 30th Division officers that helped regain the impetus in favor of the US forces. The artillery barrage effectively discouraged the Germans to such an extent that rapid progress was achieved throughout the next day. Then as the assault began to reassert its momentum the *2nd SS-Panzer Division* seemed to enigmatically disappear from view. *Das Reich*'s panzers had evidently withdrawn from the scene; their whereabouts were to remain an enigma for days to come. The notorious *Panzer Lehr Division* was on hand nevertheless. The *2nd SS-Panzer* had demonstrated the approved method of conducting armored warfare tactics to countless burgeoning panzer troops before the invasion and now it was diverting its attention to more pressing matters.

On 8 July it was reported to be somewhere in the St. Lô area and a few days later, on the night of 10/11 July, it attempted to infiltrate into the 120th Infantry Regiment's positions. The following day it mounted a bold two-pronged attack that left the rear areas of the 30th and 9th Infantry Divisions littered with burned-out German tanks. *Panzer-Grenadier Regiment 902* and a battalion of tanks, meanwhile, struck the 30th with force. During the evening of 10 July, the 3rd Battalion, 120th Infantry Regiment, was ordered to advance to Le Rocher, a little town on the northwest edge of the long ridge stretching south, parallel to the Vire River. The foot columns leading the advance met stiff resistance in some places en route, and were digging in when a column of vehicles arrived. The flanks of this position were dangerously exposed at this time, so it was decided that roadblocks should be set up to compensate for this shortfall. Not long after the position had been established a runner arrived from one of the roadblocks to the east with information that tanks, infantry, and armored vehicles were moving along the road toward the command post. Just after the messages alerting the companies had been dispatched two German tanks actually moved past the command post. Then a third German tank cautiously approached, followed at an interval by another, and then another, and finally by an armored car. A German who was standing in the open turret of the lead tank appeared to be trying to send a message.

It was at this juncture that all hell broke loose. One American lieutenant ran to a jeep-mounted .30-caliber machine gun and opened fire. Then someone fired a bazooka and redeployed to take another shot. Two officers started lobbing hand grenades into the turret of the tank and at the accompanying German infantry on the road. The first tank exploded to a chorus of screams of excruciating pain from those inside who were being slowly consumed within the impenetrable confines of this steel coffin by a rage of billowing flame. During the fog of battle one officer leading a small ammunition party tentatively approached an armored car down the road, only to discover that it was German; within moments a vicious firefight ensued that culminated in the officer and his men being wounded and taken prisoner. They were lined up behind the armored car with the accompanying German infantry as it moved away. At a nearby crossroads, just short of the command post, .50-caliber machine-gun bullets and bazooka shells continued to blaze away. By morning the 3rd Battalion, 120th Regiment had taken 60 prisoners; the toll paid in dead and wounded was never accurately calculated; and five enemy tanks along with four armored cars were effectively disabled during the fight.

Early in the morning of 11 July, while the timid sun was just revealing the extent of morning mists, German tanks rumbled menacingly across the open fields and infantry began infiltrating the 119th's positions. 3rd Armored Division's Combat Command B wasted no time in getting to the scene and by mid-morning, the attack had disintegrated. This decisive and effective response was due in no small part to individual actions such the engineer lieutenant working on road clearance near Bahais who recruited a tank and infantrymen to destroy an enemy tank and drive 20 panzergrenadiers out of a house near the river. One group of 13 tanks was reported burning, meanwhile, as a result of an air strike by P-47s. This pattern of effective air strikes against German armor was to be repeated on many occasions during the ensuing weeks of combat.

HAROLD WILLIAMS, 105TH ENGINEER COMBAT BATTALION

Our next objective was St. Lô, one of the hardest fought battles of the war. Germans were there and they were dug in. They were pretty well set up. We were the green troops. We fought for days for St. Lô. I can remember one day in particular, July 11th. We were being shelled by mortars and artillery. Rounds were coming in and you could hardly stick your head up. The reason I remember 11 July was that it was my mother's birthday and it was so, so harsh. That ended and we spent days going back and forth trying to take St. Lô. We were up against a lot of German armor.[5]

The fight was far from over, however, because a few days previous to the actions the appearance of the *Panzer Lehr Division* in the St. Lô area had been confirmed by US forward artillery observers. It later transpired that the intention of the *Panzer Lehr* was to recapture Isigny on the Normandy coast. This unrealistic ambition was indicative of the pervading desperate rationale of the German high command.

There was no doubt regarding the German resolve to attack, but they were already experiencing some critical supply problems that restricted their ability to maintain the momentum. Any gains that were made by German forces quickly dissipated when faced with relentless opposition from the Allies. A distinct pattern began to emerge that characterized the style and method of operations in the Normandy hedgerows.

The bocage wasn't the problem. The hedges that formed this feature of the countryside were planted on sizeable earthen walls that often forced advancing US troops and armor to move in single file along the boundaries of these hedges. As soon as they surmounted these obstacles and defiled into open fields they faced a deluge of bullets and shells from firmly entrenched German tanks and skillfully placed machine-gun nests. From the German side as soon as they emerged into the open they became immediately vulnerable to US artillery, armor, and troops supported by low flying P-47s and bombers. The pattern repeated itself incessantly throughout the whole campaign.

JOHN NOLAN, COMPANY G, 119TH INFANTRY REGIMENT

I was assigned as the 3rd Squad Leader, 1st Platoon, G Company, 2nd Battalion, 119th Infantry Regiment. I began my European "adventure" with a "packet" of infantry replacements that landed on Omaha Beach on 20 July 1944.

I was in an infantry replacement unit that landed on Omaha Beach on 20 July 1944. We moved inland a short distance and we were put in a hedgerow surrounding a Normandy farmer's meadow. We remained there for weeks waiting for assignment to an infantry division. During this "stay" we witnessed an unforgettable event, the bombing of St. Lô. It seemed like the flow of various kinds of Army Air Corps bombers never would end as they flew over us at a very low alti-

tude. The sound of their flight above us was a continuous roll of thunder. We were close enough to St. Lô that we could hear the sound of the bombs hitting their target. Accompanying the bombers was an occasional P-47 fighter aircraft circling around the bomber stream. The sight reminded me of a mother hen protecting her chicks. We made the best of it in the deep hedgerow ditch. We were given K-rations to eat since there was no mess or mess personnel assigned to a replacement unit. Talk about food monotony, this was it.[6]

Despite the obvious toll on the Allied effort in Normandy, it was estimated that by the end of July 1944 the German army had also incurred substantial losses. Although they defended with great tactical skill and employed every element of the environment to their advantage, it was becoming glaringly obvious that the German effort was suffering badly. In an effort to present the Allies with an appearance of cohesion the Germans had been reduced to assembling impromptu "*Kampfgruppen*" (fighting units) hurriedly thrown together to attempt to maintain the façade that they were defending from an unbroken line. They had reserves just west of the river Seine, but only one division, the *2nd SS-Panzer Division "Das Reich,"* was in close enough proximity to orchestrate a counterattack.

The hedgerow fighting badly affected both Allies and Axis forces. By late July, it was estimated that the Germans had lost approximately 400 tanks, 2,500 other vehicles, and 160,000 men. This had undoubtedly put a great strain on the Germans offensive capabilities. One of the main problems was the lack of resources such as gasoline and other necessary supplies. Bearing in mind that a division on the move needs around 7,000 tons of supplies every day it was becoming increasingly difficult for the Germans to keep up with the demand. Moreover they no longer had the capacity to effectively replace destroyed and damaged armor in any significant numbers.

Most of their divisions had sustained heavy losses but there were still one or two that were battle ready. The *2nd SS-Panzer Division* had a particular reputation for being stringent and thorough in all their dealings. Just four days after the Allied invasion of Normandy, they had been held responsible for a heinous war crime at the small French village of Oradour-sur-Glane. Soldiers of the *3rd Company, 1st Battalion, SS-Panzer-Grenadier Regiment 4* (motorized infantry) "*Der Führer,*" attached to the *2nd SS-Panzer Division,* advanced to the village of Oradour-sur-Glane. Led by the commander of the *1st Battalion, SS*-Major Adolf Diekmann, the *Waffen-SS* troops surrounded the village. Dozens of women and children were burned alive. In total 642 men, women, and children were killed at this site which is still maintained as a shrine to the victims.

SS-Oberscharführer Ernst Schmuck-Barkmann, tank commander (Panther) in *4th Company, SS-Panzer-Regiment 2* was not directly involved with the massacre. In 2002, he said:

> In early July 1944, *Das Reich* was moved to St. Lô to halt the advance of the US Army's 9th and 30th Infantry Divisions and the 3rd Armored Division. On 8 July my unit was the spearhead of the *Regiment*'s attack on the advancing American units.[7]

Later on, in his Panther I Ausf. A, Ernst Barkmann knocked out his first Allied Sherman tank near St. Lô. On 12 July, he destroyed two more Shermans while disabling the third one. During that engagement Barkmann placed his camouflaged Panther in an ambush position and waited for more Allied armor. He eventually disabled three more Shermans. The 30th Division wouldn't face the *2nd SS-Panzer* again during WWII, but they would take on the *1st SS-Panzer Division "Leibstandarte SS Adolf Hitler" (LAH)* more than once. Their first encounter would occur in the vicinity of Mortain during an action the Germans referred to as Operation *LÜTTICH*.

July had been a war of attrition for both sides. On 15 July, the 30th Division was placed under the command of VII Corps. A few days later a task force from the 29th Infantry Division captured St. Lô and by 20 July, the 30th Division's advances ground to a strategic halt. Then they began reorganizing in preparation for the next assault.

RICHARD LACEY, COMPANY M, 120TH INFANTRY REGIMENT

I joined the 30th Division just after St. Lô had fallen (the 29th mainly took St. Lô but our division helped). I joined M Company and they made me an assistant machine gunner. I said to the guy with me, "I'm glad they put me with a veteran," and he said, "What do you mean, I came up with you!" We had a lieutenant and a squad leader; each squad was supposed to have a gunner, the assistant, and three ammunition bearers, but we were lucky if we had two guys carrying ammunition. I was 18 going on 19. That machine gun weighed 45 pounds and I carried it sometimes 15 miles a day across France, Belgium, and Netherlands. Sometimes I would get a ride—we had a jeep with a trailer—but that didn't happen very often. A couple times we had the guns on the jeep and Germans started to shoot at us and the jeep driver threw our guns off and took off! We did a lot of walking there. The machine gun was water-cooled, it was a good gun. The assistant gunner fed ammo belts into the machine gun and made sure it didn't jam (once in a while, it would get jammed up). Sometimes you would have a short round or something that would cause the gun to misfire. Sometimes ammo belts would come through with a lot of tracers and the tracers could give off your positions to the Germans. We used to pull out some of the tracers and put regular bullets in the slots that the tracers were in to insure we weren't giving our position. I really never fired the gun during the war. I had a Polish guy with me and he was bigger than I was. We got along well and he did all the shooting. We were armed with a .45 pistol because we needed our arms to hold the guns. The ammunition bearers carried carbines. We would be attached to one of the rifle companies such as K or L. Maybe two guns would go with one platoon of K Company and the other two would go with another. It depended upon the circumstances. When we were down in Malmédy in the Battle of the Bulge, they stood our four guns up. Two were with one platoon of riflemen and we were with another platoon of riflemen down the road maybe two tenths of a mile so we could lay down crossfire. So that was the way things worked. The mortars would stay back a little farther. They could fire shells a longer distance.[8]

As the advancing US 2nd, 3rd, and 4th Armored Divisions, supported by the 1st Infantry Division ("Big Red One"), charged through the St. Lô gap, they successfully gained 12,000 yards and eventually facilitated a breakthrough on 27 July. In response to this rapid assault, dazed and shocked German forces fell back 12 miles and only marginally managed to prevent a retreat from turning into a complete rout. Low on supplies and shattered by continuous strafing and bombing by Allied airplanes, by the end of July they were now organizing a general retreat in an attempt to regroup, but regroup they would.

MARK SCHWENDIMAN, COMPANY I, 119TH INFANTRY REGIMENT

The hedgerow-to-hedgerow "slugging match" against dug-in German infantry-men and tanks continued until the 30th captured high ground overlooking St. Lô, France, while the 29th Infantry Division went into that important railroad center to find that it had been completely destroyed. This was now known as the St. Lô Breakthrough, which opened the gate for the armored divisions and permitted them to fan out on their drive up through Northern France. Having proved itself among the veteran divisions of the US First Army, the 30th, with the 4th and 9th Infantry Divisions, was selected to spearhead the great operation designated

as COBRA. Heavy and medium bombers, attempting to pulverize the German po-
sition in front of the 30th, dropped some of their bombs short and many casualties
occurred among the assaulting units. Despite this great difficulty, reorganization
was effected and the attack pushed on successfully.[9]

JOHN O'HARE, COMPANY E, 117TH INFANTRY REGIMENT

During World War II, US Army regulations required that young men be at least
19 years of age before being sent into combat. I became 19 on 2 June 1944 and I
landed on Omaha Beach that July.

American military units in federal service were no longer recruited and
trained based upon regional origin and they were not expected to fight as repre-
sentatives of a particular state or locality. Infantry training was standardized.
Soldiers leaving training camps with identical training were simply, but aptly,
known as "replacements." Lieutenant General Leslie J. McNair had instituted
this system when he was in charge of training all Army personnel. It is ironic that
he was killed while visiting the 30th Infantry Division to observe the effects of
the carpet-bombing, which preceded the Breakout from Normandy. Units such as
the 30th Infantry Division had been National Guard units before being called to
federal service. The 30th Division was originally made up of units from Tennessee
and North Carolina. Once such units were federalized and suffered casualties,
they were reinforced with "replacements" from anywhere in the country.

I arrived at Omaha Beach as a "replacement" and did not know what my
future unit assignment would be. After I climbed the hill above the beach, I joined
other new arrivals in a series of "replacement pools," from which we could be
assigned to any frontline unit in need of reinforcements.

The 30th Division was in need of such replacements after St. Lô was taken
and it was there that I became a member of the 2nd Platoon of Company E, 117th
Infantry Regiment. Some units of the 30th Division had been in combat as early
as 10 June and many casualties had been suffered in combat around the Vire
River. The division had also suffered many casualties when American bombers
mistakenly hit forward elements in the massive carpet-bombing raids west of St.
Lô, which were intended to open a hole in the German front line to allow the
breakout known as Operation COBRA.

My first afternoon and night after arrival in Normandy were spent on the
flat area above Omaha Beach. New arrivals were exposed to rumormongering
misfits who had somehow filtered back to the beachhead with no apparent duties.
Such soldiers were known as "yardbirds" in Army slang. I avoided contact with
them, but I could hear them telling more susceptible soldiers about the horrors they

were about to encounter and that they would not return home alive. They pointed to Army trucks piled high with body bags arriving at what later was known as the National Cemetery at Colleville-sur-Mer and they yelled, "It will soon be your turn to ride in one of those stinking 'meat wagons.'" I avoided the malcontents, although it was obvious that I was in a new world. That night, I was awakened by calls for blood donors. For the first time I heard the distinctive sound of the motor of a German reconnaissance plane. Such planes took infrared photos of American positions every night. We referred to them as "Bed-Check Charlie."

While awaiting assignment to a unit, I learned to dig my foxhole into a hedgerow and then down. The hedgerows had been there for centuries and were very stable. This technique created a safe place under many feet of soil, tree roots, and rocks. On one occasion, German planes came down over the hedgerow I was using and strafed with their machine guns. I do not know how many planes took part because I was in my cave-like shelter. One soldier said six planes were involved. No Americans were injured.

On two of the days before my assignment to the 30th Division, I witnessed the sky full of US heavy bombers from horizon to horizon and in seemingly endless processions. They were on their way to carpet-bomb the German front line along part of the road west of St. Lô to Periers in preparation for the great breakout from the small enclave where the invasion had been bottled up for weeks. I joined the 30th Division at St. Lô immediately after the bombing and took part in the breakout known as Operation COBRA.

When I joined the outfit at St. Lô, the platoon sergeant of Company E, 2nd Battalion asked if anyone had any training on how to operate bazookas. I was stupid enough to say "yes," and I was made the bazooka man. The number one rule is never volunteer; no one wanted to drag around a bazooka, two bandoliers of ammunition, a rifle, and a gas mask (which you eventually threw away). I was a now a bazooka man, but not part of a particular squad. The bazooka I was given was an early type. It operated with two D-cell batteries. It was basically a rocket fired from a tube, and the electrical charge, which set off the rocket, came from the batteries. The rocket itself had wires that you had to hook up to some quills on the back end of the bazooka. The shell had a safety that you had to remove or it wouldn't fire. It was a two-step process and your ammunition bearer had to load the bazooka and help fire it. Nobody really wanted to drag that thing around. After the Battle of Mortain, I was given a more modern bazooka to replace the battery-powered earlier version.[10]

St. Lô was now in Allied hands, but still hemmed in on three sides by opposing forces. In the closing week, when the Allies eventually began gaining the upper hand, they decided to take decisive action. This stage in the campaign would be known as Operation COBRA, saturation bombing followed by a ground forces attack. The idea of a preliminary bombardment to soften up the intended target wasn't a new one, only this time it would come from the air.

After the St. Lô–Falaise breakthrough, the German line was, at best, unstable and, at worst, extremely vulnerable. This was due primarily to poor communications and reluctance to commit available reserves. The 30th Division was charged with protecting the easternmost flank of the breakthrough corridor, an ominous task because this was the flank most exposed to potential counterattack by the German *15th Army* from the east.

As a precursor to the Allied ground assault, the US Eighth Air Force would unleash a storm of annihilation and devastation on the German positions with such intensity and ferocity that the German lines would simply disintegrate under the pressure. The air support planned to launch an initial wave of 350 fighter/bombers, followed by 1,500 heavy bombers that would canvas a target only 6,000 yards wide and 2,500 yards deep. It would be the most intense carpet bombing of a target in support of ground troops that had ever been used.

The 120th Infantry Regiment, 30th Division, would advance on the right with its sister regiment, the 119th Infantry, on the left alongside the 2nd Armored Division. The sweeping up operation would be performed by two battalions of the 117th Infantry, which were to be held as a strategic reserve for this advance.

The intended date for the commencement of this attack was initially postponed due to inclement weather; the roads ahead of the advancing forces had become quagmires unsuitable for the rapid progress required to facilitate the operation. Then before the initial P-47s were due to go in, ground troops moved back 1,200 yards to avoid any damage from their own air cover. That particular summer day had commenced with a radiant sunrise and a relatively clear sky. Characteristic light patches of hazy mist hovered in spectral wisps above the undulating ground, but visibility wasn't particularly hampered by this. Soon the skies filled with the buzz of P-47s rapidly followed by a continuous throaty bellow reminiscent of the base notes of a church organ, signaling that the heavy bombers were beginning to appear.

Back at Division HQ, some disturbing reports of apparent incidents of fratricide began to filter back from the front lines. The ground troops were sustaining some serious collateral damage from their own air cover. The friendly fire situation rapidly dissipated when the air strikes were immediately called off. Dead and mortally-wounded men, meanwhile, littered the area. Air Command complained vociferously that it was because of poor visibility that these casualties had been incurred. The allocation of blame lay squarely with the air force, but that did little to assuage the damage that had been done.

The ground attack was postponed until the following day. This time instructions were given to the artillery to hit an area designated as no-man's-land before the attack commenced. Troops withdrew from this area as instructed and awaited orders. Before long, medium range artillery began showering the whole area. The situation was then exacerbated by bombers, despite assurances from Corps that these aircraft were operating with specific instructions to hit just one road. In the event of the bombers being unable to determine the correct road, they had instructions not to release their loads. It was all to no avail because the damage inflicted on ground troops and their vehicles was even more substantial than the previous day. The 30th Division incurred 814 casualties from the two days of bombardment by their own side. One of the casualties was Lieutenant General Leslie J. McNair who had only been in Europe a few days. He was killed when a bomb dropped directly into his foxhole while observing front line troops of the 2nd Battalion, 120th Infantry Regiment. He was one of the highest ranking US officers to be killed in WWII. He also had the distinction of being the only high ranking officer to be killed by friendly fire. General Omar Bradley who was also a West Point graduate like McNair wrote:

> The ground belched, shook, and spewed dirt to the sky. Scores of our troops were hit, their bodies flung from slit trenches. Doughboys were dazed and frightened. . . . A bomb landed squarely on McNair in a slit trench and threw his body 60 feet and mangled it beyond recognition except for the three stars on his collar.[11]

German losses from the bombardment were significantly less than those of the Americans because of the depth and protection offered by reinforced concrete bomb shelters that many managed to use throughout. Despite the recriminations and attempts to allocate blame, the Air Force concluded that the off-target bombings were simply due to inclement weather conditions and errors of judgment made by certain pilots and officers in their targeting.

No single person, however, was held to account or convicted for these bombings, and no court martial was ever convened on the strength of them. The press didn't report the incident, moreover, due to it being considered as potentially detrimental to the morale of the fighting men.

FRANK TOWERS, COMPANY M, 120TH INFANTRY REGIMENT

General Omar Bradley and others were in England coordinating the battle plan and attack with the Air Corps when considerable argument arose concerning the direction of the Air Corps attack and bombing. The Air Corps wanted to bomb head on, perpendicular to the German main line of resistance (MLR), the St. Lô–Periers highway, as this would allow the shortest exposure time for the planes to be targeted by the German anti-aircraft artillery. General Bradley disagreed with this approach, as it would be too risky for such close-in bombing, in case a few bombs were dropped short of their target.

He demanded that the Air Corps plan to bomb the MLR from an east to west direction, parallel to the St. Lô–Periers highway, thus lessening the possibility of any bombs dropping short and landing on our troops poised for the jump-off.

The target date of 24 July was set, and H-Hour was set for 1130 hours. All was well so far, with everything and everybody in readiness to jump off, including General Patton and his Third Army. A few hours prior to H-Hour, all of the troops of the 30th were withdrawn 1,200 yards to the north, just in case, and to allow for any misdirected bombs or artillery shells dropping short.

About one hour before H-Hour, more than 50 battalions of various-caliber artillery fired into the target area, which was the heaviest artillery barrage since the Omaha Beach landings.

At 15 minutes prior to the H-Hour, the 30th Division Artillery fired a preparation of red smoke shells, to be dropped on the southern side of the St. Lô–Periers highway. This was to more clearly define the Bomb-Line for the Air Corps. Disaster was about to strike.

As soon as the red smoke shells were fired, landed, and exploded, and the red smoke began to disperse along the MLR and highway, just as it was planned, a slight breeze from the south came up, and the smoke began to slowly drift back towards the north. In just a matter of minutes, the red smoke was on top of our 30th Division men, waiting for H-Hour.

When the planes left England, they were operating under radio silence, and there was no means established at that time, to reach the planes to divert or call off the bombing. Ground-to-air liaison was later established, due to this incident, but even then, it was not totally perfected.

At this very same time, the high-pitched drone of the engines of over 350 P-47s, followed by the deeper drone of 1,500 heavy bombers could be heard, coming from the north! Not from the east as had been planned and expected.

Since there was no ground-to-air liaison or contact, and since the planes were required to maintain radio silence from the time they left England until their mission was accomplished, there was no way whatsoever to warn them about the northward drift of the red smoke, and to request that they bomb the area south of the red smoke and the St. Lô-Periers highway.

As the armada of planes reached the designated target area, bombs began to be released, raining down directly on the "red smoke line" and our 30th Division troops!

Such a tragedy! Could it have been avoided? Why did the Air Corps, after agreeing to bomb parallel to the MLR, bomb perpendicular to the MLR? Who was responsible for this decision change? Perhaps we will never know nor get any satisfactory answers.

On 24 July, the 120th Infantry sustained 24 men killed and 128 wounded; the 119th Infantry had 5 killed and 28 wounded, as a result of this tragedy, but the 117th Infantry escaped because they were in reserve at this particular time. Other divisions to our right and left also sustained some losses, but being in the center of the line and the main point of the planned breakthrough, the 30th took the heaviest losses.

It was a tremendously demoralizing blow to the men of the 30th! But, quite naturally, the planned attack was cancelled. It was immediately decided to execute the same attack plan the following day, 25 July, with the infantry attack at 1100 hours. In such a short time, it was extremely difficult to reorganize, resupply, and integrate a few available replacements and be ready for this second attempt at the same plan at H-Hour on the 25th.

The next morning arrived, bright and sunny, as on the day before. All was in readiness: Troops were withdrawn their 1,200 yards; artillery poured its barrage on the designated target areas and marked the MLR with red smoke shells; and they awaited H-Hour.

Unknown to most, only one thing was different. In recent days, Lieutenant General Leslie McNair who had recently left his post in Washington as CG Army Ground Forces, was assigned to a newly created position and found himself at the HQ of the 2nd Battalion of the 120th Regiment, where the most casualties had occurred the day before. His purpose was to observe the actions and readiness of the troops and the air drop; to see if it could be determined what went wrong on the previous day; and how it could possibly have been prevented.

The preparation time had arrived and the "red smoke shells" went out, falling directly on the pre-designated targets, the MLR just south of the St. Lô-Periers highway. Again, much to their dismay, the slight southerly breeze came up, drifting the red smoke back about 1,200 yards, right on top of our troops, just as it had the day before!

The sound of the droning planes was again heard to the north. With the clear sky, it was easy to see the relatively low-flying bombers as they opened their bomb bays and the bombs began falling out. To their horror, they were being dropped right on our troops once again.

For a second day in a row, tragedy struck the 30th Infantry Division, with 64 more men killed and 374 wounded and 60 missing in action. Those missing in action were presumably buried alive in this bombing, and were later uncovered and recorded. Some received direct hits in their foxholes and were totally vaporized. To add to this tragedy, Lieutenant General McNair was killed in this action! Such a tragic loss to occur on the first day of his combat observation.

Now what to do? Cancel again? Go ahead with the attack? These were the questions facing not only the 30th Division, but also the adjacent divisions—who had not been affected by the bombing, but were in complete readiness to jump off at H-Hour—and the Corps and Army Headquarters. Quickly the decision was made—to go ahead with the attack as planned. The Germans "had been warned" for two days in a row and the element of surprise was entirely gone by now.

Hastily, the front line units were reorganized as best they could under the circumstances, but there were no replacements available nor was there time for re-supplying and re-equipping the troops. They would just have to do the best that they could with what they had.

Thus, a poorly led, equipped, and demoralized army of men went forward to do the best that they could do.

They found that the Germans were not as badly hurt as they had anticipated, were well dug in, and held their defensive positions very well, but in short order, their MLR was breached. It was found that the Germans had been unable to move any armor or additional replacements up to the front, so there was little depth to the MLR. Once it had been breached, the way was open for Patton and his Third Army to break through and head for Brest.

The 30th Infantry Division was soon pinched out of the front line and went into reserve for the first time since their combat action began on 15 June. After these past 49 days, the men had the opportunity to get a shower—a first for everyone—replace clothing and equipment; take in replacements for the casualties of the bombing and breaching the MLR; and a short but well-deserved rest. A

USO show and movies were available for most and was a welcome change of activity.[12]

KING KENNY, RECONNAISSANCE PLATOON, 823RD TANK DESTROYER BATTALION

At the time our platoon worked almost exclusively with the 120th Regiment of the 30th Infantry Division. We would get right in with them. For Operation COBRA *(St. Lô) the 30th was given the job of assault division. We were all dug in, but the gun companies weren't with us. We dug our foxholes and I was all by myself in mine. I had a panel of pinkish-red, which was four feet long and two feet wide, that was used to identify the front lines for the bombers flying over. Some fighters came in first and then the bombers started dropping them "short." There was a lot of smoke and the odor of bursting bombs. We were also given smoke pots to let them know where the front was. Well, it was windy and the smoke from the pots was blowing back over our troops. That was probably part of the reason the bombers were missing their targets so badly. The panels were out but the wind was blowing the smoke.*

Lieutenant General McNair was close to where I was. Normally, if someone was hurt, a jeep would come up with stretchers, but a Cadillac ambulance came up and I said, "Somebody with some brass is hurt." It turned out it was Lieutenant General McNair. Nobody could get in touch with the Air Corps.

We were able to get in touch with the little artillery plane we called "Junior." We reached him and said, "Can you call them off?" and he said, "I'm not in touch with anybody." They finally got it called off, but a lot of damage was done. I don't know how many guys from the 30th were lost that day . . . I just don't know. They came again the next day and they dropped a few more short, but we moved forward. The Germans we encountered were out of it—just babbling from all the heavy bombing. There was a long road that went up a long grade. We were told there was a cemetery up there. A German 88, their most vicious weapon, was firing on the road and everyone was in a ditch. Later, we were able to get out of the ditch and move.[13]

FRANK DENIUS, BATTERY C, 230TH FIELD ARTILLERY BATTALION

On 25 July the carpet bombing started. In the field there, the Air Force dropped short bombs and killed Lieutenant General McNair who was in a foxhole about 50–75 yards from where I was. I recall the medics rushed to him and later one of them took his three-star helmet and put it on. We suffered hundreds of casualties, dead and wounded. The next day, there was another carpet bombing and we suc-

cessfully penetrated the German lines. That's when Patton's Third Army moved through us and penetrated farther southwest. We called it his "End around to Paris."[14]

FRANK DEEGAN, COMPANY D, 119TH INFANTRY REGIMENT

We were waiting at St. Lô. We had our machine on the back of a tank. The tank commander looked up and he said, "You better get in a hole!" The B-26s were coming over and you could see the string of bombs being dropped and it hit all around us. I jumped off and got into a hole. There was a whole lot of damage. I saw the flesh hanging off of a couple of guys on the tank who had gotten hit. Fortunately, I was not.[15]

Despite alarming incidences of fratricide, Allied air superiority had proved to be a determining factor in the Normandy battles. On the ground, however, there were significant differences in the design and capability of opposing armor. There is no doubt that technically German equipment was more advanced than that of the Allies. This prompted a further concern at the time at SHAEF. Many Allied tank crews were succumbing to a condition that became widely acknowledged as "Tiger or Panzer Phobia." They began to think that these German tanks were invincible. One Stuart light tank of the 743rd Tank Battalion fired three shells in rapid succession from its 37mm cannon almost point blank at a German Mark V to absolutely no avail. The shells simply bounced off impotently, hardly causing a scratch on the dense armor of the Mark V, which then returned fire with its 75mm and obliterated the Stuart. Such incidents didn't inspire much optimism among the tankers.

JOHN NOLAN, COMPANY G, 119TH INFANTRY REGIMENT

The Germans were fine soldiers, impressive; however, we did capture some Polish conscripts to which I can't apply that same description. They were in Merzenhausen. When I ordered the men to fix bayonets and charge, they (the Poles) were dug into a trench. We started yelling and shouting and I think they wet their pants when they saw us coming! The Germans generally had better equipment. Their MG42 machine gun could fire 1,500 rounds a minute and the MG34 could fire 800 rounds a minute. They had better tanks, Pak 40s, and 88s.

In regard to US weaponry our M1 semi-automatic rifle was a blessing, and far superior to the bolt-action rifle carried by the Jerries. Our Browning Automatic Rifle (BAR) was effective if its user learned how to clean and maintain it. Its 20-round magazine provided excellent automatic fire. Our Weapons Platoon

60mm mortars, and .30-caliber light machine guns were adequate. One major advantage we had was artillery and it was tremendous, outstanding! They really supported us. We also had large supplies of ammunition. In terms of armor, our tankers always gave us high-quality support. As mentioned, however, they had a tank that was inferior in quality to their German counterpart, the Panther. The M4, with its 75mm main gun, could only bounce rounds off a Panther. Also, their frontal armor plate was pathetic compared to the armor plate of the Panther. We always enjoyed working with the Division's armored battalion, the 743rd, as well as the 2nd Armored Division. Those tankers had guts and we got along great with them. We always got the best tank support whenever we needed it. One thing we didn't appreciate was the "American Luftwaffe"—the Army Air Corps. We didn't enjoy getting bombed by our own Air Corps! [16]

Estimates of Allied casualties for the same period vary depending on which reference or archive one reads. The most conservative estimate is 209,000 Allied casualties, with nearly 37,000 dead amongst the ground forces and a further 16,714 deaths amongst the Allied air forces. Of the Allied casualties, 83,045 were from 21st Army Group (British, Canadian, and Polish ground forces), and 125,847 from the US ground forces.

During the month of July, the 30th Division had made their mark and proved that they were more than capable of rising to any challenge that came their way. Despite having suffered a disproportionate number of casualties in comparison to some other divisions, however, their ordeal was far from over. Patton's Third Army became operational at noon on 1 August 1944, and by 2 August, Old Hickory had already endured 49 consecutive days of combat and was ready to kick back a little. For the first time in weeks they were out of direct contact with the enemy. It was around this time that staff officers at SHAEF began referring to the division as the "Work Horse of the Western Front."

MARVIN SMITH, COMPANY K, 120TH INFANTRY REGIMENT

Beyond St. Jean de Daye: Early next morning, the battalion companies in column advanced down a dirt road in a southwesterly direction with no opposition. An enemy shell screeched in, killing a battalion soldier. After considerable penetration, the lead companies encountered the enemy and the battle was joined. Company K was in reserve. I vividly remember coming upon a destroyed enemy tank with parts of the dead crew scattered about in pieces. I saw a human arm hanging in a tree. An American soldier was sprawled in the middle of a field, apparently dead. Upon examination, I found instead that he was sound asleep, exhausted. Soon Company K was called out of reserve and committed in direct action against the enemy. I sent one platoon down one side of the field and another down the other side. An enemy machine gun opened up on us, pinning down the leading troops. I watched one of our privates, the only one with very thick glasses, crawl over a hedgerow to go forward. As he got up on top, the machine gun let go a burst into him. He crumpled and lay on top.

Sergeant Willy found me and told me he was using the mortars (overhead trajectory) on the machine gun. My runner, as our own artillery fired over our heads towards the Krauts, came to me to say the enemy artillery was behind us and firing at us. I assured him it was our own artillery, as the rounds were going over our heads to our front. A few days later, I sent him for medical attention, as he kept seeing things that weren't there. He never came back. I always wondered what ever happened to him.

Night arrived and we held our position. I chose a tree right on the front line under which to set up my command post. I was exhausted and dropped off to sleep.

For another day or two we held our position. Finally, the order came to move laterally toward the east several miles. After a walk of several miles though fields and friendly territory, we were committed into another offensive action into enemy territory. We passed through a battlefield, and I was shocked at the debris left there—steel helmets, ammunition, rifles, belts, clothes, Band-Aids, canteens, shoes. Evidence showed they were in a desperate battle and that many were wounded and killed there.

After two or three days, we were very tired, and we got orders to go to the rear for a shower and rest. We visualized a week or two of rest. After one day, showering and cleaning rifles and equipment, I was bitterly disappointed to get orders that we were to proceed towards the front lines because we were desperately needed. In our clean clothes we trudged forward in columns on the long hike back to the front. How much longer could we live?

I remember seeing columns of returning troops coming out of the front. I studied their faces. You could tell whether they had been on the front or whether they were fresh troops by looking into their faces and seeing their clothes. The returning troops had drawn, strained faces. The fresh troops looked relaxed but serious.

Our battalion was ordered into the breach, and we pushed steadily forward. Here, opposition was light. Soon we were far forward, far beyond other friendly troops, with our flanks exposed. We pushed on even father, alone, into enemy territory. Night came on, and we were ordered to halt. I placed K Company in a field in reserve position. I and L Companies were forward about 200 yards, and

Battalion Headquarters was just to my front. I placed a guard at the entrance to the field and scattered my men around the perimeter.

A telephone line was laid between my command post and Battalion Headquarters. My runner dug me a foxhole. I was exhausted. The nights were cold and wet. It seemed I was constantly on the phone with Battalion. Finally, Lieutenant Harnden, my executive officer and second in command, and I fell into the hole together and cuddled to keep warm. Another body is better than an electric blanket!

I was awakened with much commotion and noise of battle to our front. I heard terrible screaming come from the enemy side, as the night battle was joined. We were behind the front in reserve, so there was no engagement for K Company at this time. In a few minutes, we were all awake and watchful. A German tank or half-track on the road approached our hedgerow, and its flame-thrower barrel was lowered. I saw a soldier coming from the tank's direction, and I opened fire. He stumbled to the ground, but it was dark and I couldn't see him because the flame-thrower had ceased to light the area. I phoned Battalion Headquarters to report the flame-thrower, but soon it retreated.

That same night a K Company guard saw a soldier approaching in front of a tank. Thinking they were friendly troops, he ran over and grabbed him and asked, "What outfit are you with?" The soldier responded, "Aach, Americans!" Both the enemy solder and the K Company soldier turned away from each other and walked into the darkness. Such is the confusion of combat.

I and L Companies to our front were battling it out in the darkness. There was much firing and screaming from the German tanks, because the tanks were hit by our fire and anti-tank guns, and some were set on fire. Finally the dawn came, and I began walking around the area. With surprise, I recognized the German helmet and odd uniform on a soldier who was lying on his stomach, either dead or asleep. It was a Kraut. I asked Sergeant Adams, who was with me, if he had shot this enemy, and he answered no. Shaking, the man slowly raised his arms. We disarmed him and sent him to the rear with another one of our men.

Since we arrived in the fields late the night before, the men didn't get well dug in. I ordered everyone to dig in promptly. In a few minutes, an enemy mortar shell came down silently with a little swish and hit with a great explosion. When the dust cleared, I walked over where the shell hit and found a K Company man dead, hit in the temple by a fragment. He had not dug his foxhole as ordered, but was in the open, cleaning his rifle.

Attack and Counterattack: I visited Battalion Headquarters to get orders for the day. We were ordered to attack at 1000 hours. We were exhausted from the *night's ordeal. How could we even move? But such is war. I was surprised to see about 20 enemy soldiers at Battalion Headquarters who had surrendered. They were smoking American cigarettes. They all looked about 15 or 16 years old.*

1000 hours rolled around, and K Company was in the lead this time in the attack. We had two American tanks assigned to us. I was glad for that. I had radio contact with their leader at all times. We started the attack. I was watching Lieutenant Hulbert run across a field, and suddenly he looked down and grabbed his arm. He had been hit. I lost a good weapons platoon leader that day due to his wounded arm.

The attack by K Company and another rifle company proceeded on towards the enemy, making progress of about 200 yards. Heavy enemy artillery fire and small arms fire was concentrating on our lines. I knew we had penetrated up to heavy enemy resistance, but I was not prepared for what happened! I turned toward friendly tanks and saw one of them on fire and a man on fire scrambling out of the hatch. I was with my most forward men, and as the enemy fire concentrated on us, we could not move forward at all. I looked around and saw no men. They were retreating on their own! It seemed we were being counterattacked. We had simply lost all momentum under the heavy enemy fire.

Being all alone with only my radio operator and runner, we retreated back 200 yards to our previous position, as did the other company (either I or L Company). The heaviest counterattack was against them, however. Much firing of rifles and machine guns was occurring to my right. I expected enemy troops and their tanks to come through the gate to my front at any moment, so I grabbed my rifle and I think a bazooka (an anti-tank rocket), and jumped into a foxhole. To my mind this would be a last-ditch effort and a fight to the death.

Several K Company men were around me. We waited for the enemy to come. The next thing I knew, I heard an extremely heavy concentration of artillery shells screaming down upon us, coming from our rear, from our own friendly sector. There must have been hundreds of shells crashing all around. The noise was terrible. It was devastating. I expected death. In five minutes, it was all over. When the dust, smoke, and debris disappeared, I looked to see what K Company men have survived, if any. I found no K Company men dead. Or alive! They had all disappeared. Battalion Headquarters over the hedge from me had also disappeared!

I found a jeep burning with several bodies. There was no radio or telephone or equipment either. The shelling had destroyed them. Colonel McCollum (the battalion commander) was alive! His second in command had been captured. Most of the men of Battalion Headquarters had been killed or wounded.

Soon, K Company men began straggling back. They had simply fled the dev-astating shell fire. They looked very sheepish, but were ready to perform again whatever orders they received. They probably had saved their own lives, however. K Company was soon ordered into yet another field with orders to defend.

My father had made for me a special eight-inch knife, which I kept in a sheath on my belt. He had mailed it to me just before D-Day as his contribution to my safety. He had made it by hand from an old steel file. After the previous artillery bombardment, I remembered I had it on the edge of a foxhole about 200 yards from my front. I started to go after it, but due to the counterattack of the day before, I was not certain if the enemy lines were clear of that area. I decided why risk my life for a knife, so I did not go after it. I valued it greatly, and of course now I wish I still had it for a keepsake.

That night I probably heard enemy tanks milling around about one mile to our front—probably refueling under cover of darkness. I dreaded these steel mon-sters, which could fire machine guns and larger armor-piercing shells directly into your foxhole. Some have flame throwers, and they could run over and crush you, if not stopped. We did have an anti-tank company with large armor-piercing shells to try to stop them, as well as our own tanks to engage them, and our own K Company's bazookas (armor piercing, hand-held weapons). We felt safe with our own tanks near us, but yet because of the noise, height, and large bulk, they could be located by the enemy and so brought dreaded fire on our position.

Later, one of my men came running up to me and said, "There is an enemy tank in the woods behind us. See it?" I looked and looked, but couldn't see it. Finally I told him he was seeing things. No enemy tank ever showed up behind us. I had instructions that another regiment would pass through the lines and press the at-tack into enemy lines. We were of little use due to our losses, the devastating ar-tillery fire, and exhaustion from the counterattack. How wonderful it was to see fresh troops pouring through our devastated and depleted ranks.

Regarding the artillery barrage, I personally believed our own artillery had fired on us in error, but our superiors told us we had bypassed a German artillery unit, and it had turned its guns around and fired on us. I had several reasons to support my view. First, it came from our right rear; the enemy is supposed to be in front. Second, the German artillery simply did not have this many shells. We had never experienced over four or five shells at a time from them. Third, Amer-ican artillery timed their guns so that all the shells hit simultaneously or within a few seconds of each other; for example, several guns would fire from three miles to our rear, another unit from five or six miles back, and another maybe eight to twelve miles farther. All units timed fire so their shells would hit the target simultaneously to avoid tipping the enemy off that shelling was coming. The Germans called it "automatic artillery" and it drove many of them crazy if they were exposed to it.

The way the artillery aimed at us hit, I'm sure it was timed by several artillery units—of Americans. Of course, our superiors would never want it to get out that our own artillery was responsible for such a devastating loss. On the other side of the picture, it is true that our 3rd Battalion had pushed far forward ahead of all other friendly units, and it could have been enemy artillery fire, although the enemy had never punished us before with such a concentration as this.

Soon we had orders to move laterally among friendly lines westward to a new sector. We walked miles through a sunken road in hedgerow country and received orders to attack to our front (south) into enemy territory. K Company was to attack to the left of a blacktop road with L Company on the right and I Company in reserve. Battalion Headquarters, having been replenished with new jeeps, radios, and men, set up in the woods to our right rear with its guards all around.

I ordered Lieutenant Nash's platoon to go into action in the fields to the left of the road and another platoon to their left. This platoon was led by a sergeant. I had lost the platoon leader, an officer. Those left in the other two rifle platoons were to follow by 100 yards in reserve. Weapons Platoon, headed by Sergeant Willy (Lieutenant Hulbert was lost to a wound), with its two 60mm mortars and light machine guns, was to follow and be prepared for firing on targets that were requested by platoon leaders.

I set up my command post two hedgerows behind the leading platoons and kept in contact by radio. The forward platoons progressed well and they must have penetrated 300 yards ahead of my command post. They were getting out ahead, so I moved the K Company command post forward. Just after we had moved about 100 feet, an enemy mortar shell hit exactly where we had been moving before. Had we stayed, I have no doubt we would all have been killed or wounded. I could hear the "whrrrr" of enemy machine guns. You could always tell the enemy's guns by their sound. I had radio reports of stiff enemy opposition, and a German tank had been spotted behind a French house.

Here we go again! Another battle joined! I was on the front lines. I received word that Lieutenant Nash had stepped on a mine, and his foot was mangled. He was being evacuated. Our troops had been stopped. I went to the lead troops. As I walked, crouched low, an enemy machine gun, or burp gun, opened up at me, missing me but kicking up dust at my feet. Some of my men I found dead.

Later, I called for our artillery to fire toward our front, where I thought the enemy was. After many rounds, I stopped it. Not wanting to expose many more men to the enemy, I ordered Sergeant Byers and his squad of four or five men to penetrate beyond our lines to test the enemy after our artillery shelling quit. It was with great shock that word come that the enemy was still very much active and had opened up machine-gun fire, killing Sergeant Byers. The rest of the squad made it back to safety. This was a hard jolt for me. In another field we had several wounded men who could not get out due to enemy fire. Someone called me and asked what to do. I said the wounded had to come out. In a gallant effort, they were evacuated, not by litters but by our men carrying them on their backs, or however they could.

Wounded: The enemy tank was still behind the French house! I could see its barrel! A call came from Battalion Headquarters that we were to pull back that night under cover of darkness, preparatory to heavy bombing by US Air Force bombers. Then we could attack after this "carpet" pulverizing of the enemy by our bombers.

I was relieved and was making my plans to get the men back to safety as soon as night came. Suddenly I heard it—the one second "swhish" of a mortar shell before it hit! It exploded right next to me. Someone, I thought, had hit the back of my wrist with a rifle butt as hard as they could. It was a fragment of a mortar round. Blood was spurting from my wrist, and I knew I had been badly hit. I grabbed the wrist above the wound to slow the bleeding. Several of the company commander's men ran for a medic. I had to put on my own bandage from the first aid kit. Battalion Headquarters called and said they would send a litter for me, but I said, "Nope, I'll make it out alone."

Soon a medic came to my rescue. He placed a tourniquet and sulfa powder on the wound. I called my second in command, Lieutenant Harnden, and explained the planned withdrawal that night and the reasons for it. I also found that two or three other men had been wounded. They were about 60 feet to my front when they had been hit. No one had been killed. Corp. Koch was my administration clerk, so I asked him to accompany me back to the battalion aid station, about two or three miles. I feared I might faint, or be attacked by enemy patrol, so he grabbed his M1 rifle. I bade farewell to those around me, and we started out, passing the body of a Kraut on the way. After many minutes of hard, tortuous walking, we arrived near the Battalion Headquarters. I saw a jeep with litters on top of it and was told to climb in as they were headed for the regimental aid station. As I lay in the back seat, another jeep approached with an officer in the front seat. Lo and behold, it was my friend, Lieutenant Shaw. He asked me what had happened. I told him, and he saluted me. I noticed he had genuine sorrow for me, and this really touched me. We must have had four or five wounded on the jeep. By now *my arm was throbbing. I groaned, but someone said, "Be quiet, and look at that poor guy above you on the stretcher." I looked. He had such bad wounds; I just gritted my teeth and hung on.*

After several miles, maybe ten, we arrived at the regimental aid station. There I was given a shot, probably morphine, and we were placed into an American Red Cross ambulance, which sped us on to a large field hospital about 10–15 miles to the rear. There we were unloaded and an Army chaplain said a prayer over each of us. Then we entered the large tent area. I was placed on a table with a doctor and nurses standing around. The doctor said he was going to operate because I had a severed artery and thumb tendon, and a severed nerve with a gash down to the bone. He gave me a shot, and I began seeing less and less, and soon was out. The next thing I knew it was morning. I was missing all personal articles—pants, shirt, underwear, shoes, and socks. I was clad in only a GI olive drab wool shirt— a very efficient US Army hospital garb for the wounded. I was glad to be alive! After a few hours we were told we would be flown back to England. We were loaded on a litter, which was strapped into a C-47 transport plane. We were airborne quickly. I felt secure and doubted if enemy planes could or would attack us. It seemed in no time we were landing at an English town near a US Army hospital. There we were met by a crew and a chaplain and were bedded down in a round-top building. We were examined and treated by doctors and attended well by nurses.

The first day after arriving at this hospital, I awoke from sleeping and heard little children laughing and playing near a playground next to the hospital. I tell you, this was like Heaven—I just loved their soft, innocent voices. It was wonderful to awaken to those voices instead of the noises and horrors of a battlefield.

I spent several weeks in that hospital, and even got a pass to go to town a time or two. I still had a cast on. Then word came to be ready to go by train to another hospital.

I arrived at a new US hospital there in England, which was housed in buildings, not tents. There I was fully ambulatory. Doctors examined me. I had passes into town; ate fish and chips; went to a movie; visited a pub; visited a church in another town; wrote letters home. Then the head doctor called me into his office. I was expecting to return to France and the front in two or three months, but he told me the severed nerve would take at least six to eight months to heal, and I was being recommended to the Medical Board for return to the United States for an operation and the eight-month healing process. I just couldn't believe it![17]

The Quartermaster set up a "bath unit" on the banks of the Vire River near Condé, and Red Cross doughnut wagons arrived in the area accompanied by movies and USO shows. The USO shows were a particular highlight for weary GIs who could expect to be entertained by the cream of the Hollywood community with such names as Bob Hope and Bing Crosby; Judy Garland; Bette Davis; Humphrey Bogart; Lauren Bacall; Frank Sinatra; Marlene Dietrich; the Marx Brothers; Carole Landis; Jack Benny; James Cagney; James Stewart; Fred Astaire; Betty Hutton; and Lucille Ball. Musicians and singers included the Andrews Sisters, Al Jolsen, Glenn Miller, and Dinah Shore, to name but a few. These shows were excellent moral boosters for the troops in the field and considered vital to the war effort. USO performers were paid $100 a week, but the big names only received $10 a day because they were considered rich enough to contribute their services.

FRANK DENIUS, BATTERY C, 230TH FIELD ARTILLERY BATTALION

We were pulled out of the line on 30 or 31 July 1944. It was the first shower I had in two months. I didn't have to shave much in those days. I got to brush my teeth and put on clean socks. We had a USO show with Edward G. Robinson and Dinah Shore. Dinah Shore went on singing songs and she kissed me on the cheek. My buddies were kidding me asking, "What did you like best the shower or the kiss by Dinah Shore?" I said it was a tie![18]

HANK STAIRS, HEADQUARTERS COMPANY, 117TH INFANTRY REGIMENT

I joined the 30th Division as a replacement. As guys were getting killed off we would come up and take their place. I landed in Normandy and I joined the 30th after St. Lô on 4 August. Three or four of us were in the process of digging a foxhole and a sergeant came back and said, "Do any of you guys type?" I replied, "I can." He then said, "Come with me." He took me to Headquarters and there was a field desk with a folding chair by it. He said, "Sit down there and type! You are the new battalion clerk." The guy I replaced was hit in the rear end with shrapnel. Edward G. Robinson had come into our battalion to give us his little entertainment bit. Someone asked if I was going to see Edward Robinson? I said, "Nah, I'm going to get caught up on my letter writing."[19]

Unfortunately this particular rest period only lasted a few days because trouble was looming and the 30th Division was going to discover the name of a French town called Mortain.

**Headquarters Company, 30th Infantry Division,
After Action Report, 12 July 1944**

As part of a coordinated attack by the 30th Division to move south from the Vire and Taute Canal and seize the high ground west of St. Lô, the 1st and 3rd Battalions, 120th Infantry, launched an attack across the Canal at 071345. The main effort of the 30th Division had struck that morning west across the Vire River in the vicinity of Aire. The 120th's attack had been scheduled for early afternoon in the hope and expectation that the enemy's line immediately south of the Canal and thus facilitate the advance of the 120th. Colonel Dirk's plan was to force crossings of the Canal both above and below the bridge over the Canal. He gave the 3rd Battalion the crossing on the right and the 1st Battalion the crossing on the left. Both Battalions ran into difficulties getting across. The 105 C. Engr Battalion was supposed to throw a total of six footbridges across the Canal in the sector, but due to a miscalculation the bridges prepared were short. It was necessary to tie two bridges together in order to get one bridge long enough, and as a result only three bridges were constructed for the 3rd Battalion's crossing. Due to the resulting delays, the artillery preparation, which in any case was not plentiful, preceded the advance of the infantry by such a wide margin as to lose much of its effect. On the left the 1st Battalion was able to wade across the Canal for the most part, and thus it avoided any bridge-crossing delays and followed right behind the artillery preparation, but the hostile fire directed against it was very considerably greater than that which was received by the 3rd Battalion. Casualties were numerous and only courageous fighting enabled the battalion to get across. Though the enemy forces opposing the 120th Infantry were estimated between 800 and 900—as against twice that number of Americans—the enemy held the higher ground and had good observation of the attackers. Once the bridgehead was established, the two battalions advanced south astride the road to St. Lô without meeting strong resistance. St. Jean was bypassed and later occupied with little difficulty. By nightfall the lines were well south of St. Jean. One company of medium tanks was attached, but they crossed the Canal too late to see much action. On 8 July the 3rd Battalion attacked SW to reinforce the 113th Cav Gp in protecting the S flank of the Corps. During the day they fought a bitter battle for the high ground north of Le Desert. Casualties were heavy, but by the end of the day the hill was in their hands. The 1st Battalion advanced on the R of the road to St. Lô, advancing its lines. The 2nd/120th, having been relieved of its mission of containing the enemy on the Vire et Taute Canal by the 2nd/134th, crossed the Canal and by the morning of 9 June [July] it had passed through the 14th Battalion. With the 1st Battalion following to its right rear, the 2nd Battalion made good progress during the morning. During the afternoon it held the ground gained despite[1] mild rumors of an enemy tank attack in force, which precipitated a frantic retreat northward on the St. Lô road by all kinds of ve-hicles, armored and otherwise; and[2] a genuine counterattack by an estimated 15 tanks of the *Pioneer Battalion* of the *2d SS-[Panzer] Division "Das Reich."* The panic-stricken movement north on the St. Lô road had no direct effect on the front lines of the 120th Infantry, but it did result in making this im-portant supply route impassable. It was apparently precipitated by the leading tanks of CCB of the 3rd Armored Division taking the wrong turn when they debouched onto the St. Lô road south of the lines held by the 30th Division. They were supposed to turn south and proceed to Vents; instead they turned north, ran into AAA batteries supporting the 30th Division, and a firefight ensued, resulting in the two leading tanks being knocked out. The tragic mis-take was discovered and the headlong retreat of the leaderless vehicles stopped soon afterwards, but all agree that it was "a terrific mess" for about 20 minutes. The genuine tank counterattack came on the extreme right flank of the 2nd/120th. The tanks got into the rear of the 2nd Battalion and cut off its communications for a while. The men did not panic, however, but but-toned up, established a perimeter defense, and with the invaluable assistance of a box barrage laid down by the 230th FA, they made things too hot for the black-shirted tankers, and the latter pulled out.[20]

823rd Tank Destroyer Battalion, After Action Report, 15 July 1944

On 7 July 1944, the 30th Division, with the 823rd TD Battalion attached, shoved off on the most difficult of all offensives—a river crossing. The river: The Vire—not very large, but an important military objective. The first re-connaissance platoon, under 1st Lieutenant Thompson L. Raney, was the initial 823rd unit across, negotiating the stream via Bailey Bridge, at Airel, France, while under heavy artillery and mortar fire. When gun positions had been selected, the second and third platoons of Company C, led by Captain Samuel D. Swanson, crossed over the same bridge to support the 117th Reg-iment. Guided by the second rcn. platoon, Company A made the crossing north of St. Jean de Daye, and went into position in support of the 120th Regiment. That first night was a rough one for Company C. After being obliged to call upon the infantry to recover an overrun gun, they "sweated out" an enemy infantry counterattack all night. Cpl. Warren E. Kuhn, at the time with the second rcn. platoon, recalls vividly that day of our first river crossing. He and Lormand and Hymel were riding the point jeep, and when they arrived at the bridge site, the engineers had not completed construction. However, as soon as the bridge was ready for use the men crossed the stream, and had advanced about 200 yards when they ran into an enemy barrage of artillery, mortar, and small arms fire. The only cover available was back across the river in a hedge-lined apple orchard. This particular field had contained a German aid station. Their mortars landed exactly in the middle of it. T/5 Paul E. Berkley was being treated for a slight wound when a mortar shell struck, injuring him seriously enough to be evacuated to England and subsequently to the States. Cpl. Kuhn also mentioned Lieutenant Pfaff's utter disregard for his own safety in looking after his men when the going was most rough. Reminiscent of this particular circumstance, Lieutenant Pfaff had been knocked to the ground by a mortar blast, but he arose immediately and ran from man to man in order to ascertain whether any of them had been hit.

S/Sergeant Eugene F. Savage tells about his first crossing of the Vire, while he was driving Lieutenant Colonel Dettmer, Battalion CO. He states, "I was too intent on getting on the other side to remember what was taking place in my thoughts. I was probably praying; one never knows. I do know that I felt as if the entire German Army was waiting, with hands on the lanyards of their 88s, for us to get onto that bridge." Savage recalled the feeling of safety that he found in the haven of a ditch alongside the road after "landing" on the Airel side of the river, and the wild dash to the comparative security of the front lines where he was "inside" artillery fire and into mortar range. Lieutenant Colonel Stanley Daum, from the Company C Command Post, controlled the employment of his units, as they made their way over the Vire River, until a Battalion Command Post was established on the west bank. Toward the end of the next day, 8 July 1944, the Battalion, less Headquarters Company, was across the river, but enemy artillery had knocked out many of the vehicles. The first prisoner taken by the Battalion was captured by Company B during the afternoon. This action produced many acts of valor. Two of the courageous and heroic deeds performed by members of the 823rd TD Battalion in the battle of the Vire River Bridgehead resulted in the award of Silver Stars for gallantry in action to Privates George R. Holliday, Jr., and Monroe J. Whitley. Their citation recorded that: "Private First Class Monroe I. Whitley, 39855073, Field Artillery, United States Army, Silver Star for gallantry in action on 08 July 1944, in France. Private Whitley was assigned to duty with a tank destroyer organization engaged in action supporting an infantry unit. During a fierce engagement with the enemy, Private Whitley and a companion witnessed an infantryman wounded by enemy fire. With complete disregard for his own safety, he left the safety of his covered shelter and advanced over terrain covered by enemy fire in order to administer first aid to his comrade. Finding him seriously wounded and in need of immediate evacuation, he returned to his original position, secured a vehicle and, completely disregarding the dangers of the undertaking, evacuated the wounded man to safety. By this heroic deed, Private Whitley undoubtedly saved the life of a wounded comrade."[21]

CITATIONS FOR FIGHTING IN FRANCE

Lieutenant Colonel William S. Bradford,
120th Infantry Regiment, Silver Star citation:
For gallantry in action on 15 June 1944, in France. While observing the forward movement of his battalion, a portion of his troops were suddenly fired upon by friendly troops. Not knowing that the fire was being received from friendly sources, it was immediately returned. From his observation post Colonel Bradford immediately spotted this action, fearlessly left his position, advanced across an open field, and ordered all troops to cease firing. The immediate cessation of this action saved many lives. This courageous action in which he unhesitatingly placed the safety and lives of his men above his own reflect high credit on Colonel Bradford and the Armed Forces. Entered military service from South Carolina.[22]

Captain Gordon W. Brown, Corps of Engineers,
105th Engineer Battalion, Silver Star citation:
For gallantry in action on 7 July 1944, in France. Captain Brown's unit was assigned to the task of building a footbridge across a river which separated our men from the enemy to enable the crossing of the infantry troops. From the beginning of these operations, the troops constructing this bridge were subjected to heavy enemy artillery, mortar, and small arms fire; and casualties were heavy. The partly-constructed bridge was hit by artillery fire, which practically wiped out the assembly section. Confusion and lack of manpower

at first hindered immediate operations, but with complete disregard for his personal safety, Captain Brown assisted in final assembly of the bridge by regaining control of the men, reorganizing, and aiding working parties. His coolness and fine display of leadership under heavy enemy fire were a proud inspiration for his men. By his courageous efforts his mission was successfully accomplished. Entered military service from Tennessee.[23]

First Lieutenant Mylous T. Golson, Field Artillery,
118th Field Artillery Battalion, Silver Star citation:
For gallantry against the enemy from 7 July 1944 to 29 July 1944, in France. Lieutenant Golson was assigned as forward observer on duty with infantry assault elements during a sustained attack against the enemy. His initiative, as evidenced by his aggressiveness in locating artillery targets, contributed immeasurably to the success of the mission. He continuously exposed himself to enemy fire to accomplish his duties. On 29 July 1944, Lieutenant Golson was painfully wounded by hostile fire. Disregarding his grievous wound, he refused to be evacuated due to the urgent need for artillery support by his comrades. He remained at his post until ordered to permit himself to be evacuated. The aggressiveness, spirit of self-sacrifice, composure under duress, and high degree of personal courage exhibited by Lieutenant Golson reflect great credit on himself. Entered military service from Alabama.[24]

Technical Sergeant John L. Gray, 117th
Infantry Regiment, Silver Star citation:
For gallantry in action on 7 August 1944, in France. Sergeant Gray was assigned to duty with an infantry assault group making an attack against enemy fortified positions. During the engagement, Sergeant Gray was wounded. Undaunted and despite a veritable hail of enemy fire power, Sergeant Gray remained on duty, giving valuable information to his commanding officer and personally leading his comrades in an attack. During the advance, Sergeant Gray was again wounded, this time mortally, but his platoon, inspired by his leadership, went on to eliminate the opposition and capture their objective. Entered military service from Tennessee.[25]

Captain Henry Kaczowka, 117th Infantry
Regiment, Silver Star citation:
For gallantry in action while serving with the 30th Infantry Division, on 10 July 1944, in France. Captain Kaczowka was assigned to duty with an infantry organization, serving in the capacity of staff officer of an attacking unit. When the forward movement of the attack was brought to a halt by a concealed enemy tank, Captain Kaczowka voluntarily moved to the front and led an attack on the fortified position. His display of personal bravery, performed at the risk of his life, so inspired the troops that they overcame the hostile resistance and the advance continued. The determined leadership and personal bravery displayed by Captain Kaczowka reflect great credit on himself and are in keeping with the highest traditions of the Armed Forces.[26]

Staff Sergeant (then PFC) Ralph E. Markley,
119th Infantry Regiment, Silver Star citation:
For gallantry in action on 13 August 1944, in France. Sergeant Markley and another soldier were serving as scouts for the advance of their company when they encountered an enemy tank. Courageously holding their ground in spite of the deadly cannon and machine-gun fire the tank directed on them, they fired a rifle grenade which scored a direct hit on the tank, forcing it to withdraw. After engaging enemy infantrymen who had accompanied the tank, the two men withdrew and reported the situation to their company. Entered military service from Illinois.[27]

Captain Chris McCullough, 120th Infantry
Regiment, Silver Star citation:
For gallantry in action on 21 June 1944, in France. Captain McCullough was observing from friendly lines while members of an engineer unit crossed a river into the enemy line to probe for mines. The enemy opened fire, wounding the engineer officer and killing one of his men. Captain McCullough fearlessly left his position, proceeded across open ground and across a footbridge—both subjected to intense enemy machine-gun fire—in an effort to evacuate his fallen comrades. He successfully evacuated the wounded officer and again entered enemy territory and returned the body of the

mortally wounded soldier to friendly soil. Entered military service from Alabama.[28]

T/Sergeant Otis D. Newton, 120th Infantry Regiment, Silver Star citation:

For gallantry in action on 9 July 1944, in France. Lieutenant Newton acted with swiftness in organizing his men into defensive positions and pointing out targets to them. During this time he became constantly exposed to enemy fire. The enemy fought continuously and Lieutenant Newton again exposed himself to murderous fire and went among the members of his platoon to effect greater efforts. Entered military service from North Carolina.[29]

Sergeant Harold E. Nyland, 119th Infantry Regiment, Silver Star citation:

For gallantry in action on 13 August 1944, in France. Sergeant Nyland and another soldier were serving as scouts for the advance of their company when they encountered an enemy tank. Courageously holding their ground in spite of the deadly cannon and machine-gun fire the tank directed on them, they fired a rifle grenade which scored a direct hit on the tank, forcing it to withdraw. After engaging enemy infantrymen who had accompanied the tank, the two men withdrew and reported the situation to their company. Entered military service from Pennsylvania.[30]

Lieutenant Colonel Lewis D. Vieman, Field Artillery, 230th Field Artillery Battalion, Silver Star citation:

For gallantry in action on 15 June 1944, in France. As commanding officer of an artillery battalion furnishing supporting artillery for an infantry regiment, Colonel Vieman voluntarily, and with complete disregard for his personal safety, stationed himself at an observation post, subject to enemy sniper fire, in order to direct the most accurate and deadly artillery fire possible upon the enemy. Finding that he could better direct this fire from a more advanced position, Colonel Vieman fearlessly proceeded with the assault infantry elements under constant enemy small arms and artillery fire, until he reached his most forward observer. From this vantage point and at great risk to his life, he was able to issue detailed instructions to this observer, thus obtaining greater effectiveness of the supporting artillery. Upon completion of these instructions, Colonel Vieman proceeded with the assault elements, still under enemy fire, until the objective was secured. This display of personal courage, devotion to duty, and the superior performance of the supporting artillery, due largely to the willingness of Colonel Vieman to unhesitatingly risk his life to better accomplish the mission of his battalion, materially contributed to the success of the entire operation. His aggressiveness and bravery gave increasing confidence to the attacking infantry and were a profound inspiration to his fellow officers and men. Entered military service from Texas.[31]

CHAPTER THREE
"THE ROCK OF MORTAIN"

On 28 July, under the auspices of General Patton, the 4th Armored Division achieve an advance of twelve miles, which allowed them to capture the town of Coutances before pushing south to Pontaubault where they would be free temporarily of Normandy's claustrophobic bocage. The town of Avranches was captured by the Third Army on 30 July, and on the following day, while Patton's divisions were pushing across the Pontaubault Bridge into Brittany, the Third Army was officially activated. He then turned his divisions east, west, and south behind the German lines and stormed ahead in search of a good fight. Patton managed to perform the unprecedented feat of getting seven divisions through the Avranches-Pontaubault bottleneck in only 72 hours. This consummate grasp of logistics was going to be very useful during the coming months. The first week of August saw General Patton's Third Army charging forcefully ahead into the recently established Avaranches breach that had now been expanded to a corridor approximately 20 miles wide. This was wholly in keeping with the General's characteristic "move fast, hit hard" strategy.

When the Allies had landed in France, the German *7th Army* controlled Normandy and Brittany from the Orne River to the Loire, and by the end of June they were still there. There had been serious discussions at the highest levels of the German army concerning the efficiency of the *7th Army* to execute its allocated tasks. It was suggested that it might be better to relieve the army of responsibility for running the Normandy battlefields and relegate it to the lesser front in Brittany. This plan was shelved after the headquarters of *Panzer Group West* were demolished by Allied bombers. By the end of June the Germans had divided the Normandy front into two sectors. *Panzer Group West* assumed responsibility for four corps on the right, while the *7th Army* retained control of the two corps on the left. There was still great reluctance among the staff at *Oberkommando der Wehrmacht (OKW,* German High Command) to commit reserves from the north. This was due to the pervading idea that the Normandy invasion was just a diversionary tactic and that the Allies were still going to land in the Pas de Calais region.

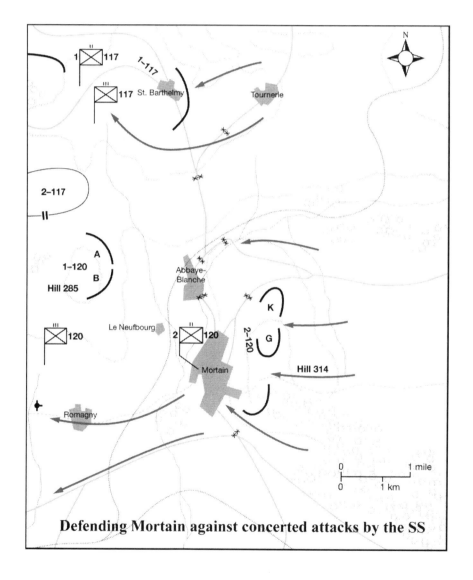

Defending Mortain against concerted attacks by the SS

In the lead up to D-Day, the Allies had commenced with Operation FORTITUDE, an intricate plan to persuade and ultimately convince the Nazis that the Allied invasion of Normandy was just a feint. The expertly organized "Army Group Patton," with its cardboard planes and inflatable tanks, had succeeded in its intent to deceive them into thinking that Normandy was indeed just a precursor to the real invasion, which would land in Calais. The Allied deception was effective throughout June and most of July. Naval activity off the Channel coast; false radio messages intercepted and reported by German intelligence; and other signs of impending coastal assault kept the Germans in a continual state of high alert and prevented the *15th Army* from being committed to the Normandy front.

At the beginning of July, the 30th Division was static and situated on the lightly held salient that jutted out among the low hills and bocage terrain east of the Vire River. Since the middle of June, while the majority of US forces had been preoccupied taking the port of Cherbourg on the Army's right, the troops near St. Lô and Caumont had remained immobile because General Bradley was reluctant to divert them. His tactical thinking was probably affected by the news that more German divisions were arriving and among them were some crack *SS* divisions. The *1st SS-Panzer Division "LAH,"* had been moved forward from *OKW* reserve on 8 June to take up position on the front in the vicinity of Caen. They were well positioned to move at a moment's notice should the need arise.

Field Marshal Günther von Kluge, commander of *Army Group B,* meanwhile, was reviewing the apparently shambolic state of his defenses. He voiced his concerns to one of Hitler's personal representatives, General Warlimont. Von Kluge aired his doubts and stated in no uncertain terms when he wrote to Hitler:

> In the face of the total enemy air superiority, we can adopt no tactics to compensate for the annihilating power of air except to retire from the battlefield. I came here with the firm resolve to enforce your command to stand and hold at all cost. The price of that policy is the steady and certain destruction of our troops. The flow of material and personnel replacements is insufficient; and artillery and anti-tank weapons and ammunition are far from adequate. Because the main force of our defense lies in the willingness of our troops to fight, then concern for the immediate future of this front is more than justified. Despite all our efforts, the moment is fast approaching

when our hard-pressed defenses will crack. When the enemy has erupted into open terrain, the inadequate mobility of our forces will make orderly and effective conduct of the battle hardly possible.[1]

Whether the enemy can be stopped at this point is questionable. The enemy air activity is terrific and smothers almost every one of our movements.[2]

Field Marshal von Kluge had commanded an army group on the Eastern Front for two and a half years before being brought to the west to replace Field Marshal Gerd von Rundstedt. Von Kluge had proved on more than one occasion that he was a more than proficient tactician despite being often overruled by Adolf Hitler. There's no doubt that as the campaign wore on, he became increasingly disaffected with Hitler's erratic behavior and punitive policies; however, he was still able to call on his own tactical proficiency when required. This would ultimately cause a great deal of disruption to Allied planning. Before von Kluge had unpacked his suitcase Hitler had alerted him to the possibility that Rommel may be hard to control. Von Kluge visited Rommel soon after arriving in Normandy and, in contrast with what Hitler had warned, he found Rommel to be most accommodating and reasonable. He found that they were on the same track regarding the next course of action needed to tackle the Allied advance.

Hitler, whose state of mind at this stage in the war was at best extremely volatile, was now becoming increasingly despondent at the possibility of the impending collapse of his forces along the western line. After a conference that occurred 29 June in Berchtesgaden, Hitler had removed von Rundstedt from command and replaced him with von Kluge. What prompted this shift was von Rundstedt's curt response to the question of how to resolve the problem of lack of cohesion in the German lines. The *Führer* asked him to propose a suggestion to deal with the problem. Von Rundstedt furrowed his heavy brow, looked up from the map laid on the table before him and said, "End the war, what other option do you have?" This suggestion was not greeted warmly by the *Führer*.

Von Rundstedt's arbitrary replacement with von Kluge was ill-advised; von Kluge also harbored serious doubts concerning the resolve and ability of his men in the field to continue withstanding the Allied onslaught indefinitely. Von Kluge implored Warlimont to allow him to commit reserves from the *15th Army*, but his pleas fell on deaf ears. The pervading opinion at *OKW* was that a limited offensive was feasible but only with the intention of stalling the

Allies while they withdrew behind the river Seine to reorganize and regroup. This opinion wasn't shared by Adolf Hitler as he pondered the maps at his HQ and emphatically restated his view that this was an ideal opportunity to decapitate the head of the Allied advance by severing it at the narrow supply corridor that ran almost 20 miles towards Avranches. Hitler wanted to send in eight panzer divisions supported by a thousand Luftwaffe fighters.

The reality of the situation determined that the German's could, at best, assemble four panzer divisions and one of these, *Panzer Lehr*, was in desperate need of refitting. Allied air superiority over the Luftwaffe was a verifiable fact, moreover, and would ensure that the few German planes that were available wouldn't even make it to the battlefield. For the generals at *OKW*, failure to comply with Hitler's advice at this juncture of the campaign was, at best, precarious; at worst, it could even mean a death sentence. According to Hitler's deranged opinion, the Avranches campaign represented an opportunity to strike a decisive blow that would break the stalemate and inevitably defeat the invasion forces. This delusional perception was based on incorrect and in some cases falsified accounts regarding the strength and availability of German divisions. Hitler always trusted his own judgment, and after the assassination attempt that would occur 20 July, he would become increasingly wary of his generals to the point of paranoia, despite the fact that very few officers in the west were ever implicated in the plot against him.

After Patton captured Rennes and spread his tentacles across the peninsula, von Kluge realized that unless immediate action was undertaken to stem the tide of men and vehicles flowing south, his forces were in serious danger of being completely obliterated. Something had to give. Up until this point the German divisions had been used sparingly, but now it was time to assemble what units were available and orchestrate a counterattack. Consequently von Kluge assembled four divisions for this effort: The *1st SS-Panzer Division "LAH"*; the remainder of the *2nd SS-Panzer Division "Das Reich,"* augmented with remnants of the *17th SS-Panzergrenadier Division "Götz von Berlichingen"* the *2nd Panzer Division*; and the *116th Panzer Division* [also known as the *"Windhund"* (Greyhound) Division]. These divisions were collectively designated to the *XLVII Panzer Corps*.

Lieutenant General Courtney Hodges, commanding US First Army, meanwhile, shifted the 30th Division to Mortain to replace the 1st Infantry Division and its attached Combat Command A (CCA) of the 3rd Armored Division. Thanks to military gridlocks on the roads heading towards Mortain, the 30th Division did not reach the town until six or seven hours after the prearranged arrival time. Within just four short hours they would become the focus of a major German counterattack.

The small town of Mortain, with 1,600 inhabitants, is near the juncture of the provinces of Normandy, Brittany, and Maine. Mortain was considered to be strategically important because, apart from other topographic features, no fewer than seven roads emanated from it and two significant rivers snaked around it.

The largest river is the Sée, approximately five miles north of the town, which flows at the base of a steeply rising ridge running almost the full 20 miles of its length. To the north of the river was a reasonably good road and on the other side of the ridge was another one running almost parallel to it. Fewer than five miles to the south is the river Sélune. The valleys of the Sée and the Sélune create a geographic feature that is known as an "isthmus," a narrow strip of land connecting two larger land areas, usually with water on either side.

Much of the countryside around Mortain was bocage, with its restricted possibilities for deployment. South of the river Sée, however, the terrain was elevated, offering better opportunities for observation by the artillery and heavy weapons.

The largest of these was Hill 314, just east of Mortain; and Hill 285, almost directly opposite. Hill 314 had a commanding view of the region and on a clear day, personnel looking out from the hill could see as far as the Domfront valley 25 kilometers to the east and beyond Avranches to the Bay of Mont St. Michel 32 kilometers to the west. Although there are no mountains as such in the immediate region, due to the rocky terrain in the area it was known as the "la Suisse Normande" (Switzerland of Normandy). [There appears to be some disparity when referring to the 1,030-feet rocky hill just east of Mortain. The locals refer to is as "Mont Joie," and the official US Army history lists it as Hill 314, but later accounts of the battle referred to it as Hill 317. For the purposes of consistency in this account it will be referred to as Hill 314. 314 is its official height in meters.]

The plan was that once the men of the 30th Division had established their positions at Mortain, they would then push east toward Barenton and Domfront. There was no indication at this time that a German counterattack would seriously disrupt these plans.

MARK SCHWENDIMAN, COMPANY I, 119TH INFANTRY REGIMENT

The armor having driven through, the 30th continued south to Tessy sur Vire to

*secure the gateway, and then on 6 August, speeded by truck south to the Mortain–
St. Barthelmy area. Taking over positions that had been manned by the reinforced
1st Infantry Division, the 30th found itself, without warning, engaged in a
struggle for existence against four German panzer divisions. During three days
and three nights of vicious fighting the 30th not only fought the German attack
to a standstill, but beat it back after knocking out many of the German tanks and
killing hundreds of attackers. The 30th's losses were heavy, too. Commenting on
the action immediately afterward, General Hobbs said, "We won't ever be in a
tighter spot and survive as a division." Division closed in to capture 172 German
vehicles including 39 tanks, six of them Tigers; 70 half-tracks; 33 self-propelled
guns; and 30 other vehicles. The German radio and captured German prisoners
nicknamed the 30th "Roosevelt's SS" troops, explaining the 30th is always thrown
in where the going is the roughest.*[3]

The primary German objective was to capture Avranches by hitting the
Allies along the area where the two almost-parallel western approach roads
to Avranches converged. The secondary objective was to capture and secure
the high ground. The German plan was called Operation *LÜTTICH*, which
incidentally is the German name for a Belgian town close to their border and
more widely known by its French name, Liege, and Flemish/Dutch name,
Luik. This was the town where General Erich Ludendorff had cleared the
way for an encirclement of the French Army in 1914.

One of most pressing problems that the German generals had to deal
with by 1944 was the complete breakdown of the system of "command and
control" that had worked so effectively at the beginning of the war. In contrast
to the flexible and decentralized Allied command structure and autonomous
control system, the Germans forces were now rigidly controlled at the highest
levels by the *Führer* himself. He personally oversaw and directed day-to-day
operations and believed resolutely in his own talent for strategic planning.
This method of controlling the battle at a distance militarily emasculated the
generals in the field who were constantly looking over their shoulders whenever the situation demanded an immediate and spontaneous response.

By August 6, with Operation COBRA well behind them, the entire 30th
Division was on the road heading towards Mortain to relieve positions previously held by the Big Red One. Many of the approach roads were lined with
cheering civilians shouting "*Vive les Allies,*" offering flowers, wine, and food;
in Mortain itself the hotels, restaurants, and cafés were doing a roaring trade
and were full to brimming with eager, jubilant customers.

RAY HOLMQUIST, 2ND BATTALION, 120TH INFANTRY REGIMENT
After the St. Lô Breakthrough the American troops broke out of the hedgerow country. Our battalion was in a depleted state; I bet we lost half our battalion. We were put into a defensive position in Mortain, France. There we were supposed to get some rest and get our battalion replenished with replacement troops. In fact, we had received a lot of replacement officers before we got there. Mortain is in a nice area, not really mountainous, but quite hilly, rough terrain. It was, in retrospect, supposed to be a resort city.[4]

It was a glorious summer's day as the 120th Infantry Regiment, under the 30th Division's leader, Major General Hobbs, disembarked, organized, and prepared defensive positions in and around the town of Mortain, which had been previously held by the 1st Infantry Division's 18th Infantry Regiment. The 2nd Battalion, 120th Infantry Regiment, moved onto Hill 314 with three rifle companies and a heavy weapons company that was equipped with several anti-tank pieces, while 1st Battalion, 120th Infantry Regiment, occupied Hill 285, which was generally regarded as the second-most commanding hill in the area. The 117th Infantry Regiment, meanwhile, settled into St. Barthelmy, just a few short miles north of Mortain, and the 119th Infantry Regiment was retained as a strategic reserve along the ridge road to Avranches. This regiment, less its 2nd Battalion, was located in an assembly area approximately three miles west of Juvigny. Old Hickory's positions collectively formed an arc that extended from Mortain in the south, north through St. Barthelmy, all the way to the high ground beside the river Sée. Shortly after arriving in Mortain they set up three roadblocks, two to the north and one to the south of Mortain, while the Regimental Command Post (CP) was established in a Mortain hotel.

JOHN O'HARE, COMPANY E, 117TH INFANTRY REGIMENT
As we approached Mortain we were attacked by British airplanes, Typhoons. They had the capacity to fire rockets and I was bounced off the ground by one that was fired by mistake. They didn't think Americans were that far up. Another fella who was perhaps within ten feet of me was severely hurt by that rocket when it exploded.[5]

HANK STAIRS, HEADQUARTERS COMPANY, 117TH INFANTRY REGIMENT
A couple days later we were carted off and taken to the area of St. Barthelmy,

which is just north of Mortain. We were taken down there by the "Red Ball Express" in trucks used for transport driven by colored guys. They did a tremendous job bringing up supplies and large numbers of troops, they were right there with us. I got off the truck and this one black man looked up in the sky and said, "Man, look at those P-47s up there circling us." Our aircraft usually ran around in fours, for some reason or another. A few seconds later, they peeled off and came down and strafed us. I know it's not kosher these days to say it, but the one black guy yelled to another, "P-47, hell! Nigger, give me that shovel!" That statement will stay with me for eternity. I tried to make myself as low a silhouette as I possibly could, laying on the ground. Fortunately, no one in our immediate area was hurt. We took up defensive positions that the Big Red One had established, including their foxholes, wire lines, and other defenses.[6]

Preliminary intelligence had indicated that there was no imminent threat of counterattack, so the 30th Division settled into their new positions in broad daylight unopposed. It had been noted, though, that in the event of a German counterattack the 30th's G-2 section was not in possession of any decent maps of the area. All they had were badly creased and almost unintelligible small-scale maps that had been passed on to them by the 1st Infantry Division. It wasn't until late in the day on 6 August that the 30th Division received maps of the relevant area; moreover, the Division's knowledge of the actual whereabouts of German forces at this time was negligible. This notable failure to provide accurate intelligence was to their detriment because a German attack was looming. The 30th Division assumed control of the Mortain sector less than four hours prior to the German attack. After more than 30 days of hard fighting and a difficult night movement to Mortain, they were exhausted. Nevertheless within a very short time they would be expected to prepare a concerted defense and fight for their lives.

In the build-up to the counterattack, the Germans were experiencing some logistical problems. At the time of the commencement of Operation *LÜTTICH* the *1st SS-Panzer Division,* which had been heavily engaged in the fight around Caen, was still a good 12 miles away from the intended assembly point. The *2nd SS-Panzer Division* hadn't received its promised artillery and tanks, and the *116th Panzer Division,* commanded by *General der Panzertruppen* (equivalent to a US lieutenant general) Gerhard *Graf* von Schwerin, failed to appear with the units needed to assist the intended counterattack. The *XLVII Panzer Corps* commander, General Hans *Freiherr* von Funck had the audacity to suggest that the attack from his right flank might be delayed by a few hours, but was informed in no uncertain terms that the attack would go ahead as scheduled regardless of his concerns. The German army prided itself on punctuality. Von Funck was told not to be distracted or deterred by these minor problems. Operation *LÜTTICH* would commence regardless.

Prior to the battle, on 31 July, Field Marshal von Kluge had visited the German *7th Army* command post at Mortain. While he was there he agreed on a plan that involved the *7th Army* attacking with three divisions: *2nd Panzer, 116th Panzer "Windhund"* (Greyhound) and *2nd SS-Panzer "Das Reich."* These represented the total armor forces available to *7th Army.* The remnants of the *Panzer Lehr Division* were no longer considered to be a viable force. Von Kluge promised to disengage every possible armored division from *I* and *II SS-Panzer Corps* currently in the *5th Panzer Army* sector and requisition them to *7th Army.* He did this because he realized that insufficient armored forces were available for the intended counterattack. The *7th Army* would be further reinforced by the *9th Panzer Division* and *708th Infantry Division.* The primary objective of the German plan was to establish a connected front line from the north that would be anchored on the south bank of the Sée River; from there they could establish a bridgehead at Avranches.

As night descended on 6 August, most of the 30th Division's units were where they were supposed to be. There had been certain problems they'd had to deal with during the day such as re-laying and duplicating telephone lines laid by the 1st Infantry Division; general digging in; and getting acquainted with the area in and around Mortain. On the whole and despite being approximately 1,000 soldiers below strength, however, they were settling in nicely. The whole position hadn't been intended for defensive purposes. When the 1st Division occupied the area, they hadn't intended to defend from these positions; consequently, telephone nets and wire lines were appropriate only for a short pause in the Allied offense and completely unsuitable for supporting a cohesive defense of the area. In preparation for the 1st Division's planned offensive action, field artillery positions had been placed too far forward, which would make them vulnerable in the event of an attack. The artillery situation could have easily been remedied with some reconnaissance, but it wasn't considered important at the time.

A normal full strength division in WWII, including attachments, was approximately 16,000 men, 9,000 of them were divided among each division's three infantry regiments. Between 3 and 5 August 1944, the 30th Division had received 780 replacements, but even when taking these into account, they were still short of fielding a full contingent by about a battalion and a half.

Notably absent when the German attack was launched against Mortain were two battalions that had been allocated to other missions: 2nd Battalion, 119th Infantry Regiment had linked up with CCA, 2d Armored Battalion in Vire on 4 August; and 3rd Battalion, 120th Infantry Regiment had been dispatched to Barenton on 6 August to assist an armored task force of the 2nd Armored Division ("Hell on Wheels"). The seven battalions that remained were stretched along a seven-mile front in the vicinity of Mortain. The 30th Division had attached the 743rd Tank Battalion to its ranks, which effectively gave them 77 tanks and assault guns.

It's possible that General Omar Bradley and some other members of Allied command may have had foreknowledge of the impending German attack, but when Major General Hobbs assumed responsibility for Mortain at 2000 hours on 6 August, he wasn't party to any of this intelligence.

Hobbs had graduated from West Point in 1915. He was regarded as a talented but impatient commander; nevertheless, his skillful handling of his hard-pressed division during the coming attack would prove decisive. He had little knowledge of enemy dispositions and wasn't even sure of the positions of some of his own divisional units. The 30th Division G-2 After Action report for August 1944 stated that on 7 August, at 0038 hours, warnings were received from VII Corps that an enemy counterattack was imminent within the next 12 hours and that it would hit from the east and north in the vicinity of Mortain.

Contrary to what German weather forecasters had predicted, there was no mist or fog to mask the columns of advancing German units. Clear visibility and control of the high ground definitely favored the American defenders.

The first serious indications that something was afoot occurred around 2200 hours. Nine German FockeWulf FW-190s began strafing a column of trucks belonging to the 3rd Battalion, 120th Infantry Regiment that had just embarked and was heading toward Domfront. A little later the 120th were reliably informed that all friendly armor had been thrown out of Barenton by a force of enemy tanks.

Up on Hill 314, the 2nd Battalion, 120th Infantry was more or less oblivious to the gathering German forces that were beginning to deploy around them. It was not until the 2nd Battalion's roadblocks began receiving small arms fire from the *"Deutschland" Regiment* of the *2nd SS-Panzer Division* that the 30th Division's command realized a serious attack was underway.

The 2nd Battalion had split a rifle company into three sections to establish roadblocks which were supported by anti-tank guns. Two of the road-blocks were overrun at once. The third remained in place and during the subsequent action it chalked up an impressive tally of hits, taking out over 40 German vehicles and tanks. The Abbaye Blanche roadblock played an integral part in the defense of Hill 314 because it controlled the main road that circumnavigated the northern edge and intersected three other smaller roads. This became one of the important enclaves during the battle. The German *2nd SS-Panzer Division "Das Reich"* attacked during the early hours of 7 August toward the road junction of Abbaye Blanche. At daybreak, on that same day, Lieutenant General Hodges and Major General J. Lawton "Lightning Joe" Collins, Commander, VII Corps, were highly conscious of the fact that this German counterattack could compromise the entire bridgehead south of the Sélune River. If the German forces north of Mortain thrust northward across the Sée River, they had the potential to cause havoc at the corps rear area and destroy supply installations there. This could result in a loss of all the ground gained during Operation COBRA.

120th Infantry Regiment, After Action Report, for the period 6–12 August 1944, dated 4 September 1944

The roadblock at the little village of Abbaye Blanche, on the northern outskirts of Mortain, is regarded by Colonel Hammond D. Birks, CO of the 120th Inf., as one of the most important factors in the 120th's successful repulse of the major enemy counterattack of August 6–12! In his opinion if that roadblock had not held, the whole position of the 120th would have been nullified and the resulting gap would have permitted the enemy to smash through the Mortain area of the 30th Division's line. In such a touch-and-battle, as the battle with that major enemy effort developed to be, the consequences of a German success in this regard might well have had disastrous implications. When, in addition, it is considered that the roadblock was held for 6 days under intensive enemy armored, infantry, and air attacks with casualties of only 3 killed and 20 wounded and that according to Colonel Birks, these slight casualties were due to the roadblock force's perfect defensive positions, it is obvious that this important road was skilfully and soundly defended. In particular, the force at Abbaye Blanche had to cover four roads: the main north-south road to Mortain, which ran right through the roadblock positions; a parallel road from the north, which by a sharp left turn joined the main Mortain road just beyond the railroad bridge; and two roads from the northeast and southeast respectively which angled into Abbaye Blanche. The control of these four roads affected an entire network of minor roads and trails. On the afternoon of August 6, Captain Reynold C. Erickson, of F Company, 2nd Battalion, sent his 1st Platoon, commanded by Lieutenant Tom F. H. Andrew, to secure and defend the Abbaye Blanche roadblock. With Lieutenant Andrew's platoon from F Company were the 1st Platoon of Company B, 823rd TD, under Lieutenant Tom Springfield; a platoon from the AT Company, under Lieutenant Sidney Eichler; and a mortar section and machine-gun section and they immediately took up dispositions for the northern end of the roadblock.

Several problems confronted Lieutenant Andrew in drawing up his dispositions. The northern end of the roadblock had to be placed north of the important bridge in order to preserve it for future Allied use, though doing so obviated the chance to canalize an enemy penetration. The river out on his right flank did not bother Lieutenant Andrew much, because he had good observation of the flat ground all around it, but the road coming in along the river from the northeast had to be covered. He had to spread his force rather thinly below the railroad bridge to counter any infiltration from the flanks, particularly among the houses and orchards along the main north-south road. He estimated that a company and a half of infantry would have really been a proper holding force for the Abbaye Blanche roadblock. There were about 70 men at his disposal. The enemy had once occupied the ground around the railroad bridge and set-up defensive positions and these Lieutenant Andrew used, for the good reason that there were no alternative defensive positions.[7]

JOHN O'HARE, COMPANY E, 117TH INFANTRY REGIMENT

On the morning of 7 August 1944, I helped set up the .50-caliber machine gun. Another GI and I set up the machine gun at the railroad overpass and we manned it until we were replaced by other soldiers (probably from the 120th Infantry). I never again went west of the railroad embankment and stayed in Le Neufbourg (the Abbaye Blanche enclave) for the remainder of the battle. I was part of Lieutenant Colonel James Lockett's Task Force for as long as it existed. On Sunday, 6 August, Company E went into Mortain but came back out through the railroad underpass to spend that night on a hill overlooking Le Neufbourg and Mortain. Company E and part of Company H of the 117th were placed in the Lockett Task Force on the night of 6 August, but did not get orders to move back east of the underpass until the following morning.

It was in my foxhole east of the Le Neufbourg Cemetery that I went beyond the "immediacy" characteristic of 19-year-olds and realized that the whole world had not changed. Only my world had changed. It was then that I had the specific thought that "Somewhere right now someone is riding a bus, and somewhere someone else is having a picnic."

Le Neufbourg was separated from Mortain only by city limit boundary lines at the north and south ends of Le Neufbourg. Le Neufbourg primarily occupied a ridge west of a gorge in the Cance River, which separated much of it from Mortain.

First off, though, we went all the way into Mortain. There was an assembly place with tanks and so on. The 1st Division had already taken the place, so we just went in and took over their positions. They brought my group back through the western edge of town onto a ridge on the other side of the river above Le Neufbourg and above Mortain to the west of the railroad tracks. We were there and the town burned while we were up there. The first night of the attack, 6 August, we could see flames all night. There was an eleventh-century church in Le Neufbourg that somehow had an automatically activated bell that rang all night. I don't know how there was an electric supply to make a bell ring all night long, but it rang. The town burned and we could see flames all over the place. The next day, we went into Le Neufbourg down a ridge road that passed that old church; when we got down to a certain point all hell broke loose. Shells of every kind—small arms, everything—hit us all at the same time. There was high ground at the end of that road and as soon as you passed that church, a few yards beyond, they could see you. So they saw us coming. I was part of Task Force Lockett that was sent to relieve the guys on Hill 314. We were put under control of the commander of the men on Hill 314, but he didn't activate us until the next morning. We could have made it up to the hill, but we weren't ordered to go until the morning of the 7th. At that time, we made an initial foray down the street and they opened up on us. We ran into houses on the western side of that street which was the main drag. That road goes down and then curves into downtown Mortain, after the gorge. We never reached that point. We broke into French houses on the side of the road. I ran through the house, out the back door, and into the backyard where I jumped into a deep shell hole. I jumped into the bottom of that thing and that's when the platoon sergeant's head rolled in with me—the rest of his body stayed up there on top, but his head rolled in. There were at least three other guys who tried to make that same shell hole and their bodies were up there at the edge of it when I finally got out of there. It was a really heavy barrage. Lieutenant Colonel Lockett said it was the heaviest barrage he'd been through and he'd been in North Africa and a lot of other places. He said, "Let's get out of here!" The remnants of the task force, Company E (which was my company), and a few guys from the heavy weapons company, Company H of the 117th (they had a few mortars), went back to the north on the high ground. I was running with the Colonel on my left-hand side going over walls back to a safer area. We came upon a wounded officer and the Colonel said, "You stay with him until we get some help." This fellow had a wounded arm. He would make it through okay so I stayed and talked with him. The rest headed for a place on the high ground behind some houses near a sunken road where there was a lined enclosure. There was a road that had embankments on both sides of it reinforced by stone. It was a pretty darn safe place.

I eventually made it there after the medics picked up the fellow who was wounded. I got in there and along came Colonel Lockett who said, "We don't have a rear guard. You, you, and you, go back and form a rear guard." So I did what he said. He went farther north and left the area. So the other guys who were told to form the rear guard just slumped back down. Everyone was worn out. I then went back alone and served as the rear guard. Fortunately, the Germans didn't come. They didn't follow us after the barrage, but they could have come up and gotten us. Three shells landed in that sunken road while I was out there on rear guard. There were eight casualties and I would have been one of them if I had stayed.

Right after that, somebody got a .50-caliber machine gun off a truck or something. Another guy and I set up the .50-caliber, pointing through the overpass. Right behind us there was another embankment and we could not have gotten out of there if the Germans had gotten through. Fortunately, they had been knocked out before they got to us.

I was reassigned back toward the main body of what was left of Company E. We made attacks down a road every morning and every afternoon. I don't remember any officers ever taking part in it, and frankly, I can remember the non-coms saying "Okay, let's get down. Let's go." We would attack and we would pass that eleventh-century church and they would open up. At one point there were 44 guys left in the company and at the end there were 33. I was untouched after the battle, and the best thing I found was that deep shell hole. It was a wonderful thing.[8]

RUDOLF VON RIBBENTROP, 1ST SS-PANZER DIVISION "LEIBSTANDARTE SS ADOLF HITLER" AND 12TH SS-PANZER DIVISION "HITLERJUGEND"

One day I was in a VW Kubelwagen exploring the area where we had our accommodation on the Seine estuary between Bernay and Honfleur, when we were attacked by a low-flying allied warplane. It was already night time when I heard its engine. Suddenly machine-gun bullets began impacting the road in front of us. I put my head between my knees in customary fashion to avoid being hit when I felt a powerful blow between my shoulder blades that temporarily paralyzed me. Bleeding profusely I instructed the driver to get me to a nearby ditch as quickly as he could because the Allied warplane was swooping low over us repeatedly firing his machine guns. I wasn't in shock though, but this was probably because I had already been wounded several times before. The driver somehow managed to drag my limp body to the ditch. As the driver applied a useless wound compress I began to lose consciousness and felt as if this was the one that would kill me. Then I decided that it wasn't my time to die yet. I felt a tingling sensation in my toes that reassured me that my spinal cord was undamaged. Within a few short moments my ability to move was restored sufficiently enough that I could raise myself out of the ditch and return to the car. I was taken to the Air Force hospital at Bernay where the surgeon told me that if the machine-gun bullet had hit one millimeter to the left it would have completely severed the carotid artery and shattered my spine. If that had been the case, he added, then an operation would have been a waste of time. I had trained my company from day one and I wanted to remain with them more than anything. When I left the hospital I was kept behind the lines until August when, due to a case of jaundice, I received convalescent leave. Many of us had been hardened on the Eastern Front. The 12th SS-Panzer Division *fought hard against the Allies and held them back for weeks.*[9]

BILL FITZGERALD, COMPANY E, 117TH INFANTRY REGIMENT
I didn't enter until 1 August, right in the middle of the battle of Mortain. I came in as a medic, my first experience in combat. For three days all I did was lift litters and run with them; and help the wounded. I didn't know where the hell I was because the front kept moving back and forth and the artillery fire was coming from east and west and south. So most of the time I was scared to death.[10]

Major General Hobbs's fears were allayed when the 4th Infantry Division, who was in the right place at the right time and well rested, placed a substantial volume of artillery fire on German movements south of the Sée River. Major General Collins attached CCB of the 3d Armored Division to the 30th Division and told Major General Hobbs to use them to take care of the situation southwest of Mortain. Hobbs decided to ignore this suggestion and use them to counter the more immediate necessity of meeting the main German thrust north of Mortain and along the south bank of the Sée River. Third Army, meanwhile, advanced northeast toward St. Hilaire that evening with the eventual objective of securing the Mortain-Barenton road south of Hill 314. Less than 24 hours after the Germans had attacked, VII Corps had successfully managed to assemble seven divisions, five infantry and two armored (less one combat command). In the event of the Germans making a more serious penetration a further US division was alerted for possible shift from Third Army. Despite this the 30th Division was fighting desperately and attempting to hold off all the German attacks, despite their numerical disadvantage.

There was no doubt that the 30th Division's defensive positions at Mortain could have been better organized, but in all fairness they hadn't really had sufficient time to get better oriented and familiarize themselves with the surrounding area. Moreover the division wasn't operating at full strength.

RICHARD LACEY, COMPANY M, 120TH INFANTRY REGIMENT

We went through several towns on our way to Mortain. Before we got to Mortain, our outfit came through with showers and clean clothes, which was good. Then the Germans brought up a lot of panzers and they moved towards Mortain. Our 2nd Battalion went up on Hill 314 along with K Company (sometimes they would take companies out of other battalions). Our company had gone by the hill but we weren't up on the top. They then moved us to Barenton, which was southeast of Mortain. It was on the lowland. They sent us down there because the Germans were trying to get through between Barenton and Mortain. We were attached to the 2nd Armored Division and all it seemed we did was fight in circles! Each day we moved and I wasn't really familiar with where we were. We were shelled and we lost some guys down there, too. We weren't aware of what was going on up in Mortain since we were south. We didn't find out about what happened until afterwards. They really had a rough time up there. The Germans surrounded the hill and captured Mortain, but they couldn't drive our men off that hill.[11]

The remaining seven battalions were enduring a bout of fatigue caused by their march from Tessy to Mortain on 6 August. Major General Hobbs considered the first German attacks as negligible and didn't take them seriously. He was concerned, however, about a possible breakthrough southwest of Mortain toward St. Hilaire. By noon of 7 August, intelligence officers assumed that the German forces behind American lines consisted of five battalions of infantry, four of artillery, and two or three of tanks. The suggestion that the Germans had launched a major counterattack to separate the US

First and Third Armies was still greeted with incredulity at command HQ. It was gradually becoming clear to all parties concerned that stopping the attack would depend substantially on the efforts of Old Hickory.

It was during the early hours of 7 August 1944 that the battle for Mortain commenced in earnest. It would culminate in a struggle for survival that would seriously test the resilience and determination of Old Hickory.

The ominous sound of German tanks moving along dirt roads in the forest of Mortain resonated through the still night air. Within moments they had infiltrated the town and were beginning to make a concerted assault on Hill 314. By 0345 hours Lieutenant Colonel Eads Hardaway, commander of 2nd Battalion, 120th Infantry Regiment, reported that part of Hill 314 was now occupied by Germans. He would eventually be captured and taken prisoner along with most of 2nd Battalion's staff officers who were at the CP in Mortain. Consequently he gave the order to eject the Germans from their tenuous foothold. This order culminated in a concentrated barrage of withering fire from Company G, 120th Infantry Regiment, which tore into the attacking Germans with such ferocity that they began to recoil and fall back. There were even reports of fierce hand-to-hand combat on the approaches to Hill 314.

MARION SANFORD, 30TH CAVALRY RECONNAISSANCE TROOP (MECHANIZED)

They removed the 1st Infantry Division and put us in the line in a place called Mortain. We were going to hold the line there. The Germans decided they would counterattack with everything they had available. They were going to Avranches to cut us in two. Patton had gone into Brittany and was moving pretty well. We were attacked. We had the higher ground on one hill [Hill 314]. The 120th Infantry had a battalion on this hill. For 5-1/2 days they were surrounded. We kept hearing that we were surrounded. Well, we were on the other side of the hill holding a road block and we didn't see a German the whole time.

The 120th lost over half their men. There were more than 500 men and more than 300 didn't walk off of that hill. They did one of the most heroic things. The Germans knew that they could not come up that hill in daytime because of our artillery. They were coming at night.

Our guys dug foxholes in the middle of the road. When a tank would come up at night, a man would jump out and try to get a hand grenade down in the tank. They knocked out tanks and piled that road up; the Germans couldn't come up that hill because it was the only road there. That lasted for 5-1/2 days. During that time, two German SS *soldiers came up and asked us to surrender. A lieutenant said he would surrender when all his bullets were gone and his bayonet was sticking in one of their bellies. They didn't like that much, but they went back and they never took the hill.*[12]

During the night, the 30th Division CP failed to competently assess the magnitude and strength of these preliminary attacks, and reported that they were optimistic that everything was fine under the circumstances. As the first wisps of ground mist began to be illuminated by hesitant indications of daybreak, however, the full force of the German attack was unleashed.

That mist began to develop into a thick fog that soon enveloped the whole area, making it impossible for the German tanks to engage the defenders at long range. This resulted in a lot of close-quarter tank and infantry attacks. While the *2nd SS-Panzer Division* executed a pincer movement at Mortain, up in St. Barthelmy approximately 50 tanks belonging to the *1st SS-Panzer Division*, and supported by panzergrenadiers from the *2nd SS-Panzers*, were converging on positions held by the 117th Regiment's 1st Battalion. During the ensuing combat two companies of the 117th were completely overrun. The 1st Battalion command group became completely surrounded and enmeshed in a life-or-death struggle as they attempted to extricate themselves from a horrific situation.

MANFRED TOON THORN, *1ST SS-PANZER DIVISION* *"LEIBSTANDARTE SS ADOLF HITLER"*

All that I knew is that we were driving in a westerly direction towards Mortain. After a couple of kilometers, the tarmac disappeared and we were driving on a dirt road which veered off to the left and then to a fork. Bearing left again, Gert Leppin, our tank commander, decided to order a rest in a wooded area. We had just finished camouflaging our tanks when a fighter zoomed in on us. We thought that we were the target, but the fighter had seen a lorry moving along the road, which he attacked with his machine guns. Clumps of earth flew around our ears and Leppin decided to change our location. We pushed the burning lorry off the road as we went. There was no sign of life.

After about 180 meters, the road brought us to a manor house that had two small lakes. This was where the men of the 8th Company, 1st SS-Panzer Regiment, *commanded by* Obersturmführer *(first lieutenant.) Josef Armberger, stopped us. They told us that Americans were in front of us and we could not drive any farther. No one had reckoned on finding the* Amis *there, at least not at this*

*juncture, because the front line was somewhere near Mortain. We quickly identi-
fied the trap that had been set for us. There were men running around the manor
house, taking up positions, impeding the advance of the Amis with their rifle fire.*

*Armberger only had one tank, a Panzer IV; and from another unit he had a
half-track and a lorry at his disposal, so he was happy when we reported to him
and provided another two tanks. He ordered our commander, Gert Leppin, to
return to the spot that we had just left to ensure a retreat, if needed. It was around
1430 hours by now. We drove back to the fork in the road, and Leppin decided to
do some reconnaissance. He climbed out of the tank and, shortly after, we heard a
cry for help. I drove away from the woods without hesitating and turned around
to get a better view. Even after turning a full 180 degrees the view was no better,
but I saw a meadow 30 meters farther on and drove to it, which is where we received a direct hit from somewhere in front and to the right of us. Our radio operator, Hans-Werner Koch, took the whole impact in the stomach and died instantly.
In starting to climb out, our gunner instantly came under MG fire, but we all
managed to climb out unharmed. Only Hans-Werner was still in the tank. An
Ami tank was hidden behind a bush about 40 meters away, and had most probably been watching us since they had captured Leppin.*

*We all huddled together against the left-hand side of the tank. The others
asked about Hans. I told them that I was convinced that he had died instantly,
and then smoke began to billow from the tank, and although we didn't want to
leave it behind, the smoke provided a screen that allowed us to return to Capt.
Armberger. He was unaware that the Amis were not only in front of us, but behind us as well—in a pincer—and we were in the middle. I had ordered two
new crew members to stay behind at a safe distance, telling them to keep an eye
on the Amis until I returned with the other tank, and reassuring them that this
would be as soon as possible. Armberger could not believe that the Amis were
closing in on us, and told me more than once that he had ordered a tank to maintain the rear positions. It took some time before I could convince him that mine
had been that rear tank. He then ordered Heinrich's tank to carry out the order
that I had not been able to achieve. Suddenly, having disobeyed the order that I
had given them, my two crew members appeared. The situation was a little too
hot for them.*

*Heinrich's tank only succeeded driving 150 meters before receiving a direct
hit that stopped it in its tracks. The shot came from an Ami who had succeeded in
getting within 80 meters of our command post. The crew climbed out unharmed
as Heinrich reported to Armberger. Without a word he took an anti-tank gun,
waded through the lake, and then shot up two Ami tanks, which prevented them*

from advancing any farther. During the night, with 40 men and one remaining tank, we crept like snails as silently as we could through Ami *lines!*[13]

KING KENNY, RECONNAISSANCE PLATOON, 823RD TANK DESTROYER BATTALION

Mortain was the next objective. As we were moving up, we understood the 30th would relieve the 1st Division and take over their old position and gun emplacements. Our fight took place in St. Barthelmy. A few miles west of us was Hill 314, where the 120th was cut off. We got there on the night of the 6th. We went out on a patrol, but it was a quiet night and we didn't come up with anything. On the morning of the 7th they started an artillery barrage, but we were dug in.

The morning was foggy and we really couldn't see a whole lot. Lieutenant Neel came up and told us to get a jeep and go up as far as we possibly could to get a view of the road and to use the radio to keep him informed. Neel was with B Company of the 823rd Tank Destroyers, and there were some 120th troops around, too. We kept the jeep concealed—it was still hedgerow country—and we made contact with him on the radio. Neel had gotten the 3-inch guns into position. As a German tank came down the road we let Neel know, and the 3-inch gunners took care of that one. Then another one came and tried to get around the first, but Lieutenant Neel took that one out, which blocked the road for quite a while. Then, more tanks came. At night, the Germans had a big tank mover, like a tow truck, and they pulled a couple of those tanks out that were blocking the way so more tanks could come through.

When we first left our platoon we were also told to take a tripod and a .30-caliber machine gun that was mounted on the jeep (each jeep had a .30-caliber on a swivel that had a 180-degree traverse on it). We pulled the pin on the .30, put it on a tripod with a good field of fire, and concealed it. When those tanks were knocked out, they called up the panzergrenadiers. Those guys started coming up and we fired at them, along with everybody else who could see them. They didn't get through and turned back.

Lieutenant Springfield, with A Company, 823rd TD, came on the radio and said, "Can you move your position to the right? Be careful. There is a hill that they are trying to get up." We got down there and at that time we had Neel on the radio. Neel was still knocking off tanks from where he was—he was on a perpendicular road set back 30 or 40 yards. He took on tanks that were very close to him and trying to get up that hill. Springfield was really firing away. We couldn't get a real good view of what he was doing. The Germans were trying to go up the hill and were really persistent. He was just picking them off. He said he figured he had knocked out 8–10 tanks and a large number of armored personal carriers. We don't know how many we may have killed or driven back with our machine gun. Although the Germans did get into Mortain, they were eventually driven back by the infantry. By the third day things let up. I don't remember anything spectacular in our area, just some infantry attacks. The three of us went back to Lieutenant Neel; he said that we would be pulling back pretty quickly and to get some rest, which we did.[14]

HANK STAIRS, HEADQUARTERS COMPANY, 117TH INFANTRY REGIMENT

The 120th Infantry Regiment was commanding the high ground on Hill 314, east of Mortain, when its roadblocks and frontline positions were quickly over-whelmed and the troops on the hill were surrounded.

Holding the Line: Meanwhile, two miles to the north, near the village of St. Barthelmy, the 1st Battalion of the 117th Regiment sustained severe losses of frontline troops. Fighting capacity of the battalion was reduced to something on the order of 50 percent. The remaining understrength frontline companies estab-lished a last line of defense north and west of the village, including clerks, mes-sengers, and other Battalion Headquarters Company personnel. A column of German tanks moved into the area along the narrow hedgerow-lined route lead-ing to the sea. A bazooka team from Company D, Private First Class Frank Joseph, Jr. and William A. Pierce, sneaked forward along the hedgerow and knocked out the lead Mark IV tank. As the second tank attempted to maneuver around the disabled leader, it, too, was a casualty to the bazooka team. Privates Joseph and Pierce were awarded the Distinguished Service Cross for their heroic actions. With exceedingly good timing, rocket firing planes of the 2nd Tactical Air Force (RAF) suddenly appeared overhead and at treetop level knocked out many enemy tanks stacked up behind the crippled leading Mark IVs. Their bravery and accurate anti-tank fire was unparalleled by Allied airmen of World War II.

All Hell Broke Loose: Our battalion commander, Colonel Frankland, had an outpost in St. Barthelmy and he did some heroic things. He was in a house when a tank pulled up outside. They were trying to get out of the area and he saw two of his men being taken prisoner by a German. The battalion commander shot the German and all of his men escaped through the back of the house.

Two of us were lying in a foxhole dug into the side of the bocage. It was sup-plemented with limbs and trees, anything we could find to put on top of it. Then all hell broke loose—small arms and artillery fire. I had never experienced small arms fire before and I didn't know where the hell it was coming from. As the small arms fire passed overhead, it cracked just like a whip. We were bombarded by "screaming meemies" which were Nebelwerfer *rockets. The* Nebelwerfer *was primarily a psychological weapon. It was a multiple-barrel (six) rocket launcher, pulled by horses. It fired artillery in clusters. When it fired, it sounded like, "Eyu! Eyu! Eyu!" You could hear the thing as it traveled from the muzzle and exploded. We were saturated with them!*

I don't remember what day but it was daylight just before noon when a sergeant came along and said, "See that hedgerow up there. The Germans have broken through and we are now the front lines. Go up there and take up a rifle position." We then did as he ordered. I took up a position in a ditch and did the best I could to look to the next hedgerow. I could hear tank tracks coming our way (to this day, when I hear any tracked vehicle, it brings back the vivid memory of the attacking armor). As I was looking at the hedgerow in front of us—I was a reasonable shot at 19 years old—I thought, "Jerry, if you come through that hedgerow, you're a goner!" No one ever got that far, though, and I never had to fire my weapon. Mortain was surrounded, but we didn't suffer like the guys on Hill 314 did. They went through an ordeal when the Germans tried to kick them off.[15]

By noon on 7 August, the fog began to dissipate and just after 1215 hours, the first of 271 RAF Typhoon fighters took off from forward airstrips in Normandy with the sole intention of strafing the massive German tank and vehicle columns now descending on all 30th Division positions in and around Mortain. Such was the confusion caused by advancing German spearheads penetrating American lines that the 120th Infantry Regiment reported being hit by friendly fire no less than 10 times during the day. Up on Hill 314, once the fog had lifted, the 120th's 2nd Battalion had a resplendent panoramic view of the whole area and was able to call in devastating artillery fire on the advancing German columns.

As the battle got into full swing, Major General Hobbs found himself confronted by three major problems. First, he needed to eradicate the German penetration northwest of Mortain. Second, he needed to block their thrust southwest and recapture the town itself. His third imperative was to reestablish contact with the 2nd Battalion on Hill 314 whose position was rapidly becoming untenable due to the fact that they were now completely surrounded.

WILLIAM GAST, COMPANY A, 743RD TANK BATTALION

The 743rd, being a separate battalion, was called upon to clean up little so-called "pockets of resistance." One of these pockets was Mortain, France, 6–12 August, when Hitler, with his 1st SS-Panzer Division, threw his punch to cut off General Patton's Third Army from the US First Army and the beachhead supply base. Casualties were heavy. Many killed . . . many wounded . . . and again, we lost a lot of equipment. We had our tanks parked in the middle of a field, camouflaged with tree branches and leaves.

I lost three tank commanders in this battle. At the same time I was driver and tank commander. An order came over the radio to deliver a message to the infantry CP. Another soldier and I got out of our tanks and on foot went to the designated CP area, equipped with a .45-caliber pistol and a .45-caliber Thompson sub-machine gun with a 30-round clip; we found the CP was all blown away, nothing there. We raced back to our tanks under machine-gun and rifle fire, with artillery and mortar shells exploding all around us, to find one of our tanks knocked out. After helping these men and receiving orders to retreat—this was the only time, during the entire war, that we were ordered to retreat—I started to remove the camouflage from my tank, when an incoming artillery shell exploded beside my tank and a piece of the shrapnel hit me in the back. I was taken to a field hospital for surgery and recovery. While hospitalized, the German bombs, intended for Patton's convoy, which was moving in close by, missed their target and landed on the hospital. More causalities; there seemed to be no end. I quickly discharged myself from the hospital and started my journey back to the 743rd . . . wherever it was.[16]

It was time to bring up some reinforcements. The 35th Infantry Division, which had previously been designated to join the Third Army, was immediately reassigned to head toward Mortain on the main road to the right of the 30th Division's line. The 12th Infantry Regiment, 4th Infantry Division, supported by the self-propelled gun unit of the 629th Tank Destroyer Battalion, was sent to attach to the 30th Division. The first of the reserves to arrive was the 2nd Battalion of the 30th's own 117th Infantry Regiment, most of whom reached the 120th's CP in Mortain by late afternoon. The first attempt to relieve the besieged defenders of Hill 314 was unsuccessful, but before long more reinforcements began to arrive, all charged with the sole intention of repelling the attacking Germans.

Even though the summit of Hill 314 was beginning to resemble a cratered moonscape, the tenacious 2nd Battalion, 120th Infantry Regiment, stubbornly continued to resist all enemy efforts to beat them into submission and drive them off this vantage point. Using the tactical advantage of clear visibility, the 2nd Battalion divided into small combat units that operated autonomously to repulse every attempt made by the determined *SS* to capture their position. These small units were frequently out of contact with one another and forced to use patrols to maintain communications. Thanks to the unrelenting efforts of forward artillery observers 2nd Lieutenant Robert L. Weiss, Corporal Frank Denius, and their team from the 230th Field Artillery Battalion, they relayed coordinates with devastating effect and repeatedly deluged the attacking *2nd SS-Panzer Division*'s columns with a ferocious rain of iron.

The first attempt to resupply the men on Hill 314 by air drop was made on 10 August. The first supplies landed 800 yards from their positions and every attempt to retrieve them over open and vulnerable terrain was met with treacherous enfilades of bullets and shells from the German positions. The second attempt at resupply failed completely. SHAEF had actually premeditated potential siege situations during their planning for the Normandy campaign and supply packages had been prepared well beforehand to accommodate these. The conditions on the hill deteriorated to such an extent that after the air drops failed to provide, even the artillery attempted to get supplies to the 2nd Battalion by firing artillery smoke shells. First they removed the bases and filled the cavities with medical supplies; although this attempt had a positive effect on the morale of the defenders, it wasn't possible to deliver much needed plasma this way. Morale was further boosted when the Germans acknowledged that two well-equipped US columns were fighting hard to get to their position.

FRANK DENIUS, BATTERY C, 230TH FIELD ARTILLERY BATTALION

Silver Star Action: Captain Merrill Alexander, an excellent leader and soldier, was our battery commander. The 120th Regiment moved towards Mortain, along with Sergeant Goldstein, my radio operator, and me. It was a sunny afternoon on 6 August when we relieved the 1st Infantry Division. I was with the leading infantry company of the 120th Regiment, 2nd Battalion, when we went up Hill 314. There were 590 of us positioned on the top of 314. In Mortain, the main street runs basically from the northwest to the southeast. Hill 314 is just east of the downtown area. "314" means that it is 314 meters above sea level. At its highest level, you can see 360 degrees around, and on a clear day you can see the Atlantic Ocean. The 1st Division guys told us they hadn't fired a shot or seen a German in several days and that we had a pretty quiet sector. We got into position in the foxholes they'd dug, which we then improved. It turned out Mortain was the target of the German counterattack with 70,000 infantrymen and 4–5 panzer divisions.

An artillery officer; Sergeant Goldstein, my radio operator; and I were positioned on the south-southwestern side of 314; another observer from the 230th, Robert Weiss, who was an excellent artillery observer, was on the other side. When we moved into our position I suggested we stay with the company commander and command post (I was just a corporal at the time). The lieutenant, who was a recent replacement, wanted to locate right on the front line, however, I told him we should locate back with the infantry company commander. We couldn't turn the radio on and direct artillery fire if we were on the perimeter defense. I was unsuccessful so Goldstein and I located a foxhole with space for 2–3 men.

That night the Germans came up the hill. The infantry defending this area had a new air-cooled machine gun that jammed and, because of our forward position, we couldn't direct artillery fire, so we engaged in hand-to-hand combat with the enemy. The German threw grenades called "potato mashers" at our foxholes. I was an artillery forward observer—my job was to direct artillery fire, not to engage in hand-to-hand combat—so during the attack we had to crawl to the company commander's command post about 150 yards back toward the interior of the hill. We were then able to call in the preset emergency barrages against the German infantrymen. During all of this the lieutenant became incapacitated, so I took over and I directed the emergency barrages along with Sergeant Goldstein. We were able to fend off the Germans that night and into the following morning.

We directed artillery fire for six and half days on Hill 314. We went from company to company, whereever the Germans attacked the hilltop, and directed fire in support of the infantry. We were able to defend every attack on our side, and Lieutenant Robert Weiss did the same on his. Most of the time, my emergency barrages were sufficient to cover us. I also directed fire to those areas where they were organizing back away from the hill, where we could see their artillery pieces and tanks moving.

We ran out of food to eat and then we ran out of water. There was a farm house on the southeast side of the hill. Some of the infantry guys crawled down at night to a well near the farmhouse. They would take some canteens and fill them up, that's how we got some water. Food—there wasn't much to eat. Goldstein and I had some emergency D-rations, a hard, rock-solid, black chocolate candy bar. You couldn't chew it. We had to use our bayonet to sort of shave it. We were constantly trying to defend and help the infantry, though, so sleeping and eating were not our biggest problems.

On the third and fourth day we were totally surrounded on the hill and com-

mand had supplies parachute-dropped to us. When the C-47s flew over they were high, to avoid the anti-aircraft fire, so the supply parachutes drifted away from us. We had to fight our way into no-man's-land to get some supplies back. On the fifth day we were completely out of medicine so my battalion commander, Colonel Louis Vieman, radioed us and he said, "We're going to try something." We had propaganda shells that were stuffed with leaflets and not high explosives. So the artillery units who were 8–9 miles behind us took the leaflets out and replaced them with cotton, gauze, morphine, and penicillin. Weiss and I then directed those shells to be fired onto the hill and then we dug out the shells!

We were relieved, I believe, on 12 August by elements of the 119th Regiment and forward elements of the 35th Infantry Division. The survivors who were left marched down that hill carrying our wounded. We had lots of guys who didn't make it. They were still up on top of the hill. Had the Germans captured Hill 314, they would have had total observation of our positions, in particular the supply lines to Patton's Third Army. Eisenhower had radioed to hold at all costs. It had been an "Alamo" situation.[17]

The enemy succeeded in sweeping around the right flank of Company E, 120th Infantry Regiment, and in doing so seized 19 of the 21 quarter-ton trucks parked there. None of the promised Luftwaffe support for Operation *LÜTTICH* ever seriously materialized, which left German ground troops vulnerable to Allied air strikes.

Two days after the battle started, the *2nd SS-Panzer Division* made an attempt to break the stalemate at Hill 314 when they sent an appointed officer to contact the beleaguered 2nd Battalion holding out there. The German officer demanded their immediate surrender with accompanying threats, but despite the desultory state of some of the men on Hill 314 the demand was categorically rejected. The Germans then continued their probing attacks, combat patrols, and barrages of heavy artillery as they persisted in their attempts to take the hill. The 2nd Battalion on Hill 314 was initially well provisioned, but after a few days of this sustained fighting, their supplies of food, ammunition, and medication inevitably began to run low. In an attempt to provide some respite from the incessant fighting, the defenders of Hill 314 implemented a rotation system comparable to the one used during "Trench warfare" in WWI. Depleted units were rotated first and their positions were improved as much as was feasibly possible, in an effort to provide sufficient cover from enemy bombardments. The wounded were quartered in deep slit trenches, but lacking adequate medical attention and the necessary supplies, they had to make do with whatever the battalion aid-men could provide.

The 1st Battalion of the 120th Infantry Regiment on Hill 285 was also attacked repeatedly by a combination of tanks and infantry. At one stage, Company A was forced to withdraw to the rear of a road cresting the hill when they were attacked by a reinforced company of Germans armed with flame throwers with the intention of preventing Company A from using their tank destroyers. The tankers simply disembarked from their vehicles and fought alongside their comrades as infantry for the duration.

The 1st Battalion, 119th Regiment was advancing against stoic German resistance via Romagny, and the 120th Infantry Regiment was advancing from Barenton. It was the latter that initiated first contact and immediately began evacuating the wounded and resupplying food and water. Of the original 700 men who reached and defended Hill 314, approximately half of them actually walked off it *corpore intact.* The front line had been stabilized less than 24 hours after Operation *LÜTTICH* had commenced and although the battle continued for several days with von Kluge committing additional forces, the Germans didn't manage to make any further gains. For its heroic stand during the German counterattack, the 30th Division, who were already known as the "Work Horse of the Western Front" added another nickname to its list, "The Rock of Mortain."

JOHN O'HARE, COMPANY E, 117TH INFANTRY REGIMENT

Historians frequently refer to the two surrounded American enclaves as "The Battalion Holding Hill 314," and the "Roadblock at the Abbaye Blanche." The "roadblock" concept appropriately describes the magnificent work done by the 120th Infantry's Anti-Tank Company, the 823rd Tank Destroyer Battalion, and the 120th's infantrymen assigned to protect their gun emplacements. The remnant of Company E, 117th Infantry, however, also active in the Abbaye Blanche area, was not bound to any specific location. It actively sought engagement with the enemy. We attacked down the rue de l'Englise every morning and again several afternoons from 7 August until the end of the battle on 12 August.

Lieutenant Colonel Mark J. Reardon (now retired), a US Army professional historian, has written an excellent book entitled Victory at Mortain, *which was published in 2002 by the University Press of Kansas. Colonel Reardon partially deals with the action of Company E as follows:*

Elsewhere within the 120th Infantry's sector, the Americans were taking the offensive. Several thousand yards to the west of the 2nd

Battalion, the survivors of E/117th Infantry girded themselves for an attack against the Germans holding Mortain. Following their catastrophic assault on 7 August, E Company numbered only 44 unwounded soldiers, but had launched an attack every morning against the Germans defending the town. On 11 August, Lieutenant Richard's rifle company once again crept along the hedges on the southeastern slope of Hill 285 before descending into the valley between Le Neufbourg and Mortain. The "lost" platoon from 629th TD Battalion provided support for the attackers.

As the Americans neared the western outskirts of the town, the Germans opened fire with machine guns. The TDs responded by hurling high-explosive rounds at the defenders. Although the American assault consisted of little more than a noisy demonstration, Lieutenant Richards hoped to prevent the Germans from sending their troops to reinforce other sectors. After skirmishing for several hours, E Company pulled back to their original positions. As they retreated the survivors of E Company rescued a soldier from H/120th Infantry found hiding in Le Neufbourg.

I do not know how many men Company E could muster before the Battle of Mortain. At full strength, a US infantry company in WWII consisted of 241 men. Perhaps the nature of my experiences at Mortain can be gauged partially by the fact my company (Company E, 117th Infantry) numbered only 44 unwounded and battle-ready soldiers after our assault on 7 August 1944. I believe that Company E could only muster 33 such soldiers on 12 August when the battle ended and I was one of them. I took an active part in every attack made by Company E during the counterattack period.

Colonel Reardon was certainly correct when he described the savage barrage, which greeted our 7 August attack as "catastrophic," but it was important that our audacious attacks continue throughout the battle. General Hobbs has been quoted with the reference to 7 August as follows: "With a heavy onion breath that day, the Germans would have achieved their objective." Perhaps the Germans misinterpreted our audacity as strength, which we did not have.

At some time after our first attack we were joined by an M10 Tank Destroyer (TD) that had made a wrong turn somewhere and arrived alone in Le Neufbourg. The M10 was basically a self-propelled 3-inch gun platform with tractor treads. Its sides were lightly armored, sufficient to deflect small arms fire, but it did not have a top. This was the "lost" TD referred to by Colonel Reardon. The tank destroyer had boxes of K-rations aboard. Except for the generosity of the M10 crew, we would have been very hungry. The M10 accompanied us on several attacks down the rue de l'Englise. It was necessary to pull the bodies of some of our dead comrades out of the roadway to avoid the tractor-like treads of the M10. On one of our sorties the M10 reached the down slope of the road south of the church and began getting small arms fire above its armored sides. Lacking roof armor the tank destroyer crew decided to back up and leave the area.

As mentioned by Colonel Reardon, during one of our attacks a soldier from Company H, 120th Infantry came stumbling out of a damaged house on the east side of the road and embraced us. He was hungry, thirsty, and unarmed so we sent him northward as we continued south. During the encirclement period, I drank water from a roadside ditch after putting chlorine pills in my canteen and waiting for an hour before drinking. After collecting water from the ditch several times I discovered a dead German lying in the dense weeds a short distance upstream.

Historians credit the 230th Field Artillery Battalion forward observers on Hill 314 with a pivotal role defeating the counterattack. On the critical morning of 7 August, fog prevented Allied aircraft from taking part in the battle. Only artillery, expertly directed from Hill 314, prevented German progress toward Pontaubault. Artillery observers on Hill 314 were in radio contact with batteries that were not surrounded. Having determined the map coordinates of roads and other approaches, the surrounded artillery observers could direct a shower of exploding shells upon targets they could hear moving even when they couldn't see them.

A large part of our activity during the battle was not directed by anyone in authority. We acted freely and spontaneously to help the common cause. Every enemy soldier deployed to counter our attacks was one fewer man available for use against the defenders of Hill 314. Every shell and bullet, fired at the men of Company E, was one fewer available to fire at the soldiers on Hill 314.

***The Stench of War:** In the cemetery in Le Neufbourg, shells had opened up a lot of the graves. There was a musty smell hanging over the place. You don't get the smell in any books or movies. Mortain was fought in August of 1944—the odors of the dead Germans and Americans! We were all there in a confined space for a long period, and those bodies, you knew they were there. When we got over to the area where the battle of the Falaise Gap was fought, there were dead horses and dead Germans all over the place. They were in the sun for quite a long time. That's a factor no one can ever put in a movie.*[18]

The battle at Mortain was a decisive tactical victory for the Allies. It culminated in the entrapment of significant portions of Germany's two western field armies in what would later become known as the Falaise Gap. They had been attacked by seasoned veterans from some of Hitler's crack *SS* divisions and proved that there was something significantly different about Old Hickory. The 30th Division had performed admirably and risen to the challenge. There's no doubt that there were many determining factors that affected the eventual outcome of this battle. The defense of Mortain would probably not have succeeded without the overwhelming air superiority the Allies could call on. Another reason for the victory was due to the use of artillery and excellent observation points. The survival of the 2nd Battalion, 120th Infantry Regiment on Hill 314, in particular, was largely due to this factor. Even with all the other elements combined, it nevertheless was undeniable that the 30th Division had tenaciously and courageously withstood a gargantuan test of their resilience and managed to survive. The US Army's "Workhorse" realized during those fateful summer months that they could win battles and they were capable of executing their allocated tasks with an almost unparalleled level of zeal and commitment.

There would be many more encounters to endure before the war was over, but those first few months in the bocage effectively determined the character and composition of this division. The indomitable resolution and fortitude that they had displayed under pressure in fierce combat inspired not only the other divisions they had fought alongside, but the whole Allied effort. Praise even extended as far as certain individuals at the German high command HQ who, out of earshot of Adolf Hitler, referred to them in no uncertain terms as Roosevelt's *SS*.

REPULSE OF THE GERMAN COUNTERATTACK
AIMED AT AVRANCHES, 7–11 AUGUST 1944
(COMMENTS OF BRIGADIER GENERAL JAMES M. LEWIS,
30TH DIVISION ARTILLERY OFFICER, DATED 25 AUGUST 1944)

The Germans had infiltrated through our front line defenses on Monday A.M. before any artillery fire was placed on them. They had not progressed much beyond St. Barthelmy, however, before all 12-1/2 F.A. Bns. were massed to interdict the two main roads leading west from St. Barthelmy. This was the artillery's most important contribution to repelling the counterattack. The 12-1/2 F.A. Bns. consisted of the following: The 30th Div.'s own 4 Bns. (113th, 118th, 197th, & 230th F.A. Bns.); two armored Bns.; the 42nd F.A. Bn (4th Inf. Div.); 1 Bn. of 155 SPs and 1 4.5 in Chem Bn. Thse were augmented by 2 Bns. of 155s, 1Bn. of

8-in. and six 105s from the 743rd Tk. Bn. (These last were in direct support and under control of the 30th Div. Arty.) The concentrations of these Bns. just west of St. Barthelmy, had to be adjusted very carefully due to the presence of friendly troops in the vicinity of St. Barthelmy. On certain missions, some of the Bns. could not be used.

Our Air OPs did invaluable work. Because of the position of the sun from 1900 to 2000, the cub planes were able to identify more targets during those hours than at any other time. Most of this time was spent adjusting on the targets. Then, when the cub planes had to come down because of darkness, the batteries would complete the firing on the observed and adjusted targets. B. Gen. Lewis believes that a record was established on 9 August, when 30 observed counter-battery missions were fully adjusted between 2045 and 2145. A tremendous drop in the enemy's artillery fire the next day evidenced the effectiveness of these missions.

Without observation from the hill (#314) east of Mortain, we would have been much in the dark. Not only did the arty observers with the 2/120 Inf. on the hill spot counterattacks forming up against the hill, they were able to locate a number of targets to the north.

After the effort to drop supplies to the 2/120 Inf. by cub planes failed on account of the heavy flak in the vicinity of Mortain (2 planes were shot up), the 230th F.A. Bn. successfully employed propaganda shells to shoot medical supplies to the isolated battalion (2/120 Inf. on Hill #314). The box score was as follows: 1st attempt: 6 shot, none recovered; 2nd attempt: 5 out of 6 recovered; 3rd attempt: 3 out of 3 recovered. Only the plasma arrived in unusable condition. Additional plasma was shot through 155's, but this was no better.

After the night of 7 August, Germans infiltrated into Romagny and vicinity presumably from the NE. The forward observers had difficulty locating targets in Romagny because of the narrow streets and high walls, but a considerable concentration was laid down anyway. On the night of 7 August, hostile tanks and infantry got into the positions of the 197th F.A. Bn. The Bn. fought as infantry all of the next morning and into the afternoon before the threat was sufficiently contained to enable the men to get on with their primary mission. In the process they knocked out one tank with a bazooka.

The most spectacular achievement of artillery during the battle—from the point of view of the amount of enemy personnel and equipment destroyed over a short time—was the intense concentration laid down on a German column moving east on the Mortain-Ger road on 9 August. Ten F.A. Bns massed on this column, causing terrible destruction on this road. The Germans fired a lot of rocket guns on the area east of St. Barthelemy and L'Abbaye Blanche. Our artillery coun-

terfired on them every afternoon in the valley of la Cance River and the draw just west of the N–S grid line.

Maintaining communications was a very difficult problem on account of the extensive hostile tank infiltration. The wire crews worked practically around the clock to keep the ground lines open, and except for occasional resorting to radio, telephone communication was employed throughout. Not that the terrain was difficult from a wire communication viewpoint; it was necessary to open up new roads and cut down innumerable hedges in order to maintain wire communications and the flow of ammunition.[19]

On 14 August, the 30th Division prepared to pull out and hit the road in the direction of Belgium, but not before they had entertained the local population, who were extremely fervent in their desire to celebrate the liberation from the Nazis. Most enemy action ahead of them had dissipated, but there were still pockets of resistance here and there. The lead units were the 113th Cavalry Group and the 30th Reconnaissance Troop. Paris was liberated on 25 August. While Third Army crossed the river Seine and entered the Marne area, on the morning of 27 August, the 117th and 119th Infantry Regiments crossed farther northeast toward to strategically significant ridgelines that were held by the Germans. Two tough days of fighting ensued until the Germans were finally dislodged but at a heavy cost to the 743rd Tank Battalion's Company B who lost four tanks due to enemy fire. After that action the chase was on and progress was swift and decisive. The Red Ball Express had a serious job on their hands to keep up with the rapid Allied advance. A division on the move needed 7,000 tons of supplies every day.

RICHARD LACEY, COMPANY M, 120TH INFANTRY REGIMENT

I got a Bronze Star in France after Mortain. We had moved out to another town in another area. We were going through a schoolyard and I was carrying our machine gun. There was a pump in this schoolyard and a rifleman had stopped there to get a drink. He got shot by a German sharpshooter. I put my gun down and ran to his aid. I really didn't do anything special. My squad was moving and they were hollering at me to come back. The company clerk eventually wrote me up for a Bronze Star. I didn't know anything about it until I got the award. The guy who got shot was hit by the bullet in his face near his eye and it went out the back. He was one of the riflemen, but I didn't know him. After that, I became a private first class and I got my stripe.[20]

KING KENNY, RECONNAISSANCE PLATOON, 823RD TANK DESTROYER BATTALION

We moved pretty well through France. There were people on the streets with flowers. We got to a town, I can't think of the name, and moved into a barn for the night. Then some Frenchman, with a little accordion maybe 12 inches long like a squeeze box, came over with 10 or 12 girls. We went to the upstairs part of the barn which had a solid floor and had a dance. The girls would go around and put a handkerchief around the back of your neck and then you would dance. They would pick out who they wanted to dance with. The guys would see some girl they liked and put the handkerchief around their neck. That lasted for at least an hour or so.

We were going through some French towns with no resistance, with the flowers and the girls hugging us. They had pulled out the women they called collaborators and they shaved their heads. They would push them up in front of us.[21]

HANK STAIRS, HEADQUARTERS COMPANY, 117TH INFANTRY REGIMENT

We traveled down to Domfront, southeast of Mortain. We didn't know it but we were part of a bigger plan to cut off the Germans. We were swinging up to close in on the Falaise Gap to cut them off. While in Domfront we were in reserve. A Red Cross donut wagon visited us and there was a jeep parked in the area with a radio. We were able to listen in on a conversation with an observation plane, one of those little Piper Cubs, that was directing artillery. He was giving a damn near blow-by-blow account of the hell that was coming down on this German column as they tried to escape. He was shouting, "Oh my God, we hit that lead truck there. They're all backed up. They can't go anyplace!" He gave us a first-hand account of what turned out to be a massacre!

That pretty well finished up our combat in France after Mortain. We left the hedgerow country, which was a great relief. We went clear across France and nothing major happened. We reached the Seine, north of Paris, and the Germans destroyed many of the bridges behind them. There were still a couple of bridges foot soldiers could cross that weren't totally disabled. We're going east on Jerry's tail and met sporadic resistance.[22]

GÜNTER ADAM, 9TH SS-PANZER DIVISION "HOHENSTAUFEN"

France, August 1944. At around three o'clock in the afternoon of 17 August 1944, Major Harzer ordered me to take over as platoon leader. He explained the situation in which the 7th Army found themselves in general terms and explained that they were surrounded by the enemy in Falaise with only the narrowest of escape routes. This was at Trun. I was told to make my way there, and after having made a recce with my platoon of the whole area, to contact our troops and guard this area to maintain the escape route. Then I was told to send two groups back, to gather the scattered troop together. I returned to the supply point, where the men of my platoon were washing and eating, and then I gave the order to "make ready." Some of the non-commissioned men then voiced opinions on how this operation should be dealt with and to them it appeared to be quite simple. Our company accountant, Sgt. Rigitini, was particularly eager to come with me. He became very agitated when I refused his request to join us because there was an empty seat in my Schwimmwagen. *I explained that this operation was not going to be a walk in the park, and then went to report our departure to the Division Staff Office. We left at around 0330 hours. At the outskirts of the town our Staff Officer and Captain Hunke, wished us "Good Luck." It was wonderful weather, the sun was shining, it was warm and there was little traffic on the roads at first, but that changed. In the distance we heard fighter bombers flying overhead, and we found it strange that they didn't appear to be interested in us. The first trickle of retreating troops marching to the west then became a torrent, which in turn became an untidy column walking three-abreast. They were the target of the fighter bombers who attacked them repeatedly. To bypass this mass—now spreading even more untidily over a large area—was impossible and impeded my advance to such an extent that I was forced to take to the fields, for which my "21 Zundapp 750" machine for off-road driving, was more than capable. The farther we advanced, the worse this situation became. Now more bombers were involved in attacking this mass and the slaughter was horrendous—it was pure hell. The sounds of the dive bombers, exploding shells, and the cries of the wounded and dying—both human being and horses—were deafening. They were all covered in smoke and dust.*

We were not their direct targets because we were not important to these slaughterers, but we became spectators of this terrible scene. Above it all, the August sun was shining. Time appeared to stand still as we slowly approached a town only to be confronted by the same scenario, masses of troops huddled together and military police trying to bring some order into the situation. I was asked to show my written order, but I didn't have one, which meant that the military police could prevent me from driving in the opposite direction to the oncoming stream of troops. I announced in no uncertain terms that, with or without the permission of this police captain, I would fulfil my mission and use force if necessary to accomplish it. The whole platoon stood behind me so I gave the signal to advance. At this moment another Schwimmwagen *stopped adjacent to me. It was carrying a major wearing a Knight's Cross who I didn't recognize. He forced his way in front of me, to guide us through the throng, forcing the way shouting and gesticulating until the way was made free for us. He explained that a bridge up ahead was responsible for the congestion. He further explained that he was on his way there and that he would be pleased to accompany us and was delighted to have the* SS *with him.*

Due to the continual air attacks, which forced the flow-back of troops to dive for cover, we eventually reached the bridge, but I still don't know to this day which town it was. Standing in our Schwimmwagens, *the major and I forced everything to move out of our way until we had reached the other side of the bridge; then the major disappeared. We had left the core of this inferno behind us and the platoon was whole. We had a few scratches, but no casualties, which was a miracle! We could not afford to lose any time and so our journey continued, and the troops who had to force their way over the bridge were now dissipating along with the air attacks. Nonetheless, we had to take to the fields again and navigate our way past columns moving in the opposite direction.*

Then the way ahead opened up and now there was nothing in front of us, only the noise of battle behind us, which was fading. We had reached high ground that gave us a commanding view of the land and of a forest area that lay around 1,000 yards in front of us. Suddenly we could not believe our eyes. Coming from the east we saw a formation of approximately 50 planes advancing towards us. We quickly took cover in some bushes nearby. Our column was so densely packed that if the airplanes had spotted us and opened their bomb hatches there would have been no escape. We would not have had a chance!

From our hiding places we could only stare at these planes as they passed overhead and we could see their bomb hatches quite clearly. If they had opened to drop their load, we could have watched the falling bombs, but we prayed that this wouldn't happen. We prayed for a miracle and our prayers were heard; once more we were undamaged. Maybe the low-lying sun had blinded them, or maybe their loads were meant for the poor beggars stuck in the Falaise Pocket? Perhaps they had already shed their load of bombs somewhere else? We had to continue and complete our mission, and by now it must have been around 6 o'clock.

I called my section leader to me and instructed him that there had to be a longer distance between our vehicles so that we would not be surprised like that again, and that included our dispatch riders. Then it was "make ready." I looked through my field glasses to look at the terrain and saw meadows, orchards, and farmhouses spread here and there, but saw no enemy movement. All appeared to be peaceful and I took my place at the spearhead. My companions were Pvt. Wessels and Pvt. Boguslayski, who was my driver. I shouted, "Let's go!" and Boguslayski put his foot down on the accelerator. He sped down to low ground where we saw the first roadside bushes, orchards, and farmhouses on our left as the road curved to the right. Suddenly, Boguslayski swung the steering wheel hard over to the left and slammed on the brakes, coming to a halt in front of an American tank parked diagonally across the road. From all sides of us we heard, "Hands up, hands up!" Still sitting in the Schwimmwagen, we were surrounded and looking at the cocked weapons of American soldiers. Boguslayski was heard to exclaim rather loudly, "Oh, shit!"

We didn't have the opportunity to get out of the car as we were searched and robbed, still seated with our hands in the air. My protests were ignored as my pistol was removed along with my money. We were stripped of everything else, including our insignia, which was taken as souvenirs; it all happened so quickly. Uppermost in my mind was that my platoon could most probably appear any minute now and I hoped that my men would not fall into this trap as we had. I told myself that their experience in previous situations would prevent this, and the Sherman moved to another position clearing the road. Two young girls of about 17 or 18 years old emerged from a farmhouse nearby. They stood and stared, then spat at us. This spiteful attitude only served to aggravate the already loaded atmosphere as the threatening situation developed into a dangerous one.

Instinctively, I knew that I had to gain a little time. The American sergeant who was in command looked through my wallet and took out a photo of Major Toldsdorf portrayed in his uniform and wearing Oak Leaves insignia. He was an acquaintance of mine from my hometown Treuberg. He asked "Father, brother?" and I answered deliberately in German, and hoped to gain a little time. While the sergeant looked at the photo of this high-ranking officer wearing insignia for bravery, though, he made his intentions clear. I was then ordered to "run towards the hedges," but I wasn't being allowed to escape to freedom. "Go on. Run!" The sergeant repeated the order in German, "Feldwebel! Lauf!" The sergeant then pointed in the direction from which we had just come. We had run into an American military lynch mob! He wanted to shoot me in the back "while escaping!" Since I didn't have anything to lose, I stood my ground, stared him in the eye, and said "No, you swine! If you want to shoot me, then go ahead, but don't shoot me in the back." He certainly didn't understand what I had said, or my gestures. Maybe his conscience began to trouble him.

He and I had been standing out of earshot from my comrades, but we walked back over to them and I found that they were digging in a trench by the roadside. They had been given the order to enlarge it. I then countermanded this order and *told them to lay down their shovels. This was the second order from this sergeant that I had revoked. Wessels and Boguslayski had not realized what they had been asked to dig, or had they? If they didn't know I was not about to tell them. My order brought a swift reaction from the sergeant, who shouted, "Kill him." Suddenly two young Americans aimed their machine pistols at me, and my last thoughts were, "This is the end, my life is over." I saw the flash of fire from the muzzles of the machine pistols and then I couldn't breathe. I attempted to stay on my feet, but try as I might, this wasn't possible. I soon lost consciousness. Before I passed out I heard shots and thought that I saw one of my dispatch riders fall from his motorbike. I do not know for sure if this was the case, and today I still don't know.*

Sometime later when I regained consciousness, it felt as if theatre curtains were being slowly raised. I was lying face down on the road. I had grit in my mouth and my face was covered in dust. I thought that something was moving close by. Every breath that I took was agony as my chest heaved, but by now I was fully conscious and I could I hear machine-gun fire in the vicinity. Still wearing my helmet, I turned my head very slowly and I could see the Amis who were quite close by in the trenches and hidden behind the hedges shooting, presumably at my platoon. My first thoughts were that I had to move as far away as I could from here, before they noticed that I was still alive; otherwise, I'd get a bullet in the back of my neck or get caught in cross fire.

I knew the trench that Wessels and Boguslayski had been told to dig in was somewhere behind me so I slowly began to drag myself to where I thought it was. Every slight movement and even just breathing was excruciating and I could not move my right leg due to the terrible pain in my right groin. There was nothing else for it. I had to move away, whatever it cost. I reached the trench and slowly sank into it where Wessels lay. His chest had been torn apart. It was just a bloody mess, but his face was untouched. He had been standing in the middle of us three and had received the full load. There was nothing I could do to help him. There was no sign of Boguslayski (I learned later in 1944, that despite being wounded, he had made his way back to our unit). As if in slow motion, I buttoned my jacket up to the top. I was quite calm and realized that I had to stop the flow of blood oozing from my wound. I always had first-aid bandages with me, but not on this occasion because I'd given them to a comrade. All that I had was a dirty handkerchief. I had received two bullets in my chest and despite the unimaginable pain, I tore this handkerchief into strips and pushed them finger-deep into my wounds. I could not ascertain if I had any other wounds. Now I had to get out of the trench. The thought that I was still in danger of being found alive was uppermost in my mind because I knew that the Amis wouldn't think twice about finishing me off! Still quite calm, I neither thought about bleeding to death nor of dying.

Thoughts of my surviving gave me the strength to leave my comrade, Wessels, there. It was hard. Once more, I pulled myself inch by inch out of the trench and crossed a road before crawling under a barbed-wire fence. The road curved here and I would no longer be in view. Somehow I managed, but I can't say how long this took me because it felt like I was moving in slow motion. I became exhausted and couldn't go any farther. I found myself parallel to the Amis, who were still firing at my platoon. Then about 20 yards away from the hedge, I saw an iron water trough sunk slightly into the ground. If I could reach the space between the hedge and the trough this would give me even better protection. Once more I had to make a superhuman effort to get there, which I eventually did, so that I could hide between the hedge and the trough. Almost instantly I heard our infantry open fire and bullets tore into the earth around me. This was a very uncomfortable situation to be in! The Amis retreated and I breathed a sigh of relief knowing that for the moment I was not going to be rudely surprised by the barrel of an American rifle being pointed at me.

All at once, there was nothing to be heard. This battle was over and I decided to wait until it was dark to try and reach German lines in the direction of Falaise. It was then that I noticed that I still possessed my watch. My jacket was no longer in good condition; my left sleeve was torn, and held together by my arm band. Being told to put my hands in the air was what saved my watch which was the only possession that I still had. My pockets were empty. The curve in the road, prevented me from seeing the "Falaise Pocket,' but I could hear the sounds of engines in the village which I had just left and could see Americans approximately a hundred yards away from me. For no apparent reason, one of them supported his rifle on top of a fence pole and took a shot at me! The bullet hit the trough, producing a fountain of water on both sides and the earth around where I was laying became a muddy quagmire.

I waited for other shots but none came so I lifted my head and saw the Amis open a farm gate for a Sherman to enter. It was coming towards me and I thought, "This is really the end for me, but then I realized that I wasn't the intended target. The squeak of the Sherman's tracks became louder and louder, and it halted just five yards away from the hedge. The commander now stood in the turret and looked through his field glasses. If he had looked down, he would have seen me, but thankfully he didn't. He concentrated on the terrain and I wondered why I'd been fired at. Maybe the rifle shot wasn't intended for me? It was a puzzle, but now I began to feel very weak. I could not have cared as I closed my eyes and fell asleep, only to be woken up by the ear shattering noise of a tank motor starting up. *The tank only moved slightly to the right of the road. Once more I dozed. This time when I regained consciousness the tank and* Amis *had gone and it was dark. All I could hear was the sound of an M42 in the distance, and then everything was peaceful once more.*

I looked at my watch. It was half-past ten, and despite the pain I had to be on my way, so I slowly got to my feet. The night was still warm as I made my way around the curve in the road, keeping away from any guards who may have been posted there. I kept the road in sight, and removed my helmet to so that I could hear things better. I was sure that someone would hear my boots, so I prepared to take them off, but this was easier said than done. It was difficult because I couldn't move my right leg, but I managed it. Now I had my boots to carry as well because I couldn't throw them away! I focused on the potential danger and decided to move away from the shadow of the hedges in case the way ahead was guarded. I had to take to the open fields but I had the darkness of the night. In stocking feet, I made my way step by step, tensely waiting for a sudden order that would shatter the silence. Due to the pain in my chest, breathing was becoming unbearable. To make matters worse, the ground under my feet was uneven, producing a torturous pain every time my left foot slipped. Eventually, I came to the outskirts of a village, which I managed to pass unnoticed. I knew that I would not be able to stay on my feet for much longer, but I really had to force myself to go a little farther.

The moon had now appeared, showing me the way. Soon another village came into view and with it the realization that I seriously needed help. I had no other choice, I couldn't go on. Almost at the end of my strength, I dragged myself *down the main road that was illuminated by street lights. All of the houses on both sides of the road were in darkness and all was as quiet as the grave. Then I heard the sounds of glasses, bottles, and conversation. I shouted as loudly as possible, "Hello, I need help!" Suddenly, there was no more sound of conversation. It was silent and so I shouted once more. Once more my cry for help echoed in the stillness; somehow I approached the very last house on the left. I couldn't go any farther. I had to gain entry to this house. There were no lights to be seen and the gate had a chain tied loosely around the posts which I undid. I made my way to the door, upon which I knocked. A young French lad opened the door and tried to shoo me away, but using the last of my strength, I pushed past him and sank to the ground. It was a barn. I asked him to get some German soldiers, but he said there were none in the area. Then suddenly, someone else appeared who lit all of the stall lanterns. It was an old woman who bent over me and inspected my wounds. She shook her head and said, "Fini!" I pointed to my groin and she looked at that, too. Her only comment was, "Nix, Monsieur." There was nothing that she could do, but she brought bundles of straw, helping me onto them and then left, extinguishing the lights as she went. But before the lights went out I saw other people, civilians also sitting around the walls. Then I was alone with my thoughts, which mysteriously led me to remember that it was 17 August and Friedrich the Great's birthday.*

Sometime later I heard the sounds of vehicles. The young lad came to me and said that there were German soldiers outside. They refused to enter the building and I was not able to go outside. They left and I'll never know who they were, but they were certainly not comrades from the Waffen-SS! *Then it was dark once more, and still. Once more my ears tuned to the sound of vehicles and I realized that a farm gate had been opened and a vehicle had driven in. I hoped once more, how I hoped, that they would be comrades come to fetch me! I saw a blinding torch-light from the barn door, and then I felt someone open my jacket and very carefully remove my strips of blood-stained handkerchief. No one spoke a word. I had to ask, "Which unit are you from?" But I received no answer. I then asked, "Are you from the* SS?" *Then, very slowly, he showed himself in the light of the torch, his head appearing for me to see his flat "soup-plate" helmet draped in a camo-net of the "Tommy." I was disappointed, but at the same time happy at the prospect of receiving some medical attention. I realized that these visitors were army medics. They tended me very carefully and applied wide bandages with sticky edges to my wounds. Then they gave me an injection for the pain and brought a litter for me. I screamed in agony as they attempted to lift me onto the litter; the pain was unbearable. I indicated that I would try myself and the man who had bandaged me said, "Sergeant-major, you are very brave." I managed to lie on the litter and was then carried outside to a jeep-type ambulance that had places for four litters inside. The tarpaulin which stretched over the sides and top had been rolled back and three lightly wounded Canadians were inside. My saviors were Canadians, and very good examples of their profession.*

I could not determine, whether it was the injection, which had started to dim the pain, or the design of this ambulance, which reduced the stress of transport. It was comfortable and soon the gum-chewing soldiers asked, "Are you SS?" *They could tell from my camo-jacket. We then drove off. The vehicle was very comfortable and it was quite pleasant driving in the fresh night air beneath the bright moonlight. The soldiers tried to start a conversation with me, but I decided it was better to pretend to be unconscious. Very soon we had joined their unit, presumably their command post. A torch was shone on me, and I heard a voice asking questions. Once more I pretended to be unconscious, and then we drove on again. My thoughts were dominated with the prospect of becoming a* POW. *I even contem-*

plated rolling off the litter and attempting to escape but there was nothing else I could do but accept my fate, whatever it was to be.

The moon had now disappeared, but it was still dark, and once more we came to a command post and I played the same charade as before. Someone searched me very, very carefully, perhaps looking for papers for identification, but had no luck. Wherever we were going, our destination had not been reached yet, so we drove on once more, turning left and driving through a small town. In the distance I could hear small arms firing. Suddenly, a volley from German infantry hit the road in front of us causing the ambulance driver to make a U-turn and put his foot down to drive back through the town. Five minutes later I heard a shot followed with someone shouting in German, "Halt! Who goes there?" The Canadians didn't respond. So to avoid being shot at again, I shouted, "Don't shoot, there are Germans here too." A German soldier confirmed that we were also German and then escorted us to a German command post. I had been saved. My German comrade was a corporal, who then accompanied us to a field hospital. He informed me that the 7th Army had narrowly broken out of the Falaise Pocket and that his unit was the rear guard. The darkness slowly faded, the heavens lit up with a red glow. I saw the retreating columns of German soldiers passing in silence. My friend, Corporal Wessels, was among them. It would be months before I could be returned to active duty.[23]

FRANK DENIUS, BATTERY C, 230TH FIELD ARTILLERY BATTALION

The 30th went on the attack toward the east of France, north of Paris. The first objectives were small towns, then we moved to protect Patton's southwestern flank during the Battle of the Falaise Gap. After that, we moved 25 to 30 miles northwest of Paris on the Seine River. We were positioned there in late August when General de Gaulle and the French 1st Armored Division entered Paris. From there, we went through WWI territory all the way north of Paris to Belgium.[24]

The 30th Division was now ordered to head toward the Belgian town of Tournai not far from the French border. They would be accompanied by the 2nd Armored Division on their left and the 28th Infantry Division on their right. The advance indicated that on the route to Belgium they would proceed through the French towns of Roye, Peronne, and Cambrai. To assist in their progress, a task force was assembled under the command of Brigadier General William K. Harrison, Jr. that consisted of: 125th Cavalry Squadron; 30th Reconnaissance Troop; 743rd Tank Battalion; 1st Battalion, 119th Infantry Regiment; Company A, 105th Engineer Battalion; 118th Field Artillery Bat-

talion; and 823rd Tank Destroyer Battalion. This was a highly mobile and
flexible force to lead the way. They set off on the afternoon of 1 September
with the 125th Cavalry on point, one hour ahead of the main body of the
task force.

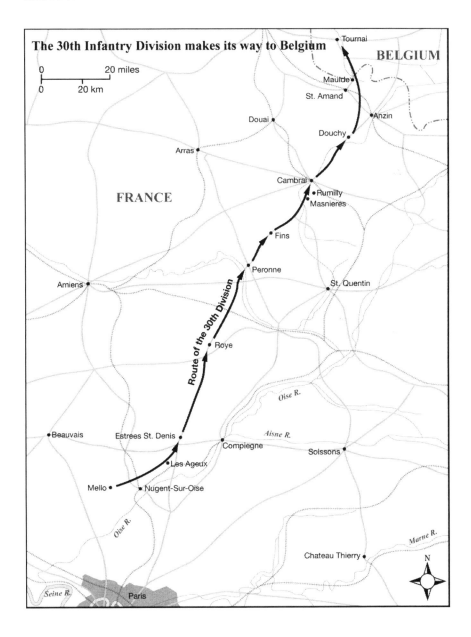

The 30th Infantry Division makes its way to Belgium

Troop A, moving up the secondary roads to the left of the route of the Division column, knocked out the occasional impediments to progress such as blown bridges, mines, as well as roadblocks manned by machinegunners and riflemen. The right flank was covered by a platoon of Troop C. During the first 35 miles of the journey there was little resistance, but at the town of Roye, Troop C was met with a burst of small arms fire as it passed through town, and civilians reported large numbers of enemy equipped with tanks just northeast of the town. These reports proved to be a little hyperbolic but a column of German half-tracks were hounded away along with a Mark III tank and a German staff car which was knocked out by a few rounds from the assault-gun platoon attached to the troop. Approximately a dozen Germans were captured and almost as many killed in a 45-minute action at Carrepuis, a few miles up the road from Roye. Similar actions occurred at almost every town along the route. In most cases the Free French Forces requisitioned German weapons and prisoners, and often assumed the task of mopping up the strays while the cavalrymen surged forward.

By early evening Troop A had reached Peronne, a town that had seen a lot of action during WWI located by the infamous river Somme. The first unit to reach the Somme was the 2nd Armored Division's 82nd Reconnaissance Battalion. They started out ahead of the 125th Cavalry and after crossing the 2nd Armored zone, they had fanned out in the direction of Peronne, where they knocked out a fairly strong enemy force stationed there and prepared to blow the bridge before proceeding.

Troop A redirected to the main road without much difficulty, closely followed by the main body of the task force. Troop C's progress was more laborious because it was confined to secondary roads, but eventually it filtered into Peronne. Gas supplies were becoming a serious problem, but the troop managed to pick up some fuel and by daybreak the following day they were ready to continue. About eight miles south of Cambrai the troop was ordered to stop to wait for the squadron fuel truck to catch up. After a fruitless hour and a half of waiting, the troop started up again because the squadron commander felt that the fuel truck probably could catch up before the tanks ran dry. Not long after they had set off again the point of the task force ran into a German column of horse-drawn carts; these were quickly dispatched as the five lead American vehicles poured machine-gun and 37mm fire into the poorly protected column.

Before long, they had almost reached the Scheldt River that runs into Belgium. The Scheldt is still one of the most important rivers in Belgium, running from the harbor town of Antwerp all the way south to the French border. It was at this juncture that the column encountered its first serious delay. The 30th Division column was still on the road but now it stretched back almost to the initial point of departure, which made it visible from the air and vulnerable to potential Luftwaffe attacks. At approximately 0300 hours, the lead cavalry platoon began taking hits from 20mm gunfire that appeared to be emanating from 200 yards ahead in the vicinity of a bridge that crossed over a stream. As the cavalrymen reconnoitered for a bypass, four medium tanks from the 743rd Tank Battalion came up past a burning German half-track spewing 20mm shells and swiftly overran the anti-tank guns on the north side of the waterway. One tank hit a mine and had a track blown off but there were no other losses. Another cavalry platoon got a quarter-ton truck across the bridge without being fired on and then proceeded about a mile past Masnières to the outskirts of Rumilly. Again the point was greeted with 20mm gunfire, which knocked out the two leading armored cars. The drive was temporarily halted. Brigadier General Harrison, who had been at the front of the task force main body all the way, was wounded by a 20mm shell as he hit the ditch from his jeep, and Colonel Edwin M. Sutherland took over temporary command of the task force, until Major General Hobbs, on his way forward in his own jeep, arrived. Medium tanks were brought up and employed yet again to knock out the enemies light anti-tank guns. A decision was made to use these tanks to attack Cambrai. They advanced with two companies of the 743rd providing a base of fire on the hill south of Cambrai, while another tank company swept in from the southeast and moved through the town. The cavalry was ordered to move up to the head of the column again as the advance was resumed.

As the head of the task force column drove past Cambrai, meanwhile, a firefight developed in the town with an enemy column that had blundered into town from the east, evidently unaware of the American presence. The 119th Infantry Regiment's 3rd Battalion was given the task of clearing the town, and as a precaution, Company A of the 823rd Tank Destroyer Battalion was left in the town to secure the flank of the main column that was due to pass through there. The head of the task force column resumed its march. Minor actions continued for the rest of the operation. Near Iwuy, about five miles beyond Cambrai, the cavalry knocked out a column of six armored cars advancing along a sunken road from the southeast. Sniper fire was encountered at Denham, and some sniper and anti-tank fire were received at Valenciennes. By this time the fast-moving point of the column had pulled away from the main body. Many vehicles had been forced to drop out due to lack of gasoline while other detachments had been dropped off to clean out snipers. At 1830, Colonel Sutherland's party, a handful of jeeps and about a platoon of tanks, crossed the Belgian border at Matilde.

Headquarters, 230th Field Artillery Battalion, Action Against Enemy/After Action Report, 3 October 1944

Advance parties left for new area in Belgium September 1st, 1944. The battalion moved out at 1830 hours for the new area in Belgium. (During night two robot planes passed over convoy.) Weather was cloudy and rain. The battalion was enroute to Belgium all day on the 2nd of September. Advance parties crossed the Belgium frontier around 1500 hours and received an enthusiastic welcome. Colonel Vieman, Lieutenant Baer, and Tec 5 Penn took three prisoners in the battalion area. Battalion arrived in position area around 0600 hours on the 3rd of September. Position was near the village of Breyelles, Belgium. South of Tournai four prisoners were taken by Sergeant Morodook and Cpl. Roberts. No firing done, length of march about 125 miles. September 4th was devoted to care and cleaning of materiel, equipment, and inspection by Staff Officers and Battery Commanders. No firing done on the 5th of September, the Belgian patriot army, L'Armée Blanche, active in vicinity. Advance parties moved out for new position area in eastern Belgium on the 6th of September. At 1845 battalion moved to assembly area near Anteing preparatory to road march. At 1450 hours on the 7th of September the battalion arrived at assembly area near Waterloo, and made a road march of 59 miles during day. Advance party consisting of Captain Stewart; Lts. Moebacher, McCrea, and Case. The survey crew and wire sections were forcibly separated from the 120th Infantry convoy by an overtaking armored convoy, and continued on the line of march, joining up with the other units later on. No firing done this day. Battalion continued to move eastward on the 8th of September. Infantry on foot due to gas shortage. Quartering party attained objective, Bilsen, on heels of reconnaissance unit. No firing done. The battalion occupied position near Vichmael on the 9th of September, the quartering party remained in Bilsen. The battalion displaced in echelons on the 10th. Quartering party re-joined battalion in Tongres. Battalion position east of Tongres, near Boire. Eight missions, 101 rounds fired. Fort Eben-Emael, about 4000 yards to the east, was taken without resistance by the 120th Infantry. September 11th, Btry C fired first rounds into Holland. One enemy plane flew over area. 5 missions, 55 rounds fired. 19 missions, 555 rounds fired on the 12th of September. Buzz bomb passed over 120th Regimental Headquarters. Battalion displaced on the 13th, crossing the Albert Canal and Meuse River, south of Visé, on pontoon bridges. Able, Baker, and Charlie Batteries crossed into Holland occupying positions near Noorbeck; Verify battery went into position in Belgium, just short of the frontier. Battalion moved to new positions near Tormars. All batteries fired into Germany, Charlie Battery first, elevation 792; range 12,200 yards. Battalion received two officer replacements, Lts. Pfeil and Cofer, on the 14th of September. Battalion still in general support. Two missions, 28 rounds fired. One prisoner captured in battalion area by 531st AAA battalion. No firing done on the 15th, received CSMO (Close Station, March Order) at 2140 hours.[25]

Private First Class John F. Cody, Medical Corps,
117th Infantry Regiment, Silver Star citation:
For gallantry in action on 7 August 1944, in France. While his company was in the act of clearing out an enemy held town, they were met by an enemy barrage of 81mm mortar and 240mm artillery fire, wounding 15 men and killing six others. Two aid men were wounded and another killed, leaving Private Cody as the only aid man left with the company. During the heaviest of the artillery and mortar fire, Private Cody searched the ruined buildings, going from wounded to wounded to administer first aid and supervise the evacuation of the more seriously wounded. As a result of his personal bravery he was directly responsible for saving the lives of a number of his wounded comrades. Entered military service from Massachusetts.[26]

Technical Sergeant Clause L. Creighton, Infantry,
117th Infantry Regiment, Silver Star citation:
For gallantry in action on 7 August 1944, in France. Sergeant Creighton was assigned duty with an infantry force engaged in an attack against the enemy. During the firefight, many of Sergeant Creighton's comrades were wounded. With complete disregard for his own safety, Sergeant Creighton voluntarily moved from place to place on the battlefield, rendering first aid and evacuating the wounded. When he himself was wounded, he continued evacuating those more

seriously hurt until he received a second wound and he had to be evacuated himself. Entered service from Tennessee.[27]

First Lieutenant Albert E. Johnson, Medical Administrative Corps, 105th Medical Battalion, Silver Star citation:
For gallantry in action on 7 August 1944, in France. When a battalion of friendly troops had been isolated in enemy territory, Lieutenant Johnson volunteered to infiltrate German lines in order that badly needed plasma would reach them. Without knowledge of German positions and as to what definite route to take, Lieutenant Johnson, with the aid of an enlisted man, drove an ambulance over a hazardous route during partial blackout in his successful effort to bring medical aid to his wounded comrades. Upon completion of the mission, finding that they could be of no further assistance to the troops, they returned unescorted to their company area. Entered military service from Illinois.[28]

Sergeant Willie L. Weaver, Medical Corps, 105th Medical Battalion, Silver Star citation:
For gallantry in action on 7 August 1944, in France. When a battalion of friendly troops had been isolated in enemy territory, Sergeant Weaver volunteered to infiltrate German lines in order that badly needed plasma would reach them. Without knowledge of German positions and as to what definite route to take, Sergeant Weaver, with the aid of an officer, drove an ambulance over a hazardous route during partial blackout in his successful effort to bring medical aid to his wounded comrades. Upon completion of the mission, finding that they could be of no further assistance to the troops, they returned unescorted to their company area. Entered military service from Mississippi.[29]

Headquarters, 30th Infantry Division, Citation of Headquarters and Headquarters Company, 117th Infantry Regiment, 20 October 1945
Headquarters and Headquarters Company, 117th Infantry Regiment is cited for outstanding performance of duty in action against the enemy on 7 August 1944, in the vicinity of St. Barthelmy, France. The enemy launched the first of a series of determined attacks, in an aggressive attempt to drive to the sea at Avranches and to split

Allied forces in France. In fog-enshrouded early morning hours the hostile troops made their first effort with paralyzing rapidity and crushing numerical superiority. Many of the company positions were overrun and a line of defense was established at the Regimental Command Post. Enemy tanks got close to the Command Post and a company of hostile infantrymen infiltrated them, threatening to encircle it. Displaying outstanding courage and tenacity of purpose, all troops of this group, including administrative personnel, fought heroically and dispersed the infantrymen to the rear while others destroyed the leading enemy tank with careful bazooka fire. Upon learning the seriousness of the general situation, the troops voluntarily moved to the front lines where for the day they fought with the front line companies and eventually repulsed the enemy attack. The devotion to duty displayed by this stalwart group reflects great credit upon each participant and is in keeping with the highest traditions of the military service.

LEYLAND S. HOBBS Major General,
US Army. Commanding[30]

PART TWO

THE RHINELAND

RHINELAND CAMPAIGN, PART 1

15 September 1944–15 December 1944

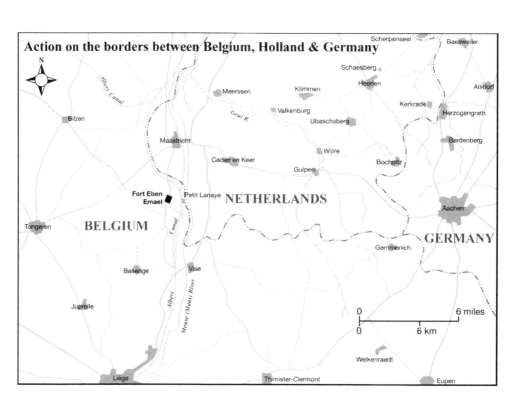

Action on the borders between Belgium, Holland & Germany

CHAPTER FOUR

TO THE EDGE OF THE REICH

The initial air of triumphalism that had pervaded the Allies since the St. Lô-Falaise breakout had steadily begun to dissipate in the fresh autumnal scenery that now greeted Old Hickory's advancing columns. While the British, Canadian, and Polish armies were hammering out a path up along the coast into the Dutch-speaking Flanders area of Belgium, the 30th Infantry Division spearheaded the route to Germany through the center of Belgium. Farther south, meanwhile, Patton's Third Army had ground to a halt on 31 August just outside of Metz. This was due to the fact that his vehicles were consuming an average of 350,000 gallons of gasoline each day and the supply route was becoming overextended. The Red Ball Express was stretched to capacity in an effort to keep Patton's men well supplied, but despite constant maligning from the general, they were struggling. On 28 August Third Army was forced to slow down when it was acknowledged that its fuel allocation was 100,000 gallons below target. There were sufficient supplies in Normandy but the Red Ball could not transport them in sufficient quantities to the Third Army's forward units. Fuel shortages and other logistical problems were also beginning to affect the 30th Division.

Since they had crossed the Belgian border, the 30th had encountered limited resistance from German troops who were now, for all intents and purposes, keeping well ahead of the Allies and heading toward their own border. Very few people, if any, at SHAEF headquarters were underestimating the magnitude of the task that the Division had now been allocated. With the columns snaking back miles along congested roads, they were hampered by driving autumnal rains and gusting winds that didn't help the situation. Pregnant blue-purple clouds hung low in the lowland sky and did nothing to lighten the mood of the men as they eventually came to halt seven miles south of Brussels in the vicinity of the famous Waterloo battlefield. It was at this juncture that they decided that the infantry should disembark and continue footslogging the following day. This was done to conserve fuel supplies for the vehicles, but it offered little consolation to the GIs who would have to wear out shoe leather trudging along these muddy, cobbled Belgian roads. Due to stops and starts it took the three regimental columns almost three days to cover 130 miles. The 113th Cavalry Squadron raced ahead toward the Meuse River, where it encountered the first signs of any concerted resistance.

JOHN O'HARE, COMPANY E, 117TH INFANTRY REGIMENT

Back in France, I was dealing with the first of my problems with my feet. I cannot identify exactly when or how my foot problems started. Perhaps it was jumping off a high wall loaded down with gear. I went to the medics who were used to seeing people who were bleeding. I said, "I think I have broken feet." They said, "Where did you go to medical school soldier?" I said, "Well, I think they're broken, I can't get my boots off. They are swollen." They then said, "We captured some arch supports from the Germans. Try these in your shoes and see if they will work." I thought this was not too good. Somewhere along the line they put me in a field hospital with tents and I slept there for three days straight. Then the front moved and the hospital moved again, so they said, "Well, we'll discharge all the patients. You have problems with your feet? We're giving a letter to your commanding officer saying that you can't take any long walks or lift anything heavy while standing on your feet. I took that back to my company commander and he said, "What a joke! There is no such job in our outfit." He was a pretty good sport about it, though. I tossed the foot supports away! We were taken part of the way into Belgium by truck to Charleroi, which is 40 miles south of Brussels. From there, we walked all the way to Maastricht. That was really bad for my feet because I thought they were broken and it just got worse and worse. I kept saying to the medics, "My right foot is broken." They asked, "How do you know that?" and said that I was a private and privates don't know anything. So I modified my stance and said, "I have a problem with my right foot, I can't get my boot off." So they x-rayed it and said, "By George, you've got a broken foot." They sent me to England and I did not return until the first of the year. So I missed the battle of Aachen and the Battle of the Bulge for all practical purposes. "Governor," who had been my ammunition bearer, had lost his leg in October and lots of other guys were dead when I returned.[1]

GEORGE SCHNEIDER, HEADQUARTERS COMPANY, 120TH INFANTRY REGIMENT

There was very little resistance across the rest of Belgium as we advanced faster than the Germans realized. On the southern outskirts of Brussels in the town of La Hulpe we spent the night in a castle on the edge of town. Just as we had experienced in Gaurain, the civilian activity was fairly normal. A friend and I decided to explore the town in the early evening. We stopped off at the first bar we saw and had a drink with some of the locals. We then moved on and came across a hospital that we entered and found a large ward. We were invited to inspect the facilities and found a wounded German soldier the Belgians were treating. We gave him a few cigarettes and went back on the street. The next stop was to talk to a Belgian standing in front of his butcher shop. He invited us in for a drink, showed us his hiding place for his illegal radio, and made conversation. He invited us to return the next day for a steak dinner and we accepted. We didn't know where he planned to get the steak since there wasn't a piece of meat in the shop. Many of the German artillery were horse-drawn and when these animals were killed the civilians would carve a nice piece of meat out of the horse's rump. I suspect our steak was to be a horse. We pulled out early the next morning and we never got our horse steak![2]

The mighty Meuse River runs through the Belgian city of Liege. It is flanked on the west side by the wide Albert Canal, which runs parallel to the river. The Meuse (Maas in Dutch) turns northeast four miles south of the Dutch city of Maastricht, which is situated 18 miles north of Liege. The area just to the east of Liege was the location of a series of forts; the vulnerability of these defenses had been emphasized when they failed to stop the Germans advancing in both WWI and WWII. On 10 May 1940, the largest of these forts, Eben-Emael, not far from the banks of the Albert Canal, had been the site of a spectacular and daring attack by 78 German paratroops. By September 1944, the Germans were using neither the natural barrier of the waterways nor the forts to offer significant resistance to advancing US forces.

In preparation for the advance that would eventually take the 30th Division into Germany, the division formed up into two columns with the 117th Infantry Regiment, which had originally been in the center column, following the 119th Infantry Regiment on its southern flank beside the Meuse River. The 120th Infantry Regiment, the other column, pushed towards Eben-Emael, not knowing that it had been abandoned already. An air strike that had been scheduled to hit the fort ahead of the advance didn't materialize, but that did not delay progress. Later it transpired that approximately 300 enemy troops who had previously occupied the fort had withdrawn over the Dutch border to Maastricht. The most assertive response to the advance up until that point was provided by a German 25-round light artillery concentration directed at the 120th's 3rd Battalion. The 119th, meanwhile, continued entirely unopposed following the river opposite the small industrial town of Visé, roughly halfway between Liege and Maastricht. It was tactically flawed that the German forces never used the potentially natural barrier of the Meuse River to oppose the 30th Division's progress.

During the night of 10 September, engineer reconnaissance established two locations that would be conducive to crossing the Meuse just south of the bridges that had been blown at Visé. Commencing in the early afternoon, Company L, 119th, was instructed to navigate their way across the canal and the river, which they did successfully. By nightfall the rest of the regiment had followed suit. Some sporadic enemy artillery rounds landed impotently in their vicinity, but no serious damage was incurred.

While the 30th Division was getting its first elements across the river near Visé, a major crossing at Liege was being forced by elements of the VII Corps. Having successfully conducted this crossing virtually unimpeded, they could now send a company of tanks and a company of tank destroyers through Liege to support the 119th Infantry. To maintain contact with VII Corps, the 113th Cavalry Squadron also crossed at Liege. The 120th Infantry, meanwhile, occupied itself with securing lock gates that were situated at the southern tip of the Maastricht island where the two waterways converge. These locks were of paramount importance because they controlled the water levels in both the Meuse River and the Albert Canal.

Once again, the 30th was being forced to undertake an amphibious crossing when at 1700 hours, with the sun casting long shadows in the ranks, a platoon of Company E from the 120th Infantry clambered down the steep banks of the Albert Canal and loaded onto assault boats. Harassed by incoming small arms fire from beyond the far bank, the officers of the 120th instructed the men to keep their heads low and move as fast as they possibly could. Their movement was aided when, completely out of the blue, a Belgian engineer suggested using two tunnels that ran from inside the Eben-Emael fort all the way down to the banks of the canal. The larger of the two tunnels opened roughly halfway down the canal bank; the other opened just one foot above the waterline, but was barely wide enough to crawl through— it was slimy, rat-infested, and extremely claustrophobic. By using these tunnels, however, they could minimize the effect of the small arms fire that had been whizzing around the heads of the GIs. Inside Eben-Emael the men of the 120th assembled to use the tunnels. There was sufficient room to crouch and shuffle through the larger of the 50-yard-long tunnels, but in the other one the soldiers were strictly confined to crawling on their bellies in pitch darkness. Neither of the tunnels had been used for a few years, and they were both in a precarious state of disrepair, but this didn't stop the Old Hickorymen. They shouldered their weapons and begrudgingly assented to crawl inside these foreboding black holes to edge their way down to the riverside. A few soldiers complained about the filth, the insects, and the voracious over-sized rats, but one by one they all went forward until the mission was accomplished and all were safely through.

GEORGE SCHNEIDER, HEADQUARTERS COMPANY, 120TH INFANTRY REGIMENT

The next area of any interest was at Fort Eben-Emael on the Belgian-Dutch border. We reached this objective in record time and caught the Germans by surprise. Fort Eben-Emael was a kind of miniature Maginot Line, built inside a small mountain or hill with the east side overlooking the Albert Canal and Holland. The Albert Canal is south-to-north flowing and is parallel to the Maas River. The Maas is the same as the Meuse River to the south in Belgium and was a major German objective in the Battle of the Bulge that we would experience three months later. The Maas River continues parallel to the canal toward Maastricht, where it flows through the city, hence the name of the city—it straddles the Maas. The canal has steep concrete sides in the vicinity of the fort, thereby providing excellent protection from the east. With this configuration, the fort had all of its guns on the east side, facing the most likely invaders. Inside the fort there were quarters for the soldiers, machine shops, a hospital, and all other amenities for a self-sufficient establishment.

We first saw the fort from the west side where we could enter it. I immediately remembered that, in training, I had seen a captured German film showing how the Germans had captured this heavily-fortified facility. They built a replica in Germany then practiced the attack until each man knew his job. In the actual attack they laid down a smoke screen over the Albert Canal then crossed in rubber boats. At the same time airborne troops landed on the fort. Entry into the fort was through air vents with the help of fifth columnists on the inside. Once inside the Germans overpowered the Belgians and captured the fort. Coming from the west, none of the fort's guns were trained on us, so the fort was taken with very little resistance. Some of the Germans didn't even know that we were there and came marching in formation to take up defensive positions. They walked right into our machine-gun company and suffered severe losses. Some of our mortars were firing from such a short distance and at such a high angle that we could hear the report of the shot before the shell landed. It was in this fort that I got the large Nazi flag that I still have.[3]

Thanks to these tunnels, the amphibious crossing was executed with remarkable discipline and precision, which was already becoming a trademark of this division. The whole maneuver was a resounding success for the 30th Division, who had managed to capture the locks intact, neutralize German demolition charges, and cross the canal in relative safety. By the time that nearby German troops realized what had happened it was already too late for them to remedy the situation, but that didn't stop them from trying. The German commander hurriedly assembled a company from remnants that were scattered around the area and decided to go on the offensive. Unfortunately, his reconnaissance was severely lacking because his unit was effectively ambushed by Company K and eliminated just a few hundred yards from where they'd started out.

The bridgehead at Visé was now consolidated with the arrival of the 117th Infantry. Just over the Dutch border in Maastricht the German authorities occupied themselves with rounding up strays and organizing the defense of this city. Their attempts to establish a line of defense just to the south of Maastricht with this ad hoc collection of soldiers and a few 30mm flak guns was a resounding failure; on 12 September at 1000 hours, the 117th Infantry crossed the Dutch-Belgian border. These were the first Allied troops to enter the Netherlands. After taking Maastricht on 13 September, they realized that they were getting precariously close to the German border in the east and it was generally accepted by all Allied commanders that the Germans were going to fight the hardest on their home ground.

FRANK DEEGAN, COMPANY D, 119TH INFANTRY REGIMENT

Fouron le Comte, Belgium. It was 12 September and our machine-gun squad was sitting near a hedge. Alongside us the commander of A Company was directing his troops. They were being held up in a little village. There was an anti-aircraft gun firing down the street. It was knocking everybody out. The commander looked over and saw us. A lieutenant came up and reported to him that they couldn't do anything about the fire. So the commander replied, "Well, pick a ma-

chine gun up and let them fire on it." As soon as my sergeant heard the commander say that he volunteered us, so we moved out. There was a street a short distance away that we had to cross to get a look at the gun. My sergeant went down the street and busted through a house. He was going to tell me where the gun was to take it out. He looked up the street and he got an idea of where the gun was. I ran over, dropped my tripod, and put the machine gun on it. In the meantime, a rifleman stepped out on the other side of the road to take a shot at the anti-aircraft gunner, but they saw him and blew his leg off. When the shell exploded, it hit me in the neck and then rolled me over. I looked up and my sergeant was looking at me. I said, "I'm hit!" and he replied, "I know. Get in here!" so I got in the house. I was moved to an aid station and while there, they brought in my company commander. He had been hit in the hand or something. I was then shipped back to Paris and was off the front line until early December.[4]

MARK SCHWENDIMAN, COMPANY I, 119TH INFANTRY REGIMENT

I was assigned to I Company, 119th Regiment, 30th Division of the First Army. I was later in the Ninth Army. Out of the 16 men that joined I Company, only five of us were alive when the fighting was over. The first action I saw was early morning at 0400 hours. It was still dark. We were moving up a road with a platoon on the right and left, ahead of us. On the right was an embankment and 100 yards ahead, the road made a right turn. A German guard who was above the road on an embankment hollered, "Halt!" We immediately crawled against the embankment. He opened a couple of bursts of machine-gun fire down the road. I just laid there, parallel with the road, with my Browning Automatic Rifle. There was a house up ahead at the turn of the road. It was starting to get light and a machine gun started firing from the house. This firing killed three of our soldiers lying against the embankment of the road. Ronald Stone from Rexburg was lying alongside of me. He borrowed my shovel and started to dig. As he threw a shovel of dirt up, another burst of fire came from the house and a bullet hit his left hand. I finally got nerve enough to fire on the house, placing a burst of fire in every window, one after the other, until it was daylight and a tank came up and destroyed the house. For this I received a Silver Star Medal.[5]

As they initially circumnavigated Maastricht, and neared the German border, resistance to the advancing US forces became more assertive. Forward artillery observers in the 120th Infantry Regiment sector noticed German reinforcements attempting to take up positions west of the Meuse River. They relayed the coordinates to supporting artillery who promptly rained

155mm and 105mm shells on them, causing the Germans to scatter and re-coil. One day later, 13 September, the 30th Division advanced roughly seven miles. While the 117th Infantry Regiment entered Maastricht and veered north, severing all roads out of the city, the 119th Infantry Regiment occupied high ground overlooking the Geul River. As expected the Germans coun-terattacked, but could only muster battalion strength. One of the reasons that they counterattacked so ferociously was to recover important documents from the attaché case of a German general's aide-de-camp. Unbeknown to the Germans these papers had already been discovered and requisitioned by Lieutenant Elwood G. Daddow; they were already providing some valuable intelligence regarding the dispositions of the German *7th Army*.

One particular map among these papers indicated the location of Nazi headquarters in Maastricht, along with the command post locations of two corps and twelve divisions. The papers also gave some important insights into the reorganization of German forces as they retreated toward their own border. Rigorous attempts by *Gestapo* officers in Maastricht to destroy other potentially useful paperwork were thwarted by Captain Melvin Handville of the division's Counter Intelligence Corps who literally walked in on these Nazis while they were in the process of destroying the documents. These *Gestapo* officers were the last remaining Germans in the city; the rest had fled and headed north during the night, blowing almost every bridge over the Meuse River as they went. Just south of there is where the countries of Belgium, Germany, and the Netherlands converge.

Thanks to the bridges being blown, Company F of the 117th Infantry Regiment were obliged to use engineer boats to cross the river to the western part of the city, where they made contact with the 120th Infantry Regiment. Now that Maastricht had been liberated, the way was clear for the arrival of the 2nd Armored Division. At 1730 hours, meanwhile, five miles west of the city of Aachen, the 120th Regiment's Intelligence and Reconnaissance Pla-toon surreptitiously crossed the German border.

At the Dutch city of Valkenberg, situated in the Geul River valley, the 1st Battalion, 120th Infantry Regiment, met some of the stiffest resistance yet encountered. On 14 September, they initiated the attack by first sending a single platoon into the town center, but before long the whole battalion had been drawn into a bitter fight. Initially they discovered a somewhat deserted town because most of the civilians were hiding in nearby caves and most of the German troops had retreated, but there were still a handful of them at the Oda Hotel in the center of town. They had remained there to guard the only remaining intact bridge over the Geul River situated near the seventeenth-century Den Halder castle.

The Germans had earmarked the line of the Geul River as a major obstacle to the Allied advance. Some soldiers from the 1st Battalion climbed the church tower to set up a machine-gun nest and obtain a good view of the bridge. From there they noticed that the view was slightly obscured by the walls of nearby Den Halder castle. Some audacious members of the Dutch resistance expertly guided two jeeps with machine guns along the small backstreets to get a better vantage point on the bridge. Snipers from 1st Battalion were brought up; they trained their rifles on the bridge to prevent the Germans from attempting to blow it up. These efforts were all in vain because within moments of the snipers lining up their sights the Germans had detonated charges, causing an almighty explosion that blew the bridge to smithereens. In the course of the afternoon the rest of 1st Battalion arrived and captured the whole town. From there they moved out to cut off the German line of retreat on the Maastricht-Aachen road. The Dutch people had suffered terribly under German occupation. They had been starved, subjugated, and repressed for four long years. Malnutrition was ubiquitous and the unshaven, war-battered, 30th Division GIs were warmly welcomed as redeeming angels. They were greeted in Holland as they had been greeted in France by grateful cheers, kisses, and waves, but this was the last friendly encounter that they would have with civilians for a long time.

FRANK TOWERS, COMPANY M, 120TH INFANTRY REGIMENT

I saw many Belgian people shame the men and women who had collaborated with the Germans. They required the women who had been consorting with the Germans to strip down naked. They would shave their heads and paint swastikas on their bodies, then would march them down the main street. It was quite a sight. It gave us a laugh to see these naked women being whipped down the street by the Belgian people (who took it very seriously because these women had consorted with German officers). They were just giving them some payback.[6]

FRANK DENIUS, BATTERY C, 230TH FIELD ARTILLERY BATTALION

I think we were the first American troops in Belgium and the first in Holland. We liberated a lot of towns, including Maastricht where we had a big battle. When we got into Holland, and just like in France, it seemed like there were rivers or canals every 30 or 40 miles, and each was a German defensive position. They easily set up snipers and machine-gun positions along them to delay the advance of the 30th Division. We had driven about 400 miles. I traveled by jeep a lot and would get out sometimes and advance with the infantry by foot. As we got closer to the middle of Belgium we faced some delaying actions, but it was not until we got to Holland that we ran into some pretty stiff German defenses.[7]

RICHARD LACEY, COMPANY M, 120TH INFANTRY REGIMENT

In Holland, they picked our section of machine guns to go across the canal with K Company in rubber rafts. There was a lock there and we set up our two guns on the lock, aiming down the road. There was a platoon of K Company riflemen in a house to our left. The next morning, when it was just about getting light, the Germans came up to blow up the locks and flood the city of Maastricht down river. There was a whole company of them, about a hundred men, and they didn't know we were there. When they got close enough, about 75 yards from us, we opened up with our machine guns. We had a perfect field of fire and they didn't have any place to go. We were shooting through an iron railing on the side of the bridge going across the canal and we made bullet holes through those iron railings. The fight only lasted about ten minutes and they surrendered. We killed 18, wounded 13, and captured about 75 of them. When I went back to Holland for a visit in 1994, I went back to where we had that battle and that railing is still there, and there are still bullet holes in it that we made back in 1944.[8]

The British, meanwhile, were poised along the line of the Albert Canal between Maastricht and Antwerp. American forces pushing east had arrived in the vicinity of the German border, but were now losing some of their initial momentum. During the hard fought battles in and around Valkenburg, the 30th Division had begun to encounter the first cohesive opposition they'd experienced since the St. Lô-Falaise breakout. German defenses in the area proved that even though they were incomplete and undermanned, they were still determined soldiers capable of offering fierce resistance.

Air reconnaissance photos indicated that there were a few long trenches already dug into hills north and east of the Geul River. As forward-combat troops of the 30th Division took up position they were subjected to the heaviest artillery barrages they had experienced in weeks. According to intelligence gleaned from the captured papers, the German *LXXXI Corps* had given instructions to the 4,500-strong *"Gruppe Jungklaus"* to establish defensive positions from the corps boundary at Valkenburg down to a wooded hill just west of Aachen. They were also designated to protect the line between the Albert Canal and the *Westwall*, the latter was better known to the Allies as the "Siegfried Line," a name that was going to resonate ominously for weeks to come among the US forces heading east.

Within three days Old Hickory had moved east from the Netherlands and was inside Germany, establishing observation posts (OPs) on the hills just west of the Wurm River, a tributary of the Rur River (also spelled Roer in Dutch and French) from where they could look down at the imposing defenses of the Siegfried Line. The initial attack there began 16 September, with the 119th Infantry Regiment on the left and the 120th Infantry on the right. Once the Siegfried Line had been reached the 117th Infantry, which was already allocated to extend the Division zone northward, would follow on the heels of the 119th. While the 1st Battalion of the 120th had managed to clear Valkenburg of its Nazis, the 120th's 3rd Battalion continued on its mission to reach Ubachsberg by nightfall. In contrast to the labored advance of the 119th, the 120th hardly made any contact with the German defenders because, unknown to the Allies, the Germans were beating a hasty retreat.

JOHN NOLAN, COMPANY G, 119TH INFANTRY REGIMENT

We had made a long trip and, personally, I was looking forward to joining an infantry unit. We joined G Company on 6 September 1944, near Tournai, Belgium. We were in some kind of a field and Sergeant Emil Galka was the platoon sergeant. He was an ugly looking Pollack, believe me! The rifle companies in the 30th Division needed many replacements by this time. A corporal, I was made a squad leader and given seven men. All were privates except for Frank O'Leary, who was a Pfc. So I made Frank the assistant squad leader. You could accurately describe us as "green as grass." It wouldn't be too many weeks of ground combat before our description could include the phrase "hard bitten." By the end of the war, our squad of eight had received ten Purple Hearts. We each had a duffle bag containing all our possessions. Galka made us put them in a pile and all we had left were our ammunition belts. They gave us an M1, then I was told they were giving us a BAR, so I had to pick a BAR man. Hedland, was really old, he must have been in his thirties. He was married and had kids; he lived out in Iowa or Illinois and was probably a farmer type. He was the sturdiest looking of all of us. I weighed only 145 pounds. I was fairly skinny so I wasn't expected to carry that thing. The BAR weighed 21 pounds and that didn't count the ammo magazines you had to carry with it, so I gave the BAR to Hedland. He eventually got killed near Merzenhausen, Germany. A panzer fired its machine gun down a street, killing Hedland and wounding others on 22 November.

Around 7 September, we were loaded in deuce-and-half trucks, and we drove to the Netherlands. The supply line ran clear back to Omaha Beach and they couldn't get enough gas forward for the trucks. They ran out of gas, so we offloaded and marched approximately 65 miles over three days. The Dutch people would grab and shake our hands. Some woman wanted my autograph, but I didn't stop to give it to her; I kept moving. The march wore out my shoes. We eventually went into defensive positions and rested after the march, but knew the 2nd Battalion would eventually go into the attack.

We were dug in on a forward slope of a field near Groenstraat, close to the Siegfried Line and pillbox fortifications. It was 19 September. We looked across the field and could see the dragon's teeth and the barbed wire. We saw a pillbox that was camouflaged as a haystack and we brought up a 155mm artillery piece to put direct fire on it. They must have broken eardrums; they blew the thing apart! We entered the pillbox and there was nothing in it.

On 26 September our squad was given its first mission: a reconnaissance patrol. We loaded all eight of us on four Company jeeps, drove to Eygelshoven, and set up in a house. We were out there in front, the company was maybe a mile or so away from us, and we felt exposed. We didn't see anyone and were told by a civilian that the Germans had left and gone back to their fortifications over the border.[9]

GEORGE SCHNEIDER, HEADQUARTERS COMPANY, 120TH INFANTRY REGIMENT

The Siegfried Line was now only 25 kilometers to the east. This was Germany's western wall of defense and was heavily fortified with pillboxes and rows of dragon's teeth snaking along the border. These dragon's teeth were reinforced concrete, angular pillars in columns two and three deep for the purpose of stopping tanks and other vehicles.

For the remainder of September we liberated other Limburg cities including Valkenburg, Heerlen, Sittard and Kerkrade, among the larger ones. After liberating these cities, we were within sight of Germany and could see the dragon's teeth. In the countryside before reaching these cities that we would become familiar with, one of our artillery must have hit a cigar factory and there were cigars littering the area. We helped ourselves to these and while sitting under a tree, I got a German prisoner to dig my foxhole while I smoked a cigar. The old fellow could have been my father and I felt sorry for him. I told him to quit digging; gave him some rations and cigars; and turned him over to our guards.

We set up our battalion headquarters in a Dutch farmhouse located next to a small convent or monastery. A wealthy person had originally built the structure for his invalid wife. From this vantage point she could look over a valley leading to her favorite town.

The day before we reached the farmhouse we were in a farm community where we had to stop for the night. Ken Bedford and I found a nice German foxhole under an apple tree, so we decided that this would be our home for the night. As darkness approached we became less willing to occupy an open hole beneath a tree, so we reconnoitered the area and chose a barn. On the barn floor there was a large threshing machine under which we settled ourselves on a bed of hay. During the night a German plane dropped some anti-personnel bombs and one exploded in the apple tree under which we had planned to stay. In the morning we examined the hole and found it riddled with hundreds of shrapnel bits.

We spent about a week in the Dutch farmhouse and in the surrounding buildings. I slept in the barn with the cows and found it quite comfortable. There were plenty of good apples from the farmer's orchard and the farmer didn't seem to mind that we found them so appetizing. A relatively new replacement, Jack Holum from Mt. Horeb, Wisconsin, and I would get a cupful of milk from one of the cows, shave bits of a chocolate D bar into the milk, and heat it for a drink of hot chocolate.

This area of Holland contained several underground coalmines with few surface features that had been destroyed by the war. Civilian life continued at a fairly normal pace after we liberated the area. In the last days of the German occupation, however, the civilians suffered considerably as the Germans herded thousands onto the highways with carts, bicycles, horses, and their belongings to delay our advance. Near the German border we could see huge piles of slag outside the entrances of the mines. From one of these slag piles we were constantly shelled with heavy artillery. We set up two observation posts a few hundred yards from the farm and in opposite directions in an attempt to get a bearing on the gun. When it fired we would get a bearing on the muzzle flash, then by plotting the two bearings on a map, we were able to locate the gun using a triangulation method of simple geometry. The problem was that our artillery spotter planes could see no guns at our triangulation point. The next day a Catholic priest visiting the convent asked if we would like to know the location of the gun that was harassing us. He located it at the same location we had but provided additional information as to why it could not be seen from the air. The gun was mounted on a railroad flatcar and was kept in the mine on an inclined track tilted toward the interior of the mine. When firing it was wheeled to the shaft opening and the blast of the shot would recoil the flatcar and gun back into the mine. It was always hidden except for the time of actual firing. We called on the Air Corps to bomb the opening with P-47s and we were not harassed for the rest of our stay at the farm.

Late one afternoon while still on the farm, a group of American bombers conducted a bombing run on the Siegfried Line within our sight. As soon as they crossed into German territory there was heavy anti-aircraft fire. The B-25s dropped their bombs, made a quick turn to the left, and headed back toward us. One of the planes was hit and losing altitude rapidly. Obviously the crew did not want to bail out over enemy lines and was waiting to reach friendly territory. We stood in open areas waving to them and firing flares to identify ourselves. Two men bailed out before the plane took a sharp dive. About 200 feet from the ground a third man jumped and he hit the ground just as his parachute began to unfurl.

The US air force and artillery had bombarded the Siegfried Line repeatedly but the dragon's teeth and the pillboxes remained mostly intact. We attacked the line the first days in October and were in Germany before my 20th birthday. We could never reveal our location in any correspondence, but we were allowed to name the country. I wrote a quick letter home with the heading, "Somewhere in Germany" and dated it 2 October 1944, two days before my birthday.

The Siegfried Line was broken after bitter fighting as our foot soldiers destroyed the pillboxes one by one. Behind the line the Germans set up a second line of defense in the flat country to the east and in the coal-mining area directly across from the Dutch border. This line of defense would prove to be as effective as the Siegfried Line itself and brought our advance to a stalemate for several weeks as we fought in the small villages in the flat sugar beet fields. The Germans dug in their tanks with only the turrets above ground. From these positions they pounded us day and night with direct fire from their feared 88s.

The nearest German town to the Dutch town of Kerkrade was Herzogenrath. These towns are so close that today the border runs down the middle of a street in Kerkrade. Residents on one side are Dutch and those on the other are German. Other towns in the area we would get quite familiar with in the next two months were Würselen, Bardenberg, Alsdorf, Euchen, Mariadorf, plus many small farm communities. We remained in this general area until 16 December when we were pulled off of the line and headed south to encounter the north flank of the German offensive in Belgium and Luxemburg known as the Battle of the Bulge. This border area was densely populated before we arrived but the civilians deserted the towns as we captured them one by one. Just northwest of Alsdorf there was a community of quaint little stucco homes for coal miners. Some of our battalion forces spent three or four days in these and received little fire from the tanks. While here we saw for the first time V-2 rockets traveling overhead. These were fired toward England from positions within Germany. As they flew overhead they appeared *as slow-moving stars arching across the sky. Years later in the States we would see some of our launched satellites inscribing identical patterns in the heavens. The V-2 rocket was quite different from the V-1, commonly known as the "buzz bomb." The V-2 was a rocket-propelled projectile loaded with a powerful explosive. The rocket was programmed by some kind of navigation instrumentation or fuel consumption to land on a specific target. It traveled at such high speed and high elevation that they were immune to destruction by aircraft or anti-aircraft fire. The V-1 buzz bomb was a slower-moving vehicle powered by an engine. It was fired from an inclined ramp and flew until the fuel was consumed, then it fell to the target. The fuel load was generally programmed so that it was expended over London. While we were in the Bulge we would see them flying overhead at a very low altitude because of the proximity to the launch sites. Sometimes they would not clear the hills of the Ardennes and explode on a hilltop.*[10]

At that moment it time, the Dutch/German town of Kerkrade was still in German hands. The local military commander made a request to the advancing US forces for a temporary ceasefire so that approximately 30,000 civilians could be evacuated. At first the US forces were hesitant because they didn't want to lose the momentum of their attack, but they eventually acquiesced to the request and allowed the civilians to leave. On the morning of 25 September this stream of refugees walked in a broad column towards the liberated town of Ubachsberg. As they left, the German occupiers of Kerkrade plundered the houses of these unfortunate people. Then another problem occurred: the ceasefire had expired but the GIs were still busy organizing the flow of refugees when German artillery started up again in earnest. Somewhere in the vicinity of Imstenrade en route to Ubachsberg, a German shell exploded in the middle of the column of refugees. Fourteen people were killed instantly and dozens were critically injured. Later it was revealed that the evacuation of this town had been unnecessary because on October 5 Kerkrade was taken without any significant opposition.

MARION SANFORD, 30TH CAVALRY RECONNAISSANCE TROOP (MECHANIZED)

When we finally got gasoline, we took the city of Kerkrade. Half of it is in Germany and half of it is in Holland. The Germans made 30,000 of the citizens go out in the road to slow us up. It was still winter and if you got off the road, you'd be mired in the mud. The Germans knew we wouldn't shoot the Dutch people, but just before we got there, the Dutch people got off the road and lay down in the mud, so we were able to get through.

We went to the Siegfried Line with the pillboxes and the dragon's teeth. Some of the engineers figured out that rather than trying to blow the dragon's teeth, they would build a bridge over them.

We'd take the pillboxes and weld the steel doors together or pile up a big pile of dirt with a tank with a dozer on it against the door where they could look out but they couldn't shoot anybody. And we'd leave the Germans in there.

We captured a German colonel one day and he was allowed to keep his cigarettes. He pulled one out without permission and one of the troopers who was manning a .50-cal told him not to smoke it. The German colonel ignored the soldier and pulled out his lighter. The American then turned the machine gun around and said, "Light it." When the colonel started to put the smokes back in his pocket, he was told to throw them all away, which he did with much regret.

A new replacement lieutenant showed up one day and was assigned to one of the platoons. He was a little bit too "gung ho" and started out on the wrong foot. He was standing with some of the men from his platoon, looking out across the way where the Germans line was. He asked if anyone knew what was between us and the Germans and he did not get a firm enough answer to suit him. The green officer decided that he was going to send a patrol down into no-man's-land that night and see what they could find out. As a general rule, lieutenants didn't make those types of decisions, especially something like what he was proposing. The senior platoon NCOs realized quickly that they had a loose cannon on their hands and went to talk to Captain Hume. He relieved the lieutenant, and after making some calls, sent the man back for reassignment elsewhere because he did not need a man showing poor judgment and putting our lives in needless jeopardy. About a week later, Captain Hume told us the lieutenant had gotten killed in action, leading a patrol where he wasn't supposed to be.[11]

BILL FITZGERALD, COMPANY E, 117TH INFANTRY REGIMENT

We got to the Siegfried Line from Maastricht. The first night on the Siegfried Line there was a lot of artillery fire. I wasn't the best medic in the world as I wasn't well trained. There was a guy with a leg wound so I put the powder on it and a big bandage. He was really wounded and I knew I wasn't the best. I was not supposed to be in combat. Coming over on the ship I broke my glasses and thankfully there was an optician who said, "Young man, you are unfit for combat." We were just moving out after we took Aachen. We drew fire and we attacked five times. We lost a lot of men that day but according to the US Army, it was a very good day.[12]

FRANCIS CURREY, COMPANY K, 120TH INFANTRY REGIMENT

The first place I went into combat was in Kerkrade and we were just mopping up the first week or so. We did not see any fighting, just guard duty and replacement duty; it was a quiet sector for us to get some more training. We didn't see any actual action. We would move up at night and occupy some foxholes of guys who were there during the day and we would pull out the next morning.[13]

Slowly but surely, the 30th Division made incursions over the border, seeped into Germany and began making preparations for what undoubtedly would be a major encounter, taking the city of Aachen.

CHAPTER FIVE

AACHEN!

The Romans enjoyed its thermal springs; Charlemagne was crowned "Emperor of the Holy Roman Empire" in its cathedral; in the Middle Ages Barbarossa and 30 German kings were crowned there; and Napoleon had annexed this famous city. They all knew and respected the German city of Aachen. Its place in history had long since been secured by great names and great deeds, but by the autumn of 1944 it awaited a considerably more ominous prospect. It was going to be the first major German city to be attacked by the Allies. The propaganda value of that was evident to both sides. Hitler was furious that an Allied army had had the temerity to set foot on German soil and consequently, gave specific instructions that Aachen was to be held until the last man. Heinrich Himmler had visited Aachen in September to remind the civilians that they would never be evacuated; by 5 September, however, Reich Defense Commissioner Joseph Grohé had sought permission from Hitler to do precisely that. Fortunately for the 160,000 civilian inhabitants, there was one particular resident German commander who had more altruistic ambitions in mind that would become apparent later in the battle for the city.

On the morning of 12 September, Lieutenant General von Schwerin positioned the *116th Panzer Division* on the outskirts of the city, and by the evening initial skirmishes on the outskirts of Aachen had commenced. During the following days and weeks, the *116th Panzer Division* would play a crucial role in its defense despite the fact that since their retreat from Normandy their numbers had been decimated. The *116th* were exhausted, disorganized, and demoralized by the fighting in Normandy, but after refitting and obtaining new recruits in Dusseldorf, eventually they would be able to field 11,500 men and 41 tanks. They were moved to the vicinity of Aachen to support the *I SS-Panzer Corps,* then commanded by *SS-Obergruppenführer* Georg Keppler.

When General von Schwerin took command of German defenses on 12

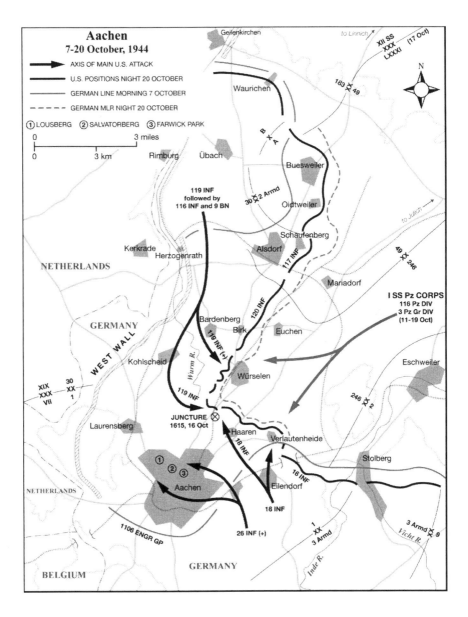

September, he had left a message with officials of the city of Aachen that was intended for the advancing US Army. In this message he stated his hope that the civilian population would be treated humanely.

> To the commanding officer of the US Forces
> occupying the town of Aachen
> I stopped the stupid evacuation of civil population and ask you
> to give her relief. I'm the last commanding officer here.
> 13. 9. 1944
> Gerhard Count von Schwerin Lieutenant General[1]

Lieutenant General von Schwerin then wrote a letter to Hitler asking him permission to surrender. The *Führer* immediately deposed von Schwerin and replaced him with Colonel Gerhard Wilck, commander of the *246th Volksgrenadier Division*. Von Schwerin was accused of defeatism and threats were made to bring him before the "People's Court" to answer these charges. To avoid this prospect he presented himself to the German *7th Army* HQ and attended a military tribunal with the intention of admonishing himself from all attributed culpability. In this unstable and volatile climate, perpetuated by an increasingly paranoid *Führer*, General von Rundstedt stuck his neck out and was quite emphatic in his defense of von Schwerin, who was then reassigned to fight in Italy. Today he's known as the "Savior of Aachen," however, and a street in the city was named in his honor.

When Lieutenant General Courtney Hodges instructed his First Army to begin a major offensive on 29 September against Siegfried Line positions around this key defensive stronghold, his objective was to open and secure a route to the Rhine River. This would effectively take the Allies into the industrial powerhouse of Germany, but there were some serious obstacles to overcome first.

In September 1944, the Germans claimed that the Siegfried Line was being defended by 25 divisions that collectively constituted around 230,000 men. This was propaganda to deter the Allies, however. In reality, many of these divisions were hastily assembled *"Volkssturm"* that had a reputation for fielding a high proportion of young, inexperienced boys and elderly men who were inadequately equipped, badly led, and poorly trained. Colonel Gerhard Wilck was not swayed by any altruistic considerations and was resolute in his intention to defend the old capital of the Roman Empire to the last street and to the last man.

General Patton's opinion of a static defense was well known at SHAEF. He had stated emphatically that, "Fixed fortifications are a monument to the stupidity of man." According to the Germans the line of bunkers that had been built in 1936 was never intended to be used purely as a static line of defense. Its purpose was to slow down the Allied advance and soften them up in preparation for a counterattack.

By the end of September, the 30th Division had successfully reached the Siegfried Line all along the entire length of its front. The bitter battle that ensued was fought in large part by the 30th Division and had commenced with an attack on the Siegfried Line south of Maastricht. It would culminate with the successful encirclement of Aachen, but there were many obstacles to overcome first. The division had a relatively short time to prepare for this new offensive.

According to Allied intelligence, the German *7th Army* was already defeated. The wrecked hulks of their tanks and trucks now littered the roadsides and dirt tracks heading east from the lowlands. The German *5th Army* was retreating from the north of the Netherlands. In less than four months of fighting, most of France and Belgium had been liberated and now the Allies had reached the German border at Aachen! There were, however, ominous indications that the "honeymoon" period for the Allies would be over soon.

Supply was still an omnipresent problem. The port of Antwerp had been captured relatively intact by the British on 4 September. It had been captured, but it wasn't operational. The problem was that the Germans still held most of the Scheldt estuary, which controlled access to Antwerp; it was going to take another few months to clear them out so that supply convoys could physically reach the port. The advance remained overextended, however, and consequently, ammunition for artillery and mortars was becoming rationed. Allied intelligence had determined that the Germans were far from being on the verge of collapse or surrender, so there was still some hard fighting to be done. South of Aachen, the US V Corps had attempted to break through the barrier of the Siegfried Line, however, dogged counterattacks stranded the Allies behind the border. The US VII Corps had succeeded in penetrating one of the two lines of the *Westwall* that surrounded Aachen. Farther north in the Netherlands, from September 17 to the 24, two German *SS* divisions had thwarted Field Marshal Bernard Montgomery's abortive attempt to outflank the Siegfried Line in the north and cross the Rhine at Arnhem. Operation MARKET-GARDEN had been an abject failure, despite Montgomery's claim that it had been a 90 percent success.

GEORGE SCHNEIDER, HEADQUARTERS COMPANY, 120TH INFANTRY REGIMENT

In one of the towns, it might have been Mariadorf, we were pinned down for several days by tank fire. The main street, the only street in town, was lined with small shops and farmhouses. Most of the buildings in Mariadorf were badly damaged and the street was covered in mud. The farmhouses were nestled among the rest of the town buildings and the barns and manure piles were attached to the rear. Ken Bedford and I found a reasonably safe place in the rear of a tavern. Our company headquarters was housed in the basement of the tavern where good protection was provided by an arched brick ceiling. Along the right side of the tavern property there was a stone wall; parallel to the wall there was a one-lane bowling alley. The other side of the alley was open to the manure pile, but the alley itself was covered with a roof. At the far end of the alley, where the pins would have been, there was another stone wall positioned between us and the Tiger tanks in the distance. The 88s fired from the tanks generally would fly over us and strike other buildings or clear the houses on the other side of the street. The worst inconvenience we experienced was the unfortunate location in the barnyard. It seems that Ken and I had chosen our bed of straw directly over the cesspool. We could hear the gurgling of the sewage and hear the gas bubbles pop as fumes of green gas rose up into our safe cover (exaggerated a little). The first night I thought that Ken was the source of the odor and he thought that I was the source, but we quickly concluded that neither of us could smell that bad and we tolerated the fumes in exchange for our safety.

Villages were taken one at a time during November and the first part of December while we closed the Aachen gap. Aachen was the first major German city captured by the Americans. This city of approximately 300,000 inhabitants was known hundreds of years before as Aix-la-Chapelle, the name the French still use. This was the home of Charlemagne (Charles the Great) who was emperor of the west from 800AD to 814 AD. Most of Aachen was in ruins, but the large cathedral where Charlemagne is buried was not destroyed. An officer and I entered the cathedral, but didn't consider it especially interesting. All of the statues and stained glass windows had been removed so the inside was drab. We stood on Charlemagne's tomb without realizing where we were. It was not until after the war while taking a course in history that I opened the text book the first day of class and saw a picture of the spot where I had stood before not knowing the significance of this treasured place.

The Rhineland campaign was probably the second hardest of the five campaigns in which the 30th Division participated, the hardest being the Battle of the Bulge. The Normandy campaign was a rough one, too, but I think that the Rhineland was worse. In this area alone during this six-week period, each of the division's regiments lost the equivalent of one battalion, or roughly one third, of its men. On one of the attacks on a village we suffered unusually high casualties. I was standing in a doorway talking to one of our riflemen who told me that before entering the Army he had worked for a mortuary in Pittsburgh and had seen many bad traffic accidents, but none like this.

In this cluster of German towns, tanks and artillery shelled us daily. Except for a direct hit by our artillery it was impossible to knock out the tanks. Bazooka attacks were not possible because of the open terrain. The best weapon was the fighter plane that could bomb and strafe them. On one occasion we had British helping us with rocket-firing Hurricanes. These were quite effective as were also direct hits with 200-pound bombs from our dive-bombing P-47s. These fighter planes usually worked in pairs, one plane firing rockets or dropping bombs, and the second plane strafing.

Late one afternoon in this area we were moving to a farm community on the far side of a hill. Only a few yards away there was a Tiger tank with its 88mm zeroed on the crest of the hill on the only road we could use. Without any passengers I floored the jeep and went sailing over the crest of the hill as the tank's 88mm landed on the right shoulder in front of me. I thanked the gunner for being a below-average German gunner. After reaching a farmhouse we were shelled quite heavily and one of our message center men was badly wounded. I found cover for the jeep in a darkened barn and while moving inside the barn I struck an object that went skidding across the floor. It was a large caliber unexploded artillery shell. Again I thanked someone, this time an unknown forced laborer who had probably assembled a dud.

Somewhere near Würselen we took cover in a small schoolhouse on Adolf Hitler Strasse. It seemed like every village had an Adolf Hitler Strasse to honor their Führer. The Germans had a machine gun at the far end of the street and were firing down the street with occasional bursts. The tracers were high and it seemed like we could avoid the overhead bullets. Further investigation revealed that the sneaky Germans were firing two machine guns. One was firing tracers high for us to see and another was firing without tracers at a man's height. The word soon went out, "Tracers high, ball low." Ammunition was commonly referred as ball ammunition.

The next morning was quiet and our rifle companies had taken out the machine-gun position at the far end of the village. Pete Perez and I decided that we would look for a radio that we might be able to adapt for use in the jeep. We drove *up the street to the edge of town where we saw a nice red brick house whose owner might likely own a radio. While I stood at the jeep Pete entered the house and shortly thereafter someone in the house took a shot at me. It cracked overhead and I took cover behind the jeep. Pete came out and I asked him if he was trying to be funny by taking a shot over my head. He said that he had not fired, but had heard the shot just as he was about to investigate the basement. We decided to look for a radio some other time and took off to the safety of our little schoolhouse on Adolf Hitler Strasse. That afternoon one of our rifle companies flushed four Germans from the basement of the red brick house. I don't see how anyone firing from the house could have missed me from such a short distance. He probably had a conscience and just warned me. I know that there were cases where a Christian would not kill the enemy in cold blood.*

All of the villages in the flat country were predominantly Catholic, as were the neighboring Dutch communities in Limburg province. Each village had a Catholic church with a high steeple that made an ideal location for observation posts. In one of the churches we drove the jeep up the steep front steps and down the main isle to the altar. The church was heavily damage and not being used, so we felt that we were not desecrating the church. From here we communicated our observations by radio relayed to us from the steeple. I remember this church in particular because there was a large crucifix of Christ over the altar. The creator of this crucifix might have been a good artist, but not a good scientist. He had defied gravity in his art. The blood flowing from the nails in Christ's hands flowed horizontally.

After taking one of these villages we thought we would try another tactic to avoid unnecessary bloodshed. We observed the next objective and had information that the Germans occupying the village might surrender. We made a white flag from a bed sheet and three of our men marched across an open field toward the village almost one mile away. One of the men spoke some German and volunteered to participate. He was only a private, but to add some authority, we pinned captain's bars on his shoulders and he was a captain for about an hour. Our artillery was trained on the village and was ordered to level the place if our truce team was fired on. If fired on, they were to drop the flag to signal the artillery to commence the artillery barrage. We watched with binoculars as they disappeared between the houses and shortly thereafter emerged with 20 prisoners. We had a representative from the Air Force on an exchange program and he was the most excited of our group as he witnessed something he never could have seen from the air.

Except for the Bulge and probably on a par with Normandy, this area between the Dutch-German border and the Rur River was where we had some of our great-

est numbers of casualties. I picked up many of our dead and hauled them back to Holland for burial. We would hook up a trailer to the jeep and make the rounds of the latest fighting, sometimes picking up Germans as well. Some of the Americans didn't appreciate having their dead buddies in the same trailer as a German, so we tried to avoid this practice. One of our scouts was a little weird. He would go out of his way looking for bodies. In civilian life he had operated a candy store. The saddest case I recall was finding one of our M Company machine gunners in a German shed. I recognized him but never knew him. He was lying on his back with a most agonizing, horrified look on his face. In his crossed hands over his chest he clutched his rosary beads with his fingers frozen halfway through his prayers. Most of our casualties from this area are buried in the Netherlands American Cemetery at Margraten, Holland, located between Maastricht and Aachen.[2]

Lieutenant General Courtney Hodges's plan was to encircle the city of Aachen with a pincer movement orchestrated by the 1st and 30th Infantry Divisions. When US forces reached the German border, however, he made his opinion known that it would be necessary to request a temporary cessation of hostilities in order to regroup. VII Corps commander Major General "Lightning" Joe Collins disagreed vociferously with this suggestion and sought First Army permission to send a reconnaissance force across the border. Major General Collins had already earned a reputation as a hard taskmaster but a competent tactician. He had commanded the 25th Infantry Division in the Pacific and it was this division that relieved the 1st Marine Division on Guadalcanal in early 1943. Collins style of leadership was exemplified by his frequent trips to the frontline areas. He harbored an impatient intolerance for those not completely committed to achieving the desired results, this didn't always endear him to some of the other generals, and his impetuosity was sometimes detrimental to the Corps. He was ignorant of the gathering German forces in and around Aachen when he gave the order to the 1st Infantry Division to check out the city and possibly even occupy it while the 3rd Armored and 9th Infantry Divisions pressed on toward the town of Düren and the Rur valley through an area that became known as the Stolberg corridor.

Now that the Siegfried Line had been physically breached in some places by the 30th Division, Allied command began focusing on Aachen on the premise that if Old Hickory's breakthrough could be amalgamated with the eventual VII Corps penetration of that city, the Allies could consolidate and support a full on advance toward the Rhine. Ominous threats from Nazi propagandists that Aachen would never fall induced both sides to up the ante for the coming offensive.

AUGUST GÖVERT, 116TH PANZER DIVISION "WINDHUND"

From inside our tank we heard a sinister and deadly whistling and noise, and we pressed against the cold steel, as if it could save our lives. Then we saw the earth shoot up in fountains when the grenades exploded, the shrapnel whined over us. Luckily we were not hit. After some time I noticed a bunker. I jumped down from the tank and ran to the bunker. I opened the door and went inside. "Come in my boy, and shut the door!" a voice said in English; so I was accidentally captured by the Americans who had occupied the bunker, but I survived the German attack. The Amis *offered me space to sit, dressed my wound on the right of my forehead, and gave me a cigarette to smoke with them. Sometime later we heard the sound of a tank in the bunker, the hum of the engine, and the clanking of chains. I said goodbye to the Americans. They let me go.*[3]

In preparation for the attack, the *Wehrmacht* reorganized and built a solid line of defense in this sector. As eventual reinforcements for German frontline troops, units of Josef "Sepp" Dietrich's *I SS-Panzer Corps* supported by the *116th Division* were placed behind the front. The *2nd SS-Panzer Division "Das Reich"; 12th SS-Panzer Division "Hitlerjugend";* and the *9th* and *116th Panzer Divisions* were also brought into the vicinity to participate in the battle.

North of Aachen, meanwhile, the fatigued but still determined 30th Division troops appeared to be on the verge of breaking out into open ground. The 1st Infantry Division, charged with seizing and holding the east-to-west ridges that were just east of the city, as well as containing Aachen itself, was already quite thinly spread and faced repeated counterattacks. The German *246th Volksgrenadier Division,* which had replaced von Schwerin's *116th Panzer Division,* now maneuvered north to oppose the 30th while being replaced in Aachen by the *12th Volksgrenadier Division.* Commanders of both armies had every intention of pressing for a quick victory before the pendulum could swing in favor of either force.

On the orders of Hitler, approximately 145,000 of Aachen's 160,000 civilian population was evacuated east, away from the city. This order was implemented under the watchful eye of *General der Infanterie* Friedrich Koechling, commander of the *LXXXI Corps,* which was comprised of four relatively incomplete divisions, namely the *183rd* and *246th Volksgrenadier;* and the *12th* and *49th Infantry.* These forces were supported by tanks from the *506th Battalion* and the *108th Panzer Brigade.* Altogether there were approximately 20,000 men. Koechling could also call on the remnants of the *116th Panzer Division* and *3rd Panzer-Grenadier Division* for support if necessary. In the city itself, meanwhile, the German soldiers were dealing with looters. Two 14-year-old boys were arrested and sentenced to be shot by firing squad in public.

Waltraud Barth was a 14-year-old German civilian from Aachen who lived through the Battle of Aachen. On the day of the execution she was in a communal bomb shelter, but had been living in a house on the edge of the city with her mother. She recalls.

> The Germans made us feel that we didn't belong in Aachen. It was as if we had nothing to do with the whole thing and as if Germany was very far away; at this time we were in Aachen but not feeling like Germans. A woman rushed into our bomb shelter and shouted in disbelief "They want to shoot the boys." It turned out that she was the aunt of one of the boys sentenced to be shot for looting. Women began to cry. There was uproar in the shelter, but for the next few hours no one was allowed to leave there. The names of those two unfortunate boys were Karl Schwartz and Johann Herren.[4]

After the 30th Division had breached the Siegfried Line, most of the German units consolidated behind natural barriers and this almost forced the Allied struggle along the rest of the Western Front to grind to a stuttering, shuddering halt. It was generally acknowledged at SHAEF that Aachen remained the primary objective behind which the German reserves would rally. The 30th Division had all but completed its assigned mission and was looking forward to some rest and reorganization when the battle began in earnest. They were to be pitched against some old adversaries and quite a few new ones that would come desperately close to denying it success.

HANK STAIRS, HEADQUARTERS COMPANY, 117TH INFANTRY REGIMENT

Aachen was part of the German defensive line, known to us as the Siegfried Line. Aachen was the first large town in Germany to fall to American forces. The 1st Infantry Division did the real work there. They were on our right and they circled around Aachen from the south and ultimately met the 30th, which came down from the north. I should mention that later on, after the fighting, the general from the 1st Division met up with our front-line guys and thanked them for their co-operation. He said, "We never could have accomplished our objective without your help."[5]

The 30th Division launched an attack on the Siegfried Line at 1000 hours, 2 October 1944. The 117th and 119th Infantry Regiments attacked alongside each other and encountered heavy resistance. In time-honored fashion, this attack was preceded by an intense artillery bombardment with the addition of 9th Air Force support. It failed to counteract the Germans. As the attacking troops advanced they continued to receive artillery, mortar, and heavy small arms fire. Despite this stiff opposition, the two regiments made steady progress and had established a small bridgehead across the Wurm River by 1450 hours. The crossing was made over previously-constructed footbridges that had been expertly assembled by the engineers who immediately began constructing a bridge to support heavy vehicles. The heavy bridge was completed by 1900 hours, allowing both tanks and tank destroyers to cross the river and provide support for the infantry. The center of the bridgehead was in the vicinity of Palenberg, approximately seven and a half miles north of Aachen.

HANK STAIRS, HEADQUARTERS COMPANY, 117TH INFANTRY REGIMENT

I believe the 1st Battalion of the 117th, my unit, was the first to hit the line up north. 1st Battalion was assigned to lead the attack, which we did, across a small stream called the Wurm River. The deepest part of the river came up to our chests. Footbridges were used in the attack and they were constructed by our engineers. They were three feet wide and maybe ten feet long. The engineer company and GIs went up to the river and they put the pieces of the bridge together for our attacking A, B, and C companies to cross. Prior to the attack, I understand there was some heavy bombing to the rear of the Siegfried Line but I don't remember that. I do remember P-38s came down parallel to our front from right to left and they dropped napalm. At the time, I wasn't aware that such a weapon even existed. The P-38s dropped napalm in the area of the line of pillboxes, but it didn't do any damage to them. The infantry attacked with bazookas, rifles, and pole charges. They put the pole ahead of them and shoved it to the opening of the pillbox as close as possible. This was the only way to really break through. Mortars helped a lot and artillery made craters, which provided some cover and protection, but not a lot.

Both B and C Companies led the attack with A Company in reserve follow-ing the two attacking companies. Headquarters Company behind A Company, perhaps 200 yards behind the attacking elements. The boys came through and secured a foothold by dark. We lost quite a few guys in the attack. During the night the Germans counterattacked us. Two of our headquarters guys said, "Come on, move to the front, there's a breakthrough. We have to establish a line of defense." The breakthrough was short-lived, but we didn't know that at the time. We were lying down and looking forward, ready to fire at anything that looked like a German. The line companies ultimately held the Germans off and once again, I didn't have to shoot.

The next day they came back to us and said, "We need some volunteers to go back on the hill to recover the dead bodies and carry them out to the road so Graves Registration can pick them up." I volunteered along with three or four others. They said, "Drop your side arms and rifle, and put on a Red Cross armband. The area is still under observation by the Germans, but we want to clear the field of those bodies." So we went down and cleared the field. I don't have much more to say about that experience.[6]

The engineers played an integral part in facilitating the advance of Old Hickory. While the infantry reduced many fortifications piecemeal, they also bypassed others. The engineers followed up on the infantry's tail and demol-ished the remaining Siegfried Line bunkers. Several methods were employed to accomplish this, the first one being to place explosives inside the concrete fortifications and demolish them. It was found that large cement blocks which were left scattered in the vicinity, however, could potentially provide effective shelter for the Germans in the event of a successful counterattack. The engineers then began welding the steel doors shut and using bulldozers to cover the angle sided openings of these bunkers with a heavy layer of earth. This method proved most effective in preventing the future use of the em-placements. The engineers also served as combat troops in both the 30th and 1st Infantry Division areas.

HAROLD WILLIAMS, 105TH ENGINEER COMBAT BATTALION

We spent days preparing for the attack on the Siegfried Line. We had to rig pole charges using sticks of TNT. We didn't use dynamite, everything was TNT. Pole charges were 3–5 feet long. We would put 4–5 sticks of TNT with a detonator. The poor fellas who carried these charges at the Siegfried Line placed them in the openings of bunkers to take care of the gun emplacements. Some of them succeeded but some of them did not. A lot of them were used. The Siegfried Line had dragon's teeth, which were big cement formations in the ground. It had pillboxes and big cement bunkers with machine guns and big guns. Some of the engineers were involved in the actual attacks. I knew one of the engineers personally who was killed there at the head of an attack with one of those pole charges, but I was not involved in that. The engineers and infantry worked hand in hand.[7]

JOHN NOLAN, COMPANY G, 119TH INFANTRY REGIMENT

We remained in Eygelshoven until we were redeployed for the attack on the Siegfried Line on 2 October, when the regiment attacked in column of battalions over the Wurm River at Rimburg Castle. G Company was in reserve and took up position in a destroyed pillbox near the castle. Somebody had thrown in a thermite grenade through the machine-gun opening and smoked out the Jerries. We spent the first night in that pillbox and all we smelled was the thermite! It was large and kind of rocky on the inside and it looked like it could hold about 10–15 men. We were pounded by artillery fire during this time.[8]

FRANCIS CURREY, COMPANY K, 120TH INFANTRY REGIMENT

The first action we had was around Aachen in the suburbs when we were near the Siegfried Line. The Siegfried Line was 8 to 10 miles wide; it included all the villages, too. We were coming into Aachen from the north from the Netherlands and the 1st Infantry Division was coming in from the south in Belgium. This was the first action I saw; being on German soil they were reluctant to give it up. Around Aachen there weren't many civilians; they had been evacuated, were seen as the enemy, and there was no fraternization. As an infantryman, we did not see many of them, and the few that we did see were elderly or very young. As far as the bulk of German civilians we did not run across them until after we crossed the Rhine. There would be farmers and you just checked to make sure they were not armed. At first, your attitude was that you're scared, then the adrenaline would kick in, but eventually it wears off. You got streetwise and you knew what to look for, you knew where proper coverage was, and where you ought to be; that cannot be trained, you have to pick it up yourself. The terrain had a lot of water, flatland, and it was just outside of small rolling hills, that was one of the difficulties crossing all of the open land. When attacking the bunkers on the Siegfried Line, sometimes you used a tank with a bulldozer to bury it, because they all had interactive fields of fire, so there was no way you could approach one per se. If you get up to it and get near the firing ports and lob something in there—some units used flamethrowers—usually if you could get up to that point they would surrender.[9]

American casualties were heavy as GIs successfully eliminated German bunkers and gun emplacements with flamethrowers and explosive charges. In the evening, however, the 30th Division pierced the enemy front and seized the town of Palenberg. On the first day of the attack, the assaulting troops successfully penetrated 1,200 yards of the German lines and worked their way into some Siegfried Line bunkers.

During the night of 2 October 1944, Germans had launched an abortive counterattack that was quickly shattered by American artillery. By 4 October, the Germans had drawn the accurate conclusion that a major incursion had been made by the 30th Division. It had been a tough call to get that far, but all in all the first day was efficacious. The attack was recommenced 5 October; the initial penetration was expanded allowing units from the 2nd Armored Division to cross the river to assist in the attack. By nightfall the bridgehead that had ben established had penetrated another 1,500 yards and occupied the German city of Übach.

HANK STAIRS, HEADQUARTERS COMPANY, 117TH INFANTRY REGIMENT

We kept moving forward and there was resistance. I can remember Übach. Jesus Christ, this is one of those strange memories I've carried with me! We were in Übach and I was running up with the rest of the attacking force. I had to jump over a dead American and as I jumped I caught a glimpse of a gold bar. He was a second lieutenant just lying there. These young fellas got their commissions quickly. They were called "30-day wonders." They were trying to lead front-line troops in the face of the enemy. Their prospects of making it through combat were pretty low. That flash of sunlight off of his gold bar really hit me emotionally.[10]

As the operations for 5 October got up to speed, ground was gained to the east in the face of steadily increasing pressure from the Germans. This culminated into heavy counterattacks on 6 October, resulting in the 30th Division losing ground during the day. By nightfall, however, they had regained most of the lost ground and captured the villages of Merkstein and Hoffstadt while generally progressing along their north-south line to include Worm. The primary objective at this time was to isolate the city of Aachen. The 2nd Armored Division was directed to make its main effort to the south and southeast to assist the 30th Division in making contact with the 1st Infantry Division. Accordingly, on the morning of 7 October, the two divisions—30th Infantry and 2nd Armored—made a combined drive southward toward Alsdorf and Merkstein Worm.

The Germans were apparently taken by surprise by the direction of this attack because no serious opposition was encountered en route; at the close of the day the advance had brought the US forces 5,000 yards closer to Aachen.

During the night of 7 October, the Germans placed additional fresh troops in the line. On the morning of 8 October they launched a determined counterattack in the direction of Alsdorf and succeeded in recapturing Birk. On 8 October the 30th Division continued its southward move in what appeared to be the relatively easy task of closing down to the Division boundary, which ran east and west through Würselen. Due to unexpected resistance it took them two days to move just 4,000 yards.

MARK SCHWENDIMAN, COMPANY I, 119TH INFANTRY REGIMENT

The next day near Kolscheid, Germany, we captured several prisoners. We went through a forest that night passing German pillboxes and stumbling over road-mines to surround the city of Aachen. That was the blackest night I have ever seen. We had to hold hands with each other to keep together. You couldn't see your hand in front of your face. Soon after this I was advanced to private first class.[11]

Long before dawn on 8 October, the 1st Battalion, 119th Infantry Regiment, had bridged the Wurm River in front of Kohlscheid and made their way to the northern edge of the town where they encountered sporadic resistance. During the course of the battle, the Regiment had to bridge it three times. First, they bridged it from the east at Rimburg, then from the west at Koldscheid, and again just south of Kohlscheid. When the leading platoon of Company A got pinned down by heavy machine-gun fire, Technical Sergeant John Overman, a mortar observer who was becoming increasingly frustrated with the situation, stood bolt upright, single handedly charged the machine-gun position brandishing his submachine gun, and wiped out three of the German crew. After that, progress was fairly rapid. The 1st Battalion had the downtown area cleared before noon and was on its way southwest towards Ursfeld and Richterich.

The 2nd Battalion of the 119th Infantry Regiment began their advance at daybreak, and soon ran into opposition from German tank, machine-gun, and artillery fire. It nevertheless still managed to disable one tank and two pillboxes. Secure footholds were finally established on the northern and western edges of Würselen. The plan was to advance along the eastern side of the city, sever the highway at a point southwest of it, and simultaneously establish contact with the 1st Infantry Division. Throughout the afternoon the 2nd Battalion held positions on a gentle slope that stretched to within 500 yards of the highway where a company of men from an attached unit of the 99th Infantry Battalion had dug in a few yards short of the highway. Overlooking the highway on the high hill directly south of Würselen was a sizeable force of German tanks and infantry that brought such heavy fire to bear on the men of the 99th that they were unable to leave their foxholes by daylight. The enemy had also pushed tanks along the road and sent six of them, accompanied by 40 infantrymen, against Company E, holding the extreme right of the 2nd Battalion west of the highway. One of the tanks, a Mark VI, was able to advance to within 175 yards of US lines.

The 119th Infantry Regiment's reserve battalion was still a mile away back in Herzogenrath when the Bardenburg counterattack got underway. They could not be committed without express permission from Division HQ; nevertheless, they attempted to move out under cover of night and were repulsed by Germans who had occupied the south of Bardenburg and the woods just beyond there. Their situation deteriorated when they became pinned down by 20mm and mortar fire from heavily entrenched German positions in the south of the town. A decision was made to pull back to the northern outskirts of the town and allow the US artillery to hammer the German positions. Weather conditions restricted the use of air support, but this factor was more than adequately compensated for by the precise and effective use of artillery that performed a magnificent job during this phase of the battle. An intense battle raged throughout the day in and around the city of Bardenburg; the forward progress of the Germans was not halted until 9 October, when they were effectively stopped in their tracks and forced to retreat. American troops entered Bardenberg and the outskirts of Würselen where the attack again bogged down. The American artillery fire was in a large way responsible for breaking the German attack during the two days mentioned. During this period observation was poor, it rained incessantly, and the XIX Corp's after action report stated, "The weather was so bad that even cub airplanes could not fly."

DAVID KNOX, COMPANY L, 119TH INFANTRY REGIMENT

The next morning, 9 October, we withdrew to attack the town of Bardenberg from a different direction. It was at this time that one of the runners, Lances, found himself taking care of two babies because the battalion would not release two civilians that he had turned in. "Someone has to do it," he said. He ended up by getting them milk and feeding them from a bottle. Things started out fine, but we soon found ourselves under the roughest artillery barrages that we had yet experienced. They started to come in while we were going through a woods. We passed through Bardenberg as a reserve company. Everything was falling in that town. We moved on through, however, behind K Company into the northern part of Würselen. We called it "The Mine," so I went down a shaft here to see what was going on, and to determine if I could find a suitable CP. The people were all packed into it for safety. We finally set up in part of the main office of the mine. Battalion was in a different part. Just after dark we received news that there was a concerted counterattack being tried by the Germans. I went out with Sergeant Norlie Williams to establish contact between our men and K Company. It was on this trip that the man behind me was shot in the arm. It was after dark so we were never able to take care of the offender. Lieutenant Drake of K Company was badly wounded that night. It was our ration driver Bosofsky who got him out of there the next morning. We were kept alerted all of that night. The next day Company K was sent back to Bardenberg to help relieve the 1st Battalion. It was only a short while after they had left that the Germans launched a counterattack in the sector that K Company had been holding. The men of the 2nd Platoon were holding this area under very extended conditions. It was while directing his men in this defense that Johnny was wounded with shrapnel. He insisted he should keep fighting, but we finally got him to go back. That was the day that I ran into a squad of "Jerries" when I crossed the street. I thought they were GIs. I got into a building in a hurry and so did they. About that time K Company returned and took proper care of the whole situation. Captain Hoperaft loaded his men down with hand grenades. His company took care of the situation in the usual style.[12]

Just north of Aachen, the 1st Infantry Division was simultaneously attacking Crucifix Hill. After the two divisions had linked up along their mutual boundary, the 30th planned to regroup and rest its battered line units prior to the next operation before heading east.

On 8 October, in the German town of Herzogenrath, the 119th Infantry Regiment discovered that the town's innocuous-looking cobbled streets were, in fact, heavily booby trapped. There were mines everywhere and in some cases the German soldiers who had placed them hadn't even bothered to conceal them. On the undulating terrain south of town they began to encounter more concerted resistance from tanks and a well-armed pillbox. The 120th

Infantry Regiment attacked across the Herzogenrath-Alsdorf road and was showered with German shells and bullets. The 117th Infantry Regiment on the left had successfully severed one of the main highways that ran northeast from Aachen; the regiment was moving ahead towards Mariaberg in an attempt to take control of the German's other main supply route to Aachen. It was tough going all the way.

JOHN NOLAN, COMPANY G, 119TH INFANTRY REGIMENT
We went into Herzogenrath and saw mines everywhere. There was a goat walking out in front of us. We all thought it would be blown up, but it survived![13]

Forward elements of the 1st and 3rd Battalions of the 117th Infantry Regiment had moved tentatively through Kol Kellersberg. They had even managed to get some of their tanks and infantry past a railroad line that was punctuated at regular intervals with German emplacements, but the situation was becoming extremely precarious. By mid-morning, withering German fire was beginning to cause serious difficulties among the ranks of the 117th Infantry's Company I, which was decimated when they attempted to cross the railroad tracks; consequently, it had only 33 men left in its three rifle platoons. Sherman tanks that were approximately 150 yards ahead of the advancing infantry were also encountering problems. When one of the tank crews ran out of machine-gun bullets, they resorted to dropping hand grenades into German foxholes.

VICTOR NEILAND, COMPANY F, 117TH INFANTRY REGIMENT
One of my first recollections was that there were a large number of towns and pillboxes along the Siegfried Line that we had to overcome. Usually we had tanks and infantry that would work together to try to take them and the surrounding defenses. The tanks would go in firing and the infantry would dismount and attack.

I had a friend with me, John C. Book, who had gone to medical school in New York. He was one of the guys advancing on the tank and he got shot in the leg, so the other soldiers took him off, thinking that was the safest thing to do. Then heavy German artillery fire started coming in and it killed him. I really felt terrible about that.

He should never have been in the infantry. It's a shame that they didn't make a medic out of him. So many guys were misplaced into the infantry because they had the highest casualty rates and always needed replacements.[14]

Then suddenly, when things couldn't get worse, they inevitably did as a hail of German shells began crashing down around the 117th, delivered by Germans attempting to dislodge the attackers and steer them away from Aachen. Back at the OP, a company of German soldiers had slipped in behind the advancing 1st and 3rd Battalions. Lieutenant Colonel MacDowell saw the German troops approaching in a skirmish line and held his breath. Watching with field glasses from a concealed position he waited until the very last minute before giving the order to open fire. The effect was devastating as almost every German recoiled and fell. Throughout the night and into the next day more German attacks hit along the line and the general consensus of opinion was that they were probably attempting to gage the strength of the attacking divisions in preparation for the impending battle.

The encirclement of Aachen was orchestrated primarily by two US divisions, the 30th Division of the US XIX Corps (commanded by Major General Charles H. Corlett) in the north, and the 1st Infantry Division of the US VII Corps (commanded by Major General "Lightning" Joe Collins) to the south.

To the north, Major General Leland Hobbs's 30th Division was assisted by 2nd Armored Division tanks while his flanks were effectively covered by the 29th Infantry Division. In the southern sector elements of the 9th Infantry Division and 3rd Armored Division were supporting the 1st Infantry Division, commanded by Major General Clarence R. Huebner.

The fighting on 9 October was heavy. The Germans launched several counterattacks in a frantic attempt to stop advancing US forces in their tracks. These attacks were poorly coordinated and poorly orchestrated and didn't involve more than a company or less in size, usually supported with between one and five tanks. The counterattacks were comfortably repulsed, but it was becoming increasingly apparent that the Germans were bringing in reserves from the east and throwing them straight into the battle. Proof that they were also bringing in fresh artillery batteries was evident when the rate of their salvos increased. Even the Luftwaffe made a rare appearance and attempted to harass the attacking troops, but they were never present in sufficient numbers to materially affect the battle.

On 10 October, SHAEF now decided that it was high time to initiate the final assault on Aachen because they were beginning to get impatient about making contact with the 1st Infantry Division and physically cauterizing the city, which had just endured three continuous days of heavy bombardment from the RAF. The end was near.

During the morning the 119th Infantry Regiment attempted to dispatch patrols to contact 1st Infantry Division patrols that were operating somewhere in the 3,000 yards that still separated the two divisions. Würselen's shell-ravaged streets were still too infested with Nazis for such a deep patrol to succeed, so early in the afternoon, permission was obtained from XIX Corps to hammer the town with artillery in the hope of battering the German defenders into submission and facilitating the desired link up with the 1st Division.

Despite the surrender ultimatum being delivered, 10 October was a day of partial inertia for the 120th's 1st Battalion, despite the opening achievements. At XIX Corps HQ attention was still focused primarily on the intended linkup between the 30th and the 1st Infantry Divisions and the expectation was that this could be achieved when the 119th's 2nd Battalion, who were the last uncommitted infantry reserves, had eliminated remaining opposition in Bardenberg. Most of the 119th, unfortunately, were still holed up in north Würselen while the rest of the infantry was strung out around the Bardenberg perimeter and under almost constant fire from German positions in the vicinity. The German forces had inadvertently forced a wedge into the 30th Division lines that, if left unattended, had the potential to eliminate the 30th's spearhead.

Corps had no other troops available at the time and knew that there was no alternative but to reduce the already thin line of defenses to force the elimination of the Bardenberg menace. During the night of the 10th, 3rd Battalion of the 120th Infantry moved out of its positions on the regiment's left flank, and became attached to the 119th Infantry with the sole purpose of cleaning out Bardenberg. Company F of the 120th filled the gap in the line left by the 3rd Battalion. General Hobbs explained to Colonel Sutherland of the 119th that there was no alternative when he said, "This thing has to drive through." It was that sense of urgency and dogged determination that helped to accomplish the task. Opposition was light when the attack commenced, but it increased as the day progressed. In the woods just south of Bardenburg German infantry, supported by tanks, harassed advancing GIs with expertly coordinated volleys. Major Howard W. Greer, commander of the 120th Infantry Regiment's 3rd Battalion, set the pace for the afternoon's activities when he grabbed a bazooka, stealthily worked his way up to within range of one tank, and took it out with one direct hit. Almost immediately another tank fired and hit the building he was in. The force of the blast covered the major in dust and debris and knocked his helmet completely off his head. A few minutes later, he had reloaded and displaced to a better vantage point to get a shot at the second tank. Once he'd adjusted the sight on his bazooka he loosed another shell that entered through the drive sprockets of the tank, incinerated all the occupants, and blew off the turret. For these decisive actions, the major was awarded the Distinguished Service Cross.

Staff Sergeant Anthony A. Tempesta, Company A, 743rd Tank Battalion, also played a pivotal role in the fight to take Bardenberg. As he led his platoon south along the main street of the town he spotted a German assault gun that was covering an intersection there. Supported by an infantry bazooka team, he moved forward into the section, aimed his cannon, and fired three shots in rapid succession. While he was maneuvering to get a clearer shot at the assault gun German snipers were actually dropping grenades from the upper floors of buildings in the vicinity. Undeterred by this distraction Tempesta not only took out the first assault gun, he went on to take out another one and disable six German half-tracks. After all his officers had been wounded, Tempesta assumed command of his company at 1400 hours.

Comparable tactics were used against half-tracks, machine guns, and a tank before the Bardenberg operation could finally be brought to a successful conclusion.

RICHARD LACEY, COMPANY M, 120TH INFANTRY REGIMENT

Our division was on the north side of Aachen. We had been taking the towns up there and we had been running into problems. It was 12 October and we came to this small town and got our gun set up. We had a nice foxhole. We had gotten a door from a house to put a roof on it. It was getting dark and I think somebody lit a fire or something. It attracted German fire and mortar shells came in. I got hit in my hip with shrapnel. A jeep come up and took me back to medical, but I wasn't wounded that bad. They sent me back and I ended up in Liege, Belgium where a doctor took out the shrapnel.[15]

While the Bardenberg pocket was being eliminated, other line troops of the Division didn't have to go looking for a fight with the Germans. The two battalions that were in up in North Würselen were hit by German tanks and infantry twice, at about 1000 and 1530 hours, but heavy artillery concentrations quickly immobilized these efforts to penetrate their lines. Just south of Kol Kellersberg the 120th Infantry Regiment's positions, arching to the southwest of that small town, were subjected to persistent strikes from tanks and infantry throughout the entire day. The most determined effort hit at

1520 hours, but was effectively repulsed by accurate, steady barrages from the 230th Field Artillery Battalion, who managed to knock out seven tanks. As darkness descended two minor infantry attacks, made without benefit of armored support, were spurned. The final two attacks of the day occurred after nightfall at 2015 hours. One small unit of German infantry still unsupported by any serious hardware temporarily managed to breach the 120th's regimental boundaries, but quickly dissipated. The other attack over in Kol Kellersberg was dealt with by the 117th Infantry Regiment.

FRANK DENIUS, BATTERY C, 230TH FIELD ARTILLERY BATTALION
Here were Goldstein and I, artillery guys, street fighting. Wherever we encountered resistance we directed artillery. Most of the buildings in the towns in Germany had cellars. When you opened the door of a building, you would throw in a grenade and then you rushed in after the explosion. That's how we fought. Block to block I would direct our artillery fire into the next area. Aachen was tough, almost like fighting in the hedgerows. I recall it was cold and rainy a lot.[16]

Major General Collins, Commanding General of VII Corps, meanwhile directed Major General Huebner, Commanding General of 1st Infantry Division, to serve a long, previously prepared ultimatum demanding the surrender of Aachen. This document was promptly extracted from the files, and on 10 October 1944, under a flag of truce, it was presented to the Germans by two lieutenants of the 26th Infantry Regiment. The ultimatum read:

> The city of Aachen is now completely surrounded by American forces. If the city is not promptly and completely surrendered unconditionally, the American Army Ground and Air Forces will proceed ruthlessly with air and artillery bombardment to reduce it to submission.[17]

The proposed terms allowed the Germans 24 hours to surrender and remove civilians from the city. These terms were broadcast to front-line German troops by American public address systems, then they were broadcast over the Luxembourg radio and leaflets were dropped into the city from airplanes. American artillery even loaded shells with these leaflets and fired them into the center of the city to ensure that everyone got the message. Lieutenant Colonel Maximillian Leyherr, who was the acting commander of the city at that time, dutifully rejected the ultimatum outright and indicated in no uncertain terms to the American lieutenants that the garrison would not surrender. He was acting in accordance with Hitler's express orders to "hold to the last man." Leyherr was relieved of executing that responsibility two days later when Colonel Gerhard Wilck, the commander of the *246th Volksgrenadier Division,* arrived on the scene. Colonel Wilck set up his headquarters in the Palast-Hotel Quellenhof, a luxurious spa-hotel that still exists today and is located beside Farwick Park in the northern portion of the city. The attacking US force was actually numerically inferior to the defending German forces. While Colonel Wilck was hedging his bets at the time and hoping for additional artillery support from the east, Major General Huebner knew the gap at Würselen was still open and from Stolberg to Ravels Hill his defenses were still sparsely spread.

Using air support, VII Corps and the 1st Infantry Division then proceeded to reduce the city. Early on the morning of 11 October, numerous white flags or bed sheets could be seen hanging from buildings in Aachen; these disappeared, however, soon after daybreak. A handful of German soldiers who made their way to the American lines and surrendered reported that the garrison commander in Aachen had taken drastic steps to forcefully have all white flags removed and to put an abrupt halt to any further attempts at surrender by the civilian population. The 24-hour period had effectively elapsed without any sign of concession from the Germans, so on 11 October four groups of IX Tactical Air Command P-38s and P-47s (about 300 planes) opened the assault. For the unfortunate civilians cowering below the city in cellars and bomb shelters, and for soldiers manning their posts, it was as if the gaping jaws of hell had finally opened. The US warplanes released more than 62 tons of bombs as they directed their efforts on targets primarily on the perimeter of the city, which had been pre-selected by the infantry and marked with red smoke by the artillery. A thunderous cacophony then erupted as 12 battalions of VII Corps and 1st Division artillery took up the bombardment. Division artillery hurled some 2,500 rounds into the city while corps artillery contributed 2,371 rounds, a combined total of 169 tons of shells rained death down onto this ancient city. Within a few short days 80 percent of Aachen's buildings were reduced to smoldering, skeletal ruins. Throughout the following days small assault teams from the 26th Infantry Regiment, 1st Infantry Division, edged cautiously through the rubble of a once beautiful city. In an effort to stave off the inevitable, Colonel Wilck appealed for reinforcements, but he received only about 150 men, which was all that remained of Wilck's own *Grenadier Regiment 404.* A battalion of *SS* that had tried to maneuver toward the city was sidetracked by one of the 30th Division's attacks near Würselen.

The 1st and 30th Infantry Divisions, in the vicinity of Ravels Hill and Würselen respectively, kept on attempting to establish a firm link. It was obvious that as long as the German *3rd Panzer-Grenadier* and *116th Panzer Divisions* remained in this sector, a major counterattack to break the encirclement could be expected at any moment.

Commander in Chief West (*OKW*) Gerd von Rundstedt took it upon himself to remind Aachen's military commander Wilck once more that in accordance with Hitler's order Wilck was to hold this venerable German city to the last man, and if necessary, allow himself to be buried under its ruins.

In response to this, during the afternoon of 19 October Colonel Wilck issued the following order:

> The defenders of Aachen will prepare for their last battle. Constricted to the smallest possible space, we shall fight to the last man, the last shell, the last bullet, in accordance with the *Führer*'s orders.
>
> In the face of the contemptible, despicable treason committed by certain individuals, I expect each and every defender of the venerable Imperial City of Aachen to do his duty to the end, in fulfillment of our Oath to the Flag. I expect courage and determination to hold out.
>
> Long live the *Führer* and our beloved Fatherland.[18]

HAROLD WILLIAMS, 105TH ENGINEER COMBAT BATTALION

We were taking Aachen. My machine gun was set up on the corner where two streets came together in a Y. They wanted my gun positioned to cover it. Then a Hitler Youth came out of the building across the street. She was a young woman and she was a fanatic, they all were. She had an axe and she was yelling in German. I yelled "Halt!" a couple of times, but she kept coming. So I stopped her with the machine gun. I'm not proud of it.[19]

On 11 October, the 1st Infantry Division reported that a battle group from the *2nd Panzer Division* had been spotted in the area. When this news filtered through to the 30th, many in the Division concluded that the battle was beginning to resemble the fight at Mortain because many of the German units now opposing them had been present there, too. Even Major General Hobbs remarked that there were indeed parallels, such as the clear weather, that allowed Allied air support to strike German armor repeatedly. The Luftwaffe was rarely seen at this juncture. A few random night sorties were observed but they never presented any serious threat to Old Hickory.

By noon, Allied dive-bombers were showering carnage on a group of approximately 40 German tanks that reduced 18 of them to incinerated metal coffins. Favorable weather conditions definitely gave the US forces a marked advantage, but even with all the air support, it was the foot slogging GI in the field that really clinched the deal. Colonel Branner P. Purdue, who had commanded the 120th Infantry Regiment for only a few days, was reported to have said to General Hobbs, "These are the bravest men you ever saw. That 1st Battalion fought them off with the outposts . . . I never did see men going like these have been going. We are as strong as strong can be."

Men of the 30th Signal Company, behind the lines once again, demonstrated the US Army's remarkable capacity for improvisation when the supply of special batteries that were used in bazookas ran out. The Signal Company devised an ingenious way of mounting abundantly available flashlight batteries on the bazooka. Virtually all the rocket launchers in the 30th Division were modified to accommodate these and kept functional thanks to this inventive spirit.

Thanks to sustained and concentrated American artillery fire, the German assaults appeared to be diminishing; despite this, they still managed to reply by throwing shells into the forward areas and into Bardenberg funnel, but they were no longer launching any serious attacks.

Lieutenant General Hodges called General Hobbs to remind him that there was still an outstanding issue to be dealt with: the 30th Division still hadn't managed to link up with the 1st Infantry Division and complete the encirclement. On the basis of this, a plan was conceived: Old Hickory was given two battalions from the 29th Infantry Division and a company of tanks. Major General Corlett, XIX Corps Commander, suggested advancing along the Wurm River through the small town of Pley. At first, it seemed like a feasible proposal, but rumors abounded that the *116th Panzer Division* was operating somewhere in the vicinity, so that idea was shelved. The ensuing three days were marked by gnawing inertia because most of the 30th Division's front, the area northeast of Würselen, was practically dormant. On 13 October, General Corlett made another suggestion to send a task force south from the Alsdorf area. General Hobbs wasn't impressed by this suggestion either because he didn't think that he had enough troops at his disposal to achieve this advance. The other reason he gave was that there were still sufficient German forces present in front of the Division to prevent this move; moreover, he didn't want the regiments out east to abandon recently-established strong defensive positions. In Hobbs's opinion, a move south would render them vulnerable to possible German counterattacks. Expanding the assault to the west would force yet another river crossing and reduce the garrison stationed in Kohlscheid.

CHARLES RICHARDSON, COMPANY L, 117TH INFANTRY REGIMENT

One day after a failed surprise attack (surprise meant no artillery support), Colonel Johnson had the survivors of his attack gather in a factory courtyard. There he told us what lousy soldiers we were . . . and cowards to boot. Someone in our berated group shouted out, "We will go anywhere. You lead us." Johnson was astonished and said, "Get the man that said that." Everyone in the berated mass started yelling and calling Johnson some choice GI names. Some officers with their heads averted were adding to the insults. Finally, as things were getting out of hand, an officer grasped Colonel Johnson by the arm and led him out of the area. As soon as we had started the "surprise attack" we were under heavy fire. We advanced a short distance, men being hit all around. Finally someone with a brain ordered, "Pick up the dead and wounded and fall back." I was walking backwards, firing short bursts in the general direction of the enemy. I nearly tripped over a wounded GI just sitting waiting for help. I asked, "Piggy-back, OK?" He pulled himself up on to me as I emptied the BAR's magazine. As I ran back, almost to a safe spot, I felt the guy I was carrying get hit and go limp. I twisted around and got him in front of me and bear hugged him the rest of the way. The medic checked the wounded GI and found his foot hanging by its tendons. The wound in his back was high into the right shoulder. They said he would live.[20]

The plan that was eventually agreed upon was enacted on 15 October. It wasn't the ideal solution, but under the circumstances, it was the best that the G-3 operations officers could muster. The following day, the 119th Infantry Regiment began driving south with two battalions. As they crossed bridges over the Wurm River that had been expertly prepared by engineers during the night, they came under heavy mortar and artillery fire. They maintained this course on the right of 29th Infantry Division's 116th Infantry Regiment. The advance was supported by two companies from the trusted 743rd Tank Battalion and an infantry battalion from the 99th Infantry Division that were earmarked to hold the ground once it was taken. For the plan to achieve its objective, the 119th Infantry was expected to cover 3000 yards in one day. Employing a diversionary tactic, the 120th and 117th Infantry Regiments successfully drew German artillery fire away from the 119th by laying down a smoke screen and raining heavy artillery on their positions.

It was at this juncture that the following incident occurred. Two platoons of the 117th Infantry Regiment's Company E were thrust forward along 500 yards of dense woodland alongside the railroad where the German main position was located. This move had but one purpose, to draw fire from the Germans and entice them into thinking that this was the main line of attack. There hadn't been time to perform adequate reconnaissance of the area and before long, sustained artillery and small arms fire caused both platoons to lose their direction. The 3rd Platoon had managed to get within 50 yards of reaching its objective, a small gap in the railroad siding, when they were mauled severely by German fire and lost all six of their number. The 2nd Platoon was forced to retreat but once they had been fortified with the 1st Platoon, they set out again and made no less than three attempts to infiltrate the German positions. The Company E commander, Captain George H. Sibbald, sent out a 10-man team to retrieve what was left of the isolated 3rd Platoon, but they failed to make contact and a general order to withdraw was issued. This would leave the 3rd Platoon to its fate, but they already knew that they had been used as cannon fodder. Many years later, Captain Sibbald publicly apologized for this action. The company was awarded the Distinguished Unit Citation for their efforts.

At 1544 hours, the 1st Infantry Division's Chief of Staff called to say that forward observers had identified friendly troops approaching from the southern outskirts of Würselen. He went on to say that a patrol had been dispatched to establish contact. During the course of the afternoon the 2nd Battalion of the 119th Infantry Regiment reached a hill just south of Würselen, opposite the main highway roughly 1000 yards away from the outposts of 1st Division's 18th Infantry Regiment. It was at this juncture that it was generally agreed that contact had indeed been made. It was, in fact, a patrol from the 119th Infantry Regiment led by Private Frank A. Karwel—who was wounded shortly after it set out—and his fellow GIs, Privates Edward Krauss and Evan Whitis—who went on to establish actual physical contact with the 1st Division at 1815 hours. As the two privates edged tentatively forward they saw silhouettes of figures in American uniforms on top of a hill. Within moments they were within shouting distance. One of the men on the hill shouted, "We're from K Company. Come on up." Private Whitis responded, "We're from F Company. Come on down." He later explained that,

"They out-talked us and we pushed on up." Within half an hour the news had been delivered to Army HQ, the Aachen gap was now officially sealed.

After Aachen fell, VII Corps and the 1st Infantry Division formally thanked the 30th for its vital work in enabling the city to be taken, and the Division received widespread media recognition for its part in this vital battle. Sometime later, in the last week of October, Major General Clarence R. Huebner of the 1st Division appeared unannounced at a 119th regimental outpost and introduced himself to the surprised soldiers there. He said "I wish you'd get it around to your people that we never could have taken Aachen without your help."

With the encirclement of Aachen achieved, the focus shifted to the center of the city, where troops of Huebner's 1st Infantry Division were steadily driving forward block by block to extinguish the city's trapped German garrison. Fruitless attempts by the German *3rd Panzer Grenadier* and *116th Panzer Divisions* to break through the encirclement further exacerbated an increasingly desperate situation but by nightfall on 19 October, the German commanders had decided to abandon the defenders of Aachen to their fate. The attritional battle for Aachen drew to a close when Staff Sergeant Ewart M. Padgett and Private First Class James B. Haswell, two POWs from the 1106th Engineer Combat Group who had been taken early on in the fighting, carrying a white flag, dashed into the middle of Lousberg Strasse. As they anxiously waved the flag the firing dissipated. An American rifleman leaned out from a nearby window and waved the two men forward. Sergeant Padgett beckoned to two German officers behind him to follow.

Assistant Division Commander, Brigadier General George A. Taylor, accepted the German surrender. At 1205 hours on 21 October, it was all over. That evening before sunset, GIs swept through every corner of the city, rounding up 1,600 German POWs as they went. Colonel Wilck and his headquarters staff, defiant to the very end, were nevertheless taken prisoner.

HERMANN WOLZ, *STURMGESCHÜTZ BRIGADE 341*

On 14 October 1944 our first battery command from the corps, with all available guns of the brigade, were told to march as "armor-piercing unit" in the almost surrounded city of Aachen. Around 0900 hours I reported to Corps and was ordered to move to Würselen and to Aachen. In Würselen I was with an SS *battalion of the* Leibstandarte Adolf Hitler *under* Obersturmführer *Rink.*

Between Würselen and Aachen on both sides of the proposed route was a completely open area, which was occupied by the Americans. This strip of land between

Würselen and Aachen (about 2–3 km deep) was constantly patrolled by between 25 and 35 Sherman tanks that commanded this approach completely.

Our unit was supplemented with only 8 assault guns (including two howitzers), so it seemed impossible to me. All the guns had been fired from the many locations as we waited for the US tanks; this was supposed to happen in the morning between 0900 and 1200 hours. On the advice of a commander of an artillery unit in Würselen, I found a way through Wolfsbusch, west of Würselen, because the Americans had this site occupied with only a few troops. I attacked the Americans from the northwest toward Aachen. Around noon I placed my battle group under Colonel Wilck, battle commander of the troops in Aachen.

Over the next days there was a lot of street fighting; the assault guns, because of the numerous roadblocks, couldn't operate properly. In addition to this the opponent benefitted from all cellars being interconnected in Aachen because of the earlier air attacks. They appeared again and again through these underground passages. Enemy troops behind us and in front of us weakened our positions. This was street fighting, as I recall, several gunners and radio operators drove their vehicles with their heads looking out of the turrets.

By the time Aachen capitulated we had only one last gun in the vicinity of the road underpass at Schloss Rahe that fired throughout the morning of 21 October 1944. Between 0600 and 0700 we used up our last ammunition. Then we blew up the gun and pulled back to edge of Aachen.[21]

The 30th Division, since the start of the Aachen campaign on 2 October, had incurred almost 3,000 casualties and taken 6,000 prisoners, which was a testament to the ferocity of the fighting that they had endured up until that point. They claimed to have destroyed 20 German tanks: 12 destroyed by 105mm howitzers; five by supporting tanks and tank destroyers; and three by bazookas. The 1st Infantry Division's casualties were heaviest in two of the battalions of the 26th Infantry Regiment and totaled 498. On occasion the battles in the 30th Division sector had assumed the character of an armored duel, although it had primarily involved infantry units. Both sides had tank support and few units, German or American, experienced much success unless supporting tanks were on hand. By their own count, the Germans lost 45 tanks.

GEORGE SCHNEIDER, HEADQUARTERS COMPANY, 120TH INFANTRY REGIMENT

While we were in the Würselen-Alsdorf area we were given a two-day rest in

Holland. We were taken to the Rolduc Abbey near Kerkrade, across from the German border. The rooms in the abbey were empty and we slept on the wooden floors. We were treated to hot meals and a USO show. During meals a USO band played for our dining entertainment. As part of the USO troop a guitar player/singer/ composer came on stage and sang his most famous composition, "You Are My Sunshine." He was Jimmy Davis, who later became the governor of Louisiana.

Until now I was classified a scout and observer. One of our message center jeep drivers was killed while taking one of the villages. He was a big likeable Greek from the Boston area who found pleasure in collecting postcards he would find in homes. We called him Tiny, not because he was tiny, but because his family name was Constantine. Our message center had two jeeps that were used for all kinds of jobs, from running food and ammunition to rifle companies, to picking up bodies. One of the main duties was driving rifle company runners to and from their companies. I was asked if I would take Tiny's place and I accepted. I continued to serve as a scout when needed, and would soon be using my French language skills during our re-entry into Belgium during the Battle of the Bulge.

Even though Aachen, the first major city in Germany, had fallen, there was still serious work to do. The way ahead was not going to be easy for the Allies. After arriving in the Aachen sector in mid-October, General der Panzertrupppen *Hasso* Freiherr *von Manteuffel and his* 5th Panzer Army *staff had organized a comprehensive digging program involving the troops, some men of* Organization Todt, *boys of the Hitler Youth, and the civilian population. Extensive minefields were laid, both in front of the main line and on approaches to second, third, and fourth lines of defense. Arrangements were made with the* 7th Army *about controlling the water level of the Roer River by utilizing the Roer River dams, most of which were still undamaged. During the three weeks in which the* 5th Panzer Army *commanded the Aachen sector, it organized an impressive battle position, complete with several lines of defense, coordinated artillery positions, barbed wire entanglements, minefields, and anti-tank obstacles. Now it was just a question of establishing when the Allies would strike.*[22]

CITATIONS FOR ACTIONS AROUND AACHEN

Private Harold G. Kiner, Company F, 117th Infantry Regiment, near Palenberg, Germany, 2 October 1944. Medal of Honor citation:
With 4 other men, he was leading in a frontal assault 2 October 1944, on a Siegfried Line pillbox near Palenberg, Germany. Machine-gun fire from the strongly defended enemy position 25 yards away

pinned down the attackers. The Germans threw hand grenades, 1 of which dropped between Pvt. Kiner and 2 other men. With no hesitation, Private Kiner hurled himself upon the grenade, smothering the explosion. By his gallant action and voluntary sacrifice of his own life, he saved his 2 comrades from serious injury or death. Entered service at: Enid, Okla. Birth: Aline, Okla.[23]

Staff Sergeant Jack J. Pendleton, Company I, 120th Infantry Regiment, Bardenberg, Germany, 12 October 1944. Medal of Honor citation:
For conspicuous gallantry and intrepidity at the risk of his life above and beyond the call of duty on 12 October 1944. When Company I was advancing on the town of Bardenberg, Germany, they reached a point approximately two-thirds of the distance through the town when they were pinned down by fire from a nest of enemy machine-guns. This enemy strong point was protected by a lone machinegun strategically placed at an intersection and firing down a street which offered little or no cover or concealment for the advancing troops. The elimination of this protecting machinegun was imperative in order that the stronger position it protected could be neutralized. After repeated and unsuccessful attempts had been made to knock out this position, S/Sgt. Pendleton volunteered to lead his squad in an attempt to neutralize this strongpoint. S/Sgt. Pendleton started his squad slowly forward, crawling about 10 yards in front of his men in the advance toward the enemy gun. After advancing approximately 130 yards under the withering fire, S/Sgt. Pendleton was seriously wounded in the leg by a burst from the gun he was assaulting. Disregarding his grievous wound, he ordered his men to remain where they were, and with a supply of hand-grenades he slowly and painfully worked his way forward alone. With no hope of surviving the veritable hail of machinegun fire which he deliberately drew onto himself, he succeeded in advancing to within 10 yards of the enemy position when he was instantly killed by a burst from the enemy gun. By deliberately diverting the attention of the enemy machine gunners upon himself, a second squad was able to advance, undetected, and with the help of S/Sgt. Pendleton's squad, neutralized the lone machinegun, while another platoon of his company advanced up the intersecting street and knocked out the machinegun nest which the first gun had been covering. S/Sgt. Pendleton's sacrifice enabled the

entire company to continue the advance and complete their mission at a critical phase of the action. Entered service at: Yakima, Wash. Birth: Sentinel Butte, N. Dakota.[24]

Staff Sergeant (Sergeant-Major) Anthony A. Tempesta, Company A, 743rd Tank Battalion, Distinguished Service Cross citation:
The President of the United States takes pride in presenting the Distinguished Service Cross (Posthumously) to Anthony A. Tempesta (33082666), Staff Sergeant, US Army, for extraordinary heroism in connection with military operations against an armed enemy while serving with the 743d Tank Battalion, attached to the 30th Infantry Division, in action against enemy forces on 11 October 1944, in Germany.

Staff Sergeant Tempesta displayed marked personal bravery in a combined infantry-tank attack upon a German village. During the day's engagement, while continuously exposed to hostile fire, he directed the fire of his tank in destroying two anti-tank guns and six vehicles mounting 20mm guns. In addition, Staff Sergeant Tempesta inflicted heavy casualties upon infantry ranks and made dangerous reconnaissance missions on foot to locate enemy strongpoints. Upon learning that all officers had been wounded, he voluntarily assumed command of the entire company and successfully led his tanks in the accomplishment of a difficult mission. Staff Sergeant Tempesta's intrepid actions, personal bravery, and zealous devotion to duty at the cost of his life, exemplify the highest traditions of the military forces of the United States and reflect great credit upon himself, the 30th Infantry Division, and the United States Army.[25]

Lieutenant Karlheinz Zillies, 3rd Panzer-Grenadier Division, Knight's Cross Award:
For defending both sides of Würselen, September–November 1944. On October 21 the enemy penetrated several hundred yards in the direction of Würselen. Lieutenant Zillies realized that the Americans were about to encircle his position, so he assembled the remains of his company among the ruins in southern Würselen until they could retaliate and take up new positions. In these 24 hours, with his small unit he destroyed 7 Sherman tanks. Although no anti-tank weapons were available to him, his unit defended their position with machine

guns, pistols and hand grenades. In the bitter fights that ensued they blocked the American advance repeatedly. Only when Lieutenant Zillies had led the battalion and established a new line of defense were they able to penetrate the American line. For this heroic act Lieutenant Zillies is awarded the RITTERKREUZ "Knight's Cross." [26]

Brigadier General James M. Lewis is seen awarding Bill Gast of the 743rd Tank Battalion the Silver Star for his heroics on 9 August 1944. Earlier, as driver in his M4 Sherman, Gast landed in support of the first wave of infantry on D-Day at Omaha Beach. "We learned that out of 15 tanks of A Company, five of us made it. I have something that bothers me to this day—the beach was covered with dead and wounded soldiers. There is no way of telling if I ran over any of them with my tank."—*courtesy Bill Gast*

Above: Frank Towers, Liaison Officer with Company M, 120th Infantry Regiment. Frank served with the 30th all the way across the ETO and after the war kept the memory of Old Hickory alive serving as historian and editor of The 30th Infantry Division in World War II website.—*courtesy Frank Towers*

Right: Axis Sally referred to the 30th Infantry Division as "Roosevelt's SS" in her nightly radio broadcasts. In response, Major E.L. Glaser unofficially modified the 30th Division's insignia to reflect this hard-won battle honor.—*courtesy Hank Stairs*

Ssh! U.S.—'SS'

Sally's Sallies Suggest New Shoulder Patch For 30th Div.

WITH 30TH DIV.—The Joes of the 30th Div. have thrown one of "Sally's" sallies right back in the Nazi propaganda gal's face.

Sally had been saying in her nightly English language broadcasts that the 30th boys were "F. D.R's S.S. troops." The boys rather fancied the idea. They pointed out they really were Elite Troops, a chosen few, and top-notch fighters. Maj. E. L. Glaser, of Palm Beach, Fla., decided to adopt the designation and make a new division patch to go with it.

The result was a design, now under consideration at division headquarters, which combines the O and F of the 30th's Old Hickory with the two flashes of lightning which comprise the S.S. troopers' insignia—and to top it off, the president's well-known initials.

Above: The 30th received its baptism of fire in the hellish hedgerows of Normandy. Harold Williams recalled, "We were herded into one of the openings into one of the fields. It might have been 2–3 acres. A bulldozer was near me punching holes in the hedgerow so we could move forward. The driver was shot—one...two...three! Then a buddy of mine took it upon himself to do what he could. He jumped on the dozer and that was the end of him. He was shot. There was mass confusion. Nobody knew what was happening."—*courtesy National Archives*

Above: King Kenny served in the 2nd Reconnaissance Platoon, 823rd Tank Destroyer Battalion. He received a Purple Heart and a Bronze Star for his actions during WWII. Company B of the 823rd, including 2nd Recon Platoon, received a Presidential Citation for its brilliant anti-tank defensive actions around St. Barthelmy near Mortain. Kenny said that camaraderie between the men made the 30th the great unit it was.—*courtesy King Kenny*

Left: John O'Hare, Company E, 117th Infantry Regiment, on the front lawn of his parent's home in St. Louis, Missouri, as he was leaving for the war in Europe in June 1944.—*courtesy John O'Hare*

General Omar Bradley launched Operation Cobra to break out of the Normandy hedgerow country. Sadly, the preparatory carpet bombing by thousands of Allied aircraft killed and wounded hundreds of GIs, including many Old Hickorymen, in the lead assault units.

After a slow start, the operation succeeded and unhinged the German defenses, opening the door for fast-moving maneuver warfare and ultimate Allied victory in northwestern France.—*courtesy Warren Watson*

Tough, exhausted Old Hickorymen of the 120th Infantry Regiment rest briefly during the fighting at Mortain. The strain of battle is clearly evident in this photograph. The 120th fought a close-quarter engagement with enemy panzers and infantry, and despite the overwhelming odds, emerged victorious.—*courtesy National Archives*

In this aerial photo of Mortain taken after the war, the rocky ground and trees of Hill 314 can be seen in the upper right, while the destroyed town can be seen to the left. Also noteworthy are the plentiful and deadly hedgerows which dominated the Normandy countryside. —*courtesy Warren Watson*

Left: Frank Denius was a forward observer in Battery C, 230th Field Artillery Battalion. He received two Purple Hearts for wounds sustained in Normandy and the Battle of Bulge, and four Silver Stars for gallantry in action. When his lieutenant became incapacitated, Frank took the initiative and played a critical role directing artillery fire from Hill 314 in Mortain, which helped break the back of the German panzer offensive.—*courtesy Frank Denius*

Right: Gunter Adam was a platoon leader in the *9th SS-Panzer Division "Hohenstaufen."* His incredible odyssey through the Normandy battlefield began when he was captured and shot by American GIs. —*Martin King*

Marion Sanford, along with troopers from the 30th Recon, can be seen standing in the center of the photo to the left of the man holding the captured Nazi flag. —*courtesy Marion Sanford and Jeff Rogers*

Right: Hank Stairs served with Headquarters Company, 1st Battalion, 117th Infantry Regiment. This photograph was taken in Kerkrade or Herleen, Belgium, after the assault on the Siegfried Line. "We had two or three days of R&R. We actually slept on bunks and ate off of real dinnerware!"—*courtesy Hank Stairs*

Center: Old Hickorymen had to overcome a wide range of deadly fortifications in their assault on the Siegfried Line. In this photo, a GI from the 119th Infantry Regiment surveys a pillbox that was cleverly camouflaged to look like a house.—*courtesy Warren Watson*

Below: Frank Towers took this never-before-seen photograph on 24 December from a mountaintop position above Malmédy just seconds after Allied aircraft flew over and mistakenly bombed the city filled with American troops. To this day, Frank Towers believes that 24 missing men from the 30th sadly perished in the air raid.—*courtesy Frank Towers*

In the counterattack to close the Bulge, members of the 30th Division moved through Baugnez where the Malmédy Massacre took place on 17 December 1944. In this never-before-seen photo taken by Frank Towers at the crossroads, a fresh coat of snow had fallen, which covered the bodies of 84 American soldiers seen as mounds beneath the snow. The dead had yet to be recovered from the field.—*courtesy Frank Towers*

Right: John Nolan joined the 30th Division as a replacement on 6 September 1944. He was assigned as a squad leader in the 1st Platoon, Company G, 119th Infantry Regiment. He was "green" and was given seven "green" privates. By the end of the war he and his squad had earned ten Purple Hearts; only one man came out unscathed. At the end of the Bulge fighting there were just 14 men remaining out of 40 in Nolan's company.—*courtesy John Nolan*

Left: Richard Lacey fought with 2nd Platoon, Company M, 120th Infantry Regiment. An assistant machine gunner, Lacey received a Purple Heart for a wound received near Aachen. He returned to action at the Battle of Bulge and recalled walking past the Malmédy Massacre site before the bodies of the dead American soldiers had been recovered. "We walked right by that corner and all of those guys were laying out there. . . . It was tragic," he said.—*courtesy Richard Lacey*

Manfred Toon Thorn was a "tankie" in the *1st SS-Panzer Division "Leibstandarte Adolf Hitler."* He was awarded the Iron Cross 2nd Class for his actions in the Ardennes Offensive.—*Martin King*

Mason Armstrong, Company F, 119th Infantry Regiment, is seen shouldering a bazooka. On 18 December, Armstrong knocked out two half-tracks and disabled a third from Kampfgruppe Peiper's spearhead. He fired a bazooka like the one shown here from inside the second story of a house in Neufmoulin, Belgium, to stop the German advance. He was awarded the Distinguished Service Cross for his actions. —*courtesy Joseph Crea*

Members of the 30th Division prepare to cross the Roer River on LTVs (Landing Vehicle Tracked), otherwise known as "Alligators."—*courtesy Warren Watson*

Right: Francis Currey from Company K, 120th Infantry Regiment, single handedly fought off a strong German attack and rescued his comrades (two of whom were wounded) on 21 December 1944 in Malmedy, Belgium. Currey was awarded the Medal of Honor for his incredible acts of valor that day.—*courtesy National Archives*

Center: Harold Williams, 105th Engineer Battalion, poses in front of a knocked-out German *Sturmgeschütz (StuG)* assault gun in Germany. The *StuG* was destroyed by bazooka fire. Flanking Williams are Max Humphreys (left) and a man Williams knew as Hatto (right). Williams recalled that this photo was taken the day they learned of President Roosevelt's death.—*courtesy Harold Williams*

Below: Infantrymen of the 30th Division and tankers of an M4A3E8 Sherman from the 743rd Tank Battalion work closely together near Brunswick, Germany.—*courtesy National Archives*

Left: Photo of Victor Neiland (back row, right) with his squad from Company F, 117th Infantry Regiment taken 5 April 1945 at Horst Wessel Square in Hamelin, Germany. Standing left to right are Max Moeller, John Moore and Neiland. Kneeling left to right are Frank Patullo and John Volpe.—*courtesy Victor Neiland*

Center: This photo shows the "Death Train" and survivors near Farsleben, Germany, where approximately 2,500 Jewish prisoners were freed on 3 April 1945 by the 743rd Tank Battalion and infantry from the 119th Infantry Regiment. The train and its SS guards were transporting the Jews from Bergen-Belsen to another camp for extermination when it was liberated.—*courtesy National Archives*

With only 32 kilometers to go until Magdeburg, Frank Denius, a forward artillery observer with 230th Field Artillery Battalion, took this photo from his jeep as artillery shells landed nearby. —*courtesy Frank Denius*

Members of Company E, 117th Infantry Regiment, and an M10 tank destroyer (possibly from the 823rd Tank Destroyer Battalion) during a brief rest late on the second day of the Battle of Magdeburg. Resistance had virtually ended except for a few snipers and shells fired from the other side of the Elbe. Note the man near the back of the TD drinking from a bottle. He is likely drinking champagne from the hotel wine cellar found intact earlier.—*courtesy John O'Hare*

Several of the most highly decorated 30th Division enlisted men and officers meet with their commanders before boarding the *Queen Mary* at Southampton, England for redeployment to the United States. Francis Currey is third from left in the front row and Frank Denius is second from left in the back row. —*courtesy Frank Denius*

Last reunion of the 30th Infantry Division Veterans of WWII, 17–18 April 2015 in Nashville, TN. Pictured back row left to right: Jack Eddins (119th, Co. D), Eugene Pflughaupt (120th, Co. G), Bill Drasal (117th, Co. E), John O'Hare (117th, Co. E) and Peter Munger, Sr. (120th, I & R). Pictured front row left to right: William Hornsby (120th, Co. G), Marion Sanford (30th Recon.), Roger Casey, Sr. (119th, Co. D), Henry Kaczowka (117th, 1st Bn. HQ), Victor Neiland (117th, Co. F), Richard Lacey (120th, Co. M), Jack Kraus (119th, Co. A), and Frank Towers (120th, Co. M and Div. HQ).—*courtesy Larry S. Powell*

30th Infantry Division
"Old Hickory"
Nashville, Tennessee
April 18, 2015

CHAPTER SIX

ADVANCE TO THE EAST

Since 19 September, the 1st Infantry Division, along with the 3rd Armored Division, had been making forays into an area between the cities of Aachen, Düren, and Monschau known as the Hürtgen Forest. Lieutenant General Courtney Hodges had personally authorized and endorsed this action for the purpose of eliminating German resistance there. It wasn't even debated at the time that entering those densely forested primordial woods of tall fir trees, deep gorges, high ridges, and narrow trails area would eradicate all tactical advantages that the US forces had employed since the battles in Normandy. The canopy of the forest was so thick that when the GIs ventured in, they were in almost pitch darkness after about 30 yards. This also meant that it was nearly impossible to operate at anything above squad strength. The situation was exacerbated by the strong German defenses located deep in the forest and protected by pillboxes from the Siegfried Line.

American units were furnished with maps that didn't accurately show the steep contours of this region, and when the attacks bogged down, no one above the rank of captain ever went to see what the problem was. For the unfortunate infantry the forest presented a hellish tableau full of booby traps, mines, tree bursts, and an enemy determined to thwart their every move. The divisions that were poured into the Hürtgen Forest came to know the area as the "meat grinder" and casualties were excessively high in proportion to the ground actually gained. Ernest Hemingway compared it to the WWI battlefield at Passchendale.

General Hodges delegated the job of clearing out the forest to Major General Leonard T. Gerow's V Corps. Gerow, in turn, passed the mission on to Major General Norman D. Cota's 28th Infantry Division. It cost the 28th Division, whose red keystone shoulder patch became known as the "Bloody Bucket," almost 80 percent of its number and even then the task wasn't successfully accomplished.

During the first week of November, an abortive attack on the town of Schmidt in the Hürtgen Forest had set the tone for the coming weeks in that area. The 28th Infantry Division was up against Old Hickory's former adversaries, the German *116th Panzer Division*. The *116th* knew the terrain in the Hürtgen and knew how to best use it to their advantage.

While the 28th Infantry Division endured the stalemate in the Hürtgen Forest, US divisions in and around Aachen prepared for a drive to the Rhine River. The plan was that the British 21st Army Group would clear the west bank and protect the northern flank of this offensive. Even by the middle of the fall, however, there was still glaring disagreement among the senior commanders at SHAEF concerning which steps to take next. When General Eisenhower met Field Marshal Montgomery and General Bradley in Brussels on 18 October to discuss future plans, he once again hammered home his idea of the "broad-front" strategy. Eisenhower had first proposed this idea after the St. Lô-Falaise breakout. Patton had disagreed vociferously with the suggestion. General Eisenhower and his advisers suggested that with winter fast approaching, the best policy might be to hold in place, then to launch a final victorious offensive in the early spring.

The problem for many Allied commanders was Eisenhower's credibility as a strategist. Although he was a respected and much admired leader, his emphasis was usually more inclined toward maintaining the equilibrium among his commanders rather than initiating bold military strategies. The "wait until spring" idea was not received well and eventually three mitigating factors helped dissuade Eisenhower from this course of action. First, due to the attritional nature of the fighting, the German army was incurring casualties of up to 4,000 per day. Second, a winter sojourn would give the new Germans divisions time to train, prepare these troops for combat, and enable German industrial production to turn out more tanks and guns. Third, a sizeable pause in the fighting might enable the Germans to accelerate their jet production and discover the proximity fuse that would enable them to blast Allied bombers out of the skies.

Although Bradley and Montgomery's opinions on how to proceed were diametrically opposed, Montgomery still fervently supported the idea of his Allied spearhead in the north supported by US divisions. Bradley wasn't particularly enamored with this idea. Supply was an omnipresent problem for the Allies so before he could begin any concerted thrust east, Montgomery had to clear German forces out of the Walcheren peninsula west of Antwerp, which would drastically shorten supply lines. Eisenhower knew that a push to the Ruhr River was an imperative. He had even made plans for this before the Allied invasion of Normandy. The Ruhr valley was the pumping heart of Germany's industrial might; moreover, the Allies wanted an economic objective that, if achieved, would substantially hinder Germany's means of continuing the war. If they could capture the Ruhr industrial area this would effectively deprive Germany of 65 percent of its production of crude steel and 56 percent of its coal.

It was tentatively agreed that the British 21st Army Group would attack east of Eindhoven and head towards the Ruhr to establish bridgeheads over the Rhine and Ijssel Rivers. Hodges's First Army would make the main thrust in the center for the 12th Army Group. He would be charged with the task of establishing a bridgehead across the Rhine south of Cologne. Lieutenant General William Hood Simpson's Ninth Army would protect the First Army's left flank between Sittard and Aachen until the Ruhr was crossed, and then they intended to veer northeastward toward Krefeld. Bradley had repositioned the Ninth between the First Army and the 21st Army Group on 22 October to avoid them from being requisitioned by Montgomery. According to Bradley the motivation for doing this had no tactical basis other than to prevent Montgomery from using the veteran First Army for his own purposes. After weeks of meticulous planning the attack was finally launched toward the Roer River.

The 30th Division, meanwhile, was given the job of eliminating the German salient that jutted out west toward Aachen. Their flanks would be protected by the 29th Infantry Division in the north and the newly-arrived 104th Infantry Division ("Timberwolves") in the south. While the 119th Infantry Regiment remained in Würselen, the 117th and 120th Infantry Regiments lined up between Alsdorf and Euchen. Patrols in that vicinity didn't encounter any serious German opposition, so everything was set for the standard military advance. This reconnaissance established that the German line ran along the line of a railway embankment. The "Work Horse of the Western Front" was going to have to work for it again.

GEORGE SCHNEIDER, HEADQUARTERS COMPANY, 120TH INFANTRY REGIMENT

Near the end of November I was asked to sign a statement that I had been given the opportunity to vote in the November presidential election. I had just turned 20 in October and was not yet 21 years old and could not vote, so I refused to sign. The officer in charge of obtaining the signatures understood my position and politely asked that I not cause any trouble. He said, "Sign the damn form!" I signed.

East of the German villages clustered along the Dutch border and in the coal mining area the terrain is flat and the main crop was sugar beets grown for human and animal consumption. In this sugar beet country the farms were not isolated units among the fields. They were in small communities and the fields stretched from one village to another. From one vantage point it was common to see three or four of these communities, each identified by a Catholic Church steeple. Between the villages and among the beet fields the Germans had dug deep zig-zag trenches for defense. These fields and villages were not very well defended and we took them one at a time. In one of these villages I decided to take a bath in one of the farmhouses. In the kitchen there was a large shell hole in the ceiling and the floor was wet and muddy. We found a large wooden tub big enough to sit in and set it in the middle of the floor. On the kitchen stove we heated water in a bucket one bucket at a time until the tub contained sufficient water for a bath. I removed all of my clothes and was sitting in the tub completely lathered when our own fighter planes attacked us. We were so close to the German lines that we were often vulnerable to such attacks by mistake. Our P-47s were dive-bombing and strafing us. The first plane would strafe then the next would drop 200-pound bombs. There were only three or four planes, but they continued their mission, diving, bombing, and pulling out; circling around and coming back to strafe. At the first attack I dove into the cellar and into a coal bin. The adhesion of the coal dust to the soapsuds outfitted me for the lead in a minstrel show. After the first pass there was a short lull in the activity so I returned to the tub in the kitchen. Having washed off the coal dust I lathered again only to be interrupted by the planes on their second approach. I did a second performance in the coal bin. I tried a third attempt at bathing, again to no avail. In disgust I surrendered to our Air Corps and dressed myself after scraping off most of the coal dust and soapsuds.

Across from our farmhouse the planes strafed one of our gun emplacements and wounded some of the gunners. We got the identification of the planes and upon relating this information to the Air Corps they admitted that they had attacked. Their excuse was that they had seen fires in the village and thought that we were still fighting for its possession. They had decided to help us out by dropping a few bombs and strafing.

There was a bit of humor to the incident. The coalmines in Holland were not destroyed because of their protected locations underground. The facilities included showers that were used. Upon entering the mine, clothing was removed and a hot shower was enjoyed. After showering you were given a set of clean clothes that had been disinfected for body lice. On the day of the friendly bombing a truckload of our men had gone to Kerkrade for showers and were on their way back when the planes began their runs. The truck was near our village but in the open country with the German trenches. The men abandoned the truck and ran into the trenches for cover. They were well protected, but emerged soaking wet and muddy from the trenches that were half filled with muddy water. Their de-loused uniforms were now dirtier than their uniforms had been before the showers.

The next day we took the neighboring town; Ken Bedford and I laid claim to a farmhouse bedroom. We found a large satin comforter, apple green on one side and pink on the other. Wrapped in this we bedded down for the night. All night we kept itching from some kind of crawling critters running races up and down our backs. In the morning we removed our shirts and long john undershirts and found hundreds of lice lined up in formation in the undershirt ribbings. We took another trip to the coalmines and a new set of de-loused clothing.

By the middle of December we had crossed the Inde River, a short distance to the east, and reached the banks of the Ruhr River. Upstream the Germans controlled the dams that could be opened to flood our area and bog down a crossing. If we did successfully cross the Ruhr and were allowed to establish a bridgehead, the dams could be opened and we would be at the mercy of the 6th SS-Panzer Army on the other side. While contemplating the next move, the counteroffensive of the Ardennes (Bulge) began and we were pulled off to go south and engage the Germans in the Bulge.[1]

Throughout the third week of November, the 119th Infantry Regiment was still fighting the *3rd Panzer-Grenadier Division* house to house in the shattered town of Würselen. The town was beginning to resemble a mini-Stalingrad. But by the 18 November, German units there pulled back to the Linden-Neusen area along the line of the highway and the 119th finally succeeded in capturing the whole town.

The 117th Infantry Regiment was preoccupied taking Mariadorf. During the previous day, the 1st Battalion of the 117th had been faced with stubborn resistance and due to the inclement weather conditions it hadn't been possible to call in desperately-needed air support. By early evening they had laboriously cleaned out the remainder of the opposition, but at a cost. While the 117th's 2nd Battalion advanced towards Höngen against a withering hail of German artillery and mortar fire, the 1st Battalion made preparations to attack the town of Warden.

According to after action reports, when 1st Battalion jumped off at 0730 hours on 18 November, their initial thrust was parried by powerful screens of enemy artillery, small arms fire, and direct fire from dug-in tanks. After being repulsed at 1115 hours the attack was renewed, but once again the devastating superiority of opposing fire power cost Company B more than 70 men and halted the advance short of its target. Determined to press on with the attack, at 1515 hours, after an intensive artillery barrage, 1st Battalion with the addition of Company F, launched a coordinated attack against the heavily-defended town. In an effort to make faster contact with the Germans, the 30th Division GIs mounted tanks, four men upon each one as they moved forward. Three rifle companies and eleven tanks charged at the city simultaneously from three angles. The Germans dug in their heels and resisted the drive fiercely by using reinforced concrete emplacements, houses as strong points, and with the support of at least four direct-fire assault guns. During the engagement hand-to-hand fighting occurred as 209 prisoners were captured along with a hoard of ammunition and two self-propelled assault guns and eventually the town was taken by the 117th.

A message intercepted by intelligence at Corps revealed that a ridge between Kinzweiler and St. Jöris had been selected as the new main line of defense for the German forces. On 19 November, the 117th Infantry Regiment's 2nd Battalion attacked south in the direction of Kinzweiler while its 3rd Battalion launched an attack against St. Jöris. By now the 117th was making a habit of moving forward sitting on the available armor; this method, along with preceding each attack with intense artillery, was proving to be so successful that both objectives had been taken within 30 minutes. The 117th incurred only light casualties and managed to round up a further 223 German prisoners to join the existing collection.

On 21 November, the 30th Division moved out at night, charged with the task of clearing out Ninth Army's inner wing near the original line of departure and during the initial assault they gained 3-1/2 miles. The 120th Infantry Regiment and its attached 743rd Tank Battalion quickly overran five villages. The 120th Infantry's most advanced position ended just four miles from the Roer. They had encountered some sporadic resistance but there were no concerted German counterattacks to dissuade them from their trajectory. It was overly optimistic, nevertheless, to suggest that the Germans were a spent force or that they were withdrawing in disarray.

Rumors began to circulate that the Germans were massing forces just east of the Rhine, but there was no serious intelligence at the time to substantiate these claims. Some even said that the 30th Division's old adversaries, Josef "Sepp" Dietrich and the *1st SS-Panzer Division,* were among these troops, but again this was just a rumor wasn't it? By 30 November, Old Hickory had accomplished its contribution in the historic drive to the Ruhr River and in the process they had incurred 160 men killed and 1,058 wounded. General Simpson, commanding Ninth Army, was so impressed by the magnificent display of combined armor and infantry tactics that had been used by the 30th Division that he actually persuaded them to re-stage them for the benefit of newly-arrived commanders.

On the whole, the drive to the Ruhr had been a disappointing maneuver because although quite a bit of territory was claimed by the Allies, they hadn't really been able to exploit these minor victories sufficiently. Hemmed in by a checkerboard of villages and towns, it had been a slogging match that hadn't really enabled the US forces to break out into open ground. They had now set themselves up, moreover, with the daunting task of actually crossing the Ruhr River at a future point in time. Farther south in the Hürtgen Forest, torrential rain and mud had all but brought the advance there to a halt. The whole area was simply not conducive to the Allied way of fighting. To the right of the town of Schmidt in the Hürtgen Forest, the Schwammenauel Dam was still intact as were many of the dams that supplied the Ruhr industrial zone. Between 4 and 11 December, the RAF dropped approximately 2,000 tons of bombs on these dams, but hadn't managed to breach any of them and had been largely ineffectual. Calling for air support in the Hürtgen was often counterproductive because of the dense canopy, so it was all left to the infantry to do the hard work.

RICHARD LACEY, COMPANY M, 120TH INFANTRY REGIMENT

Recovery and Return to the Front: [After I was wounded outside Aachen] they put me on a hospital troop train to Paris and I was there for several days. They then loaded me into a C-47 and flew me to England. I wasn't really wounded that badly and I was surprised that they sent me back so far. I ended up in England in a hospital but I was one of the walking wounded. There was a farm next to the hospital so I got acquainted with some of the gals who were working over there. I watched them milking their cows and I even had a cup of tea with them one afternoon. I was eventually sent back and crossed the channel on Thanksgiving on another English ship. We had cold canned turkey and I slept in a hammock.

We landed in La Havre and we loaded on 40-and-8s (40 men or eight horses) from World War I. They were crowded and we didn't have any food or any toilet facilities. The cars were pretty well filled. The train would stop for a few minutes so the guys would run off and go out in the farm fields and pull up beets and potatoes to get something to eat. The train would start up and we'd run back to get on the train. As one fellow ran to jump on the train he was caught under the wheels and it cut his legs off. We went to a place near Paris in the country outside and stayed overnight there. A colonel came down and lined us up there. They starting asking questions about the train and we told them—we didn't have any food, it was crowded, and we didn't have any toilet facilities. He said to me, "Are you anxious to get back to the front?" I wanted tell him, "Are you crazy?" Instead I told him I was anxious to get back to my own outfit. The conditions on the train were a lot better afterward and I eventually rejoined my outfit in the Netherlands.[2]

Even though the 30th was due some R&R, plans were being made for a new assault on the Ruhr. At the end of October, they had set up a recreation center in the Dutch/German border town of Kerkrade in buildings belonging to the centuries old Rolduc College. It was a place where the GIs could get a hot shower, clean clothes, a clean bed, and three meals a day.

HANK STAIRS, HEADQUARTERS COMPANY, 117TH INFANTRY REGIMENT

After Aachen, we went to the town of Alsdorf. We were there for weeks and we had a chance to take a bath. It was our fall bath—you take one spring, summer, and fall in the infantry! It was a real treat. It was in a coalmine facility. While in Alsdorf we also used to listen to Axis Sally because she played big band music. She would come on, though, and do things like tell us what our password for the night was, which was kind of a blow in the ass![3]

There was no shortage of entertainment there, either. The 30th Division Band that had been assigned to guard duties at Division CP for the duration had discovered some abandoned German instruments and began making music again for the troops. Apart from that there was the excellent USO to provide entertainment from home, and movies were shown three times a day. There was no compulsory training to do, so the soldiers could sleep for as long as they wanted in the separate cubicles that allowed privacy and provided comfort for these battle-hardened but weary foot-sloggers. The regiments took turns to move away from the front line and use these excellent facilities. The hiatus was to be short lived, though. Those ominous rumors about the Nazis amassing forces for a possible massive counteroffensive were going to become more than just rumors.

CITATION FOR ACTION IN GERMANY

Staff Sergeant Freeman V. Horner, Company K, 119th Infantry Regiment, Wurselen, Germany, 16 November 1944. Medal of Honor citation:
S/Sgt. Horner and other members of his company were attacking Wurselen, Germany, against stubborn resistance on 16 November 1944, when machinegun fire from houses on the edge of the town pinned the attackers in flat, open terrain 100 yards from their objective. As they lay in the field, enemy artillery observers directed fire upon them, causing serious casualties. Realizing that the machine guns must be eliminated in order to permit the company to advance from its precarious position, S/Sgt. Horner voluntarily stood up with his submachine gun and rushed into the teeth of concentrated fire, burdened by a heavy load of ammunition and hand grenades. Just as he reached a position of seeming safety, he was fired on by a machine gun which had remained silent up until that time. He coolly wheeled in his fully exposed position while bullets barely missed him and killed 2 hostile gunners with a single, devastating burst. He turned to face the fire of the other 2 machine guns, and dodging fire as he ran, charged the 2 positions 50 yards away.

Demoralized by their inability to hit the intrepid infantryman, the enemy abandoned their guns and took cover in the cellar of the house they occupied. S/Sgt. Horner burst into the building, hurled 2 grenades down the cellar stairs, and called for the Germans to surrender. Four men gave up to him. By his extraordinary courage, S/Sgt. Horner destroyed 3 enemy machine-gun positions, killed or captured 7 enemy, and cleared the path for his company's successful assault on Wurselen. Entered service at: Shamokin, Pa. Birth: Mount Carmel, Pa.[4]

PART THREE

THE ARDENNES

ARDENNES-ALSACE CAMPAIGN

16 December 1944–25 January 1945

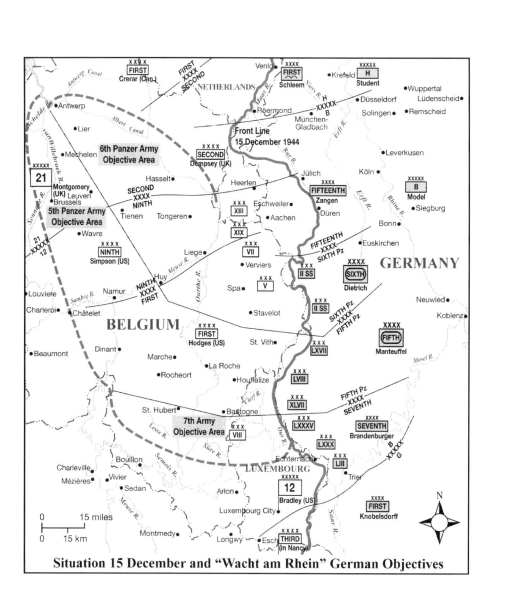

Situation 15 December and "Wacht am Rhein" German Objectives

CHAPTER SEVEN

THE THIN GREEN LINE

W hile the 30th Division caught up on some R&R, the 28th Infantry Division, which had taken some heavy casualties in the Hürtgen Forest, were sent south to an area that was generally regarded as the "quiet sector." They desperately needed to refit and add new recruits to replace those lost in the deadly Hürtgen Forest, which had consumed 80 percent of their men. Their new position was just below the freshly-arrived 106th Infantry Division and covered an unconventionally wide area. The space extended way beyond the normal division front at the time but that was also the case for the other divisions in the Ardennes. The 106th, for instance, was covering a front of almost 26 miles when guidelines had stipulated that an effective division front should not exceed 5.5 miles. To the north of them the 99th Infantry Division fared no better. Both of these divisions were part of Major General Leonard T. Gerow's V Corps. The 99th was also stretched out beyond what they could reasonably be expected to hold in the event of a German offensive. A greater cause for worry was the 4.5-mile gap that existed between these two divisions with the German village of Losheim at its center.

General Patton had casually mentioned that the Germans were still capable of mounting a powerful offensive if they wanted to, but nobody at SHAEF suspected that a counterattack would occur in this sector. Patton had positioned his whole Third Army in the Alsace region in northern France because if the attack came he assumed that it would happen there. He based his assumptions on the fact that this area had indeed changed hands on a number of occasions during the previous hundred years. Alsace looked like any other southern German place with its half-timbered houses and cobbled streets. Many there still spoke German and referred to Alsace by its German name, *Das Elsass*. The Germans knew the terrain there all too well. They had targeted the area in 1940 but whether or not it would be suitable for a new offensive remained to be seen.

While Adolf Hilter was recuperating from the abortive assassination attempt that had happened at the "Wolf's Lair" in July 1944, he began formulating plans for a new offensive in the west. Despite being extremely wary of his generals after this incident, he still maintained that a concerted push west would divide the Allies and facilitate the re-taking of the vital port of Antwerp. The latter was now operational; consequently, supply lines for the Allied armies in the north were no longer dependent on Normandy and the Channel ports. Canadian units had cleared out the Walcheren peninsula and effectively opened the estuary to allow Allied shipping to reach Antwerp.

During August and September, meanwhile, Hitler was still ruminating about opening a new front. His volatile state of mind at the time was such that not many of his generals had the nerve to openly question or contradict his plans. Field Marshal Walter Model was, in fact, one of the very few high-ranking officers who dared to disagree with Hitler, despite the *Führer's* insistence that his plan could succeed and divide the Allies. He based his opinions on the assumption that there was already a glaring lack of cohesion among the generals at Allied command. There had indeed been some disagreement there regarding the advance toward Germany after the Normandy campaign, but this didn't effectively distract from the fact that the Allies were still materially in a stronger position than their German adversaries.

A particular problem for the Allies at this time was the glaring lack of accurate and verifiable intelligence regarding the buildup of German forces in the west. Bletchley Park had intercepted communications that indicated that some German divisions were being moved west from the Russian front, but no one at SHAEF regarded this information as anything more than an indication that they were preparing to defend their homeland when the Allies went on the offensive again in February 1945. Even when two German prisoners were inadvertently captured by the 28th Infantry Division on the Luxembourg/Germany border, no one believed their claims that a massive German counteroffensive was imminent. Some days prior to the attack, the German armies had imposed radio silence on all their units; although some US division commanders suspected that something was afoot, there was still no definitive intelligence to corroborate this.

At 0530 hours on 16 December, however, their suspicions proved right.

Along an 89-mile front that stretched from Monschau on the southwestern edge of the Hürtgen Forest all the way down to Echternach in the south of Luxembourg, a tirade of German wrath was unleashed against unsuspecting GIs as barrages from at least 657 artillery pieces, along with 340 rocket launchers, thundered into the murky pre-dawn skies and crashed among the unsuspecting thin green line of US troops there.

Over at First Army HQ in Spa, General Omar Bradley received the news with incredulity. He wasn't the only one who didn't consider this to be an all-out offensive, but as the day wore on it was evident that these were most definitely not simple probing attacks. As German 88s and *Nebelwerfers* reaped havoc among front-line US divisions, word reached the 30th that something serious was going on down in the Ardennes. Three German armies had attacked simultaneously along the whole line there. In the northern sector they were primarily *SS* units, some of which had been specially imported from the eastern front solely for this offensive. These battle-hardened veterans were not afraid of cold temperatures and were spoiling for a fight with the intrusive Americans.

RICHARD LACEY, COMPANY M, 120TH INFANTRY REGIMENT

The SS *troops were better than the regular German soldiers. I'm sure they drafted a lot of younger people, especially towards the end of the war. They had teenagers out there shooting. The* SS *appeared to us to be better trained troops. I don't know how to describe it, but they were harder to fight. They had more guts, I guess.*[1]

The 30th was also battle-hardened; most of them had taken on *SS* troops before and come out on top. It was time to take them on again. When the attack occurred the 30th Division was positioned to the west of the Ruhr River and largely oblivious to events that were occurring down south in the Ardennes. Once again, they were going to put into practice all the valuable knowledge that they had gained from the previous months of fighting. They were going to prove beyond any doubt that they were more than capable of taking on any job that was given to them. In addition to being pitted against the *SS,* there would be an enemy with which they had already had some experience, but not to this extent. The weather would be more debilitating in the Ardennes than anything they had dealt with before. The November rains had caused cases of trench-foot and hypothermia throughout the ranks, but nothing could have prepared them for what was in store when they reached the Ardennes region of Belgium.

FRANK TOWERS, COMPANY M, 120TH INFANTRY REGIMENT

Some of the most intense and vicious fighting of the entire war took place in this area due to the cold weather, lack of warm clothing, food, supplies, and ammunition. Temperatures hovered below freezing during the day, often with wind and snow; and temperatures as low as -20 degrees Fahrenheit at night. During this December-January period, we endured the coldest winter on record up to that time, according to local authorities. Although fighting was severe and continuous, we actually had more casualties from frostbite of the feet and hands than actual wounds from enemy action. This required an enormous number of replacements throughout these two months. The logistics of keeping us supplied with ammunition, food, and replacements was an on-going nightmare for our service units.[2]

Accurate intelligence was still a problem but verifiable news had filtered down from G-2 that there was something serious going on down south; even so, the news was received by his unit laconically and not immediately acted upon. The thick mist that covered the whole area prohibited any serious air reconnaissance. On the morning of 17 December Major General Hobbs was waiting for a transport plane to take him to England for a seven-day furlough when he got a call from Lieutenant General Simpson informing him that the 30th Division was to be temporarily assigned to V Corps, with the additional instruction to get the men ready to move out with all haste.

The 30th Reconnaissance Troop and the 119th Infantry Regiment led the way, arriving in the vicinity of the Belgian town of Malmédy by 1630 hours on 17 December. They were closely followed by the 117th and 120th Infantry Regiments, the 120th having turned over their sector to the 29th Infantry Division moments before they hit the road. The long regimental columns interspersed with tanks and tank destroyers meandered south almost unopposed. A couple of stray German fighter planes dropped a few flares on the columns. It was about this time that the ominous tones of Axis Sally could be heard on frequent broadcasts informing the troops mockingly that, "The fanatical 30th Division, Roosevelt's *SS,* was going to save First Army."

MARION SANFORD, 30TH CAVALRY RECONNAISSANCE TROOP (MECHANIZED)

Everything changed for us on December 16th. For the better part of four weeks, we had been in reserve and taking it easy in the coalmine in Kerkrade while enjoying our R&R. A good many men from Recon were on leave elsewhere, including most of the senior enlisted leadership. We were expecting to be out of action until after the first of the year, or at least that is what the rumor mill was telling us. We were enjoying our time off of the line, anyway, and were expecting a joyous Christmas, given the circumstances.

About midmorning, someone from the HQ section came into our room and passed the word that we were to be ready to move out in 30 minutes. We were caught by surprise and started scrambling to get our gear ready to go. We had no idea where we were headed or why, but at 1100 hours we moved out, driving south. I usually rode in the half-track with Sims, Sutton, and Duggan, but because Sergeant Tidwell was on leave, I was the senior enlisted man present in the maintenance section so I rode in the jeep.

It was a cold, raw day and I sure missed the warmth of my usual vehicle. When we pulled out, a drizzling rain was falling, but somewhere down the road near Belgium it turned into sleet. We continued driving and some time during the night snow started falling. The jeep was crowded with equipment and supplies, so I had to put my leg on the outside and rest my foot on the fender extension, where it caught the rain and splash from the front wheel. By nightfall, my pants leg was frozen stiff.

I did not know it at the time, but I probably met Steve Rouse headed in the opposite direction. He was part of First Army Headquarters at Spa and they were moving back because the Germans were getting too close to their position. That was part of the reason we had to remove the rear fenders from the armored cars. Their trucks kept bumping into our vehicles and bending the fenders in as they were driving north and we were driving south. During the night and next day we more or less hacked the fenders off using axes and sledgehammers. Otherwise, they would have torn up the tires.

At one point during the drive we were strafed by a German plane, but none of Recon's vehicles were hit. As the German lined up his plane for the strafing run, we bailed out of our vehicles and sprinted into the fields and woods lining the roadway. I plopped down beside a soldier and covered my head as the plane shot up the area. When the attack was over, I reached over, bumped the other soldier on the leg and told him, "Let's go." It was only then that I realized that the man was dead and had been that way for a long time.[3]

ED MIDDLETON, 730TH ORDNANCE COMPANY

When we got down there we took a 17-mile front along the Amblève River which ran from Malmédy to Stavelot to La Gleize and to Stoumont Station. Just north of the front lines, we stopped at Spa for a short period. First Army had retreated from there. We moved into farm yards to set up our shops to do repair work. It was near zero-degree temperature and we eventually had waist-deep snow. For-tunately, not being in the front line, we could sit down and change our shoes and socks to keep from getting frostbite. At the same time, we had to keep our infantry and artillery firing.[4]

HANK STAIRS, HEADQUARTERS COMPANY, 117TH INFANTRY REGIMENT

We got on trucks and headed south. We were in a convoy traveling at night, without headlights. Sometimes we had a guy walking out in front of the truck so we wouldn't crash into the truck in front of us. While going down to the Bulge the guys were listening to Axis Sally on the radio. She said the 30th Division was heading south and would be annihilated by the German counteroffensive. She also referred to us as Roosevelt's SS Troops.

Jerry flew over us and dropped a few bombs, but he didn't know where he was dropping them. We stopped and someone shouted, "Bail out and get down!" We never fastened our helmet chinstrap and I wore GI glasses at the time, so my helmet came crashing down on my glasses and sliced open the bridge of my nose. That was my only chance for a Purple Heart! We reached a town called Malmédy and stopped there. I think the 117th was the first regiment to get into the town. The Germans hadn't taken it yet and the Air Corps didn't know it and they bombed us, again! I thanked God we survived.[5]

FRANCIS CURREY, COMPANY K, 120TH INFANTRY REGIMENT

We were gearing up to cross the Roer River. One day during the middle of the night they told us to get our stuff together, the trucks are leaving. Take everything with you, you're not coming back! We kept going and going. German planes were strafing us and we were jumping off the trucks and getting into ditches while the trucks fired back at the planes. The truck drivers were all colored. As the German planes were strafing and coming in, this man of color manned a .50-caliber gun on the truck. When a plane came in, he let him have it good, tore the wing off the plane, then it crashed. The other truck drivers carried him on their shoulders! If anyone deserved a Silver Star, it was him. It was like watching a movie. That event delayed our convoy for a few hours.

I did not have all of my stuff. I had my BAR, my clothes, my pack, and en-trenching tool, that was it. The war was going to be over by December so of course I only had a light field jacket and no winter clothes at all, period! I remember going thru Spa and Francorchamps, which was the last stop until we trucked into Malmédy.[6]

FRANK DENIUS, BATTERY C, 230TH FIELD ARTILLERY BATTALION

On the morning of 17 December, Captain Alexander, my battery commander, called me and told me that we had orders to move the Division. One of my responsibilities as Chief of Detail was to head up the quartering party. When the artillery battery moved, I was in an advance party tasked with locating the position where to put the battery. Captain Alexander called me and told me to get my radio sergeant (Goldstein) and jeep driver (Louis Sberna) and report to Division Headquarters. We met at Division HQ and started out, heading south. We had no maps and we did not know what our mission was. Ironically, we later learned about our mission by a radio broadcast from Axis Sally! Later in the day, it got cold and windy, not snowing yet, with a little rain, then it got dark. The entire 30th Division's advance units were strung out on the highway and we did not know where exactly we were going. All we knew was what Axis Sally told us—the German army had broken through and was on its way to Antwerp. She also mentioned that what was left of the 30th Division, after being mangled at Aachen, was moving down to stop Peiper. That wasn't true, we weren't mangled ever! We were an alert fighting division.

During the move the Germans dropped flares on us and we were strafed by German planes. Later that night I found a spot to locate the artillery battery between the highway that goes from Aachen to Malmédy, about 40 miles south of Aachen. When my battery arrived around midnight, I pulled them off and put them into position. We went into perimeter defense because we had no idea where the Germans were and we had no idea exactly where we were. Early the next morning we moved towards Malmédy. By then, we knew where we were going and why. The first thing I did was get in my jeep with my driver, Sberna, and Sherman Goldstein to head to Malmédy to locate a new position for the battery. When they came along I put them in position and got them oriented. That night I went up on a hill to observe the 120th Regiment as it headed into Malmédy (the 117th went to Stavelot and the 119th went to La Gleize and Stoumont). That's when we took up defensive positions to defend against Peiper's advance. At that time, Lieutenant John Jacobs joined us.[7]

The *1st SS-Panzer Division "Liebstandarte SS Adolf Hitler"* led the advance into the Amblève River valley and collided with the 30th Division. *LAH* was part of General Josef "Sepp" Dietrich's *6th Panzer Army*. Dietrich was a committed Nazi, and while other German commanders secretly muttered their disapproval of Hitler's plan, Dietrich supported it wholeheartedly. Such was his enthusiasm for the plan that the Germans called "*WACHT AM*

RHEIN" (Guard on the Rhine) that Hitler gave him the task of leading the "spearhead" toward Antwerp. The unit on point was known as *Kampfgruppe* (battle group) *Peiper*. Its leader, *Obersturmbannführer* (lieutenant colonel) Joachim Peiper, was a handsome 29-year-old veteran with a fearsome reputation for being very thorough when in combat. He had served as an adjutant on Heinrich Himmler's staff before commanding various panzer units attached to the *1st SS-Panzer Division*. Peiper was Himmler's "blue-eyed boy" and Himmler always maintained a fervent interest in Peiper's military career.

On the eastern front, his unit had been known as the "Blowtorch Battalion." The "blowtorch" reference came from their overly enthusiastic use of flamethrowers. Their method of fighting had been brutal and merciless. They would capture a Russian village, burn everything to cinders, and kill everything with a pulse.

Even though Peiper was a combat veteran he still hadn't grasped the logistics of organizing an invasion column, and from the outset he created gridlocks that impeded his own advance. On the morning of 16 December, Lieutenant Colonel Peiper had driven out to the *12th Volks-Grenadier Division* advance command post. This division had been given the task of making a gap in the lines of the US 99th Infantry Division north of the Schnee Eifel through which his armor would be committed. Peiper was infuriated when he discovered that this order hadn't been executed to its full extent; consequently, as the day continued Peiper's column remained practically inert on the roads to the rear until he personally took charge of the situation. The main problem facing his advance was a blown railway overpass that hadn't been efficiently repaired. It wasn't until late in the evening that he managed to get underway via an alternate route that wasn't really suitable for his heavy tanks.

The following day brought more problems for *Kampfgruppe Peiper*. Unable to take the route that he had intended, combined with the dogged resistance of the 99th and 2nd Infantry Divisions, his unit was effectively funneled into an area where he didn't want to be, the Amblève valley. Peiper's command was used to fighting in the vast open spaces of the Russian plains where it was possible to maneuver. His unit was not designed to be confined to the narrow and constricting roads; small villages and towns; hilly terrain; and the densely-wooded boreal forests of the Amblève valley. Peiper, moreover, harbored a festering dislike for Sepp Dietrich, the butcher's son from Bavaria. By that stage in the war Dietrich was an alcoholic who rarely exhibited the necessary lucidity required to orchestrate a major offensive. He'd become no more than a Nazi sycophant who acquiesced willingly to his *Führer*.

When the 30th Division arrived the following day to take on *Kampfgruppe Peiper* in the Amblève area, they discovered that the task force from the 99th had already been involved in a fierce running battle with the *SS*. Brigadier General Harrison, the 30th's assistant division commander, instructed the 117th Infantry Regiment to continue on and secure the towns of Malmédy and Stavelot. The 119th Infantry Regiment stopped at Hauset, just inside the Belgian border, and bedded down for the night. A task force from the 99th Infantry Division was also ordered to go to Malmédy. They arrived there at 2130 hours and found that 60 men from the 291st Engineer Combat Battalion had already set up some roadblocks and were laying mines south of Stavelot. Within two hours of arriving on the scene the task force became embroiled in a vicious firefight with leading elements of *Kampfgruppe Peiper*.

The *1st SS-Panzer Division* and *Kampfgruppe Peiper* had been given the instruction by *6th Panzer Army* commander, Josef "Sepp" Dietrich, to subjugate all opposition by whatever means. This was a thinly-veiled order to indulge in a killing spree and take no prisoners. Perhaps the most infamous example of these orders being followed to the letter occurred at the Baugnez crossroads on 17 December. On that fateful winter's day in 1944, the spearhead of Peiper's *Kampfgruppe* executed more than 80 American GIs in cold blood, while more than 40 escaped the slaughter. It is generally agreed that at approximately 1300 hours on 17 December 1944, the lead vehicles of *Kampfgruppe Peiper*'s 15-mile-long column approached the crossroad at Baugnez, a few miles north of the town of Malmédy. They ran into a small American convoy of 26 vehicles belonging to Battery B, 285th Field Artillery Observation Battalion (FAOB) that had been sent down from Germany to join the 7th Armored Division near St. Vith. A short but violent firefight ensued, and the men of the FAOB, lacking any heavy weapons to defend themselves and after taking casualties, decided to surrender. They didn't have the option to retreat back down the road to Malmédy because engineers had felled trees behind them that toppled in a lattice pattern on the road, making it virtually impassable. As the exchange of fire subsided, the GIs were told to lay down their weapons, whereupon they were herded into a nearby field next to a structure known as the Café Bodarwe.

According to eyewitnesses, half-tracks and tanks from *Kampfgruppe Peiper* pulled up opposite the field where the surrendered Americans were gathered. The *SS* were seen loading their weapons, then the *SS* troops suddenly opened up with pistols and machine guns on the US prisoners standing in what would become known as the "Massacre Field." GIs crumpled to the ground while terrified US soldiers who were not hit in the initial fusillade suddenly began to run. There was more fire and additional prisoners fell screaming to the ground. Within a matter of a few minutes, pools of blood and writhing bodies littered the field. Then a small group of *SS* men began to walk among the injured and the dead, with their pistols out. Any bodies that showed signs of life were instantly dispatched by the *SS;* personal valuables such as watches were taken from the dead Americans. The incident has been covered many times in many books and there are those who claim to be able to provide the definitive account, but the authors of this volume are not among them. Despite what has been written by other historians, there is indisputable proof that many of the casualties at Baugnez suffered close-proximity head wounds, which concurs with reports by survivors that many of the wounded were shot point blank. Escapees who made their way back to the 291st Engineer positions in Malmédy would later tell their stories and those quickly made their way through the American ranks, steeling GI resolve to blunt the German assault, and fueling their abhorrence of the *SS.*

HAROLD WILLIAMS, 105TH ENGINEER COMBAT BATTALION

There was an area of the Bulge near Malmédy where a lot of US soldiers were lined up and shot by SS. *It was called the Malmédy Massacre. I saw those bodies. They were snow-covered and the bodies were there. Fighting was still going on and when the Allied troops found out about this, the first thing that went up and down the line was, "Take no prisoners." Those next few days I don't think there were many prisoners taken. The* SS *were arrogant; they were good fighters, no question about it. They were harder to come up against than the regular German Army. They were the elite and brainwashed to do anything. You couldn't reason with them.*[8]

FRANK TOWERS, COMPANY M, 120TH INFANTRY REGIMENT

It was around 18–20 December when we found about it [the Malmédy Massacre]. We discovered the bodies. There were a few men who survived the massacre and from them we knew what had happened. It gave us an anti-German feeling. Not that I was actually involved, but I heard of cases where we had captured Germans. Our troops would take a few of them with one guy as a guard to a prisoner-of-war cage, but we would hear, "These prisoners tried to escape, so I had to shoot them." I know this happened on a few occasions.[9]

RICHARD LACEY, COMPANY M, 120TH INFANTRY REGIMENT

They moved our positions around and we were in the area where the Malmédy Massacre took place. The outfit that picked up the bodies hadn't gotten there yet. By then we had snow on the ground. We walked right by that corner and all of those guys were laying out there. I know a few of them got away. It was tragic.[10]

HANK STAIRS, HEADQUARTERS COMPANY, 117TH INFANTRY REGIMENT

We eventually passed the spot where the Malmédy Massacre occurred. There was no fighting going on and we were in reserve. We were going up to support elements that had already attacked, through. The Graves Registration boys were already there and they were sweeping the snow off, loading the corpses up like cordwood onto trucks. It was a pretty shocking sight![11]

A squad of men from the 291st Engineer Combat Battalion, which had been sent from Malmédy to Stavelot to construct a roadblock on the road leading to the town's only bridge over the Amblève, was the only combat unit in the town at this time. They were soon augmented with a platoon from the 526th Armored Infantry Battalion, but this task force was still insufficient for the job at hand. Stavelot was recognized as a key enemy objective for three specific reasons. First, on the south side of town there was an excellent bridge over the Amblève River. Second, two road networks to Liege converged just west of Stavelot. Third, one of these roads passed through Spa, which was the US First Army headquarters at that time and only nine miles away.

The task force sent out two platoons and two tank destroyers to cover the bridge over the Amblève River south of the town, but they were set upon by SS troops before they could get into position. Inexplicably, as the day came to a close Peiper halted his advance and stopped on the south side of the river. He later claimed that he mistakenly thought that a full US division was bearing down on his position, but this respite cost him valuable time that he could ill afford at that point in the offensive. Early the next morning, German tanks began moving toward the bridge and were immediately fired at by three US 57mm anti-tank guns; they managed to successfully disable the first two tanks, but then the German 88s retaliated. One anti-tank gun was destroyed and one escaped while the other continued firing until it was just 40 yards from its target. A torrent of German shells rained down on the position, which inevitably forced the last remaining gun back over the river. The whole premise of the German attack had been based on the crucial elements of speed and surprise. The "surprise" was complete, but the "speed" was in danger of dissipating.

MANFRED TOON THORN, 1ST SS-PANZER DIVISION
"LEIBSTANDARTE SS ADOLF HITLER"

On 17 December 1944, we participated in the Ardennes Offensive. When people read about the experiences of a tank regiment they rarely imagine themselves inside a tank actually driving it. They either do not know or cannot imagine how the war looks through a 25cm-square window. That is how it is for a "tankie" when he drives to the front, however, and that's how it was on 16 December 1944. In the very early hours of the morning, in accordance with our orders, we left the Schmidtheim Wald to advance to Losheim.

Our convoy made a short pause just before reaching Losheim before moving on again. We were not in "Breitkeil" formation (an inverted wedge formation) and so we did not need to concentrate as hard, just follow the tank in front. It was at Honsfeld that we met some weak resistance that broke the uneventful routine a little.

It was just before Büllingen that we spotted a small airfield on the left hand side of the road. I did not know at the time, but this was one of two in the possession of the Americans. It was manned by the US 2nd Infantry Division. The other one was out of view behind the hills and manned by the US 99th Infantry Division (called The Battle Babies) and from this airfield all of the planes but one got safely away. We could clearly see two planes ready to take off. We destroyed one before it could take off, but the other flew away.

About 15 minutes later, and after a fork in the road, my path was blocked by a tank that I thought had hit a mine. It had been destroyed by a bazooka. Once in Büllingen, we had the chance to refuel at the American petrol dump, at their cost, which was situated near the road to Bütgenbach. This was rudely interrupted by heavy artillery fire coming from Elsenborn, so we made our way once more to Morschheck where we had a break.

During the previous October we had been re-fitted with tanks, men, and provisions in Geber near Siegburg. One of the new men was Unterscharführer *(junior squad leader) Horst Pilarcek. He was two ranks higher than I was, and had not come from a tank unit. Even though he wasn't an officer they made him our tank commander.*

From Morschheck we advanced through Schoppen, Ondenval, and Thirimont. We were the second tank in the vorhut *(advance guard) of the* spitze *(spearhead) in Preuss's* Panzer-Grenadier Regiment 2. *At the church in Thirimont, we turned left to take a route over the fields to gain time, which was a sad mistake. Up until this point we'd had snow, which had thawed and turned to rain. It was no surprise when the lead tank sank in the quagmire and damaged its tracks. On the regimental commander's orders we returned to Thirimont to advance through Bagatelle as the lead tank.*

On the Thirimont-Bagatelle road at about 800 to 900 meters Pilarcek saw an American column moving over the Baugnez crossing on the parallel road in the direction of Baugnez/Engelsdorf. Suddenly I heard my name as Pilarcek said. "Manfred, what should we do? I don't have any experience with these situations." He couldn't provide any clear instructions and so I assumed the jobs of driver and commander until this action was over. It was a unique situation. Pilarcek earned my respect that day like no other in my time as a soldier because he was honest, honest enough to reveal his inadequacy in the situation. He was willing to ask for help and even hand over his command. This would not have happened with a real officer and it is something that I have never forgotten.

I gave the "Fire" order to the gunner and we destroyed the first two vehicles of the moving column. The front of the column had already passed the crossing, and trucks coming up from behind crashed into the damaged vehicles. I could see no other damaged vehicles behind the trees and bushes from this distance, but I knew they were there. When we reached the crossing a few minutes later, we saw a scene of chaos. Then Commander Potchke from the lst Battalion gave us the order to follow Sternebeck, who was already on his way to Engelsdorf (Ligneuville). We realized that he was ahead of us by about ten minutes. We hadn't seen him. He had also attacked the convoy but had received orders to advance to Engelsdorf as quickly as possible. After the attack, the Americans could have re-assembled and boarded their vehicles with their weapons. We drove on to Engelsdorf without delay. Later in Lutrebois, Pilarcek became ill with cartilage problems and for the rest of my service as a soldier I never saw him again. In Lutrebois we took 150 prisoners of war, including a medical orderly, and sent them to the rear to the volksgrenadier division. This was standard practice for a tank unit. I never saw these prisoners again. Then due to brake failure, my tank had to be repaired in Rodt near St.Vith. As I arrived there I was informed that my father had died and that I had been given leave. I was asked where I had been, and at the same time, I was informed that the EKII (Iron Cross 2nd Class) was waiting for me along with a new promotion to corporal, which took place before I left the woods on 5 January 1945. The EKII was awarded upon my return to our base at Espelkamp, near Rhaden, in northern Germany.[12] [N.B.: In a telephone conversation with author Martin King, Manfred Toon Thorn denied ever having been at Baugnez.]

Peiper had almost circumnavigated the valley of the Amblève River to the south when he headed for Engelsdorf (Ligneuville) earlier on 17 December, but now he was precisely where he didn't want to be, down in the valley. Apart from the danger of losing the momentum he was now going to be confronted by elements of the 30th Division. Peiper's situation didn't look too promising because at the western end of the valley the small village of Werbomont had been marked as the disembarkation point for the 82nd Airborne Division that, like the 30th Division, had been rushed from their reserve position to take the fight right to the *SS*.

By the time that the 117th Infantry Regiment was heading south through Eupen and Spa, they encountered columns of US vehicles moving in the opposite direction. General Bradley, meanwhile, had given orders to move First Army's headquarters south to Luxembourg. Bradley now fully comprehended that this was no minor enemy incursion; it was an all-out counterattack by a determined enemy. Down in Luxembourg Bradley would be in closer proximity to Patton's Third Army and he understood well that when push came to shove Patton would never evade a potential fight.

105th Medical Battalion, 30th Infantry Division, After Action Report, December 1944

On 17 December 1944 at 1200 we were notified that the Nazis had broken through the line between the V and VIII Corps. We were told to be ready to move in 6 hours. At 1650 the division moved out. Each collecting company of the battalion moved with its combat team. The 1st Platoon of the clearing station, Bn. Hq., and the medical supply section of Hq. Det. moved out at 1940 following CT 119. Midnight found the battalion disposed approximately as follows: Company B had proceeded to Malmédy in support of CT 117, which had been ordered to seize and hold the town. The rest of the battalion was still enroute, with Company A bivouacked for the night at Eynatten, Belgium; Company C also at Eynatten; Bn. Hq., 1st Plat. of Clr. Station and Med. Supply Section of Hq. Det. in Germany just north of the Belgian-German border near Hauset, Belgium. The collecting companies were ordered to evacuate casualties to the nearest Evac. Hospital direct. These hospitals were located in Eupen and Verviers, Belgium.

On 18 December 1944 Company A moved down to vicinity of Aywaille, Belgium, in support of CT 119, which was fighting north of Stoumont. Co. B remained in Malmédy. Co. C moved to north of Malmédy. Bn. Hq., 1st

Platoon Clr. Station, Med. Supply Section of Hq. Det. moved to Francor-champs, Belgium. The collecting companies evacuated 27 patients direct to Evac. Hospitals on 17 and 18 December. The 30th Div. was transferred from XIX Corps, Ninth Army, to V Corps, First Army.

On 19 December 1944 normal evacuation through the clearing station was resumed. CT 120 took over Malmédy and CT 117 shift to La Gleize-Stavelot sector. Collection Co B moved to vicinity of Francorchamps, Belgium, to support the new disposition of troops. Meanwhile Bn. Hq., 1st Plat. of clearing station and med. supply section of Hq. Det. moved to Spa, Belgium, a position more centrally located for the 3 collecting companies. By this time a definite line had been established in the division's zone and it was holding well.

On 20 December 1944 Company C moved to site of 67 Evac. Hospital in Malmédy, Belgium, and the remainder of Bn. Hq. and Hq. Det. which had been left behind at Kohlschied, Germany, moved down to Spa, Belgium.

On 21 December 1944 counterattacks against the 120th and 117th were repulsed. Co. C, which had been in the path of one of the counterattacks, withdrew to its previous location north of Malmédy, Belgium. Since its ambulance route had been cut by the counterattack it was necessary to evacuate 27 patients direct to an evac hospital in Eupen during the night. The 30th Division was relieved from V Corps and assigned to XVIII Corps.[13]

By early morning 18 December, the 117th Infantry Regiment had reached their assembly area at Malmédy as ordered by Brigadier General Harrison. This ancient Ardennes town still has a twin-spired church at its center and is surrounded by steep, wooded hills on three sides. At the time the 117th arrived, most of the German troops had absconded, and the remaining inhabitants were living in their cellars below the town.

MARION SANFORD, 30TH CAVALRY RECONNAISSANCE TROOP (MECHANIZED)

It was snowing hard outside when Sergeant Stuart came in and picked out four of us to go man an outpost on top of a large hill a little bit down the road. Word had come down that tanks were headed our way. We carried a bazooka and .30-caliber machine gun up to the hill and tried to dig foxholes, but the ground was getting hard from the frost and we didn't get them very deep. As the morning wore on, it was snowing like nobody's business.

We had not been given any real cold weather gear and were having to rely on what we had been issued after the shower outside Mortain back during the summer. We were wearing every article of clothing we could get our hands on, which for me was long and short underwear; a cotton shirt and trousers under a wool shirt and trousers; and boots with wool and cotton socks. On top of all that, I was wearing high-bib tanker pants and the tanker jacket. Under my helmet, I was wearing a wool beanie hat, which we always wore in cold weather. I had wool gloves that I wore under a pair of leather gloves. I had to take off the leather gloves to fire my weapon, though.

Even wearing all that, I was about to freeze to death, exposed like we were out on that hill. Later in the afternoon I went back to the barn to find Sergeant Stuart. I told him that I didn't think that there was any way that tanks could get to the hill and then up it. In the first place, it was too wooded at the base of the hill and there was no road through it. Also, as hard as it was snowing, I didn't think that any infantry could climb the hill to support the tanks. I also told him that we were freezing to death and I worried that we were going to get frostbite.

Sergeant Stuart listened to me, decided that I was right, and ordered us down to an old house that was nearby. It had a large fireplace and he let us build a fire in it, since it was getting dark and the smoke would not show. We wrapped ourselves in blankets and huddled around the fire trying to get warm. We were listening to military traffic on the radio and the BBC, so we knew that the "balloon had gone up." We didn't know the name of it yet, but the Battle of the Bulge had started and we were in for a serious fight.

We moved around a good bit over the next few days but never were sure exactly where we were, other than we were in Belgium, near the town of Malmédy. We spent a great deal of time manning roadblocks, wondering when the Germans were going to appear around the distant curve. There were also rumors that Germans were roving around in the rear areas dressed as Americans and were causing all manner of havoc. I don't know how much of that was true, but very few soldiers were taking any chances with someone they didn't know. It became overly important to know the daily passwords when traveling and sometimes that still was not enough. It became common to pepper traveling soldiers with such questions as who was dating who in Hollywood or what was going on with various baseball players.[14]

A few miles northwest of Malmédy, on the road to Francorchamps, was the location of Depot Number 3, a huge Allied fuel dump that contained

997,730 gallons of gasoline—more than enough to get the attacking German tanks all the way to Antwerp. It was only being guarded by a handful of poorly-equipped Belgian soldiers. The 117th Infantry Regiment immediately got to work setting up roadblocks and preparing to meet the *SS*; while 3rd Battalion of the 117th set up those roadblocks, 1st Battalion of the 117th moved past the fuel dump in Francorchamps and disembarked a few miles north of Stavelot, roughly five miles southwest of Malmédy.

At Stavelot, in their haste to get into the fight, 1st Battalion didn't wait for the artillery to set up and consequently had to retreat after being overwhelmed by *SS* armor streaming through the town. At this stage of the attack Peiper still had his massive King Tiger IIs on point, but that would change as he progressed toward the Meuse River, which is situated 42 miles west of Stavelot. Some of his tanks ventured north to see if there was a more accessible route than having to traverse the base of the Amblève valley. They were stopped dead when Major Paul J. Solis of the 526th Armored Infantry Battalion seized some of the gasoline from the Francorchamps dump and got his men to pour it in a deep groove in the road before igniting it. The result was a blazing wall of flame that made a perfect anti-tank barrier, promptly causing the German tanks to do an about turn and return to Stavelot. This operation used 124,000 gallons of gas and it was the closest that *Kampfgruppe Peiper* came to discovering the great stores of gas that definitely would have fueled his drive to the west.

For the next job, the 117th Infantry's 2nd Battalion was reinforced by the 291st Engineer Combat Battalion. They dug in along the embankment of the railroad that ran between Malmédy and Stavelot before setting demolition charges on the viaducts that converged just outside Stavelot and laying minefields on the approach roads there. All the footbridges that crossed the Amblève River in that sector had already been blown. The town itself became a harrowing battleground where men of the 1st Battalion of the 117th dodged between exploding masonry to avoid being blown to pieces by the German tanks that were holding out there. The town square became a no-man's-land littered with dead and dying soldiers from both sides. During the afternoon of 18 December, 16 P-47 fighter-bombers flew under the low clouds to strafe Peiper's column as it headed west. His situation was further exacerbated when, due to the high hills in that region, the column experienced loss of radio contact with other units of the *1st SS-Panzer Division*. Peiper also assumed at this juncture in the battle that the German *3rd Para-*

chute Division, consisting of *Parachute Regiments 5, 8, and 9,* was in close proximity to his unit when in fact, they were still a few miles to the east confined to the hills around Malmédy.

As a precursor to the actual attack, the drop zone of Lieutenant Colonel Friedrich August *Freiherr* von der Heydte's *Kampfgruppe* had been set 11km north of Malmédy, with the main objective being a cross-road junction there. The assault had commenced with 112 Junkers-52 troop carriers that also carried 300 straw dummies to be dropped as decoys. Due to the poor visibility and low clouds only 10 aircraft actually made it to the drop zone. Some paratroopers landed 50 miles behind German lines and some were even reported to have landed in Holland. Only 125 made it to the actual drop zone, which was roughly one-tenth of the original force.

While a battalion of *SS* remained in Stavelot to protect Peiper's supply route, he headed west toward the town of Trois Ponts ("three bridges").... Well, it had three bridges before Company C, 51st Engineer Combat Battalion arrived there, then it didn't have any bridges after the engineers blew them up to block Peiper's advance.

Farther west, at a roadblock near the hamlet of Neufmoulin, Pfc. Mason Armstrong, an expert bazooka man from Company F, 119th Infantry Regiment, peered into the gloom from the upstairs window of a roadside house. Three German half-tracks carrying soldiers from *SS-Panzer-Grenadier Regiment 2* approached the roadblock in the dark. As they turned the sharp corner, 40 yards from the roadblock the lead vehicle turned on its lights. Mason Armstrong had positioned himself well, with a machine gunner on the second floor. From this vantage point he managed to fire three shots as a group of three half-tracks full of German infantry began to ascend the hill. The machine gunner who gave Armstrong cover was killed after one of the half-tracks fired at the house. Armstrong survived and managed to take out two of the half-tracks and disable the third. Armstrong's action helped prevent one of the *SS* spearheads from advancing, and once again, another part of the German thrust was stopped by a small group of well trained, courageous soldiers with initiative who took the fight to the enemy.

To the Family of the Late Mason H. Armstrong:
I have just received word from Mr. Frank Towers, Secretary-Treasurer of the 30th Infantry Division Association, that your beloved Mason H. Armstrong of Altoona, Alabama, passed away last May 2000.

I do not have any specific family names in my possession so I have addressed this letter to his family.

Our F Company records show that Mason joined our company of the 2nd Battalion, 119th Regt., 30th Division in October 1944 as an expert bazooka man. I had just taken command of F-119th because our valiant Captain Melvin Riesch had been killed in action. I was the only officer left in the company. I assigned Mason to 2nd Lieutenant Ken Austin's 3rd Platoon. In mid-December 1944, the entire 30th Division was trucked from its "on-line" position in Germany on the Ruhr River to help contain a German counteroffensive in the Ardennes Mountains of Belgium. The six weeks battle that followed became known as the famous "Battle of the Bulge."

On December 18, 1944, our F Company came to a tiny community known then and now as Neufmoulin. It was comprised of three or four houses where Lienne Creek joins the Grandmont Rivulet. I sent Austin's platoon on ahead where he finally set up a roadblock and awaited the enemy. The darkness of night was upon us.

We didn't have long to wait. The Germans came crashing down the highway that leads into Neufmoulin from the east and ran right into Austin's men along the road and in the few houses of the hamlet.

By this time Mason had managed to reach the second floor of one of the homes (now called the Lambotte House) and managed to fire his bazooka from a second-floor widow. He got off three shots, knocking out two armored half-tracks and crippling another. We stopped the enemy and turned him away right there in Neufmoulin and Mason's heroics helped far beyond the call of duty. As his commanding officer, I recommended the Distinguished Service Cross be awarded to Mason for his gallantry in action. The enclosed papers will indicate that he received the award after the war was over. This is the second highest award in the Nation's recognitions of bravery in action.

I want all of the members of Mason's family to know that Mason H. Armstrong proved to be an excellent combat soldier. Again, I submit my deepest sympathy to all of you. You have lost a loved one and I have lost a cherished friendship and one of our Nation's finest soldiers.

May God Bless all of you.

Edward C. Arn, Captain U. S Army (Retired)

P.S. I am 92 years old. I do hope you'll forgive my typing mistakes.[15]

Major General Hobbs now personally directed the 119th Infantry Regiment on their way south to meet their old antagonists, the *1st SS-Panzer Division*. The 2nd Battalion of the 119th went as far west as the town of Aywaille before reaching Werbomont. After carefully studying reconnaissance of the area, it was determined that the *I SS-Panzer Corps* was operating with the *1st* and *12th SS-Panzer Divisions* in the vicinity of Malmédy and St. Vith. The 120th Infantry Regiment had taken over the defense of Malmédy from the 3rd Battalion, 117th Infantry. At that particular time the 117th was urgently needed farther west where the fight was intensifying by the hour. Stavelot, meanwhile, had become a town divided between east and west, with US and German forces both fighting hard to extend their grasp. They were becoming embroiled in a savage house-to-house, street-to-street battle for supremacy where every shot and every grenade counted. This close proximity struggle frequently degenerated into frantic hand-to-hand combat that tested the mettle of both sides to the utmost.

Firing from the steep slope at the north side of the town, a platoon of 3-inch towed tank destroyers from the 823rd Tank Destroyer Battalion had made good use of this vantage point to effectively disable some Mark VI tanks and a few half-tracks. Just before nightfall, two American companies were effectively holding half of the town and had contacted the 117th Infantry Regiment's 2nd Battalion, who were between Stavelot and Malmédy, and had been reinforced by a tank platoon from the 743rd Tank Battalion. Artillery support was also on hand because the 118th Field Artillery Battalion had pressed forward under fire to establish a position northeast of the town.

HANK STAIRS, HEADQUARTERS COMPANY, 117TH INFANTRY REGIMENT

I was with Lieutenant Colonel Robert E. Franklin when we, 1st Battalion, 117th Infantry de-trucked at the top of the hill leading into Stavelot. Remnants, as I recall perhaps 30 men from the 526th Armored Infantry Battalion, were at roadside as we arrived. With a rifle company deployed on each side of the road we attacked down the hill. Company C, in reserve, Heavy Weapons Company, along with Battalion Headquarters Company, walked the narrow road passing thou-

sands of burned, bloated gas cans. The dump was still hot and smoldering, Sunday, 18 December 1944. Fast forward. Our battalion captured the town and controlled the Stavelot bridge, cutting off Peiper's supply line. The Battle of the Bulge continued.

Lieutenant Murray sent word to the front to "shoot anything that moves." The rest of the evening was spent with little interruption. Next morning the attack was renewed, the battalion's mission being to push forward a couple of hundred yards and set up a defense on the Amblève River, which flowed north-south across the eastern part of Stavelot. All Germans had withdrawn from the main part of town during the night, so A and B Companies reached the river with little difficulty by 1000 hours. A single bridge crossed the Amblève. The point platoons of A and B had hardly begun preparing holding positions near the bridge before the enemy made another of its daring but foolish attempts. Five American jeeps, again filled with Germans in GI uniforms, suddenly appeared and made a wild dash across the bridge. Our soldiers didn't have to think twice this time. They promptly opened up, knocking out every jeep and killing most of the occupants. Only one of the vehicles had managed to reach the friendly side of the river. The tactical situation quieted down. Company B fanned out to the left portion of Stavelot, while Company A, very much stretched out, did likewise on the right. Company C, in reserve; Company D's mortars; and Battalion Headquarters all remained on top of the hill overlooking Stavelot.

I recall another memory while in Stavelot. We were still short of the river looking across "no-man's-land" for about half a mile. There were puffs of smoke from artillery on the hillside across the river. Then, much to our surprise, a German plane came out at rooftop height right up the river. When it got to our immediate front he made a slow roll over and the pilot fell out and the plane just kept on going. Then, a guy on my right said to one of the other guys, "A Company will have his flight suit off of him before he hits the ground!" The comment was fitting and comical because that wasn't A Company's area, it was B Company's. That tells you a bit about A Company! [16]

Farther west, the 30th Division's attack was gathering momentum, supported by IX and XXIX Tactical Air Commands, who had joined the fight and were proving their worth. Planes from the 365th Fighter Group, reinforced by the 390th Squadron (366th) and the 506th Squadron (404th), swooped down on German armor wherever they could find it. They even made it over to Stavelot where they tipped the balance in favor of the US forces there. This wasn't entirely the old pattern of air superiority repeating itself like it had in Normandy because the ground troops still had to deal with the lion's share of the fighting on the ground.

By dawn 19 December, the 30th Division's line extended over 17 miles and there was almost constant fighting along each mile of the front. The *SS* were as determined to reach the river Meuse as the 30th Division was to prevent them from doing precisely that. Due to the unfavorable terrain *Kampfgruppe Peiper* was severely restricted in their ability to maneuver effectively enough to deploy their superior tanks. Those hills and trees were causing increasing claustrophobia for the *SS* column as 30th Division units and 82nd Airborne Division effectively occupied the high ground and lobbed mortar and bazooka shells onto the winding trails at the base of the valley. After a while, Peiper began to regard his magnificent King Tiger II tanks as an encumbrance and consequently placed them all to the rear of his column as he slogged doggedly forward, encountering the growing resistance now along his route to the Meuse River. He was becoming so exasperated by the US engineers blowing every bridge in his path that he was even seen beating the hood of a half-track with the rifle butt of an MP40. It has been suggested that after four years of almost constant combat, Peiper was beginning to display emphatic signs of conditions that can only be described as post-traumatic stress disorder. The odds against him were increasing, but for the time being that didn't nullify his fighting spirit.

Horrendous freezing weather conditions didn't help the situation for either side as temperatures plummeted and blizzards began to blow through the Ardennes, forming snow drifts deep enough to cover a man.

MARION SANFORD, 30TH CAVALRY RECONNAISSANCE TROOP (MECHANIZED)

In Belgium, we began to see a problem that we had not expected. Snow would pile up on the armored cars when they were parked. Later on, the crew would get in, crank it up and drive off. The snow on the rear deck would then melt and drip through vents and into the engine compartment. The water would eventually seep into the distributor cap and cause the engine to spit and sputter before dying. We told the crews to sweep off the rear deck before moving, but they often forgot, so as a result, we had to spend a lot of time drying or changing distributor caps that December.

We were working on an armored car one afternoon when we heard a V–1 Rocket (buzz bomb) heading our way. I didn't like those things at all. They had an engine out the back end that looked like a long syrup bucket and they sounded like a lawn mower to me as they flew along. The Germans launched the rocket toward a target and set the engine to cut off after it had flown a certain amount of time estimated for the rocket to reach the target. Without the engine running, it would drop like a rock and make a huge explosion that could bring down large buildings.

We had been seeing the buzz bombs fly over us since September and were not too worried about them because they were not accurate at all. As long as the engine was running on the thing, we didn't have to worry about it landing on top of us. They were really more of a terror weapon than anything else. Anyway, we heard a buzz bomb coming directly at us and then its engine cut off before we could see it. We started to scatter, but it was still hidden by hills and trees so we didn't know exactly where it was, and really didn't know which way to run. When it finally came silently over, we looked up and saw it glide by about 200 feet in the air directly above us. It sailed on by and blew up when it hit the side of the hill about a quarter of a mile way.

It was a cold winter and we never seemed to get warm. It was dark by 1600 hours and it would not be daylight until around 0900. The nights were long and I hated them. A lot of times we were able to sleep in cellars. There wouldn't be any heat, but it was a lot better than staying outside, plus it was safer there if artillery started falling around us.

I was fortunate that I was able to ride in a half-track. It was open-topped, but was warmer than any other vehicle we had, since it had metal sides all around. The engine was in front and we could get some heat off of it as we rode along. The trucks and jeeps were miserable. There was no heater and they were all open to the elements. The guys in the armored cars had it the worst. In addition to not having a heater, the engine was in the back, so the heat could not get to them as they drove. Sometimes when we felt we were in a safe area and it was not snowing, we'd sleep on the hood if the engine had been running recently.[17]

JOHN NOLAN, COMPANY G, 119TH INFANTRY REGIMENT

The conditions during the Bulge can be described in one word, miserable! I can't be more descriptive or succinct than that. During the Bulge each man in the platoon had "piled" on enough clothes to keep warm, especially when on the march. When we were able we carried blanket-like sleeping bags that had a full-length zipper. We had excellent gloves, a wool inner glove, with an outer leather shell. No one froze to death. The cold, coupled with the snow, slowed us down greatly. So did our footwear, which was four buckle galoshes over GI shoes and leggings, plus the weight of our weapons, ammunition, gas mask, and other gear that was in the pack on our backs. The Jerries, since they had fought in Russian winters, were better equipped and clothed.[18]

In addition to the miserable weather conditions, the GIs began to hear about another potential menace. Rumors abounded that there were German *SS* troops wearing American uniforms and, according to reports, they were all over the Ardennes. This was a major exaggeration, but there were indeed some German troops who were thus attired. They were known as members of the *Panzer Brigade 150* (or *Brandenburger Brigade*) and had approximately 2000 men in the unit. It was claimed that 150 of these men could speak perfect English. Sometime after the war, Lieutenant Colonel Otto Skorzeny described their mission, called Operation GRIEFF (Griffon), as an unmitigated disaster. He added that most of this specially chosen 150 were incapable of putting three English words together in a sentence. Skorzeny simply hadn't had the time to train them up to his high standard. They used captured Allied equipment (particularly tanks and jeeps), uniforms, identification papers, that had been hurriedly accumulated at the front and sent to Skorzeny's headquarters. Although he was personally very dismissive of the effectiveness of these troops, the psychological effect on the Allies was quite profound. Skorzeny was known as "Hitler's Assassin" and had indeed been quite successful in the past. He had rescued Mussolini from the Italians, conducted various clandestine operations, and when the Hungarian Regent, Admiral Miklós von Nagybánya Horthy, began to show signs of questionable loyalty by declaring an end to the war, Skorzeny was dispatched to Budapest to kidnap Horthy's son. As a direct result of this, Horthy was forced to revoke his declarations and abdicate.

There was no doubt that Skorzeny was a dangerous adversary, but by the time he got to the Ardennes those days were over. Disguised jeep parties did go into action with varying degrees of success on 16 December, but the *Brandenburger Brigade* would be engaged as a unit only in a single and abortive skirmish near Malmédy five days later. One particular bazooka man took the initiative on one occasion to fire a direct hit at a jeep carrying four GIs. It was a gamble that worked because all the jeeps occupants were indeed Germans wearing GI uniforms. The bazooka man had taken the shot purely on the premise that regulations restricted the number of passengers to two, and that jeep, driver included was carrying four which, in his opinion made it a justifiable target.

KING KENNY, RECONNAISSANCE PLATOON, 823RD TANK DESTROYER BATTALION

We were off the line cleaning our weapons when someone on a motorcycle said, "You gotta get going right away." We loaded up—likewise, the whole division was loading up—to head south to the Malmédy area. It was night and the Germans were dropping paratroopers in. When we got into Malmédy we made our headquarters in a large factory. There were a lot of civilians in there, too, but not near us. Our lieutenant ordered us to go out and to try to make contact up by the railroad tracks. We took 5–6 guys to do that and could hear tanks—nothing awakens you more than the screech of tank tracks. We reported back that the Germans were on the other side of the railroad tracks. Our next mission was to go check the woods to make sure there was no enemy close by. The lieutenant said, "We're not sure that there are not some enemy paratroopers in there." So we moved out on foot to the woods. I said, "There are some guys up there." So we spread out into a skirmish line so we could surround them. There were three guys standing there talking. One guy had a US officer's uniform on, a dress uniform mind you, which was a giveaway. The other guys had GI uniforms on, just the ODs. We captured them and two others surrendered to us. We weren't sure what to do with them. One of our guys said, "I'll take care of the officer." He got him by the scruff of the neck, pushed him ahead and the next thing I heard was BOOM! He killed him! The other Germans were standing just shaking in their boots. We told the lieutenant that we had some prisoners and someone needed to take them back.[19]

Once again, the 30th Division was staggered with supply problems, but on this occasion they had made contingency plans to deal with it. A column of trucks belonging to the 117th Infantry Regiment's Service Company was dispatched to a supply depot from where it returned laden with artillery, mortar shells, and bullets. It had been accurately determined already that *Kampfgruppe Peiper's* target was probably Liege where massive stores for the First and Ninth Armies were located. The best roads to reach this objective were along the *Hohes Venn* (high fens) north of Malmédy, where the terrain was more suitable for the movement of massed tank and troop formations. Unfortunately, fierce defense at the twin villages of Krinkelt and Rochrath from the 99th Infantry Division, and tenacious resistance on the Elsenborn Ridge held by the 2nd Infantry Division had forced the *SS* to concede the initiative and become funneled into the Amblève River valley area.

This left Peiper with only one viable route to the Meuse River and that was via Stoumont, Remouchamps, and Aywaille. If he could break the resistance there, he would reach the main north road to Liege. Peiper was fully aware that time was of the essence now as he acknowledged another pressing problem: fuel. The German tanks and vehicles consumed a lot of gas and it was becoming almost untenable to keep refueling them every few miles. He'd been fortunate enough to capture a US fuel dump at Büllingen, but that was 25 miles away from his current location. As the freezing fog descended on the Ardennes reducing visibility to a few yards, the *SS* were heading for a show-down with US forces at Stoumont.

Very early on the morning of 19 December, while the 119th Infantry Regiment less one battalion had started positioning itself on a few hills situated on the north bank of the Amblève River, a few miles east of this position Peiper was gathering his forces in and around the small village of La Gleize. After studying maps of the area he made his move. Two platoons of the 743rd Tank Battalion had just maneuvered into position at the eastern edge of Stoumont around the village of Targnon, when *Kampfgruppe Peiper* lashed out with an all-out infantry attack, supported from the east with tanks blazing away and doubling up as assault guns.

The terrain between La Gleize and Stoumont opens into some low-rolling plains at the base of the Amblève River valley that made these limited maneuvers possible, but unfortunately, the weather was still bad and fog still restricted visibility to around 30 yards. In an attempt to counteract Peiper's moves, ten tanks from the 743rd Tank Battalion responded immediately to the attack and went into action. After a while they were running short of ammunition, but not before they had effectively knocked out six Mark IV tanks and incapacitated three Mark V's.

Approximately 100 GIs were captured as the roadblock to the west of Stoumont began to falter against this fierce *SS* onslaught. Despite encountering stubborn resistance, it took *Kampfgruppe Peiper* about two hours to successfully enter and occupy Stoumont. The ferocity and determination of this attack on the US forces, which were lacking effective and vital artillery support, caused them to pull back from the town. Their tactical retreat was covered by the 1st Battalion, 119th Infantry Regiment who subsequently exposed the possibility of a new threat.[20]

DONALD STRAND, COMPANY D, 119TH INFANTRY REGIMENT

Very heavy fog continued and the previous night, the Luftwaffe was dropping supplies in our midst, thinking it was German-held ground. This day (19 December) we received tank support from the US 740th Tank Battalion; but with tanks that were back for repairs at Sprimont that had no sights, we set them up on road-blocks, one of which was the curve in the road where we had dug in along the railroad tracks.

I was given a mission about 1100 hours that day to go on a reconnaissance toward La Gleize to find our line of the 3rd Battalion of the 119th Regiment. I ran into a group of GIs pulling back and talked to an officer who I knew real well, and all I found out was utter confusion. Later, I found out that over 100 GIs were captured that day from the 3rd Battalion and I came back and reported this to my battalion commander. Our decision then was to stay in our dug-in positions and wait for the Germans to attack us.

Around 1500 on 19 December, we could hear German tanks ahead of us coming down the road toward our position. As I said previously we were dug in on the curve in the road with our tank supports and waited. When the Panther tanks came around the curve in sight of us, our tanks cut loose at them; without any sights on the tanks, their aim was off—the shells hit the cobblestone road and ricocheted up under the belly of the tanks where their armor was thin and exploded the tanks. These young inexperienced tankers of ours fired four shells and knocked out three Panther tanks. Later on, this proved to be the furthest advance that the Germans made in the Battle of the Bulge.[21]

Once Peiper had taken Stoumont, he opened the option to turn north on a small road that led over the ridge in the direction of Verviers. This would bring the *SS* to the rear of the US forces. The potential threat was detected and dealt with by 80 GIs from the 3rd Battalion, 119th Infantry Regiment, commanded by Captain Carleton E. Stewart. Supported by two 90mm AA guns and a tank destroyer, they were sent to block this potential route of advance. So far, the *SS* had inflicted serious losses on the 3rd Battalion, which had been forced to abandon most of its equipment, at the cost of 267 officers and men.

The fuel depot on the road to Francorchamps had been saved thanks to some quick thinking and an almighty puddle of burning gasoline that dissuaded the *SS* from attempting to take it, but that wasn't the only fuel dump in the vicinity. It was at this juncture that Peiper missed yet another badly needed opportunity to refuel at another Allied depot situated beside the hamlet of Bourgomont just one mile north of La Gleize. As a small German convoy of two armored cars, two tanks, and two *Jagdpanthers* packing 88mm guns approached to within 500 yards of the depot, a fierce firefight ensued. The front of the depot was protected by a minefield that prevented the convoy from closing in on their target. After about 20 minutes of fierce fighting, the German tanks withdrew under a hail of fire from four .50-caliber machine guns and two 90mm AA guns.

It was now high time to address the imbalance and bring in those much needed reserves. On 20 December, Brigadier General Truman E. Boudinot of Combat Command B of the 3rd Armored Division organized three task forces to go immediately to the assistance of the 30th Division. The largest of these was Task Force Lovelady, led by Lieutenant Colonel William B. Lovelady, which was organized around the 2nd Battalion, 33rd Armored Regiment and attached units. The other task forces of Combat Command B were Task Force McGeorge (Major K. T. McGeorge) and Task Force Jordan (Captain John W. Jordan).

Task Force McGeorge was designated to drive south from La Reid, attack La Gleize, and pass through elements of the 30th Division. Task Force Jordan would take Stoumont while the primary objective was handed to the largest of the three task forces, Task Force Lovelady was to clear the road from La Gleize to Stoumont while Task Force Jordan would take the town and then turn east to join Task Force McGeorge in La Gleize.

As they moved into position on 20 December, Task Force Jordan's column didn't encounter any opposition until they were just north of Stoumont where they inadvertently stumbled upon *SS* tanks and anti-tank guns, which effectively halted their advance. Although US engineers had blown most of the much-needed bridges along the Amblève River, including the main one at Stavelot there was still a hole in the US line. A German engineer unit had reinforced a small footbridge just east of Trois Ponts; since the night of 18 December supply trucks and reinforcements had been using this bridge to supply much-needed gasoline to *Kampfgruppe Peiper*, but the amount was insufficient to enable the latter to make any concerted drive westward. In an effort to effectively cauterize *Kampfgruppe Peiper*'s supply line to Stoumont, Task Force Lovelady set about establishing three roadblocks along the main road between Trois Ponts and La Gleize. Just as the column was making the turn south toward Trois Ponts, however, a small German column of artillery, infantry, and supply trucks appeared. They were on their way to reinforce *Kampfgruppe Peiper*'s main thrust. Task Force Lovelady pounced on the column immediately and forced them to scatter before continuing on to complete the initial mission to establish the roadblocks. The net around *Kampfgruppe Peiper* was now falling into place and gradually tightening.

Bitter fighting in the streets of Stavelot had already dislodged *SS* forces there, but they still attempted to force inroads to retake the town that re-mained vital to their supply route. The *SS* even went as far as wading through the icy waters of the Amblève a few yards south of the destroyed bridge where the riverbank wasn't as steep as it was in Stavelot. Company A of the 117th Infantry Regiment responded by firing a fusillade of artillery and mortar shells at the Germans who resisted stoically and even managed to occupy a few houses in the south of Stavelot. It was becoming clear that, in a vain effort to protect their supply route, the Germans hadn't left sufficient troops in place to protect the bridge. Most of the bridges on *Kampfgruppe Peiper's* intended route had been blown, so it was now imperative for them to recap-ture Stavelot in order to supply the forces that were north of the Amblève River in the vicinity of Stoumont, and to protect an escape route if it was needed. During the afternoon of 19 December, the *SS* launched two coun-terattacks to recapture Stavelot and on 20 December, they orchestrated three further assaults, but none of these efforts achieved the desired results. For the US troops there, it would take a further two days of sustained combat to completely eradicate the German threat to Stavelot.

RUDOLF VON RIBBENTROP, 1ST SS-PANZER DIVISION "LEIBSTANDARTE SS ADOLF HITLER" AND 12TH SS-PANZER DIVISION "HITLERJUGEND"

The Battle of the Bulge was an irresponsible gamble, in my opinion. The Amer-icans were preparing for an offensive from Aachen to the Rhine and were pound-ing us hard with their artillery. Every artillery barrage that preceded this one paled into comparative insignificance. Heinrich Himmler had been ordered to return from his vacation because of the Ardennes offensive.

A few days into the Battle of the Bulge I recall talking to a tank commander who was irresponsibly standing in full view on the back of his tank. "Get inside your tank, you're causing a draft," I yelled at him. I was almost inside and as he prepared to climb in a shell exploded right behind us. He hadn't even closed the hatch when this happened. Thankfully it didn't do much harm to me but if it would have hit just a few moments earlier it would have reduced me to mince-meat. Either way I was hit in my mouth by a small fragment of shrapnel, a very unpleasant and painful wound I can assure you. The tank commander, a good friend of mine who was due to be married, was killed outright. [22]

Rumors abounded that the *SS* were massacring civilians as they pushed west. When American soldiers occupied the western perimeter of Stavelot and entered the villages of Ster, Renardmont and Parfondruy, they discovered gruesome confirmation that the German troops, who had occupied these places, had indiscriminately murdered innocent civilians. In the homes and outlying buildings of these localities, the GIs saw the irrefutable evidence of these atrocities with their own eyes. They counted the dead bodies of 117 men, women, and children, all killed by small arms fire.

Task Force Jordan, attached to the 119th Infantry Regiment, resumed the attack on Stoumont. Only meagre results were achieved until 22 December, however, when, following a heavy artillery preparation by the 391st Armored Field Artillery Battalion, a coordinated attack was launched by a battalion of the 119th, plus Company F, 36th Armored Infantry Regiment, supported by the tanks of Task Force Jordan. This attack took both Stoumont and the adjacent town of Rouat.

119th Infantry Regiment, After Action Report, 2 January 1945
18 Dec: 1340 CT 119 moved southwest by motor, following the route, 00970, EUPEN, VERVIERS, THEUX, REMOUCHAUMPS, to positions in vicinity of STOUMONT, and WERBOMONT, BELGIUM, closing at 2100. The 2d Battalion, attached one platoon of self-propelled tank destroyers; one platoon of medium tanks, which did not arrive until 19 December 1944; and one platoon of Anti-Tank Company; and with Cannon Company in direct support, occupied a defensive line east of WERBOMONT. Roadblocks were established on all roads leading into the sector. Company F, on the right, received enemy small arms and tank fire from vicinity of VEUGY. The bridge at 569935 had been blown earlier in the day by friendly troops. Contact was made with the 82d Airborne Division in vicinity of WER-BOMONT. The 3d Battalion moved into Stoumont and dismounted from trucks. A defensive position was organized around the eastern edge of the town and all roads were blocked and mined. At 2130 a patrol from Company HQ reported approximately 40 enemy tanks in the vicinity of 633024. Company A minus one platoon, 823 Tank Destroyer Battalion, was attached to the battalion. The 400th Armored Field Artillery Battalion was attached to the CT and placed in direct support of the 3d Battalion, but did not get into positions until the following morning. Elements of the 110th and 143d AAA Gun Battalion were placed in positions to provide anti-tank support to the 3d Battalion and cover the roads in the vicinity of the regimental command post. The 1st Battalion, in regimental reserve, established roadblocks on all roads in the vicinity of the regimental command post (608040).

19 Dec: At 0615 an enemy attack was reported forming along road in front of Company I, just east of STOUMONT. At 0645 the enemy attack, comprised of tanks and infantry, began, and by 0715 the 3rd Battalion was being slowly pushed back and one tank destroyer had been overrun. At 0735 four tanks of Company C, 743rd Tank Battalion were sent to Company I and one battery, 400th Field Artillery was in position to give artillery support to the battalion. At 0810 an enemy Mk V tank was knocked out by friendly tank fire, but the enemy continued to force the 3d Battalion back. By 0910 Company I was back to the church in STOUMONT and still withdrawing. By 1010 the situation in the 3rd Battalion was becoming critical, all supporting tank destroyers had been overrun and. the battalion was forced from the town. At 1050 the 90mm AA guns knocked out three enemy Mk V tanks and two Mk IVs were KO'd by bazooka fire. The 740th Tank Battalion, minus, was attached to CT 119 at 1100 and sent to support the tanks of Company C, 743rd Tank Battalion, which, by this time, were almost out of ammunition and fuel. At 1210 the 3rd Battalion had fallen back through the 1st Battalion, where it was reorganized and sent to establish a roadblock on the road leading north from STOUMONT through ROUAT. The tanks with the 3rd Battalion were attached to the 1st Battalion and at 1230 four self-propelled tank destroyers and two medium tanks from the 2nd Battalion joined the 1st Battalion. By 1500 the 1st Battalion plus attachments stopped the enemy attack about 200 yards east of STOUMONT station. 80 men from the 3rd Battalion with two 90mm AA guns and one self-propelled tank destroyer were reported on the road just north of ROUAT. Later in the day this force was increased to 150 men and a platoon of medium tanks was attached to it. At 1520 CT119 was attached to the Airborne Corps. 2nd Battalion held its position until it was relieved by the 82nd Airborne at 1330. The Battalion was moved to an assembly area just east of REMOUCHAMPS. Company E was employed for protection of the regimental command post. By 1600 the enemy attack had been definitely stopped and the 3rd and 1st Battalions were organizing positions for the night as shown on overlay, this headquarters, 19–22 December 1944. Before 2000 three more enemy Mk V tanks were KO'd by our tanks.

20 Dec: 0830 the 1st Battalion, attached one company, 740th Tank Battalion and one platoon, self-propelled tank destroyers, 823rd Tank Battalion, attacked east toward STOUMONT. Five enemy minefields were encountered between 607040 and 629030. All fields were covered by automatic and anti-tank weapons. By 1720 the battalion was 500 yards east of STOUMONT, where it dug in for the night. One tank had been lost when it hit a

mine. At 1030 Task Force Jordon, Combat Command B, 3rd Armored Division, passed through the 3rd Battalion and attacked south toward STOUMONT, but was stopped 500 yards north of the town by dug-in enemy tanks. The 3rd Battalion attempts to assist the task force, but was held up by the same fire. The 2nd Battalion was moved to an assembly area just east of HALT DE LORCE. CHEVRON. A patrol was sent out and contacted Company I, 504th Parachute Infantry at 609021. A roadblock was established at this point. At 2300 approximately 100 enemy infantry attacked the chateau (628032) occupied by the 1st Battalion and by 2330 had taken all but one room of the building. This room held out until ordered to withdraw at 1545 the next day. It was used as an observation post to direct tank destroyer fire into the rooms occupied by the enemy. Brigadier General Harrison arrived at the command post at 2200 and took command of Task Force Harrison, consisting of CT 119 and Task Force Jordon, Combat Command B.[23]

For two days *1st SS-Panzer Division* made no serious attempts to capture the town of Malmédy. German patrols constantly scoured the approach roads and reported that they were all blocked. They had obviously recognized that while possession of Malmédy would give them access to the main road to Spa, it would also entail becoming embroiled in another house-to-house fight. After considering the options on the morning of 21 December, the *SS* struck Malmédy after deciding that it was a possible, but not preferred, way of securing their objectives.

On 21 December, between 0300 and 0400 hours, a company of German infantry launched a diversionary attack from the southeast, striking a roadblock of the 1st Battalion, 120th Infantry Regiment, near Montbijou, about a mile outside of Malmédy. By daybreak, the attack had been repulsed. The main attack was launched shortly after from the southwest. One column of armor and infantry advanced directly toward the town along the Route de Bellevaux, a secondary road that roughly parallels the Stavelot-Malmédy highway. A second column attacked north on a small country road that joins the Stavelot-Malmédy highway in the vicinity of the bridge of the Avenue du Pont du Warche.

The German column consisted of three American jeeps; one half-track; one American M8 armored car; and one Mark VI and two Mark V tanks. The two Panther tanks had been carefully disguised as American M4A3 tanks, by the addition of a false front and back of ordinary sheet metal. In an attempt to further confuse the Americans, the markings of a fictitious armored unit had been painted on the tanks. Actually, it was so dark at the time of the attack, that the German efforts to simulate a US column were superfluous. Three of the lead vehicles hit mines, and were simultaneously fired upon by two TD guns. One of the TD guns was knocked out, but the Mark VI tank was damaged and forced to retire. American rifle and machine-gun fire, pinned down the attacking infantry, and then artillery and mortar fire was brought down on them and the stranded column of armor.[24]

FRANK DENIUS, BATTERY C, 230TH FIELD ARTILLERY BATTALION

The 230th was in support of the entire division area. All the regiments were on the line. We directed artillery fire constantly in support of the defense of the 120th and the other regiments during the attack by the Germans. The Germans were trying to find a way to penetrate our lines. They would come at us in one direction in an area and move to another one. Their tanks had to cross many river bridges. They were also running out of fuel. Eventually, we had snow and it was close to zero. The weather conditions made it almost intolerable.[25]

The brunt of the attack was broken after an hour, though some firing continued for the rest of the morning. An estimated 100 German infantry were killed and three prisoners were taken, two from the *3rd Parachute Division* and one from the *1st SS-Panzer Division*. Two of the US jeeps and the M8 armored car were recovered in useable condition. The second German column advanced toward the Stavelot-Malmédy highway at approximately the same time that the first column was hitting the roadblock manned by Company B, 99th Infantry Battalion (Separate). The attack of this column was handicapped by the fact that its route of approach to the Stavelot-Malmédy highway was subject to observation from the high bluff, one kilometer to the west. The Germans knew that the 30th Division had roadblocks on the highway that wound up the side of this bluff, as patrols had probed at these roadblocks in the last two days. By striking two hours before daylight, they undoubtedly hoped to break through onto the highway while it was still dark. They had the good luck to attack a roadblock which was manned by only one platoon from Company K, 120th Infantry Regiment. Also, the crew of one of the two TD guns supporting this roadblock happened to be away from their gun, reconnoitering for better positions at the time of the attack. Finally, although there was a full platoon of TDs on the high bluff to the west; they were towed guns, set up to cover attack along the road that winds up the bluff, and because of their immobility, only one of them was moved into a position from which it could fire on the road along which the German column was attacking. This gun caused the Germans a lot of trouble, however.

After 21 December the Germans made no serious attempt to capture Malmédy. The defenders of the town had no easy time of it, however, because the US Air Corps erroneously and tragically bombed the town on 23, 24, 25, and 30 December. The 1st and 3rd Battalions of the 120th Infantry Regiment there actually suffered more casualties as a result of these bombings than they did from fighting the Germans during the entire time they were defending the town of Malmédy.

FRANK TOWERS, COMPANY M, 120TH INFANTRY REGIMENT

Initially, the Division Headquarters was in the town of Francorchamps, which

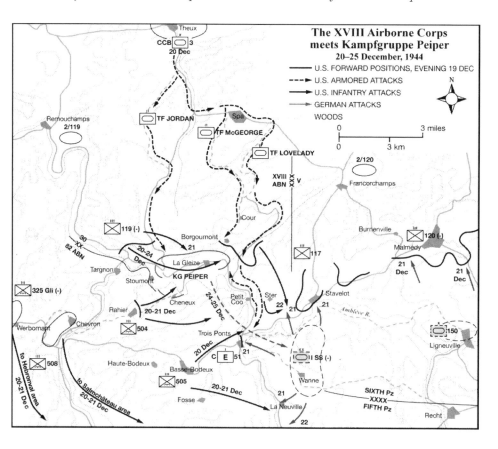

was a small resort town north of Malmédy. I continued my liaison roll contacting the Regimental Headquarters, which was in Malmédy. The route from Francorchamps to Malmédy was kind of a circuitous route because this was very mountainous country. I found a shorter route on a back road up and over a mountain. It took 10–12 miles off my trip. The day before Christmas, I was on a run from Division to Regiment. I was up on top of the mountain and I heard the buzz of planes. I told my driver to stop so I could watch the planes. I could see them coming from the north and I was thinking, "What the hell are they going to do? Somewhere, the Germans are going to catch hell today." At that point on the mountain, we could look down on the city of Malmédy. We could see the whole city spread out down there. All of the sudden, as I had witnessed before in Normandy during Operation COBRA, the bomb bay doors opened. I thought, "What the hell are these guys doing?" Then I saw the bombs coming out right there in front of me! They dropped down in the center of Malmédy. Then another flight came over and they did the same thing. We had two flights that came over and bombed the center of Malmédy! I could see the City Hall down there. That was where I was headed. We then moved down the side of the mountain to try to help some of the people who had been bombed and injured. At the time, there was no radio communication because of the mountain; you couldn't send radio waves through it and there was no telephone communication. I had to get back to Division and tell them what had happened in Malmédy. They needed engineers and the medical battalion up there as quickly as possible. People needed to be dug out and taken care of. Our battalion aid station had been hit and badly damaged. We couldn't help the civilian people in addition to our soldiers. After waiting, the 105th Medical Battalion arrived and the engineers came to help clear out some of the streets and to dig people out of the rubble. There was fire and smoke coming from the debris on the ground; it was a terrible situation. We had a lot of injuries. In fact a hotel was being used as the headquarters for three companies and each one had their kitchen in this hotel and it took a direct hit, so three kitchens were destroyed. To this day, I think we still have 24 men who are missing in action—the mess sergeants and cooks, everyone who were in that hotel. The downtown area was completely destroyed. The town square and everything around it, was demolished, but the cathedral was untouched.[26]

RICHARD LACEY, COMPANY M, 120TH INFANTRY REGIMENT

I came back from the hospital in England on 16 December and that's when the Germans started the Battle of the Bulge. I met my new lieutenant and the fellows who were in the outfit had been through heavy fighting. I met the guys again that had been with me when I got wounded. There were a lot of replacements. They loaded us up in trucks and sent us down to Malmédy. Our air force bombed us there and destroyed the town. The men from our mortar platoon were in the basements of the houses there and they got killed. Our whole kitchen crew, 4–5 guys, our cooks, they were there, too. Our Company headquarters was also in town. All together we lost 45 guys during the whole war in our company and I would dare say there were probably 15–20 who were killed in Malmédy when the air force bombed us.[27]

FRANCIS CURREY, COMPANY K, 120TH INFANTRY REGIMENT

We moved up from the bridge to a hillside. It looked like the bombers were at the same level when the opened up their bomb bays. What a tough thing. It was sickening but there was nothing you could do about it. Christmas was just another day.[28]

Francis Currey was a Browning Automatic Rifleman (BAR) when he went into action at the Battle of the Bulge. He was only 19 years old, but he was nicknamed "Fearless" by his squad-mates. On 21 December, he and his small platoon were sent to cover the bridge on the avenue du Pont du Warche that leads west out of Malmédy. He'd been told that there was no German armor in the area and that he shouldn't expect to see any. His squad was assigned to defend that bridge with little more than small arms. Within hours, they were facing a column of German tanks intent on flanking his battalion. Currey repeatedly braved enemy fire to inflict heavy losses on them, while doing so he managed to rescue five American soldiers who had been pinned down in foxholes almost directly opposite Currey's position. In recognition of this courageous feat, Sergeant Currey was awarded the Medal of Honor. Eisenhower later said, "If the Germans had taken the bridge at Malmédy and the US Army Depot at Liege, the war would have been six weeks longer. So actually, I personally approved the citation."

RICHARD LACEY, COMPANY M, 120TH INFANTRY REGIMENT

We set up positions on the edge of town. Our two guns were about two tenths of a mile from where the other two were with a platoon from K Company near a paper mill. For some reason I had gone into town to company headquarters, I cannot remember why. The Germans made an attack off the hill with tanks and infantry and drove our fellows back to this paper mill. My lieutenant was killed along with our platoon sergeant. Our guns were out in the open. Our artillery

observer called for artillery fire on the Germans and they eventually pulled back.
This is where Francis Currey won the Medal of Honor.[29]

FRANCIS CURREY, COMPANY K, 120TH INFANTRY REGIMENT

Medal of Honor Action: We were spread so thin. Our company had maybe three
or four trucks and they spread us all over. We unloaded and the junior officers
were just as confused as we were. I don't think they knew what the hell was going
on. It was almost a complete breakdown in communications. We were placed at a
key bridge, just a single squad, probably ten of us at the time. They took a couple
men away at some point to another platoon that was short. Our company had the
whole line from Malmédy to Stavelot. You had all these roads that had to be
blocked. Despite the fact that Malmédy was a key area, we were all there was to
guard this valuable bridge. There were just eight of us to hold that entire sector!
Across the river on the other side was the Company CP with six men. They had
to run the whole show.

We dug in beside the bridge. There was a factory on our left and there was a
little park and a house across from the factory. We had four foxholes, with a field
of fire on one side right next to the house. The factory went right down to the
Warche River, right on the edge of it. With me were Ray Snow, Raymond Gould,
Warren Schinn, Irving Kuskin, Adam Lucero, and Gordon Gunderson. Snow
was our assistant squad leader. At the bridge, the squad leader we had was taken
away. He had to go someplace else. Everybody had left us the day before saying,
"You guys are on your own, good luck!"

A US Army hospital had been set up in the factory. They departed the day
before and left everything; they loaded their trucks with patients and just left. We
went in and looted it, even their mailroom. Christmas packages for the officers
and nurses hadn't been delivered; we ate like kings!

Also, the day before the attack, a large patrol had come through. At that time,
the Company commander was still across the river with his headquarters in the
garage. I could hear him talking with the patrol leader, "We have completely
surveyed and the Germans can't operate armor in the area. The most they can
do is infiltrate infantry, so one squad should be enough to handle it."

The German attack started about 0400 hours. You could hear them. The dis-
tance was probably about a mile from the bridge to Malmédy. One tank came
along and he was barreling through pretty good. He got to the edge of the bridge
and slowed down. My foxhole was right against the bridge where I had a good
field of fire. I can close my eyes and visualize the guy. He was standing up in his
turret, his tank was just creeping along, and then he looked down at me. I stood

up and said, "What the hell is this…this freakin' German tank!" Instinctively, I raised my BAR and started firing but he beat me and got down in the turret. He moved across the bridge and the headquarters guys on the other side, before they took off, took the tank out. The German infantry then started infiltrating.

I had one advantage over the others in my squad, I had had officer training. I could recognize a good officer and a shit one. I was 18 years old and I had a mind like a sponge, I could absorb everything. I knew what we needed to do. The guys looked at me to be in charge. So I said, "Let's get the hell out of here and get over to that factory." We could not hold out where we were. They would take us out in less than hour, period!

We ran towards the factory from the foxholes at an angle. The tanks could fire at the factory but they could not hit us. Infantry had a good shot, but not the tanks. The only one who got hit moving was Kuskin. I was still in a foxhole, and he was too damn slow. He was coming from across the street and he wasn't fast. I said to Snow, "Dammit, Kuskin just got it." The factory had windows all the way down it. Nobody was given orders what to do. We moved from window to window firing. By the time they got a tank oriented on a position, we were long gone from the windows we had fired from before. We were running back and forth taking a few shots out of a window and then moving on. This continued until noon. We also moved Irving Kuskin inside.

I didn't have to tell the guys to do anything. They would cover me. We worked together long enough and we had teamwork. I knew that I would be covered. We had plenty of ammunition that an anti-tank (AT) outfit had left in their half-track with us when they went out way in front. I found the bazooka in the half-track along with the anti-tank grenades. The bazooka requires a two-man team. It's a tube and you put it on your shoulder to fire it; flashlight batteries power it. When the bazooka fires a 2–3 foot flame comes out the back. So you had to trust the loader.

The first tank we took out had turned sideways so that the gun was facing toward Malmédy and his back was toward us. The tank was at an angle but he had the turret turned to cover the city. I had a good shot at it. He was blind and didn't see us at all. You had to get within 50 feet because that was the range of the bazooka. Lucero loaded the bazooka. I fired and hit it where the turret turns on the chassis. It went right in there. Of course it really screwed it up and they got the hell out of there. I later found out the tank crashed into a building because he was in such a hurry to get out of there!

There were three tanks in front of me, one in the middle and the others on the sides. The anti-tank gun had been demolished. I wanted to get a better look.

There was a little hedge so I crawled down and saw guys from the AT outfit trapped in foxholes down there. One of them was a sergeant and he was closest to the gun. I said, "They haven't seen me yet, that hedge is blocking me. This is what I am going to do. Is that your half-track down there?" He said, "Yes." I then asked, "Do you have anti-tank grenades?" He replied, "Yes, I have a couple boxes of them." I then told him, "I'm going to go back and bring them up. How about a launcher?" He said, "Yes, I'll tell you where to find one, you have to have an M1 to use it." I said, "You guys just sit tight!" There was a lull, no fighting was going on. It was a stalemate.

I went back to the half-track and got a box of grenades and the other stuff. They still hadn't seen me. The AT sergeant then said, "We've got one guy who is pretty well shot up." I said, "I'm going to fire these grenades." This was part of my training. I was taught at Benning that an anti-tank grenade will not take out a tank. But when it hits the tank it will make a hell of a big flame, a lot of smoke, and a lot of noise.

The tanks were not spread out. So I started to fire these grenades, a few here, a couple there. I used them up. The tankers abandoned the tanks; they must have thought a big AT gun was firing. I then set up a .30-caliber machine gun. It had been used to back up the AT gun. I then sprayed the area with machine-gun fire. I told the trapped AT crew to get out one by one, but to make sure that someone was with the wounded man. I was the last one out with the sergeant.

We also had an artillery observer with us. He called in artillery and the only weapon he had was a .45. I told him to get out of there and get back with his unit. The Germans had withdrawn from the valley and were heading up the hill north of us and the artillery strike destroyed their attack.

So there we were, it was night and it was dark. We found a jeep in a court-yard left behind from the hospital. There were six of us at the time. We were talking about what we were going to do. We couldn't leave Kuskin behind. Warren was the one who could drive a standard transmission. We had a two-stretcher mount on the jeep. We had the wounded guy from the AT outfit and we had Kuskin. Schinn drove the jeep and I rode shotgun on the back tire. If we were stopped, I was going to engage the Germans while the rest of the guys could take off. The others held down the stretcher mounts. We could only drive about five miles an hour.

There we were, six guys with two wounded in the middle of Belgium, and we had no idea where the hell we were. We started and went back over the bridge. All we knew is we had come in that way, so we went out that way. We didn't know what was on the other side. We crossed the bridge, and that goddamn German tank was still burning. They had abandoned it long before we left. We never got challenged. As we went through, Schinn could barely see the sides of the road. Finally, we ran into another regiment in the division. They challenged us because we were coming in from the German side. Finally, we got that straightened out and they let us in. They surrounded us and they took our weapons, our jeep and our wounded. I remember they took us to company headquarters and they didn't know what the hell to do. They thought we were Germans. I remember they had this kid, must have just been come in as a replacement. I remember telling someone, "Jesus Christ, tell that kid to point that fucking rifle someplace else, or take it away from him!"

We finally got up to regiment and they finally realized who we were. By noon the next day, we were back with our company. By that time, they had stabilized the front and by the next day, we were right back in the same foxholes by the bridge where we started out and that goddamn tank was still idling. You should have seen the fucking headquarters people who came down to see the situation! [30]

120th Infantry Regiment, After Action Report, 3 January 1945
The attack toward K Company's roadblock began as an infantry attack. There was no artillery preparation, in fact, no artillery support at all. When the advancing enemy infantry got within three or four hundred yards of the roadblock's outpost, they were discovered and fired upon. A spirited firefight immediately developed. Under the cover of machine-gun and direct fire, the attackers advanced and took possession of a house in the vicinity of the crewless TD gun, about 200 yards from the positions of the defending platoon. The enemy made this house into a strong point and built up a line east thereof. Practically all of the hostile infantrymen carried automatic weapons. After about six hours, during which the men of Company K fought off all efforts of the German infantry to overrun their position, the supporting hostile tanks moved forward up the road in an effort to break the resistance, which the infantry had been unable to do.

In the face of this threat, all of the defending platoon, except for a few who were so badly pinned down so that they could not move, retreated to a paper factory on the north side of the Stavelot-Malmédy highway. In the confusion of making this shift in position, the leading tank reached the intersection without being fired on and turned west. It advanced up the highway about two hundred yards, apparently in an effort to get onto commanding ground. Fortunately, Lieutenant Arnold Snyder, a mortar observer with the 3rd platoon, who had left the roadblock on foot to confer with the Company

K commander at his CP about getting artillery support, spotted the oncoming German tank in time to get a bazooka and get into a position from which he was able to knock it out from the rear. As a second enemy tank approached the main highway, a bazooka team consisting of Pfc. Francis Currey and Pfc. Adam Lucero, put a round into the turret of the tank, which prevented its firing.

The enemy tank driver backed it off and the crew abandoned it. Lieutenant Claire Farley, commanding the platoon of towed TD guns on the bluff west of the roadblock, meanwhile ordered Sergeant Stinett to move his gun into a position from which he could fire across the river onto the road where the enemy armor was advancing. From this position, Sergeant Stinett's gun scored effective shots on five enemy tanks along the road. Two other TDs of Company B, 823rd TD Battalion, were able to place flanking fire on the enemy column from the east. These latter guns were covering a supporting roadblock on the Stavelot-Malmédy highway, seven or eight hundred yards east of Company K's roadblock. With the help of supporting infantrymen, the crews of these two guns, which were self-propelled M10s, took up the hastily-laid mines and advanced to positions from which they could fire in the direction of the house that constituted the enemy's strongpoint. The hostile tanks took cover behind this house, but a couple of rounds from the M10s knocked down the covering wall of the house, and exposed the target. Two of the tanks were hit and burned. The combined TD fire from the west and east broke the back of the counterattack, although the enemy did not withdraw until after dark.[31]

KING KENNY, RECONNAISSANCE PLATOON, 823RD TANK DESTROYER BATTALION

Later, we held the position in the north with the 82nd Airborne Division. We didn't get many tank attacks, but we held the line. By that time I was a sergeant. I had the map, and I was figuring out the way for the squad to go up to a town that started with an A, but I can't recall the name. We started taking artillery or tank fire. Fishback, my best friend, was driving an M8. I said to him, "Stan, you're attracting shell fire. Get that thing out of the way!" He said, "I can't see where I'm going." So I got out in front of him and I tried to direct him to back up by the side of a building, then a lot of mortar stuff came in, and that's what got me. They were probably aiming for the M8 because it was visible. I got into a building, and there were 2 or 3 of our guys there. They asked, "Are you hit?" I said

"Yeah, I am, in my shoulder and my back and it really burns." They lifted my shirt and got a guy to take me in a jeep back to an aid station. My lip was cut and my two front teeth were knocked sideways. They bandaged me up at the battalion aid station.

I ended up on one of those GI ambulances and I could sit up. When we got to the next destination they had colored troops who were litter bearers and, boy, they were really gentle with the litters. They would set you on the ground, a doctor would come by to do a quick survey of what your problem was and tag you, so when they moved you inside (it was a school building with a bunch of desks) the doctors could do their thing. From there the doctor removed some of the shrapnel and he may have sewn my lip up, I forget. Then I got in another ambulance and went back to Liege to the 116th General Hospital which was a very large tent hospital. Lying in bed there, buzz bombs were coming and you could hear the engine going. When it shut off you didn't know where it was going to land. They had no guidance system in them. The Germans were just trying to go for an area with those things. It would be quiet and then KABOOM! *They didn't hit the hospital. I don't think they missed it on purpose, it was just luck. After about 20 days or so, the nurse came by and asked how I felt and I said I felt fine. She took a look at my bandages and said, "We're going to re-bandage you and send you back."* [32]

Despite the growing opposition, *Kampfgruppe Peiper* was still maintaining the momentum in their drive to get to the river Meuse, but it was becoming an increasingly desperate struggle. As more American units arrived in the northern Ardennes, Peiper must have sensed that his chances were gradually diminishing, but that didn't stop him. If anything, it increased his determination to achieve his objective despite the odds. His subordinates noticed that all was not well with their leader; he was having trouble dispatching clear orders and his speech was becoming, at times, almost incoherent.

While the 117th Infantry Regiment was attacking La Gleize on 20 December, the 1st Battalion of the 119th Infantry Regiment attacked from the west, supported by Company C of the 740th Tank Battalion. Before long they ran into a Mark V maneuvering along the road, but the leading American tank knocked it out. A little farther along the route Lieutenant Galloway's platoon demolished two German half-tracks. At the big "S" bend east of Targnon, close to Stoumont, the 740th Tank Battalion lost its first tank when it struck a landmine. The attacking force still managed to advance approximately two miles. As dusk approached they were roughly 350 yards west of Stoumont.

Just north of the La Gleize–Stoumont road, situated on high ground overlooking Stoumont stood a large building which housed a sanatorium for sick children and aged people. It's still there today. A few platoons of Companies B and C drew the conclusion that this building would make an excellent location for their CPs. At that moment the *SS* were in possession of it, but after a fierce firefight they were ejected and three or four platoon CPs were set up in the building. Companies B and C deployed north of the road, while Company A set up south of the road. GIs discovered that some of the sanatorium's inmates were hiding in the cellars beneath the building, but they were evacuated to a safe zone the following day.

Around 2300 hours, the Germans launched a powerful counterattack to recapture the sanatorium. Between 50 and 100 *SS* infantry, supported by several tanks firing from the road north of the sanatorium, charged toward the building shouting, *"Heil, Hitler!"* This culminated in a bloody close-quarter fight, which carried on for several hours. Such was the ferocity of this assault that the GIs were compelled to evacuate the sanatorium's main building. Eleven GIs, led by Sergeant William J. Widener, held out in an adjoining building, while the rest of Companies B and C established a firing line along a privet hedge just 30 yards away from the sanatorium. This tactical withdrawal was the result of the German's superior firepower, which was augmented by the Panther tanks that were brought up to within close proximity of the sanatorium. Three of Captain Berry's tanks attempted to counter the hostile tank fire from positions along the road just south of the sanatorium but were repelled. The uneven terrain proved to be a major obstacle. Ascending up this slope was further exacerbated by the muddy conditions that kept the US tanks there confined to the road.

FRANK DEEGAN, COMPANY D, 119TH INFANTRY REGIMENT

When I returned to my unit, I reported to my lieutenant and he told me to report to my squad who were billeted in German houses. My sergeant had been granted a 30-day furlough home just two days before I returned. It wasn't long after the beginning of the Battle of the Bulge. When I left the hospital they gave me new clothes and an overcoat, which had brass buttons. During the Bulge, we were lined up on a road near railroad tracks where we spent the night. I left my coat there because I didn't want the Germans to take the brass buttons. Later, I sure wish I had kept it!

At Stoumont Station, we got up and moved out on a road where there was a lot of different equipment. There were Sherman tanks, mechanized artillery, and

TDs (tank destroyers). The Germans were up the road, so two TDs pulled up and knocked out 3 or 4 German tanks that had come up. That was unusual because we had inferior armor compared to the Germans.

The unit commander took us over the mountain to Stoumont. There was a sanatorium there and we were going to take it. We ended up spending days fighting over it, back and forth. We had our machine gun set up on the side road near the sanatorium. There was a German medic coming down over the field and someone hollered, "There's a German there!" Then someone yelled, "Hold your fire, Red Cross!" This guy came down to the field and he ended up making three trips. Everybody was keeping an eye on him with their rifles. He brought down ammo on his third trip so the word "Fire!" was passed along. We fired on him and he went down like a bulldozer blade!

After that, we got into the fight in the sanatorium building. There was a wall blown out and we had a machine gun set up there. In a desk there I found a couple of rosary beads in it, which led me to think, at the time, the place was a convent for nuns. I took 3 or 4 rosary beads and I eventually gave them to my mother and sisters. During the back and forth fighting we had a machine gunner who got trapped in the sanatorium cellar. We had to send him ammo to keep him in the fight. We got him out in the end.

We then made our way to Stoumont up a mountain. Riflemen set up along a stone fence there and we set up the machine gun next to them. We needed ammo but before I could go down to get it the Germans opened up on us. We were in a bad position and had to leave the gun as everybody retreated back to our lines. We'd been about 150–200 yards outside of our lines when this happened. After a while, my sergeant came up to me and said someone had reconnoitered the area we'd just retreated from and they hadn't found any Germans. So he asked me to go up to get the machine gun. One of the ammo bearers came with us. We made it up to the crest of the mountain and were almost to the gun. My sergeant was about five yards in front of me to the right and the fellow behind me was another five yards off to the right as well. Just then I saw my sergeant duck and start running back. I figured he had heard or seen something. I wheeled around on my right leg and stepped out—and then I went down! A shot from the Germans hit me in the femur, broke it and cut my sciatic nerve. I found myself lying there, between Stoumont and Stoumont Station, and I figured this was where I was going to die. I started to think—I had come up with two friends and both of them had been killed. I had been wounded twice and now this was the third time.

The first thing I did was pull out my .45 and then I checked the lay of the land on the right, center, and left. As I looked left, my sergeant and the other guy were up against a wall. I told them to get the hell out of there, so they left. I just laid there and watched. I figured the Krauts were going to come up and see me. The only thing I could do was to wait for that to happen. I figured there was no use treating my wound (which I should have done). I was stuck in the middle of the road and I wasn't going anywhere, my leg was busted. I must have passed out for a time. I had a recollection that I saw stretcher bearers. It could have been from a dream. I don't know if it happened or not. Americans eventually came and got me and took me to a hospital. That was the end of my combat. When I woke up back at the hospital there were several bottles hooked up to me and a nurse sitting on a stool right alongside my stretcher. I looked up I saw the bottles and I said to her, "It looks really bad." She said, "No, no, no." She jumped up and motioned down the hall to a Chaplain to come in and he gave the last rites! I made it, though, and eventually made it back to a hospital in Virginia, where I recovered.[33]

The next step was to place all of the forces involved in the reduction of the enemy column caught in the Stoumont–La Gleize pocket under one command. Brigadier General Harrison was charged with this command, called Task Force Harrison. His plan of attack for 21 December involved a pincer movement moving toward Stoumont from one direction while coordinating a simultaneous attack on La Gleize. The 2nd Battalion of the 119th Infantry Regiment was to make a wide envelopment to the north, then turn south and attack Stoumont from the east, setting up a roadblock between Stoumont and La Gleize to protect its rear. The 1st Battalion, 119th Infantry, supported by Captain Berry's tanks and a company of TDs, would recapture the sanatorium and move into the town from the northwest. Task Force Jordan and the 3rd Battalion, 119th Infantry, would advance on the town directly from the north.

At about 1000 hours the following morning, 22 December, General Harrison came up to the front lines just west of the sanatorium to consider the most favorable options for attacking this imposing building. He immediately noticed that it was suspiciously quiet there, when he was approached by two civilians who reported that the Germans had vacated the building during the night. The General sent up a reconnaissance patrol to investigate and discovered that the place was indeed deserted. The 1st Battalion re-occupied the building without firing a shot. They discovered a couple of seriously wounded GIs that the Germans had left behind in the sanatorium. They confirmed that the enemy had vacated the building some time before dawn at around 0400 hours. In the town of Stoumont, meanwhile, there were still ominous indications that the *SS* was still there, but when the 1st and 2nd Battalions attacked from the west, only rear guards were encountered. By mid-morning Stoumont was finally and firmly in American hands. Aerial reconnaissance discovered an estimated 12 enemy tanks travelling on the road between Stavelot and Trois Ponts. When the Americans later captured this road, it was found that the enemy had improved a footbridge across the Amblève River, one kilometer east of Trois Ponts, so that it could support their heavy tanks. General Harrison estimated that the enemy force in La Gleize consisted of at least one panzer battalion and two panzergrenadier battalions. In addition to its impressive firepower, this force held the ground commanding the approach from the east. He readied his men and prepared to fight a hard battle, but as it turned out, he didn't actually get one.

JOHN NOLAN, COMPANY G, 119TH INFANTRY REGIMENT

We eventually deployed to La Gleize. I can remember the terrific shelling; we had great artillery and they shelled the hell out of La Gleize. It was surrounded, except for one road leading out. G Company was given the mission of setting up a roadblock on that road using anti-tank mines, which were given to my platoon. Major Harold "Hal" McCown, the battalion commander, and his radio operator went along with us. We were going down a steep hill not far from our objective, the road we were to cut off, when the Jerries counterattacked through the woods on our right. They captured the battalion commander and others from his party. We got the hell out of there as quickly as we could! We had lost our battalion commander, but the platoon got back to its original location. Major Nathaniel Laney, the battalion's executive officer, took over. Later, on Christmas Eve, Major McCown escaped from capture and returned to retake command of our 2nd Battalion.

We were then ordered to attack La Gleize. I believe that Major Laney and all of us at the time thought Joachim Peiper and the SS were going to shoot our battalion commander. We were really pissed off and I believe he gave us the order to "take no prisoners" in the attack. Several members of the 1st Platoon and I were the first ones in La Gleize. I don't know how we made it in first, but we did. I found a Jerry medical captain named Willy Dittman who had on a beautiful gray coat with both Red Cross and SS armbands. We didn't shoot them because they were medics. That was the first time I knew we were up against the 1st SS-Panzer Division. The platoon didn't stay in La Gleize more than an hour because we were ordered to go down and secure the flank in case of counterattack.[34]

At 0300 hours on 24 December *Kampfgruppe Peiper*, now reduced to approximately 800 men led by Peiper himself, had surreptitiously slipped away from La Gleize under cover of darkness. Major McCowan (commander of a battalion in the 119th Infantry, captured on 21 December while assaulting Stoumont) was the only one of the 171 American prisoners in La Gleize to go with the column. The rest were simply left there in the basement beneath the former Town Hall. At the commencement of his great drive to the Meuse River, *Kampfgruppe Peiper* consisted of 5,800 men that were later augmented by an additional battalion from the *SS-Panzer-Grenadier Regiment 2*. Now, there were only 800 left to sneak back through the woods to their own lines. As he moved back east he was forced to abandon 80 wounded in the Château de Froid-Cour and just over 300 in La Gleize.

The tally in abandoned and destroyed German armor totaled around 87 tanks; 70 half-tracks; at least 14 flak wagons; 25 75mm assault guns and 105mm and 150mm self-propelled howitzers; plus trucks and smaller vehicles.

While the Germans were secretly crossing the Amblève River on a small bridge south of La Gleize, at 0500 hours that morning, GIs in the vicinity heard the first tank blow up and inside of 30 minutes, the entire area formerly occupied by *Kampfgruppe Peiper* was a sea of fiercely burning vehicles. This last desperate act was the work of a small detachment Peiper left behind to complete the destruction of all of his equipment. The gas tanks of most of the vehicles were empty, corroborating the belief of General Harrison and Major McCowan that Peiper did not have sufficient gasoline to move his armor back through Trois Ponts, even if he had not been forced to fight.

The 170 US POWs, most of them from the 3rd Battalion, 119th Infantry, that had been left behind by Peiper were in relatively good condition, although a few of them showed signs of shellshock due to the terrific pounding that the US artillery had inflicted on Peiper's remaining men in La Gleize while they were captives there. Peiper later disclosed to Major McCowan that seven of the prisoners there had been shot while attempting to escape.

MARK SCHWENDIMAN, COMPANY I, 119TH INFANTRY REGIMENT

At a rest center, we had Thanksgiving dinner for breakfast because we were alerted to move out. We were fighting by noon the next day. It was 17 December and we were on trucks joining a convoy of vehicles about two miles long. A German plane flew over dropping flares, but he flew on by. We traveled all night and the next day. The whole 30th Division was on the move. We learned that we were headed for the Bulge. We traveled until we came to a small town that the Germans had left. We stopped there and were too tired to even dig foxholes, so we curled up and went to sleep in one of the houses. Patrols were sent out to see what they could find. A short distance from this town they saw several German vehicles and armored tanks. The battalion commander didn't believe the report, so didn't prepare for any action.

We awoke at 0400 hours, ate K rations, and prepared for deployment. As soon as it was light, the Germans started to come into town. They had tanks, half-tracks, and infantry. We only had infantry, two tanks, and a 90mm gun. They knocked out one of our tanks and the gun, then the other tank ran out of ammunition so it left. We started to pull back, but it was too late. I was captured because of two German tanks that had a cross fire of machine guns that would have been suicide to run through. They shoved us out of the building and lined us up, making us put our hands on our heads. As soon as we did this, our sleeves came down and before I knew it some German had my wrist watch. They marched us back about a mile and searched us more thoroughly. Then they lined us up again, took us back another two miles, and put us in the basement of a house. While marching back, we saw our jeeps and half-tracks they had captured and they were using them. They put 172 of us in a basement with only two small windows and a door that was closed most of the time. We could only sit down by spreading our legs and having someone sit between them. In the basement was a pile of raw potatoes, which was all we had to eat for five days.

The Germans couldn't get out to get us any food because they were in a pocket surrounded by our forces. I went out of the basement on a detail mainly to get some fresh air. I carried 88mm shells from one tank to another. During the fifth night in the basement and the morning of 24 December, the Americans really turned loose the artillery, which set fire to tanks and many buildings. During all this shelling, one of the fellows suggested that each of us offer a silent prayer for our safety and wellbeing. I don't think there was anyone who didn't offer a prayer for our deliverance. We were lucky to have been put in a basement of a building; it probably saved our lives. The Americans who were not captured then liberated us and we returned to our outfits, thankful to be free and to see our old buddies. This was a wonderful Christmas present. A Christmas never goes by that I don't think of this experience and thank my Heavenly Father for my freedom.[35]

When General Harrison's troops attacked at first light on 24 December, only Companies E and G faced any real resistance against some 50 SS-panzergrenadiers in the woods just north of La Gleize. It was first assumed that their fierce fighting was because they had not been told that Peiper had given up the town, or because they wished to die rather than surrender. It was later learned that Peiper had distributed a code word to his troops in the event of them having to make their escape; these *SS*-panzergrenadiers never received Peiper's code word—"Merry Christmas"—and subsequently they fought almost to the last man.

When the Americans got into La Gleize, they found that the small detachment which Peiper had left behind had done a very poor job of destroying all of the discarded German equipment. Many vehicles were found to be in perfect working condition. After the Battle of the Bulge, Joachim Peiper spent a while in a German hospital recuperating from this traumatic experience. Behind his unit in the Belgian Ardennes lay a trail of murder and destruction on a scale that had never been experienced in this previously sedate part of Belgium. He would eventually be brought to account for his transgressions, but first the Nazis had to be defeated. Roosevelt's *SS* had once again checked the real *SS*, but their fight wasn't over yet. They had spent the past few weeks on the defensive, but now they were gearing up to chase the Nazis right back to the German border and beyond.

CITATIONS FOR ACTION IN THE ARDENNES

Staff Sergeant Paul L. Bolden, Company I, 120th Infantry Regiment. Petit-Coo, Belgium, 23 December 1944. Medal of Honor citation:
He voluntarily attacked a formidable enemy strong point in Petit-Coo, Belgium, on 23 December, 1944, when his company was pinned down by extremely heavy automatic and small-arms fire coming from a house 200 yards to the front. Mortar and tank artillery shells pounded the unit, when S/Sgt. Bolden and a comrade, on their own initiative, moved forward into a hail of bullets to eliminate the ever-increasing fire from the German position. Crawling ahead to close with what they knew was a powerfully armed, vastly superior force, the pair reached the house and took up assault positions, S/Sgt. Bolden under a window, his comrade across the street where he could deliver covering fire. In rapid succession, S/Sgt. Bolden hurled a fragmentation grenade and a white phosphorous grenade into the building; and then, fully realizing that he faced tremendous odds, rushed to the door, threw it open and fired into 35 SS troopers who were trying to reorganize themselves after the havoc wrought by the grenades. Twenty Germans died under fire of his submachinegun before

he was struck in the shoulder, chest, and stomach by part of a burst which killed his comrade across the street. He withdrew from the house, waiting for the surviving Germans to come out and surrender. When none appeared in the doorway, he summoned his ebbing strength, overcame the extreme pain he suffered and boldly walked back into the house, firing as he went. He had killed the remaining 15 enemy soldiers when his ammunition ran out. S/Sgt. Bolden's heroic advance against great odds, his fearless assault, and his magnificent display of courage in reentering the building where he had been severely wounded cleared the path for his company and insured the success of its mission. Entered service at: Madison, Ala. Birth: Hobbes Island, Iowa.[36]

Sergeant Francis S. Currey, 120th Infantry Regiment, Malmédy, Belgium, 21 December 1944. Medal of Honor citation:
He was an automatic rifleman with the 3d Platoon defending a strong point near Malmedy, Belgium, on 21 December 1944, when the enemy launched a powerful attack. Overrunning tank destroyers and antitank guns located near the strong point, German tanks advanced to the 3d Platoon's position, and, after prolonged fighting, forced the withdrawal of this group to a nearby factory. Sgt. Currey found a bazooka in the building and crossed the street to secure rockets meanwhile enduring intense fire from enemy tanks and hostile infantrymen who had taken up a position at a house a short distance away. In the face of small-arms, machinegun, and artillery fire, he, with a companion, knocked out a tank with 1 shot. Moving to another position, he observed 3 Germans in the doorway of an enemy-held house. He killed or wounded all 3 with his automatic rifle. He emerged from cover and advanced alone to within 50 yards of the house, intent on wrecking it with rockets. Covered by friendly fire, he stood erect, and fired a shot which knocked down half of 1 wall. While in this forward position, he observed 5 Americans who had been pinned down for hours by fire from the house and 3 tanks. Realizing that they could not escape until the enemy tank and infantry guns had been silenced, Sgt. Currey crossed the street to a vehicle, where he procured an armful of antitank grenades. These he launched while under heavy enemy fire, driving the tank men from the vehicles into the house.

He then climbed onto a half-track in full view of the Germans and fired a machinegun at the house. Once again changing his position, he manned another machinegun whose crew had been killed; under his covering fire the 5 soldiers were able to retire to safety. Deprived of tanks and with heavy infantry casualties, the enemy was forced to withdraw. Through his extensive knowledge of weapons and by his heroic and repeated braving of murderous enemy fire, Sgt. Currey was greatly responsible for inflicting heavy losses in men and material on the enemy, for rescuing 5 comrades, 2 of whom were wounded, and for stemming an attack which threatened to flank his battalion's position. Entered service at: Hurleyville, N.Y.[37]

CHAPTER EIGHT
COUNTEROFFENSIVE

The spectacle of winter in the Ardennes has all the hallmarks of a beautiful picture postcard. It's a breathtaking landscape full of snow-laden pine forests punctuated by half-timbered houses in towns, villages, and hamlets, connected by winding country lanes that meander along gentle sloping hills and valleys. For the visitor in peacetime, it's a veritable winter wonderland, but for the Joes of Old Hickory who found themselves there during the biggest land battle in US military history, it was a freezing, miserable fight for survival in some of the most inhuman conditions imaginable. The snow there was thigh deep in some places and the thermometer had plunged below -25 degrees Fahrenheit, but despite the inclement weather, the Allied counteroffensive was planned to go ahead commencing 2 January.

KING KENNY, RECONNAISSANCE PLATOON,
823RD TANK DESTROYER BATTALION
Another sergeant and I joined a unit of the 120th as they were moving across a field. Some of the guys had pulled bedsheets off of beds and they made camouflage coverings out of them. The rest of us had overcoats and it was miserable. The highest I saw the snow was out in that field where it was about knee high. We had combat boots on, but they did not want you to take them off because you would get swelling and frostbite. Someone said sure, take your boots off, they cure frostbite with whiskey![1]

Their purpose was to eliminate the remaining bulge in the line and while the 82nd Airborne Division began its push southeast, the 30th Division spent the rest of December and the first days of January 1945 clearing the northern Ardennes of German stragglers. They cooperated in providing a small diversionary attack below Malmédy; then a few days later, supported by the remaining, severely mauled men of 112th Infantry Regiment, 28th Infantry Division, they were on the move again, attacking south toward Spineux and Wanne. Then on 9 January, in the sector held by the 30th Division and the 424th Infantry Regiment, the only remaining regiment from the ill-fated 106th Infantry Division (their two other regiments had been captured at the beginning of the Battle of the Bulge), they occupied the Wanne-Wanneranval region that was previously held by the 112th Infantry Regiment, 28th Infantry Division.

On 13 January the 30th Division initiated its southerly attack. The 119th Infantry Regiment assaulted the line held by the *Volksgrenadier Regiment 293*, concentrating its attack on the town of Hedomont. It was taken by the infantry after an intensive artillery barrage drove the enemy from their defensive positions. The following day, the Germans were rousted from their positions in Bellevaux. The 119th then moved through area, which had been taken by the 120th Infantry Regiment the day before. The fighting for the 119th was rough.

JOHN NOLAN, COMPANY G, 119TH INFANTRY REGIMENT

We received orders to close the "Bulge" and return the line to its 16 December location. Our battalion would attack, moving south from Malmédy, to seize the town of Bellevaux that was situated behind a high ridge. Company G would lead the attack and our platoon would be the lead unit to carry the assault up the narrow road to the heights above the town. In preparing for the attack our platoon was told to leave sleeping bags in the rear with the company mess truck. The plan was to bring them forward the night after we had captured the objective. I decided to put my gas mask in my haversack instead of carrying it slung under my left arm. For a GI the gas mask carrier was considered a good place to "stash" personal belongings. In mine I carried letters received from home, writing paper, a shaving brush, razor and soap, and a coal miner's carbide canister filled with tea bags.

Our platoon moved to the line of departure in darkness and at dawn the attack began with combat engineers moving forward to remove any anti-tank mines. We then were to clear out any German opposition so our supporting tanks could follow us then deploy in the open ground to support our attack. As we moved forward we learned the engineers had discovered an extensive minefield on the road. It was late in the morning before we could move across a footpath the engi-

neers had opened through the mines. We continued the attack up the road to seize and hold the ridgeline until the tanks could catch up. The platoon slowly trudged its way up the steeply sloped, narrow road that ran a quarter of a mile to the top of the ridge. The snow was a foot deep and it was slow going as we made our way up the hill with combat boots and our four-buckle galoshes.

Ernie King's squad led the attack. As the platoon sergeant I decided to be up front with Ernie's squad; the other two squads in the platoon deployed in single file behind us. Cletus Herrig was the lead scout with Bob Friedenheimer the second scout. As the platoon approached the crest of the ridge, Herrig spotted German soldiers in foxholes and yelled back that they were dug-in some 30 yards ahead. Cletus could speak German so we told him to call to them and demand that they surrender. I thought I could fire a rifle grenade into their position, but when it landed, the deep snow cushioned the impact and it failed to explode.

Cletus kept trying to talk them into surrender, when suddenly all hell broke loose! No one who has ever heard the sound of an MG42 German machine gun open fire will ever forget it. This machine gun was pointed down toward the ditch line where we were crouched, spraying us with bullets. The first burst hit four of us before we could find cover in the ditch below the machine-gun's trajectory. Herrig was hit along the top of both shoulders, Friedenheimer was hit through the lung, I took a bullet in the back of my pack and was knocked down to my knees. Behind me was Milton Cohen, a private, one of the 18-year-old replacements that had joined us two weeks earlier. He was hit in the teeth with the bullet exiting his head behind his right ear, and I will never forget his plaintive call for his mother. Ernie King was the only one of the first five who was not hit by the initial burst of fire from the machine gun.

Having been knocked down I immediately thought, "I just got lucky, I am on my way to the hospital and off this damn hill, and hope my wound is not too severe." My back was hurting and I assumed that I was bleeding from a puncture in my back. I rolled over and took the pack off my shoulders to see what had happened. To my surprise a German machine-gun bullet was lying on the hole in my pack with a shred of rubber attached to it. I picked it up, it was still warm, then put it in my pocket as a souvenir of the occasion. Later I opened my gas-mask container and discovered that the pack fabric, the gas-mask container fabric, the rubber face mask, the metal gas-mask canister, and the handle of my shaving brush had slowed the bullet to a stop on the surface of my field coat. It gave me one hell of a thump on my back that was sore for a few days afterward. This was the only day in combat I had ever carried my gas mask in my pack and it had saved my life.

That first burst of machine-gun fire put our platoon down hugging the *ground in the ditch beside the road. We were stunned, and began to assess the extent of our casualties; we were grateful to find that no one had been killed. For the wounded among us immediate evacuation to the rear for treatment at the battalion aid station was made more difficult by the sporadic machine-gun fire. The Jerries had us pinned down and we could not move forward in the face of their machine gun fire on the road and ditch line. The phrase "all hell broke loose" again applied to our situation when the Germans began to drop 81mm mortar rounds down on our position. There are few things more fearful to an infantryman than incoming mortar or artillery fire. To compound this fear the Jerries included in their barrage "screaming meemies," enemy rockets that made a horrendous noise, and caught us unprepared as targets for this form of artillery. When they came in on us I perceived their sound was comparable to a railroad boxcar flying sideways through the air with both of its doors open. I found out later that the German name for this weapon was* Nebelwerfer. *As a rocket it did not compare with the accuracy of mortar or artillery fire, but its high pitched screeching noise made it all the more terrifying.*

The "screaming meemies" did not get us, but the 81mm mortars did. From their defensive positions the Germans were masters at pinning down advancing infantry and then raining mortar rounds on them. The mortar shells were falling on the road behind us and on the remainder of the platoon. An 81mm mortar shell fragment hit Vic Kwiatowski in the head, seriously wounding him. Mortar shell fragments hit Bob Heider in the neck, shoulder, and back. Jones got hit in the head by a fragment that penetrated his steel helmet, and the mortar barrage also wounded the second squad BAR man, Charles Holverson. Clarence Overton was killed. Our progress halted, we could not go forward and were not going to retreat. The immediate requirement was to evacuate our wounded. Smitty, our platoon leader, was in the middle of the platoon column and organized the effort along with the platoon medic to remove the wounded from the hill. Those that could walk moved to the rear. A door was taken from a nearby house and brought forward to use as a stretcher for Vic and others more seriously wounded from the barrage.

Ernie King and I stayed to the front keeping down low in the ditch beside the road. We were concerned that the Germans would mount a counterattack on our position after their first machine-gun burst. Artillery support fire began, but we were too close to our enemy for the artillery to continue and be effective. Any artillery rounds falling short would have landed on our platoon deployed along the road. The tanks would eventually move forward and up the hill to support us when the minefield was cleared. In the meantime we scanned the hedgerow along the crest of the ridge and a row of trees about 30 yards away that ran down the hill paralleling the road. We spotted a German soldier on the other side of the line of trees crawling down the hill in an attempt to outflank our position. Both King and I shot at him, but at the time, we could not see whether we got him. We finally received word that two light tanks had moved through the cleared minefield and would support the 3rd Platoon in its attack through the field on our left flank to knock out the machine-gun emplacement.

The attack by the 3rd Platoon was a sight to behold, with a deafening crescendo of small arms fire and cannon bursts. Each platoon of Company G had a slightly different character regarding weapon preference. Our platoon had no particular love for the Browning Automatic Rifle (BAR); it was a 21-pound load to carry and a weapon that required constant maintenance to keep it operational. Each of our three squads was issued a BAR, however, the 3rd Platoon thought the BAR was a great weapon and almost every third man in the platoon carried one. Sergeant Frank Wease, the 3rd Platoon sergeant, carried one and encouraged the weapons use.

In the combined infantry and tank attack up the hill Wease deployed his platoon abreast in a line on each side of and between the two light tanks. The tanks were armed with a 37mm main gun on the turret and a .30-caliber light machine gun that protruded from the front of the tank where the machinegunner sat beside the tank driver. There were about 14 men with BARs in Wease's platoon and the remainder with M1 rifles. Coming up the hill with the tanks in the middle of the formation, they were all firing as they moved forward. Each tank's main gun, its machine gun, the BARs, and the M1 rifles of the 3rd Platoon created a sheet of fire concentrated on the enemy position at the crest of the hill. There was no way the 3rd Platoon could be stopped by any counterfire from the entrenched German troops. Wease and his men, with their tank support, surged through the enemy line along the trees on the ridge. The German troops who were still alive immediately surrendered. Several minutes had passed when Sergeant Wease brought some prisoners down the road where we were located. All of us were furious at the casualties they had inflicted on our platoon, and wanted to shoot them, but Wease would not let us. Later, after calming down from the days' events, I was grateful that Wease had restrained me from taking such a rash act. I had never shot an unarmed prisoner, and didn't want such a thing on my conscience. After the attack King and I went over to the hedgerow where we had shot at the German crawling down the hill. We found him dead. Someone in the attacking 3rd Platoon had taken his pistol as they moved up the hill in the assault.

Late afternoon had come by the time our company had seized the ridgeline above Bellevaux. We received orders to set up a defensive position, the days were short in the middle of winter and night would soon fall. The 3rd Platoon was to occupy that part of the ridge they had captured earlier in the day. Our platoon deployed in a stretch of open field to their right, where digging a foxhole was very difficult. To get beneath the frozen ground required an extraordinary effort. Fortunately, someone in command had realized this problem, and before the attack thought to issue a quarter-pound block of TNT with a fuse and blasting cap to every other man in our platoon. Instructions had been given on the proper method to assemble the explosive device: dig a small hole in the ground, put the charge in the hole, light the fuse, and move away quickly before it exploded. The resulting explosion broke up the frozen crust so that a foxhole could be easily dug in the softer ground underneath. We were also told that the blasting cap was volatile and could explode if jarred violently, or exposed to excessive heat. This required that every man carrying a block of TNT, with its fuse and blasting cap, carefully wrap each separately, hoping they did not get hit, or in some way inadvertently ignite the blasting cap and TNT while they were carrying it.

Those of us in the company that survived this day's combat were faced with enduring a cold winter's night on a Belgian mountain. Previous to the attack we were told to lighten our equipment load by leaving our sleeping bags in the rear area. Then after the attack our sleeping bags would be carried forward for use that night; this did not happen. The snow cover and steep incline of the winding road to our defensive position made it impossible for our company truck to move close enough to deliver the promised sleeping bags. We were in for a very long, cold night of lying in the open on frozen, snow-covered ground, or in hastily-dug foxholes. The rifle squads on the defensive line got busy breaking up the ground with TNT then dug their foxholes for the night. We, in the platoon headquarters, were not issued blocks of TNT, so lying on top of the snow-covered ground was our only option. Lou LeFever, always a great forager, went down the hill and found a barn with some hay in it. He brought as much as he could carry to our position behind the ridgeline. We scattered the hay in the drainage ditch where previously the machine-gun fire had pinned us down. We lay in the hay putting the remainder on us. We huddled together in the "spoon position"—Smitty, the platoon leader; Lou LeFever, the platoon runner; Mullins the medic, and me, the platoon sergeant— I don't remember who was in the middle, or who was on the outside of our sleeping "formation," but I do remember that it was very cold and were all shivering and hoping for morning to come quickly.

The next morning G Company was ordered to advance over the ridge and down the road leading to the town of Bellevaux, our next objective. The 3rd Platoon would lead the attack, with the 2nd Platoon in support. The 1st Platoon, having been severely mangled the day before, followed in reserve, with my position being at the rear of the platoon column. It was a cold, dark morning as the remaining members of the platoon reluctantly shouldered packs and rifles to prepare themselves for another day of combat against a determined enemy. As we moved single file down the road toward Bellevaux one of the men from the platoon, Samuel Klugman, dropped out of the column. I walked over to find out why. He pulled off his glove and showed me his right hand, saying his hand felt frozen. The hand looked blue and rigid so I told him to go to the rear for medical treatment. This was our last casualty from the attack the previous day, the worst day of my life.[2]

The 120th Infantry Regiment also went on the offensive on 13 January. They set off at 0800 with the 3rd Battalion on their western flank and advanced through the towns of Geromont and Baugnez (site of the infamous Malmédy Massacre), eventually reaching positions on Houyire Hill. They lacked any concerted armored support because the only route available for accompanying tanks and tank destroyers proved impassable.[3]

RICHARD LACEY, COMPANY M, 120TH INFANTRY REGIMENT

Finally we started to attack south. We were carrying our guns, wading through snow about a foot deep. The Germans were holding out in a town down south. We tried to get that town but couldn't take it. It took a couple more days and finally we were able to capture it. We were attached to K Company, seemed like we always got into trouble with K Company.

We set up our guns to cover an intersection and there were riflemen up along the road. A German armored vehicle, like a tank with a gun on it, came through. It was hit and stopped. Someone had fired a bazooka; I guess it was one of the riflemen because we didn't have bazookas. Then two Germans started coming out of it. We started to open fire on them and we saw the two Germans drop down back into the vehicle. It was cold and there was shelling. A branch came down and hit me on the side. It didn't really hurt me but I got another Purple Heart. It started to get dark and there was no activity. We were there alone, just our machine gun and crew. The gunner, the big Polish fella, got his pistol out and said, "I am going up there to see what was going on," because everything was quiet. He said, "You stay here, you're now the gunner." We stayed there and after dark our platoon sergeant came up and got us. So, we pulled back into some woods. The ground was so frozen we couldn't dig holes. I went back to stay with the company overnight and then I rejoined the fellows. There were so many guys who got trenchfoot injuries because of the cold weather and snow. They kept telling us to take our boots off and to rub our feet. Eventually we managed to advance to an area just outside of where the 7th Armored Division had been fighting. That was the end of our part of that battle. We pulled back to a rest area.[4]

VICTOR NEILAND, COMPANY F, 117TH INFANTRY REGIMENT

We were attacking south to Ligneuville. We got up at 0400 hours; packed our roll and got our supplies of Ks; and started out at 0500 on a road. It was quite cold in the morning, still very dark and snow everywhere. We walked through Malmédy, which had been wrecked by the air corps, and it was still smoking. We went past the massacre field. We stayed in a house for an hour or so then moved out in a different direction than we thought we were going to go. We walked and it was very tiring. I saw GIs evacuating by ambulances and also Nazi prisoners.[5]

By this date the counteroffensive had expanded far enough to the east along the battle line to fully bring the rest of the 30th Division into the fight. Their first and most important objective at this time was the capture of the German-speaking Belgian town of St. Vith. While the 117th and 119th Infantry Regiments were doggedly advancing south in difficult conditions and against tough resistance, the 120th Infantry began a punishing three-day fight to take the town of Thirimont, a small town on a ridge that provided a commanding view of the east flank of the assault. This area was defended by *Volksgrenadier Regiment 293.* The 2nd Battalion attacked on the left towards Thirimont; Companies E and F were halted in their tracks by heavy artillery and mortar fire; and by late morning Company G had bypassed enemy positions in the southern sector. At 1145 hours the Germans even farther south of that position struck Company G with about 100 men, but were repelled. The attack continued pressing forward unabated, but Company G was taking many casualties. Without adequate reinforcements on hand to plug the gaps, they were eventually compelled to pull back.

Frustrated by this lack of progress, Major General Hobbs attempted to direct Company G to return to Thirimont and finish the job, but the company wasn't reachable by radio. The battle reached its climax on 15 January when the German troops attacked with a mixed battalion that contained elements of the *3rd Parachute Division* and the *348th Assault Gun Battalion.* The German *3rd Parachute Division* had earned quite a fearsome reputation in Normandy, but was by now battle weary and demoralized to such an extent that they no longer proved to be as menacing as they had been during previous encounters.

FRANCIS CURREY, COMPANY K, 120TH INFANTRY REGIMENT

Thirimont, it was only a little village. It was impregnable. We had to go in from the flanks. This one place was defended by some of Hermann Göring's paratroopers, which was one of their better units. They were all young guys and all had automatic weapons. Our squad was sent up a hillside to take this one point. It was an open field there, so you couldn't take the whole squad. We—Lucero, Gould, and I—figured, hell, just the three of us could advance fast. We didn't realize, however, that we were taking on the regimental headquarters for the paratrooper unit!

We took a lot of automatic fire when we started crossing that field. They started opening up on us; Lucero and I made it, but Gould didn't. I got hit in the arm and was kind of numb for a while. Lucero and I got inside the building and we drove them upstairs, but we couldn't go up and the Germans couldn't come down. We managed to get the rest of our squad there. That night our company executive officer showed up to see what the hell was going on up there. We had all afternoon to plan out what to do; meanwhile, they were lobbing grenades. A couple guys from another squad came in and got hit by the grenade fragments. It was a stalemate. We couldn't go out or anything because they hadn't taken the village, so my idea was to set the goddamn barn on fire. It was a hay-barn combination. So I set it on fire and let the other guys get out one at a time. Our executive officer knew exactly where our line was at the time. As for my arm, it was two days before I could get to an aid station. The doctor looked at it and he said, "Boy, that's nice and clean—bandage and back you go." It got me another Purple Heart.

By the end of the Bulge we had no officers. So a day or two after Thirimont, some officers of the 120th called out, "Company K, who's in charge here?" We looked around and I said, "I guess I am." They asked again, "Who are your officers?" I replied "We don't have any." They replied, "Oh. . . . just fall in."[6]

On 12 January, along a 750-mile front in the east, the Red Army had launched a massive offensive that would inevitably distract German High Command (*OKW*) and draw their attention away from the Bulge.

Around this time, conditions on the high ground between Malmédy and St. Vith deteriorated significantly when blizzards set in, impeding both sides in the ensuing bitter struggle. It was enough to test the resilience of the toughest, battle-hardened troops of both sides, but once again, the Old Hickorymen stepped up and drove the Germans back. On 20 December, the 117th Infantry Regiment descended on Sart les St. Vith with such speed and ferocity that they took the defending Germans there completely by surprise. The 119th Infantry Regiment made equally devastating progress at Hinderhausen. Having eventually taken Thirimont, the 120th Infantry Regiment advanced into the adjoining villages of Ober-Emmels and Nieder-Emmels in the German speaking part of Belgium only to be hit there by friendly artillery, but they completed their objective relatively undeterred. Unfortunately, the 30th Division was no stranger to collateral damage.

VICTOR NEILAND, COMPANY F, 117TH INFANTRY REGIMENT

Company F was out in a field one day and German artillery started coming in something fierce. It was too late to dig foxholes, so we had to use what the Germans had left. I was with a bazooka team, a couple of little guys. We jumped into the holes and those two left their bazooka and all of their equipment including their carbines outside their hole. The two of them fit pretty well in their hole and I took the next one.

The artillery resumed and it was very accurate landing all around us. One shell hit right between us and the explosion buried the bazooka team. Once the artillery stopped at dark, I got up and out of my hole. I wasn't covered with too much dirt and debris, but the other guys were literally buried, so I had to dig and pull them out. They were shaking like crazy! It was terrible and that round destroyed all of their stuff, including their bazooka, supplies, and carbines. We had to hurry back to the rest of the Company to get new equipment.[7]

FRANK DENIUS, BATTERY C, 230TH FIELD ARTILLERY BATTALION

We stopped the Germans in late December and then went into the attack in mid-January 1945. We were trying to pinch off the salient the Germans had created. I was sent along with a company behind the German lines, along with Jacobs and Goldstein. Our mission was to get behind their lines and interrupt their rear echelon. When it was time to head out, we watched where and when the Germans patrolled; they would pass about every seven to eight minutes, and during the gap in time we would slip across 10 to 12 guys. Eventually, we moved about 200 across and they didn't know we were there. We fired artillery into the rear areas, but they eventually found us and started firing at us with rockets. Other American armored units were supposed to relieve us but, they couldn't get through. So we were there for three nights instead of one. I had frozen feet, hands, and extremities. I was also wounded in my right leg just above the knee by a rocket shell fragment on 25 January.[8]

While the 9th Air Force pummeled retreating German columns with impunity, US forces finally began to mass and converge on St. Vith; by 23

January. it was back under Allied control. The 30th Division continued to push south but by now there was no longer any determined effort from German forces to prevent their advance. They ran into a few pockets of resistance, but for all intents and purposes, the back of the German foray into Belgium had been significantly broken and was rapidly deteriorating into a chaotic retreat. A massive pincer movement involving the First and Third Armies had finally squeezed the German forces into submission and forced them well back behind the Siegfried Line from where they started. The two US armies met at the town of Houffalize on 16 January, and by 28 January, the Germans had been pushed back to their original starting line beyond the Belgian and Luxembourg borders. It had been the largest land battle ever fought by US forces; by the time it was over more than 600,000 US troops had reached the Ardennes. Old Hickory's fight in the Belgian Ardennes was over, but their war was destined to continue, and to a man, they were hoping it would all be over soon.

PART FOUR

GERMANY AND VICTORY

RHINELAND CAMPAIGN, PART 2
26 January–21 March 1945

CENTRAL EUROPE CAMPAIGN
22 March–11 May 1945

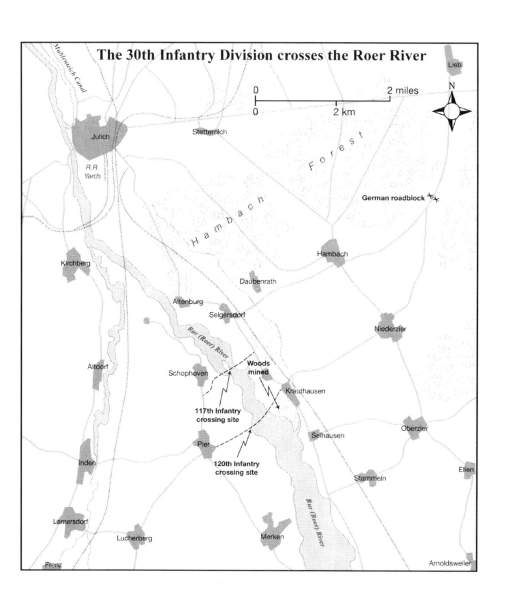

The 30th Infantry Division crosses the Roer River

Lieb

0   2 miles

0   2 km

N

Muhlenteich Canal

Julich

Stetternich

F o r e s t

H a m b a c h

German roadblock

R.R. Yards

Kirchberg

Hambach

Daubenrath

Altenburg

Selgersdorf

Niederzier

Rur (Roer) River

Altdorf

Schophoven

Woods mined

Krauthausen

117th Infantry crossing site

Selhausen

Oberzier

Pier

120th Infantry crossing site

Inden

Stammeln

Ellen

Lamersdorf

Rur (Roer) River

Lucherberg

Merken

Frenz

Arnoldsweiler

CHAPTER NINE

SETTING THE PACE

The Battle of the Bulge may have been over, but the war in the west still had to be won. As the Old Hickorymen huddled around campfires and hearths of bombed out buildings in the vicinity of Liernieux, those who had survived the previous months of fighting must have been deeply contemplating thoughts such as, "What would the US Army want them to do next?" "When would it all be over?" and the most pervasive, "Would they survive to tell the tale?" So many had been lost or wounded since the desperate fighting in the Normandy bocage. As was usual during the all too infrequent times of inertia, rumors abounded. One rumor even audaciously suggested that they were going to have to do the Siegfried Line campaign all over again.

Behind the 30th Division was the liberated country of Belgium and ahead of them the ominous open ground of the Schnee Eiffel region of Germany beckoned. It had been agreed at Allied HQ that the 30th Division would remain as part of the Ninth Army, which in turn would remain part of 21st Army Group. Since 21 December, they had been commanded by Field Marshal Montgomery. Needless to say, his appointment had not been a popular one.

The order finally came through to the 30th Division to head back north to the area above Aachen. To some, after the claustrophobic densely forested northern Ardennes, it came as a relief. At least they were going to open plains where they could maneuver and advance to what would hopefully be the final victory. It would entail a few river crossings first, but these obstacles weren't deterrents to the 30th, who had crossed numerous rivers and canals since arriving in Normandy back in June 1944. They had learned a lot about navigating these waterways and had even demonstrated their aptitude to other divisions behind the lines.

As the Allies resumed the offensive in February 1945, all that stood in the way of victory and the unconditional surrender of Germany were battered and weakened German forces and a series of river obstacles, the first of which was the Roer River. On 23 February 1945, the 30th Division prepared to cross the Roer in assault boats alongside the 84th, 29th, and 102nd Infantry Divisions. The plan to cross this river was called Operation GRENADE and was initially scheduled to commence 10 February to coincide with the Canadian attack to the north, but was delayed until 23 February 1945. Operation GRENADE was intended to be a large-scale river crossing operation in which US Ninth Army and VII Corps of US First Army would navigate the river with six divisions. The most detrimental obstacle to the Allied offensive was not the river, but the seven dams that regulated the flow of the Roer and its tributaries.

The two largest dams there were the Erft and the Schwammenauel. The larger of these two dams, the Schwammenauel, lay at the southern edge of the Hürtgen Forest beside the town of Schmidt. Some of the bloodiest fighting in the western theatre had occurred when the Allies had attempted to take control of this dam. They had failed in that objective and German control of the dams still posed a serious threat to the Allied advance because their destruction had the potential to cause flooding throughout the whole Roer River valley.

Now the Germans were faced with two options. They could destroy the dams and cause flash flooding throughout the valley, or they could destroy each dam's outlet valve, and by gradually releasing vast amounts of water they could systematically flood the whole area. They decided on the second option and began releasing a steady stream of water into the Roer Valley. At midnight, 8 February, the Germans had blown the sluices that controlled the water level emanating from the Schwammenauel dam. Allied plans, codenamed Operation GRENADE, were temporarily postponed because in some sections the river rose to depths of 10 to 11 feet and flooded broad areas. Where the Roer River overflowed its banks some areas extended as far as 1000 yards wide. By unleashing this water the Germans created a sizeable flood barrier in front of Ninth Army that extended right up into the British sector to the left of that position. The Roer River and German defensive positions beyond its banks provided the primary defensive barrier against the attack from the west.

Under normal circumstances the river was 60 to 85 feet wide, but with the flooding and winter conditions in February and March, it had increased to between 900 and 1,200 feet wide, with a water level of 12 feet in places. Intelligence reported that opposite the US Ninth Army, the German *15th Army* was defending the Roer sector with approximately 30,000 men, supported by 85 assault guns, 32 tanks, and 30 battalions of artillery. This later proved to be a gross overestimation of German strength in the area.

While Patton was descending on Trier through the Saar-Moselle triangle, Eisenhower agreed to support Field Marshal Montgomery's attack through the *Reichswald* (German imperial forest) with a supporting attack to the south of this position. Montgomery's attack in the north, code-named Operation VERITABLE, began on 8 February. Infantry with tanks of the Canadian army's I and II Corps jumped off 9 February to initiate the spearhead, reinforced by British XXX Corps. They assaulted the Siegfried Line defenses in and around the dense *Reichswald*. Despite the attackers' greater numbers and air superiority, stubborn German resistance and poor weather slowed up the advance considerably.

A two-week delay in the American sector finally came to an end on 23 February. This was going to be the last decisive battle of the war in Europe. The Germans supplemented the natural obstacle presented by the Roer with a series of field fortifications that were laid out in three lines. The first line coursed along the Roer's east bank, while the other two lines ran six and eleven miles behind the first, with the third running parallel to the Erft River. They had placed trenches and anti-tank obstacles designed to impede the US forces mobility and to force them into close-quarter fighting in the adjacent towns and villages that would serve as strongpoints.

Once again the 30th Division was going to lead the way. The 119th and 120th Infantry Regiments were designated to be the main assault troops with the 117th Infantry retained as the strategic reserve. There must have been a pervasive feeling of *déjà vu* through the ranks when at 0130 hours, engineers moved stealthily toward the river carrying heavy sections of the footbridge they planned to assemble under cover of darkness. They set to work in time honored fashion, and a few hours later, as a thin, ghostly veil of pre-dawn mist covered the area, the skies were suddenly illuminated by the eruption of a thunderous Allied artillery barrage covering a 25-mile stretch of the river from the south of Düren to north of Linnich. Old Hickorymen gritted their teeth and prepared for yet another crossing.

They would use amphibious tractors called Alligator LVTs (Landing

Vehicle Tracked) and M2 assault boats. M2s weighed 410 pounds, were manned by three engineers, and could carry a 12-man rifle squad or mortar crew. The principal use for the M2s was to ferry the assault waves of infantry. They were far from being ideal for this purpose because they were built of plywood and were cumbersome and noisy when they collided with other boats; moreover, they didn't have outboard motors so the crew and infantry squad provided the propelling power with paddles.

Now the war was full on again and the use of artillery would be on an overwhelming scale. The 30th Division front extending to around 800 yards was supported by three battalions of artillery from the 2nd Armored Division's self-propelled guns along with Corps and Army battalions that collectively provided 246 pieces. Accompanying this tirade of shells were 36 guns from the 823rd Tank Destroyer Battalion. As the attack went in the Germans were caught unaware and, consequently, only light resistance was encountered during the crossing. To the left of the 30th's position in Broich the main thrust was provided by the 29th Infantry Division.

While work was underway to construct the footbridges, a highly effective smoke screen was provided by the 82nd Smoke Generator Company, which allowed the work to progress virtually unimpeded. Germans beyond the far bank of the Roer had no idea that these bridges were being built, as most of them were hiding in the cellars during the punishing Allied artillery barrages.

The crossing got underway at 0330 hours when one Alligator, operated by Company C, 234th Engineer Combat Battalion, loaded up its passengers and began to wade down through the swampy area to the riverbank. Shortly after, when the necessary signal had been given, three other troop-laden Alligators followed. No serious resistance was encountered except some light mortar and artillery fire that splashed ineffectively into the river without causing so much as a bow wave. All but one of the M2s also made it to the far shore unimpeded. Only one boat, carrying men from the 119th Infantry Regiment, was swept downstream. The only obstacle to progress after landing on the far shore were the mines that caused a few casualties who were quickly transported back across the river. Two hours after the crossing had started, two infantry companies had been safely transported to the far bank; according to the infantry battalion commanding officer, that was sufficient for the time being. The engineers, meanwhile, had successfully assembled a footbridge.

The bridgehead across the Roer River in the vicinity of the German town of Schophoven was quickly established by the 119th and 120th Infantry Regiments; on the following day, at 1630 hours on 24 February, the 117th Infantry, initially in reserve, was brought up to strengthen the forward units of the division. As they scurried up the far bank of the Roer and headed east, Company L of the 117th, making their way through the woods toward Steinstrass, stumbled upon three German half-tracks each packing 20mm AA guns and carrying infantry. Suddenly it was like being back in the Ardennes as machine-gun and rifle bullets splintered the wood and whizzed between the fir trees accompanied by tracer rounds aimed at the Germans. A lieutenant from Company L then ordered his men to fix bayonets and charge. The ensuing charge was so effective that it didn't lose momentum until it was halted by a roadblock just in front of the town.

VICTOR NEILAND, COMPANY F, 117TH INFANTRY REGIMENT

On the 14th we saw German planes in a spotlight dropping flares and bombs. Our heavy guns were firing. "Bed-Check Charlie" was bombing and strafing. During this time we practiced carrying boats to the river.

On the 23rd there was a terrific artillery barrage in the morning. We were up at 0400 hours and rode on trucks to the end of the town. There were smoke screens and then we crossed the Roer. There was a big traffic tie-up, but we got over. There were houses burning and we saw English tanks and artillery come in.[1]

HANK STAIRS, HEADQUARTERS COMPANY, 117TH INFANTRY REGIMENT

We got across the Roer and into Germany. Here, I had my first experience seeing a jet plane. It was a bright, sunny day and we were out playing touch football in the open fields. This German jet plane shot in from Germany towards the west at treetop level. It was about a quarter of mile from where I was standing. It reminded me of a cigar with wings. I later found out it was an Me 262 aircraft. We then attacked north and were fighting-alongside the British. I liked fighting with them because they would shoot the hell out of a town with artillery before they made an attempt to move into it.[2]

The 117th Infantry's 1st Battalion remained in regimental reserve and in late afternoon, moved to the site where the 119th Infantry had crossed, near Schophoven. After crossing the river, the 30th turned south to Krauthauzen, then northeast to Niederzier more than two miles east of the Roer, and remained there to await further orders. Company B left at 0145 hours on 25 February and led the battalion northeast along the highway toward Steinstrass, through the Burge woods. The mission of the 1st Battalion was to protect the right flank of the 117th Infantry, which also was the flank of the 30th Infantry Division, XIX Corps, Ninth Army, and the 21st Army Group.

By this time, within 21 hours of the commencement of the crossings, the engineers had successfully managed to construct a bridge over the Roer that was capable of supporting tanks. They were far ahead of the 36 hours first estimated to complete the task. Thanks to this level of efficiency, the 30th Division was ahead of the 29th Infantry Division in the north. German prisoners taken immediately after the crossing gave the GIs some encouragement when they spoke of the discouraged condition of their comrades.

The crossing of the Roer was justifiably acknowledged by the Allies as a tactical success. With the destruction of the discharge valves at the dams by the Germans and the subsequent flooding in the valley, they did not expect an attack in that area until the flooding had subsided and the ground in the flood plain had dried sufficiently to allow heavy vehicles to cross. The decision to commence the assault on 23 February before the flooding had subsided, coupled with several false artillery preparations prior to 23 February, enabled the Ninth Army to achieve tactical surprise and consequently gain the advantage over the German defenders.

It became apparent that many of the German units encountered just after the crossing were now in full retreat. The only concerted defense that the 30th encountered was in the small town of Köngishoven, which was in their opinion, one of the few remaining places being defended with any spirit and skill. A German battalion commander, who was taken as a POW, paid the 119th Infantry Regiment a great compliment for their action there when he said that he had witnessed the best example of effective infantry tactics that he had ever seen in 17 years of army life. At this juncture in time, after the first successes, there was no real incentive to continue the advance northward. It hadn't all been plain sailing for the Old Hickorymen. The Corps commander had called off the advance fewer than 24 hours after the attack had gotten underway. The 30th Division, meanwhile, was strategically checkerboarding its regiments along the front line almost as quickly as the G-3 could relay instructions.

From this point on, there was no longer any organized defense ahead of the Old Hickorymen; they were only too ready to contend with the disorganized sporadic interludes provided by town defenses, which were manned by whatever troops and tanks the local commander could requisition.

A combat command of the US 2nd Armored Division moved in temporarily to protect the division's right flank east of Steinstrass, but they were probably surplus to requirements at the time. Captured German commanders complained vociferously of being abandoned to their fate by armor that had pulled out prematurely without giving prior notice to their comrades. German resistance in this area was rapidly dissolving into a shambolic display of mismanagement and self-preservation. They realized too late in the game that the main objective of this Allied thrust was to capture the industrial German heartland of the Ruhr valley and beyond that, the city of Düsseldorf. Nevertheless, the Roer River crossing was a categorical victory for US forces. The river was crossed, objectives were seized, and the bridgehead was established, all events occurring ahead of schedule and with minimal casualties.

The Roer River crossing was, for all intents and purposes, one of the slickest, precise operations of World War II. The 30th completely hoodwinked the Germans by crossing over an area that was considered impassable due to flooding. The skill and speed with which this crossing was executed allowed the supporting artillery batteries to relocate and provide close support wherever and whenever it was needed. Granted there had been some collateral damage, but this was minimal in comparison with other assaults. The 30th's display of military prowess and efficiency raised the eyebrows of the most battle-hardened veterans and they set the pace for the rest of the Ninth Army. This was further proof, if it was needed, that those Old Hickorymen could overcome almost any obstacle and rise to the challenge. Now the final challenge was fast approaching. After the successful crossing of the Roer, attention was now focused on the mighty Rhine River.

Pfc. Arlon L. Adams, 119th Infantry Regiment, KIA on 24 February 1945 in the Roer River assault, the 119th crossed and attacked just south of the Hambach Forest. Pfc. Adams was awarded the Silver Star and the Bronze Star.

3rd Battalion, 119th Infantry Regiment, Combat Journal After Action Report, 17 March 1945
23 Feb: Large artillery saturation began at 0240 hours. Regiment attacked across Roer River to Schophoven in a column of Battalion in order of lst, 2nd, and 3rd. This Battalion started to move to Schophoven at 0610. Remained here until 1900 when they crossed the Roer River and passed through the 1st and 2nd Battalions of this regiment and attacked Hambach. Battalion

crossed the line of departure at 2300 and reached objective at 2330.

24 Feb: This battalion attacked to the northwest toward Stetternich at 1500. Company K as the assault company with tanks attached. Company I on the right with tanks in support of Company K. Company L remained in Hambach in regimental reserve. Company K reached its objective in short time. Positions consolidated by Companies I and K at about 1700 hours. Captured considerable number of prisoners, 20 120mm mortars, and ammunition. At ___ hours elements of the 1st Engineers, this regiment, and the 117th Infantry Regiment, passed through Hambach attacking to the north and the northeast.

25 Feb: At 1200 hours this battalion, with 2nd Battalion on the right, attacked to the north to seize Rödingen and Hollen, respectively. This battalion attacked with I and K in the assault; Company L in support; with Company A, 744th Tank Battalion; and 1st platoon, 823rd TDs; attacked at 1300. 1st elements of Company I in south edge of Rödingen. K Company on the left was held up by intense tank and small arms fire from Welldorf and Güsten on their left. By 1530, Companies I and L and one platoon K Company had captured all but the west end of Rödingen at 2000 hours. The balance of K Company with tanks attached forced the enemy out of the west end of Rödingen and the town was taken at 1700 with a force of 150 men with tanks (five) were assembling to the northeast for a counterattack on Rödingen. This attempted organization was broken up by heavy artillery concentrations. By 0200 hours, 26th February 1945, the battalion objective was completely cleaned out and organized defensively. During the night Colonel R. A. Baker, Regimental commander, visited the Battalion Forward CP and presented Major Carlton Stewart, Battalion commander, with the Oak Leaf Cluster to his Bronze Star on behalf of General Hobbs.

26 Feb: Situation and positions unchanged. Battalion Rear CP moved to Rödingen, closed in town at 1600.

27 Feb: Situation and positions unchanged.

Lieutenant General William H. Simpson, the Ninth Army commander, wrote this letter on March 15, to the Division commander:

It was a distinct pleasure for me last October when I learned that the 30th Infantry Division was being assigned to the Ninth Army, a pleasure all the more keenly felt because of the fact of my previous association as one-time commander of the Division. I have been happy to share with you the pride of accomplishment that has characterized the history of your Division since the initiation of operations on the Continent. The operation just concluded again furnished your Division with an opportunity to distinguish itself. I scarcely need point out that this opportunity was accepted and completely exploited by the Division, thereby adding another glowing chapter to the record. Particularly gratifying to me was the surprise which was achieved in your crossing the Roer River at an unsuitable site, and the ingenuity with which your organization overcame the difficulties of building up a bridgehead despite meager access and egress roads. Your expeditious clearing of the Hambach Forest and the firm protection which you furnished the Army right flank, materially assisted the Army to successfully execute the maneuver by which the enemy was turned out of his positions and driven to retreat across his own line of communication.

It was characteristic of your Division that, with the original mission accomplished, you were ready and waiting to execute another mission—that of further securing the Army's right flank and facilitating the capture of the key strongpoint of Neuss. It is with great personal pleasure that I acknowledge the splendid job performed by the 30th Infantry Division and express my commendation of the individual contribution made by every officer and man.[3]

CHAPTER TEN

THE FINAL PUSH

The stage was now set for the final river crossing. This time it was going to be the Rhine, the last great water barrier before descending on Berlin. Behind the lines, not far from Maastricht, the 30th Division set about making preparations in their usual meticulous style. They staged a preparatory crossing of the Maas River using the latest amphibious vehicles available to the US Army. No stone was left unturned as the engineers cleared old German minefields on the banks of the Maas and set up practice crossing sites. All of the assault troops earmarked to participate in the crossing began rehearsing what they would be required to do when they got to the Rhine. The 30th Division practiced with the consummate skill they had molded to perfection during the past months of combat.

The imposing bridge at Remagen had been taken intact by the 9th Armored Division between 7 and 8 March 1945, enabling US forces to establish a bridgehead on the eastern side of the Rhine. Ninth Army now held the west bank of the Rhine, from the south of Düsseldorf to the mouth of the Lippe River at Wesel.

Field Marshal Montgomery, commanding 21st Army Group, now planned to strike east on a narrow front that would bring them into close proximity to the northern edge of the Ruhr cities. Once there, they would make contact with First Army, completely encircle the industrial heartland of Germany in the Ruhr area, and take possession of the area that Allied air command had failed to completely destroy. This plan also incorporated what would become the last great airborne assault of WWII, to simultaneously drop the British 6th Airborne Division ("Red Devils"), commanded by Major

General Eric L. Bols, and the US 17th Airborne Division ("Thunder from Heaven"). Their objective was to first seize the bridges over the Issel River (Ijssel in Dutch), then eliminate German forces from the Diersfordt Forest, which would clear the way for ground forces crossing the Rhine and prevent enemy reinforcements from reaching the beachhead.

Montgomery was a fastidious and meticulous planner who rarely considered any offensive unless the odds were decidedly in his favor, and this time they most definitely were.

The Germans were now finding themselves the disagreeable target of a massive pincer movement with General Patton's Third Army attacking from the south; Ninth Army attacking from the east; and British and Canadian Allies bearing down from the north. Many of the German divisions were mere skeletons of their former selves, reconstituted and reorganized with troops that were, in many cases, way below standard. The morale among German troops was inevitably poor but there were still a few divisions, such the *116th Panzer Division* and the *15th Panzer-Grenadier Division,* that still had enough fight in them to give the Allies a headache; unfortunately for them, they were a distinct minority. They were, moreover, insufficient to the task of defending the whole northern sector against the inevitable Allied tsunami now coming in from the west.

The Old Hickorymen were again given a vital role in the planned assault that would cover an area approximately five miles wide, which was roughly the textbook standard for a division front in WWII. First, a massive artillery bombardment lit the skies in one of the most impressive and powerful barrages of WWII. Then zero hour arrived and the GIs quietly made their way down to the riverside with tracer bullets whizzing above their heads. Just to the north of the 30th Division's position, under cover of darkness, British commandos removed the safety catches on their weapons and at 2200 hours they stealthily boarded the boats that would carry them to the west bank of the Rhine.

The 30th Division commander had decided to simultaneously engage all three regiments for this crossing. At 0100 hours massed 30th Division artillery thundered away with a barrage that lasted more than an hour and sent more than 20,000 rounds of smoke and high explosives to the far shore.

The 119th Infantry Regiment began crossing in the north, just southeast of the village of Büderich, near the confluence of the Lippe with the Rhine. The primary thrust in the center was provided by the 117th Infantry Regiment at the village of Wallach, with the 120th Infantry Regiment attacking two miles to the southeast near a big bend in the river just northeast of Rhein-berg. Each regiment used one battalion in the assault. Each assault battalion was organized into four waves with two-minute intervals between waves. Each battalion was equipped with 54 storm boats carrying seven men and a two-man crew each, and 30 double assault boats capable of transporting 14 men and a three-man crew. Machine guns firing tracer bullets guided the first wave, while colored aircraft landing lights illuminated the path for those who followed after. Once again, elaborate preparations had been undertaken along with detailed reconnaissance to avoid any unexpected barriers to their progress.

HANK STAIRS, HEADQUARTERS COMPANY, 117TH INFANTRY REGIMENT

We used sand tables to prepare for attacks, including the Rhine River crossing. The boys from the Operations section (S-3), the boys from the Intelligence section (S-2) and a number of us from Headquarters assisted in the construction of the sand tables. The table was elevated, about waist high and six by eight feet. We made a miniature image of the area we planned to attack. We reconstructed the contours and terrain features such as hills, villages, and forested areas. We used small blocks, little bits of grass and shrubbery, etc. The battalion commander could then instruct his company commanders and their staff exactly what their respon-sibilities were. Everybody was told where they would be, when they would jump off, what obstacles would be encountered, what terrain features were on their front, how they were expected to move, and phase lines for the attack. Everyone down to and including squad leaders visited Battalion Headquarters to be in-structed on the sand table.

We were headed to the Rhine and it was pitch black. There was a sedan nearby painted khaki, sitting right on the trail. We said, "Hey, it's gotta be someone important." The story we got later was that Ike and General Simpson from the Ninth Army were in the car that very dark morning. To reach the river we had to drag our boat up the side of the dike and down the other side into the water for the attack, which we did. The guy who had been hit in the ass with shrapnel who I replaced in France was in front of me carrying the boat. The poor guy was abso-lutely scared out of his pants. I said to him, "Come on, we'll get through this." He was really afraid of getting hit again. As we headed across the river there was a guy in Navy fatigues sitting in the rear of the boat. I said to him, "Hey you're in the Navy, what the hell are you doing up here in a boat working for the Army?" He replied, "I'm taking you across the river, only I get to come back!" The Germans could have really given us hell, but there was very little resistance.[1]

JOHN O'HARE, COMPANY E, 117TH INFANTRY REGIMENT

We were south of Wesel and we were the Americans farthest north crossing the Rhine. We were placed under command of Field Marshal Montgomery for that crossing. I don't know why, but we were. Where we crossed it was almost a palisades area; it was not an easy bank on our side. We were in an assembly area near the east bank of the Rhine for four days before the Navy took us across.

Before we crossed, one of the tanks up with us on one of the bluffs had a radio which could pick up broadcasts, not just chatter between tanks and commanders. We were able to hear the songs being played by Axis Sally. She got on and said, "30th Division, we know where you are, and we know you have earned the reputation as Roosevelt's SS. Let us tell you what's waiting for you on the other side of the Rhine River. We have screaming meemies, we have 88s, we have bayonets—all of which will tear your guts out. In the meantime, other men will have a good time with your wives and girlfriends back in the United States. You are the ones taking the brunt of the war." It was the whole propaganda thing. Supposedly this woman was coming from Radio Arnhem, which was Dutch, but it was obviously a German propaganda station because every now and then they would talk about Bolsheviks being beaten down on the Eastern Front. They played music though, and it was just a joke.

When the day arrived to cross the Rhine, they loaded us on an amphibious vehicle which the Navy had. The whole propulsion system depended on tracks on both sides. We started off at about 0400 hours and it was dark. They lost sight of the vehicle ahead of them and they made a wrong turn somewhere climbing. They must have had a path staked out to go down the bluffs. We bumped into some rocks and the amphibious vehicle turned on an angle. Since I was holding the bazooka on the back end of the thing, I could see what was going on and I could see treetops below. Looking down, I said, "Oh my God, we're on some sort of palisade here. We're partly hanging off and we're at a terrible angle. We could fall off of this thing!" We got off the rocks and got in the river, but one side of the vehicle had been damaged by the rocks and wasn't responding. We went around in circles! They figured out that if they made the circles big enough we could get across. We were on the river for quite a while and I was holding my bazooka, so I could not crouch below the side or the front. The vehicle had fairly flimsy metal for armor. I could see shells landing in the river.[2]

**KING KENNY, RECONNAISSANCE PLATOON,
823RD TANK DESTROYER BATTALION**

I remember when we crossed the Rhine we were to go in boats—not motorboats, but boats with paddles. We were lined up on top of a hilly area with the river down in front of us. It was dark, nighttime. A bunch of guys were next to us and I looked over and saw their faces were blacked-up. They were sharp, a bunch of Canadian commandos. We got to the water and they had a boat for us. It was big and we rowed that thing until we hit land. Turned out there was an island in the middle of the river and it hadn't been plotted for us. We kept paddling the boat and finally pushed across to the other side but met no resistance. We went forward for the next 24 hours and just kept moving. Later, General Simpson wrote a letter commending the Division (he once commanded) for its success in crossing the Rhine. Before we crossed that day, we were in a wooded area and the bombers came over, mostly B-17s. They were in tight formation. You could see some get hit and keel over. Some guys jumped out and sometimes nobody got out. The guys on the ground would shout, "Jump! Get out! Get out!"[3]

MARION SANFORD, 30TH CAVALRY RECONNAISSANCE TROOP (MECHANIZED)

Early on the morning of 26 March, we drove across the Rhine River on the longest pontoon bridge I had ever seen. The infantry had crossed earlier, pushing east, and had expanded the bridgehead sufficiently to allow the bridge to be built by the engineers. We did not receive any fire as we slowly drove across, our vehicles spaced so as not to overload the pontoons. It was still an unnerving ride, since the bridge moved and swayed up and down and from side to side with the current and the load it was supporting.

It had been raining heavily for several days and the river banks were muddy as we climbed up to the soaked river bank beyond the bridge. We stopped on a small rise and were waiting for instructions about which way we were to go. We were fairly relaxed and didn't expect any problems as the line was several miles away, so we were mostly just standing around the vehicles, jawing with each other.

We were not there for ten minutes when three large German artillery shells landed practically on top of us, one not more than 10 feet from our half-track. The shells impacted deeply into the mud and, by the grace of God, none of them exploded. It shook us up pretty badly because if any of the three had gone off, we would have most likely been killed or, at the very least, badly injured.

I had not fully settled down from our near miss when we were instructed to drive on a bit farther to an assembly area and wait. After a while, General Harrison, the Assistant Division Commander, drove up and had a short meeting with Captain Hume and several other Recon officers. Captain Hume was told that Recon would be joining a task force that General Harrison was forming. The task force was made up of our troop and detachments from an engineer company, an infantry battalion from the 119th Infantry, tanks, tank destroyers, artillery, anti-aircraft, medical, and ordnance.[4]

When the crossing got underway the Germans were crouching in a dike that ran parallel to the west bank of the Rhine with their helmets pulled low. The thick smoke screen and constant accurate shelling rapidly caused them to become demoralized and disoriented. They were never going to be able to put up any concerted resistance and, according to one GI, it wasn't much of a fight. The artillery had performed well and the 30th Division captured all the planned objectives in rapid succession. Company K of the 120th Infantry Regiment took the initiative to expand their territory farther as they mounted a company of light tanks from the 744th Tank Battalion along with two platoons of the 823d's tank destroyers.

JOHN O'HARE, COMPANY E, 117TH INFANTRY REGIMENT

We were close to the town of Spellen. I know that because one of the guys had gone into a German house nearby and had come out with a fireman's helmet that had the name Spellen on it. We got pinned down in the forest there for quite a while. The 116th Panzer Division *had been resupplied and was back in Germany. They came up and closed up against us. I don't know how far in we were from the river itself, but they closed in on us and did a lot of damage. Eight other guys and I found a trench that the Germans had dug. They periodically would build trenches because of possible air raids and they would jump into them. This was a forested area, so not only had the trench already been dug by the Germans, but there were a lot of logs piled up. We got word that the Germans were heading our way for a counterattack so we just took advantage of the ready-made holes and put logs on top with dirt over them. While we were there the* 116th Panzer Division *came up and started shelling pretty wildly; they cut down the forest around us. We spent the next couple of days down in this hole. We were in there for about 48 hours sitting with our knees under our chins. And every time a shell would land, some of the dirt from above would fall down our back and shirt. There was a tank knocked out really close to us and it burned furiously. The tank had been parked and the GIs inside had found some wine somewhere—they were all drunk. The Germans pumped a round in and set them on fire. What was amusing was the artillery observers were in the hole with us, so we joked, "Why isn't our artillery doing something?" but we knew why—because they were seeking cover in the hole with us!*[5]

HANK STAIRS, HEADQUARTERS COMPANY, 117TH INFANTRY REGIMENT

On the other side, I heard someone yelling; it was a Jerry who had a broken ankle. I said to him, "The medics are right behind us, they'll take care of you. Can I have your watch?" So he gave me his watch and I left. We got to this little village and there was a house. I had gotten separated, but I caught up later. I went into the farmhouse to see if anyone was in the cellar. There was old gentleman and three ladies. I was hot and sweaty so I took off my helmet. I saw a baby basket sitting back in the corner and I was going to toss my helmet over into it when I caught myself. I thought "I'd better be careful that there's nothing in there." So I went over and looked in. Sure enough, there was a baby. I stayed but two seconds in that place and went up the ladder out of the basement and caught up with the troops.[6]

KING KENNY, RECONNAISSANCE PLATOON, 823RD TANK DESTROYER BATTALION

We crossed and went into this town. The residents had cleared out but there were a bunch of Russian girls there. I think they were slave labor. They looked like they could play fullback for Notre Dame! They had a bunch of booze and some guy said it could blind you. One girl said she wanted to dance and kiss me. She bit me on the lip and that was my last date with her![7]

FRANK DENIUS, BATTERY C, 230TH FIELD ARTILLERY BATTALION

I missed about 5 weeks of combat from 25 January until early March. I was able to get warm again and I was given a lot of medicine. You weren't totally alert all the time when you are taking that medicine! I traveled back riding in a hammock in a boxcar (40 and 8). They put colored gauze on my arm to let nurses know what shots I needed, but I hid the gauze under my sleeve so that I could sleep! I went back to England and I was ambulatory for ten days or so. While I was there, my job was to take the wounded ambulatory patients on marches. I also went to different wards where guys needed exercises, arm exercises, etc. I was in charge of that for about a week, then I was shipped back to my unit.

I rejoined my unit just on the west side of the Rhine. We, as well as all our artillery, crossed the Rhine in LCIs and a pontoon. There were a lot of German soldiers moving west because they wanted to be captured by the Americans, not the Russians.[8]

The Old Hickory habit of riding tanks into battle to get to the enemy faster was repeated for one final time, and by 1730 hours, the way ahead had been completely cleared of German troops. Within 24 hours of crossing the Rhine, the 30th Division had advanced over six miles. On top of that, their engineers had stunned division command again and completed a bridge across the Rhine in just nine hours.

117th Infantry Regiment, After Action Report, 28 March 1945. Interview Major Julius W. Singleton, S-3, 117th Infantry at Waldeslust (382372), Germany, with Lt. Henderson.

We moved the regiment into assembly area near Wallach (200335) on the evening of 23 March 1945. The 1st Battalion made the initial crossing, taking Ork (218339) with Companies A and B abreast. 150 prisoners were captured there. The 2d Battalion went through Ork and took objective Folly (240345), and from there went into Katie (245353). Ginny (265350) was captured by the 1st and 2d Battalions, the 2d on the left and the 1st on the right. Following that the 1st and 3d Battalions captured Sue (290360). In that attack we employed the 3d Battalion on the left and the 1st Battalion on the right, clearing the objective by 0600 25 March 1945. At 0900, using the same formation, we took objective Anne (315375). It was ours by 1500. Company B went on in and captured the town of Hunxe (332388). At 0200 26 March, the 1st and 2d Battalions jumped off for objective Sally (355375). As soon as that capture was affected, the 3d Battalion passed through the 1st, and together with the 2d Battalion on the right, went on to objective Lilly (395375). That objective was cleared by nightfall. By that time we had moved ahead of the rest of the division, and our flanks were exposed. The next objective was Marie (420376) which we attacked at midnight, using again two battalions abreast, 3d on the left and 2d on the right. We were on the objective by 0445 27 March 1945.[9]

119th Infantry Regiment, After Action Report, 24 March 1945

At darkness on 23 March 1945, we put our boats in position behind the seawall and promptly pulled the men back into the houses. We estimated that it would take 30 minutes to carry the boats from the seawall to the launching site. Our assault was executed using two platoons of Company G on the left and two platoons of Company A on the right. These elements used storm boats exclusively in the crossing. We kept the storm boats on the foreshore until the assault battalion was entirely across, so that there wouldn't be any confusion from two-way traffic on the river. Direction was maintained by using machine-gun tracers and by the use of colored lights on the far shore. Cooperation with the engineers was grand. In crossing, the last battalion to cross ran into difficulties because the engineer guides couldn't find the right boats. That was the only mix up. The initial battalion, the 2d Battalion, drove directly inland to its objective. That objective was the portion of highway running north and south along the 22.5 grid line within the regimental zone. The 3d Battalion crossed in alligators end storm hosts and went through the 2d, into objective Patty (115351). There was not much resistance in there and the cap-strong resistance, but the combined strength, together with the fact that our light tanks were moving up to join the infantry, broke the resistance, and we crested over the railroad. This gave us complete control of objective Joy (238365). Hedy (247374) which included the town of Friedrichsfeld, and Jo (255360) were the next objectives. These had another railroad embankment running through them, but not on as high an embankment as the one running through Joy. In attacking these two objectives we used the 1st and 3d Battalions, 3d on the right, in a coordinated assault. Again the main opposition came from guns guarding the underpasses. The enemy realized that the underpasses were essential for our getting tanks through. The railroad embankment was an effective anti-tank barrier. Except for the underpasses there was not much defense. Once they were in our control, we had the entire objective.[10]

120th Infantry Regiment, After Action Report, 25 March 1945
Character of terrain, of hostile observation, and of enemy fire: The terrain was flat, divided by hedgerows, canals, and two railroad embankments; and containing woods, orchards, open fields, and several towns and villages. Hostile observation was excellent during daylight hours. Enemy fire consisted of artillery, mortar, 20mm, self-propelled gun, tank, rocket, and small arms fires; and aerial strafing.

Visibility, time of day, and atmospheric conditions: Visibility was excellent during daylight, the night was dark; time from 0200 to 1800; weather was good.

Location of enemy: In depth from the right (east) bank of the Rhine River to include the high ground approximately seven miles east thereof.

Morale: Our force, superior; enemy, good.

Effect or result of actions: In 16 hours these men covered the phenomenal distance of 6.2 miles beyond the far (east) bank of the Rhine, surging two or more miles ahead of friendly troops to their flanks, despite the fact that the curvature of the river caused the 120th Infantry Regiment to start behind all other friendly troops. As the result of the penetration, attacks by friendly forces on both flanks were facilitated. Furthermore, the regiment was in position at dawn on 25 March 1945 to capture an area on the high ground seven miles east of the Rhine upon which the enemy was endeavoring to establish his main defense line. The regiment seized this high ground early on 25 March 1945 while elements of the enemy were in the process of occupying it. Rapidly continuing the attack on the same day, the regiment overran and tore to pieces in one engagement two battalions of *Panzergrenadier Regiment 60*, which, according to captured officers, were rushing forward to occupy the high ground which the regiment had captured three hours earlier. As the result of its long drive on 24 March 1945 the regiment was able to quickly seize an exceptionally strong defense area which dominated all of the Division zone and also the northern portion of the zone assigned to the division to the right (south). The early seizure of this area prevented many casualties among all friendly troops in the vicinity because its capture would have been difficult and costly if the enemy reserves had had a few more hours for occupation and organization of the high ground.

Casualties sustained: 82.

Detailed resume: The 120th Regimental Combat Team started its attack across the Rhine River south and southwest of Mehrum, Germany, at 0200 hours on 24 March 1945.[11]

The German response to the Allied assault had been to commit the *116th Panzer Division* that had faced the 30th Division on numerous occasions in the past months. Despite only having two operational divisions available for combat, the Germans still managed to surprise the Allies with their speed and accuracy. The *116th* had practically welcomed the final opportunity to pitch themselves against their old adversaries in the 30th Division. While other Allied divisions raced ahead, the 30th remained in place to take on the *116th Panzer Division* and eradicate them once and for all. The reputation of the *116th* with their own army wasn't quite as illustrious as it was with the Allies. They were frequently accused by German generals of turning up unprepared to fight. Despite this, their battle honors were irrefutable and they had participated in many major engagements. The division had been originally created from the remnants of the *16th Panzergrenadier Division* and

179th Reserve Panzer Division in March 1944 and, quite a few of their men were seasoned veterans who had seen action on the Eastern front. They had fought hard during the Allied landings in Normandy and had even become trapped in the Falaise pocket. After Normandy their numbers were reduced to 600 men and 12 tanks, but after some refitting they were sent to defend Aachen. Now part of the *XLVII Panzer Corps,* under General Blaskowitz's *Army Group H,* on 24 March 1945 the division was ordered to halt the advance of the US 30th Infantry Division south of the Lippe River.

Positioned near the Dutch-German border, the *Greyhound Division's Panzergrenadier Regiment* 60 commenced its assault the next day, and by nightfall on 26 March 1945, the division had staggered the US 30th Infantry Division's attempts to breakout to the east. By 28 March 1945, the division held Dorsten, but was successfully outflanked when the British 6th Guards Armored Brigade bypassed the city. By 4 April 1945, the division was ordered to form and hold a north facing line of defense behind the Rhine-Herne Canal to preserve reinforcement of the north face of the Ruhr Valley. But by 18 April 1945, there was a definite cessation of all resistance in the Ruhr Pocket, and the remnants of the *116th Division,* along with their commanding officer, surrendered to the US Ninth Army.

Despite difficulties encountered while facing off against the *116th Panzer Division* and attempting to break out to the east, the ground and amphibious operations proved to be a resounding success and a veritable testament to the iron discipline and expertise of the 30th Division. Unfortunately, the airborne part of the attack, Operation VARSITY, hadn't fared so well.

The British 6th Airborne Division had suffered 590 killed and another 710 wounded or missing. Several hundred of the assumed MIAs turned up later and managed to link up with their units. The US 17th Airborne Division sustained 430 killed, with 834 wounded and 81 missing. Casualties among the glider pilots and the troop plane pilots and crews included 91 killed, 280 wounded and 414 missing in action. Eighty planes were shot down, and only 172 of the 1,305 gliders that landed in Germany were reusable. A total of 1,111 Allied soldiers had been killed during the day's fighting. In comparison, on D-Day, the 101st Airborne Division had lost 182 killed and the 82nd Airborne Division 158. Operation VARSITY, executed on 24 March 1945, was the single worst day for Allied airborne troops in WWII. Much of the damage inflicted on the airborne was due to the well-prepared German AA defenses that protected the Ruhr area. It was a staggering blow, nevertheless, to the final airborne assault of the war in the west.

HAROLD WILLIAMS, 105TH ENGINEER COMBAT BATTALION

It was early evening and a lot of Allied paratroopers were being dropped. As they were coming down, ack-ack guns were firing at them. Some of them went limp as they were coming down. It was sickening to us to see them fired upon and shot as they were coming down.[12]

Now that the Rhine had been crossed, Field Marshal Montgomery gave new orders that would guide the Ninth Army across the north German plain toward the Elbe River, deep inside Germany. Four Allied armies had successfully negotiated the last great barrier and now they could begin thrusting into the German heartland. On 1 April, Adolf Hitler responded to the rapid Allied advance by issuing a proclamation calling on all Germans to become "Werewolves" to prey on Allied troops, Jews, and those Germans who cooperated with Allied forces. Despite the late date of this statement, Hitler was serious. Despite the collapsing German defense, 30th blood would continue to be spilled along the rapid advance into the German heartland.

KING KENNY, RECONNAISSANCE PLATOON, 823RD TANK DESTROYER BATTALION

On the other side of the Rhine, it was pretty fluid. I recall it was called the "Rat Race." The regiments in the 30th were leap frogging. One would go to a town, one would jump over, and another would go to the next town. There were a lot of small areas that we simply bypassed. That was the way it went. They would form task forces named after the commander's last name (like Task Force Jones). Some had tanks, some TDs. They were not big forces. Recon was in front and we were supposed to be five minutes ahead of the force, and stay in radio contact all the time. There wasn't much resistance when we went into these town. In one town, however, there was a red cross hanging out of a window. I went in and they had a nurse who could speak English. I told her we wanted all their walking wounded up and out and on the road; affix a bed sheet to a pole; and just keep walking back towards the main force. We couldn't bother with prisoners. This one guy came up to me in a brown uniform (the German's were a greenish color) and he had ten or more guys with him. He handed me his pistol. He kept saying, "Hungar! Hungar!" Someone finally came up and said, "He's Hungarian, take his pistol." I guess they were Allies with the Germans and I didn't know it, so I took his pistol and had him walk the other way. They looked like an Italian company with this guy strutting down the road with his 10 guys after having given up! We went up another 100 yards and the road stopped. I took a right and I felt antsy. I stopped and said, "Send up a bazooka." So they brought a bazooka up and we moved another 100 yards; it was farmland. Suddenly a German just on the other side of a ditch got up with a Panzerfaust. *It was like a bazooka. I motioned to him to put it down. He was apparently confused and it occurred to me that he was going to raise it. I had a swivel machine gun on the front of the jeep, so I took him out. Then 10 or 12 Germans stood up in the field, so I just started spraying it. Something caught my attention on the left side, so I swung my machine gun around and started firing. The next thing I knew I was flying—it had to be armor piercing from a cannon, a tank, or something. They hit the right side of the jeep. As I was in the air, I looked up and the wheels were flying above my head. The driver apparently had gotten out and tried to run. He was cut down.*

The guy on the back of the jeep, next to a large high-mounted .50-caliber, was a fellow named James. He was a replacement. As the jeep was hit he landed in the dirt with me. I motioned to him to get into the ditch. Close by, there was a culvert and there was a guy already in there. I put my finger up to my mouth signaling him to be quiet and he told me, "Ruski Ruski." I guess he was a slave laborer; so we kept him quiet until after dark when we started crawling up the ditch toward where we knew our guys would have stopped in the town. There were two or three of our guys lying dead in the ditch. The first thing you'd feel was their combat boots. I lifted one fella's head and I knew him, his name was Hansen. We moved on up the ditch and I told James, the replacement, "You go up and see if you can call out, hopefully to the GIs." So he called out and the outpost replied, "What's the password?" James yelled back to me, "What's the password?" I didn't know. The only one I knew was to say, "Sure" and they would reply, "Cure," but that was an early one. I said just to tell them we were GIs. We were told to come forward and moved into our lines. We then delivered the Russian to some guys who could question him. After knocking out the jeep, the Germans also knocked out the M8s, which were abandoned and ended up in the ditch—the platoon was out of action. A day or two later I was riding on the back of an M10 or a tank when we got the word that Roosevelt had died.[13]

JOHN NOLAN, COMPANY G, 119TH INFANTRY REGIMENT

The attack in Hollen, Germany, happened on 26 February 1945. We were attached to the 2nd Armored Division. It was a classic tank-infantry assault across flat ground. The attack started from positions about a half mile away. It was over open ground, but we had 26 Sherman tanks that we marched between. That is not always a good thing and 16 tanks were lost in the attack. I remember a Panther tank taking position in an orchard on the outskirts of Hollen. It was shooting solid shot rounds. A shell knocked an open hatch off the Sherman right next to me. If it had not been solid shot, I'd be dead. It sure did shake up the tank commander whose head was in the opening. The Germans or German civilians had dug five-foot-deep slit trenches about 40 yards in front of the first houses. My platoon was able to occupy these trenches as the Nazis fled back to the houses during our advance. The Panther crew was very aggressive, though, as most all of the German tank crews were, and would not retreat to its orchard position. I always preferred anti-tank rifle grenades and thought I'd take a crack at the Panther. Well, I missed the tank but brought a tree branch down on the tank commander's head. This did not make him too happy and the Panther proceeded to try and bury the platoon in the trench. Lt. Giblin sent lead scout Hall from Virginia into the town first. Before Hall left he offered the Lt. some of his chewing tobacco to "calm" his nerves and off he went. Private Raymond Butts also entered the town with a bazooka. He was able to get to a second-floor position and shot a round into the Panther's turret. As the crew tried to escape the burning tank, Lt. Giblin used his grease gun to elim-inate them. Private Butts earned the Distinguished Service Cross for his action.[14]

JOHN O'HARE, COMPANY E, 117TH INFANTRY REGIMENT

I lost some buddies who were close to me. One of them, Edwin Fuller of California, a young Browning Automatic Rifleman, was shot so close to me that I was covered with his brains. He was shot in the head. He happened to have a Browning Au-tomatic Rifle. I was one of the two guys who knew where his body was, so I had to go back and find it, clean it up, take off his ammunition belts and bring that Browning Automatic Rifle back to the group so someone else could use it. I was covered with pieces of brains and blood because he was within arms-reach. I knew they were shooting at me. They were trying to get me but he had a bright spot on his helmet so they got him. We had gotten separated from our friends and the three of us were walking over a hill after we crossed the Rhine River along a ridge. We were a bit too high on the ridge. The enemy was in a stone house, which we didn't see but they saw us and opened up. I crawled up to a point where I could see the stone house and started shooting into the windows. This fellow, Fuller, came up with his Browning Automatic; he was not quite in position when they got him. I think it was because he used his helmet to warm water in. The paint on my helmet was absolutely intact and they didn't see me. I was already shooting at the win-dows, assuming that's where they were shooting from. I figured I could get a better angle on the stone building. Somebody opened up on me with a lot of small arms fire. They didn't get me. I found my ammo bearer in Shaner's squad with the pla-toon, and joined them. He told them that Fuller and I had been killed.[15]

JOHN NOLAN, COMPANY G, 119TH INFANTRY REGIMENT

The initial reaction when we received an attack order was—looks like we've got to do it, so let's get it over with! Final checks would be made with the men in the platoon making sure they knew what they had to do. We would also check to be sure they had enough ammo. If it was to be a bayonet attack, we would be sure they had their bayonets affixed on their rifles. It was a grim time and it was the ultimate test of individual "intestinal fortitude."

The "hard lesson" I learned over time was that a cohesive attack was possible and success probable if you had just a few veteran "stalwarts" in each rifle squad. The stalwarts "carried" the "less enthusiastic" into battle.

We were attacking in the mountainous Teutoburg Forest region and it was 3 April. I tried to get as many bandoliers of M1 ammunition as I could from supply. I had the men hang them around their necks, a couple each if they had them. I lined them up with bayonets on and they held their rifles at their hip level. We marched forward, shoulder to shoulder. We opened fire as fast as we could pull the trigger and reloaded as we kept moving. The sheet of fire, we believed and later proved, would prevent counterfire. As far as I can remember nobody was hit during the attack. We went down the side of the hill using this marching fire. When we got down to the bottom, there was an anti-tank gun and some gunners, and we killed them.

I lasted from 6 September to 7 April when I was hit. The Jerries came in at night on a counterattack. Our platoon ran out and started shooting at them and I got hit. Luckily, the round hit my rifle while I was holding it right above my left hand. It went into my left arm and I still have the slug in my left arm today.[16]

VICTOR NEILAND, COMPANY F, 117TH INFANTRY REGIMENT

We captured Hamelin. Our squad was the first one into Horst Wessel Square. There was a prison there and we released the prisoners. Unfortunately there was too much sniper fire going on, so we had to put those prisoners back in.

We looked through the rooms in the prison and it was loaded with stuff the Nazis had taken from the prisoners. There were watches, eyeglasses, and so on, all neatly packed in boxes all over the place. We took a few things, but being infantry we couldn't carry much. We even found a camera, but we had to leave it behind because it became too heavy. It was a nice town, but we were always moving and couldn't stay.[17]

The next item on the agenda for the 30th Division was the attack and capture of the city of Magdeburg that occurred in April 1945. This was to be the final action of the 30th Division before they reached the Elbe River. On the morning of 16 April, the 120th Infantry Regiment was ordered to make preparations to attack the city. While those preparations were underway, an attempt was made to obtain an unconditional surrender from the German staff, but at this juncture they were still reluctant to sign. Initial plans to send one regiment to attack Magdeburg were discarded and replaced with new directives to involve two divisions whose assault would be preceded by a massive air strike. Artillery units encircled Magdeburg to provide close support for the attack. Just a few days prior to the attack a horrifying discovery had been made in the forest beside the small town of Farsleben.

FRANK TOWERS, COMPANY M, 120TH INFANTRY REGIMENT

The 30th Infantry Division had just liberated Brunswick, and our next objective was Magdeburg on the western bank of the Elbe River. Unknown to us at this time, the Elbe River had been designated as the "political boundary" between the Allied and Russian armies.

In between Brunswick and Magdeburg was the city of Hillersleben, where there was a large German Luftwaffe airbase with many two-story barracks buildings housing German personnel who had recently been evicted from Hillersleben by the 30th Infantry Division.

At this point, a small task force, led by the 743rd Tank Battalion, with infantrymen of the 119th Regiment, was mounted on their tanks. As they were forging ahead toward Magdeburg, they entered the small town of Farsleben, about 10 kilometers west of Magdeburg, with the mission of clearing out all of the German soldiers who may be waiting there for us, and may have set up an ambush.

Upon entering and capturing the village, no German soldiers were found who may have been intent on setting up an ambush when we appeared. The lead elements of the 743rd Recon, however, discovered a long freight train on the railroad track, which had been guarded by several Nazi guards. The engine was standing ready with a full head of steam and awaiting orders. The guards and the train crew fled the area as soon as they realized that they were well outnumbered, although they were rounded up in a short time.

While the train crew was awaiting orders where to go, many of the occupants of some of the passenger cars had dismounted and were relaxing on the ground near the train.

This train which contained about 2,500 Jews, had a few days previously left the Bergen-Belsen death camp. Men, women, and children were all loaded into a few available railway cars, some passenger and some freight, but mostly the typical antiquated freight cars, termed as "40 & 8." WWI terminology, this signified that these cars would accommodate 40 men or 8 horses.

They were crammed into all available space and the freight cars were packed with about 60–70 of the Jewish Holocaust victims, with standing room only for most of them, so that they were packed in like sardines.

Why those people had not been exterminated earlier we never did learn. The Nazis, however, were attempting to move them out of Bergen-Belsen so that the advancing Allied army would not see the condition of this mass of frail humanity, if it could be called that. They had been moved eastward from the camp to the Elbe River, where they were informed that it would not be advisable to proceed farther because of the rapidly advancing Russian army. The train then reversed direction and proceeded to Farsleben, where they were then told that they were heading into the advancing American army. The train halted at Farsleben and was awaiting further orders as to where to go next. The engineers had then received their orders: to drive the train onto the bridge over the Elbe River and either blow it up or just drive it off the end of the damaged bridge, with all of the cars of the train crashing into the river, and killing or drowning all of the occupants. The engineers were having some second thoughts about this action, as they would be hurtling themselves to death, too. This is the point at which they were discovered, just shortly after the leading elements of the 743rd Tank Battalion arrived on the scene.

Some of these prisoners had dismounted from the passenger cars and were milling about near the train and relaxing, as best they could, under the watchful eyes of their Nazi guards. Those in the freight cars were still locked in the cars when discovered.

The men of the 743rd Tank Battalion and the 119th Regiment, who discovered this train, could not believe what they were seeing, nor what they had upon their hands at this moment. Upon speaking to some of those victims, a few of whom could speak a little English, they began to learn what they had uncovered.

They immediately unlocked all of the freight cars and allowed these pathetic victims to be released, dismount from the cars, and enjoy their first taste of freedom. Many were hesitant at first because they had been advised by their Nazi guards that, "If and when they ever became prisoners of the Americans, they would be executed immediately." Little did they know what to expect at the hands of these savage Americans.

Being packed in these antiquated freight cars for a long, undetermined time, receiving rations only once a day, consisting of a thin and cold potato soup, it was surprising that more of them were not dead.

They were packed in there so tightly that they did not have room to sit or lay down, so they just had to stand upright until they collapsed and crumpled to the floor because of exhaustion. They had no sanitary facilities except a single bucket in one corner of the car, which most could not even reach as the sudden necessity arose. The consequence was that most, in having to relieve themselves, just urinated and had bowel movements, and just let it run down their legs! Such a stench! Such humiliation for these people to have to endure! Needless to say, the stench from the cars was almost unbearable, and many of our men had to rush away and vomit.

We had heard of the cruel treatment that the Nazis had been handing out to Jews and political opponents of the Nazi regime, whom they had enslaved, but we thought that it was propaganda and slightly exaggerated. As we went along, it became more apparent that this barbaric savagery was actually true. The stories of German inhumanity were being corroborated before our own eyes. The condition of these people had deteriorated to the lowest level imaginable.

During this European war, I was a first lieutenant and was a liaison officer between the 30th Infantry Division HQ and the 120th Regimental HQ. During this time I was closely associated with 1st Lieutenant Floyd Mitchell (now deceased), who was the liaison officer from the 743rd Tank Battalion. We became very close friends during the war, exchanging many stories and assisting in our duties along the way. It was through Floyd that I had the experience of visiting the site of this tragic scene at Farsleben.

After the initial discovery and capture of Farsleben, the 743rd Tank Battalion had to move on toward Magdeburg and assist in the attack on this city as quickly as possible. At this point, the custody of guarding this very sad group of humanity fell to the 823rd Tank Destroyer Battalion.

Of primary importance was getting food, water, and medical assistance to these victims. Our 105th Medical Battalion was called upon to survey the group and provide immediate attention to those most in need. The 823rd Tank Destroyer Battalion commander, Lt. Col. Dettmer, immediately contacted the Burgomeister of Farsleben, and without any hesitation, ordered the Burgomeister to order his citizens to gather up all of the food, clothing, soap, and sanitary supplies, to help these victims. Second, they were ordered to offer them any housing facilities that were available, particularly for the elderly and those families with children.

The German people caused these victims to be in the situation in which they were found, so it was felt that it was their responsibility to rectify what they had done to them over the past five years. At first they rebelled at these orders, but upon the threat of execution of the Burgomeister, and with a pistol held to his *head, the citizens of Farsleben complied and went about the task that they had been ordered to do.*

At this time the Burgomeister *began to cooperate, and told his citizens to take some of these Jews into their homes and give them some comfort, which they did, very grudgingly. This was the first taste of "Home" for many of them after some months or years of inhuman incarceration.*

Since my duties as a liaison officer were at a minimum at this point, I was placed in charge of procuring sufficient vehicles on which these 2,500 Jewish victims could be loaded, and to relocate them to Hillersleben, about 10 kilometers distant.

It must be noted here that in most cases, it was not possible to drive directly from "point A to point B," which may in fact be only 5 to 10 kilometers. With bridges on all main roads either bombed or deliberately blown up by the retreating German army, it required navigating over many secondary and unimproved farm roads to find a suitable route to get from "point A to point B," which in some cases was 25 to 30 kilometers.

Having driven over these roads for the previous few days, I was relatively familiar with these deviations, and was thus chosen for this job.

After loading up these Jewish victims on our trucks and navigating the convoy over a circuitous route, we arrived at the designated site in Hillersleben, where their custody was turned over to the American Military Government for further processing.

First they were deloused! Their bodies and clothing were totally infested with lice, so they were heavily dusted with DDT; stripped of their clothing, which was burned; given a shower; then re-supplied with adequate clothing, which had been furnished by the people of Farsleben.

Settled in to their new surroundings, here they were given appropriate medical care according to their needs, and fed with adequate but rationed food. They were eventually processed for repatriation to their homelands.[18]

At first, Allied generals regarded Magdeburg as a relatively easy objective and they all hoped that the garrison there would surrender without a fight. The surrender ultimatum had been issued, but emphatically rejected by the German colonel there who accentuated his resolution to resist by placing *SS* soldiers around the perimeter of the town. So having failed to secure the surrender, the 30th Division, supported by elements of the 2nd Armored Division, was ordered to attack from the north while other US units moved in from the southern perimeter. Looking above they would have seen the terrifying spectacle of 15 German Me 262 jet fighters streaming through the air to strafe their positions, but their appearance, albeit impressive, was far too late to alter the inevitable outcome of the fight. The battered and haggard remnants of the German *12th Army*, although comprised mostly from hurriedly assembled units, provided sufficient resistance to prevent an easy assault on the town. After two days of fighting against the overwhelming power of the 30th Division, however, they finally capitulated.

JOHN O'HARE, COMPANY E, 117TH INFANTRY REGIMENT

Silver Star Action: Our objective was Magdeburg on the Elbe River. It had been an important German city since the Middle Ages. Like many European cities the western approach to Magdeburg involved an abrupt transition from crop land to urban development and multi-story buildings. The crop land seemed very flat and expansive. It had no cross fences or outbuildings for an unusual distance. My company, like the others involved in the attack, was spread out in an attack pattern with men far enough apart to limit casualties from a single artillery or mortar shell. Tanks of the 743rd Tank Battalion were interspersed among us in the usual fashion. None of us rode on the back of the tanks this time.

The 2nd Armored Division had attempted to enter the city the day before but was repulsed. Now the 2nd Armored and the 30th Division were attacking together. As we progressed through the fields, one of the tankers yelled at a few of us nearby. He shouted, "Let's have some infantry out there in front of the tanks, there could be krauts out there with Panzerfausts." *We joined the good-natured banter replying, "You have armor all around you. We are just wearing shirts!"*

As usual, I was carrying an M1 rifle, a belt, two bandoliers full of ammunition, two hand-grenades, a bayonet, and a bazooka. To the dismay of some of the boys who feared an explosion, I habitually carried a high-explosive rocket in the bazooka. The rocket was locked in place inside the bazooka, but a safety device remained in place and the wires necessary for firing were not attached to the ignition system. In addition to me, our bazooka team included Howard "Duke" Benz and Al Riccio. "Duke" and Al each carried a canvas bag containing three rounds of bazooka ammunition in protective canisters. Both of them were married and each was the father of at least one young child.

This attack differed from others because for the first time I could see B-17 "Flying Fortresses" in action. They were bombing the downtown area as we approached through the fields. In the distance, I could see individual bombs join the stream flowing out of the planes.

As we entered the urban area, we passed the first two streets without incident. When we reached the wider third street we quickly realized that well-hidden snipers would have a commanding view of any movement we might make. Across the street was a three-story apartment building. It apparently extended on the right to an intersecting side street. There was a bar on the first floor near the side street. A recessed doorway apparently led to the apartments upstairs. The apartment entrance seemed to be wide open. Without any coordination, four of us quickly dashed across the street and into the apartment entrance.

We had learned the art of street fighting in other cities. We sensed that the third street would soon become a hot spot. Sometimes there is a brief window of opportunity, perhaps seconds, when spontaneous, audacious moves will succeed. Perhaps it is that instant when a defender is shocked by his first glimpse of a determined enemy invader. The opportunity fades quickly, but young men are capable of quick, decisive moves and they are fast runners.

Claude Hudson, Louis Polasek, a man whose name I can't remember, and I dashed across the street and through the open apartment door without any pre-arrangement. We intuitively knew it was a "now or never" opportunity. First, the four of us searched the second- and third-floor apartments. We found them unoccupied and learned that although the building wrapped around the corner, there were walls separating the apartments facing the two streets and there were no connecting corridors. Polasek and the other man took up positions near the most strategically located windows. Hudson and I went back down to further explore the first level.

On the first floor, a corridor ran from the main apartment door to the bar on the corner, but once again a wall separated the bar from the rest of the building that faced the side street. A quick glance through the swinging half-door leading to the bar made us aware that a barricade of rubble had been bulldozed into place on the side street near the back end of the bar. We knew that barricades were often found near German "strong points" and this began to resemble one. We considered the Germans to be very efficient and reasoned that there must be some connecting link uniting the entire building. Through elimination, we concluded that the connecting link must be the basement. When we opened the basement door and started down the stairs, we realized that there were no windows to admit light. We also found the basement flooded with water up to our knees. There was a shaft of light apparently coming from a side door well down the corridor. We waded through the water in the direction of the light source. When we got close, we could see stacks of shells for a big gun on the stairs leading up to the side door. We were suddenly aware that we were in a German ammunition dump and realized that it must be there to serve a big gun on the side street. Hudson and I were the only Americans with this knowledge.

We went back to the ground floor. Once again I looked over the half-door leading to the bar and this time I focused very carefully on the entire barricade across the side street. There it was! *The muzzle of some type of cannon projected through the barricade at a point very close to the building we occupied. At about the same time of this discovery we heard the sound of tank motors. Rushing to the main apartment entrance, I saw three American light tanks slowly moving up the street in the direction of the side street. They were unaware of the anti-tank gun. I realized that my shouts of "Stop!" could not be heard due to the noise of the tank motors, so I held up my hands and used body language to signal the "Stop!" message.*

The commander of the lead tank stopped it and stuck his head out to find out why I was making such emphatic gestures. He was immediately shot in the head by a sniper and slumped back into the tank. Now the three tanks were stopped in the street. They could not have effectively dealt with the hidden anti-tank weapon. Their vulnerable sides would have been exposed long before they could make a left turn down the side street to face the gun and even the armor on the front of a US light tank would have been no match for a German anti-tank gun. It was my time to do something!

Returning to the bar area, I tried to visualize how I could approach the anti-tank gun with my bazooka while keeping the element of surprise.

The big plate glass windows of the bar facing the side street had been blown out long before, perhaps during an air raid. The sill which had supported the windows about two feet above the floor level remained in place. I decided on a course of action and began to implement it. With my bazooka in hand, I began crawling on the floor of the bar. First, I crawled along the west wall of the room and then crawled parallel to the side street, always keeping below the top of the sill which had formerly supported the large windows. When I got close to the barricade, I turned on my side. I took the rocket out of the bazooka, removed the safety device, then locked it back in the tube. Next, I attached the ignition wires to the appropriate quills at the back of the bazooka and it was ready to fire. I suddenly stood up as close to the barricade as I could get and fired point-blank at the gun. My own explosion instantly blew me backward, off my feet, and I was once again invisible to the enemy below the two-foot sill. After crawling back to the bar entrance, I rejoined my Platoon for our next movement. Much later, I was surprised to learn that I had been cited for gallantry in action and awarded the Silver Star.

Years later I learned that the action had been observed from across the street by Major Warren Giles and he recommended the award. Major Giles rose to the rank of Major General before the end of his service.

The Battle of Magdeburg lasted two days. During the afternoon of the first day we reached a point where forward progress was stopped because an anti-aircraft 88 had been deflected to fire at street level. Our platoon was passing through a small urban park when we were stopped by the artillery fire. A little hillside had been cut into to build a small kiosk or newsstand. While we were forced to halt and take cover, I crawled into the kiosk low spot and stretched out. Apparently my feet remained in view by the soldiers following me. "Doc" Toothman, our platoon medic, observed that my feet were not moving. He called my name several times but received no response so he came running over to me. When he arrived he realized that I was sound asleep. He gave me a kick and said, "Damn you, O'Hare! I came running down here because I saw your feet were sticking out and not moving. I called but there was no answer—and I find you asleep!" We were very good friends, but often engaged in a special "soldier's humor."

Still later on the first day of the battle, we reached what had been a tall building close to the downtown area. It had been a fine hotel. The building was in ruins but someone discovered that the wine cellar was intact. We had no water but after this discovery we were well supplied with champagne. The wine cellar had been "liberated." It took most of another day to reach the Elbe. It had been decided at Yalta, or another Big Three Conference, that we would stop at the west bank of the Elbe, so we ended our forward motion at Magdeburg. The wine cellar was declared "Officer Supply," but GIs of questionable discipline were placed on guard at the hotel and the "Supply" continued to shrink.[19]

KING KENNY, RECONNAISSANCE PLATOON, 823RD TANK DESTROYER BATTALION

The next big thing I remember was a major attack on the city of Magdeburg. We bunked down in a house the night before at a location from which we could see Magdeburg. The next morning, around daylight, we were to move out, and it was going to be our last major attack against Magdeburg. The next day I was lying in a field waiting for the word to "jump off" when another soldier lay down next to me. He had a "bird" on his shoulder. It was Colonel Branner Purdue, commander of the 120th Infantry Regiment. He said, "What time do you have?" I told him, "About five minutes to go until jumping off." He said, "Good luck!" I jumped on the back of a tank with another guy and since I always fired at church steeples because the Germans would use them for observation for artillery spotting, I fired its .50-caliber machine gun up into the steeple. The tanker then broke open the hatch and said, "You're killing us in here. The noise is driving us crazy!" So we jumped off, this other guy and I, and we moved up to a bunch of zigzag trenches that had been abandoned.

There was no resistance until we got into town. An infantry guy from one of the other companies came over, maybe from the 120th, and said, "I don't know where I am supposed to be. I can't find my squad." I said, "Well, stay with us." I was near a telephone poll, they were aluminum or metal, and all of a sudden there was a boing! *Some German from a window was shooting at me. I told the infantry guy, "Take him out, he's shooting at me!" I got real thin in a short period of time, I can tell you that!*

Somebody then said, "That's a bank, get a bazooka and let's see if there's a safe!" So we went into the basement and blew the safe with a bazooka, but there was nothing in it, just some Czech money, which we took. We were near the river and there was a big warehouse full of liquor there. We said, "Don't tell anybody," but shoot, within two hours, vehicles were backing up to it and loading up on all the booze. It had been a German booze warehouse.[20]

VICTOR NEILAND, COMPANY F, 117TH INFANTRY REGIMENT

We moved out the next morning at 1000 hours. We were very disappointed as we had just finished fighting in Rogatz and had lost a lot of people there. We slept in a bed in a house that some Danish people owned. There were three of us to a bed and we sure were disappointed to move out for Magdeburg!

We walked a long way, stopping and digging holes. . . . Artillery was going over us as we approached Magdeburg. There was small arms fire and many bullets came very close. We kept going with tanks and artillery supporting us.

We finally made it into town. . . . Some of the other platoons caught hell. . . . We started searching houses and broke down doors. . . . Tanks assembled in the main square. . . . A tank kept up firing its machine gun and shooting its 75mm and knocked out a [German] 40mm gun which had inflicted many casualties on our company. Panzerfausts *were being used against our tanks and we were subjected to sniper fire. We started out and advanced by the railroad bridge until we hit the river, searching houses along the way. . . . Mortars and heavy machine guns moved in with us later. . . . There was incoming and outgoing artillery fire.*[21]

FRANCIS CURREY, COMPANY K, 120TH INFANTRY REGIMENT

Madgeburg got worked over that morning by the Air Corps. I had a lead platoon group in our sector and the Germans had time to organize a defense. They had the streets pretty well covered, especially the key intersections. The street we were coming in on was at the main intersection and there was a machine gun dug in about halfway up; we couldn't move.

I thought, "What the hell are we going to do now?" I was a platoon leader at the time and I don't think I had a guy in my platoon that was over 21 years old. I met with my three squad leaders and said, "You see the third story up there? There is a balcony, which is right over that German machine-gun nest. There's a side door there. If we can get to the staircase, we can get up there." We backtracked down the block. There was a steel door and we started hammering on that god-damn door. We got it open, we ran up one landing, two landings, and then we got there and there was someone in there. The door was locked. I had a whole squad with me, Schinn's squad as well. We kicked in the front door, and there was a German family, a woman, a teenage girl, and a guy. The guy was shaving and the mother and the daughter were having breakfast. They were nonchalant and kept on going like we didn't exist! There was the kitchen, the living room, then the balcony. I took my helmet off and took a look over the balcony and there were the three Germans in the machine-gun nest. Schinn had the best BAR man I had ever trained. He was good so I told Schinn to send him. I told him, "Sneak up and first take a peak, get ready, get yourself set, take your BAR, lean over the railing and give him the whole goddamn clip. Make sure you get all three." He went up and I went with him. He just edged out of that balcony onto the railing and Wham!, *he got all three of them. He was a good BAR man and a good guy.*

Later, on one of the bombed-out streets, I took the lead. We came up to an intersection, which was also pretty well bombed out, so I decided to scout ahead. I approached a stoop near a door. European stoops are four or five feet high, four steps, and then a door. I saw the door start to open so I ducked behind a pile of rubble. As I was watching, a guy stuck his head out. It was a German soldier. He saw nothing and came out on the steps. I was carrying an M1 and I got him right in the chest. He tumbled ass-over-head down those steps. I waited a second to see and there was no movement. I went up to him and he was dead, he was a German MP. He had a nice Luger holster, brand new. I took the whole thing, belt and all. I had a feeling this was the last of the war. On the other side of the river we are coming up to Berlin. While making sure to get his Luger, I observed there was a live German soldier beyond the pile of rubble. Son of a bitch! He had a goddamn gun aimed right at me, not very far away. Oh, shit! How careless could I get? I steeled myself and he fired at me. He had a single-shot Mauser and it put a hole in my pack. By the time I fired mine, he was gone. It turned out it was a nice 1942 Mauser Luger!

We came to the main square. There was a big German pillbox right in the middle of the square. We couldn't do anything about it. I told the guys, there was just one firing point and to stay away from it. No one was firing from it, but they weren't surrendering. I got one of my guys up onto our shoulders onto the roof of the pillbox. It had a flat roof. There was a vent pipe coming out. He took a phosphorus grenade and dropped it down there. It went off and they came out. This guy, a German officer, said, "That's the Lord Mayor of Madgeburg." He first asked me to give my rank and then he said he wouldn't surrender to me. He needed to surrender to an officer. My company commander came by and I said, "Hey, Plummer, I have this guy here and he won't surrender to me. He will only surrender to you." The German officer came back and I thought we had Hermann Göring there, a big fat slob with the uniform and the medals and all that. He gave Plummer the Hitler salute and he said, "Sir, I am the Lord Mayor of Magdeburg." Plummer looked at him and said, "Shit, get in line with the rest of them!"

That was the end of the war for us. We had a young German soldier, maybe 18 or 19, our age, who was hit in the thigh and our guys were giving him a cigarette and chatting with him. So we decided to check out a German army hospital south of there and we decided to take him there. He received the German equivalent of the Purple Heart, which he gave to me for a few packs of cigarettes.[22]

HAROLD WILLIAMS, 105TH ENGINEER COMBAT BATTALION

We were so happy that Magdeburg was the last big thrust. It was hard for us to imagine that the Germans who were giving up were old men, a bunch of pretty scary looking people. Some were no more than 15- or 16-year-old boys. They had used every resource to resist to the end. There were lines and lines and lines of prisoners. Still coming through to the front were US tanks and trucks with materiel. It must have been mind boggling for the prisoners walking one way on the autobahn to the American side with all this equipment coming at them.[23]

On 18 April 1945, the war in Europe had witnessed its last battle. A few days later on 25 April, units from the Soviet Red Army made contact with US troops in the vicinity of Torgau; during the night of 4 May soldiers from Company G, 119th Infantry Regiment met with their Russian counterparts beside the banks of the River Elbe. Major General Hobbs sat down to dinner with Russian General Bagilevsky at the 117th Regiment's CP in Magdeburg. While they were communicating through translators, a message came though that Germany had agreed to unconditional surrender. The war was officially over and now, at last, the Old Hickorymen could finally lay down their arms and look forward to returning home.

HANK STAIRS, HEADQUARTERS COMPANY, 117TH INFANTRY REGIMENT

After Magdeburg, the war was over for us. We were ordered to halt at the river and wait for the Russians. It was a disappointment for us because we had fought our asses off all that time and we should be able to charge in and take Berlin. Sometime around 7 or 8 May, 4 or 5 of us decided to go down to a bridge to meet the Russians. There was no verbal communication whatsoever. They wanted

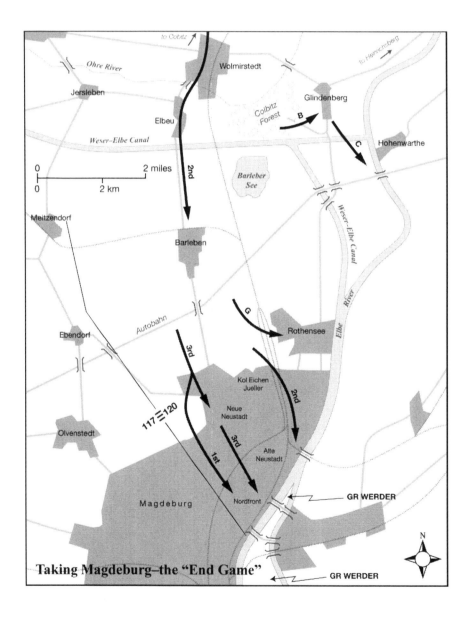

Taking Magdeburg—the "End Game"

*American cigarettes, which, of course, we gave them. I had alcohol and lemon pow-
der in my canteen, so I offered a Russian a drink. He took it and then he offered
me a drink, which must have been high-grade vodka. I took a mouthful and swal-
lowed it. It was like fire going in and the whole way down. I couldn't speak; it
sure cleaned the passage way out!* [24]

KING KENNY, RECONNAISSANCE PLATOON,
823RD TANK DESTROYER BATTALION

*Engineers had built a flat boat, and we would go across the river at night and
party with the Russians. Officials had given the Russians our plates to make
money which we called "Eisenhower Marks" and they were identical to ours. These
guys had satchels full of money. So we'd take out a dollar and write our name on
it and give it to the Russians. They would reach into their bag and they didn't
know a one dollar bill from a thousand dollar bill, and they'd take a hundred. He'd
write his name on it, and we'd say, "Okay." That was good business! The war was
over on 8 May. We did have a ceremony with the Russians, but I wasn't there.*

*After that, we started moving south to little towns and because I was a ser-
geant they gave me the authority to have the "say-so" in that town. The people
would line up in the morning to ask for permission to visit the next town. We had
a guy who had been a German guard at a prisoner of war camp. We had met some
GI prisoners and they said he had been really good to them, so we made him chief
of police. We called him Dick Tracy. There was a game reserve nearby and he'd
bring back deer for dinner. He'd shoot them with machine guns (we let him take
the jeep with the machine guns). We ate grouse, pheasant, and venison. Women
there were doing our laundry and they would fix the meals. We lived in a civilian
house. Later, we moved to a town called Ash, on the Czech border. We had the
Czech money (from the bank) so we decided we might as well use it. We had to go
through a Russian outpost and just waved, but we didn't speak Russian. We went
into the town and got lace tablecloths and wooden flutes. That was on 3 June, my
21st birthday. Earlier on that day, the guy who called for the bazooka to blow the
safe, said to me, "Hey it's your birthday. I've got a jeep so let's go to Czechoslova-
kia." I thought he had cleared it, but he hadn't. We took the jeep for a joyride. Later,
the Captain said to me, "Kenny if it wasn't for your record, you would be a private!" We moved down south, then left from Marseilles, and came home. They
had a band to greet us and a big sign up on the hill that said, "Well done."* [25]

VICTOR NEILAND, COMPANY F, 117TH INFANTRY REGIMENT

In early May, after several weeks of isolated fighting, we moved south near the

Czech border to prevent the SS *from regrouping. Nothing developed. We did round up* Werewolves, *however, who were teenagers who threw hand grenades through the windows of the nice houses we stayed in at night.*[26]

FRANCIS CURREY, COMPANY K, 120TH INFANTRY REGIMENT

We went down to Bavaria as the army of occupation; that was the best part of my army life. It was beautiful country. They sent us to disarm the German army down there. When in Bavaria, you would take over a village and then you were the mayor. You would set up roadblocks and other GI stuff. I had my own jeep and a driver. I was checking roadblocks one morning, going down this highway, and I had a rifleman with me in the jeep. Right in front of us came a German pickup truck with four soldiers, towing a cannon, going down to where they were sup-posed to surrender. We pulled up behind them. So there were these four Germans with rifles; they'd never seen combat but they were still soldiers. They were glaring at me and I told the soldier in the back, "For God's sake, don't put your hands on that rifle!"

I was at Division Headquarters at that time because I knew my medal was coming through. I had nothing to do so I used go down to my old company and my old platoon. I went down to where they were disarming a group one day and got shot! The first sergeant, we had gone through the war together, was responsible for me. My God! When they took me in the ambulance, First Sergeant's face was white. He said, "What the hell!" They took me all the way back to different hos-pitals in France where they took the bullet out. I was located with the enlisted men. I remember this one colonel in charge of the hospital came up to my bed, and said, "Who in the hell are you?" I told him I was a tech sergeant and about the medal, and he said to me, "This general keeps calling me and wants me to give him a personal report on you every morning."

We left there in August 1945. We were scheduled to go to Japan for the inva-sion, but by the time we got home and had the 90-day furlough the war was over.[27]

Many Allied divisions fought with great distinction during WWII, but there were few that spent as many consecutive days in combat as the 30th. Eventually they would return home, try pick up their lives where they left off, and just carry on. On 25 November, the 30th Division would be deacti-vated, but none of those who were there would ever forget.

VICTOR NEILAND, COMPANY F, 117TH INFANTRY REGIMENT

The 30th Division was outstanding. We had good leadership, especially the assis-

tant division commander, Brigadier General Harrison. He was excellent and he was always out front. He led the division through the breakout in Normandy and in the Bulge he led our effort at Stoumont. Also, Major General Hobbs was an excellent division commander. He kept us well supplied and equipped. He instilled the importance of keeping the units well supplied throughout the division. Our unit had a lot of experienced leadership—captains, majors, and colonels—and that really helped. They always knew what to do. We also had excellent artillery and our positions were well protected. We had high morale and that started from the beginning with all the guys from the Carolinas and Tennessee.[28]

KING KENNY, RECONNAISSANCE PLATOON, 823RD TANK DESTROYER BATTALION

The camaraderie existed not only between units, but between personnel within units. I remember after I got knocked out at the end, I went up the next day after the town was taken to look at the jeep that I was knocked out in and the damaged M8s on the side of the road. I was looking at the jeep and a replacement said to me, "Was that your jeep?" and I said, "Yes." He said, "I wouldn't want your job." I then said to him, "I wouldn't want yours." It boiled down to the squads. We trained together and we were ready, we knew each other. We knew the names of one another's families and girlfriends. Most of the guys weren't married; I don't think anyone was married. We had been together from January 1943 to May 1945. You counted on them. If somebody told me to go and get a couple of guys to go forward, I knew whoever I took with me was going to have my back. Eisenhower said the war was won on the initiative of the NCOs. The Germans waited to be told to do something and they did it. An American non-com would say, "Spread out, I'll take the right, you take the left." The non-coms took the initiative without being ordered to do so. If they got in a tight spot they took over.[29]

JOHN NOLAN, COMPANY G, 119TH INFANTRY REGIMENT

I joined the 30th Division as a replacement on 6 September 1944 at Tournai, Belgium. I was assigned as a Squad Leader of the 3d Squad, 1st Platoon, G Company, 119th Infantry Regiment. I was "green," and was given seven "green" privates. By the end of the war my squad of eight had "collected" ten Purple Hearts. One member never got hit. Of the other seven, one got three, one got two, and five got one each. I believe not more than three were "accrued" during the Bulge. I "picked-up" mine near Hildeshine on 7 April 1945. I remember one or two occurred when we attacked Merzenhauzen on 22 November 1944. You must understand that G Company was home to us, and when we got hit we made sure that when the hospital(s) released us we made sure to return to our home. *Of the eight members of the original 3rd Squad, we had one KIA. It was David Hedland, our BAR man. At the end of the Bulge there were only 14 remaining of the almost 40 in the company. We watched each other's back. Every attack, there was a chance we were going to get hit; we were a band of brothers. We accomplished our objectives expeditiously. We did it as quickly as possible. The 30th was top notch!* [30]

You could take the men out of the division but you could never take the division out of the men. There would be annual meetings, commemorations and memorials but the reunions would become less well attended with each year that passed, although the memory of those days, weeks and months in Europe would remain with those men for the rest of their lives. Now their skin may be wrinkled with age and the hairlines may have receded, maybe their eyes and ears don't work like they used to do, but in their hearts they are young warriors and the deeds of Old Hickory will live on.

CITATION FOR ACTION IN GERMANY

First Lieutenant, Raymond O. Beaudoin, Company F, 119th Infantry Regiment. Hamelin, Germany, 6 April 1945. Medal of Honor citation: He was leading the 2d Platoon of Company F over flat, open terrain to Hamelin, Germany, when the enemy went into action with machineguns and automatic weapons, laying down a devastating curtain of fire which pinned his unit to the ground. By rotating men in firing positions he made it possible for his entire platoon to dig in, defying all the while the murderous enemy fire to encourage his men and to distribute ammunition.

He then dug in himself at the most advanced position, where he kept up a steady fire, killing 6 hostile soldiers, and directing his men in inflicting heavy casualties on the numerically superior opposing force. Despite these defensive measures, however, the position of the platoon became more precarious, for the enemy had brought up strong reinforcements and was preparing a counterattack. Three men, sent back at intervals to obtain ammunition and reinforcements, were killed by sniper fire. To relieve his command from the desperate situation, 1st Lt. Beaudoin decided to make a 1-man attack on the most damaging enemy sniper nest 90 yards to the right flank, and thereby divert attention from the runner who would attempt to pierce the enemy's barrier of bullets and secure help. Crawling over completely exposed ground, he relentlessly advanced, undeterred by 8 rounds of bazooka fire which threw mud and stones over him or by rifle fire which ripped his uniform. Ten yards from the enemy position he stood up and charged. At point-blank range he shot and killed 2 occupants of the nest; a third, who tried to bayonet him, he overpowered and killed with the butt of his carbine; and the fourth adversary was cut down by the platoon's rifle fire as he attempted to flee.

He continued his attack by running toward a dugout, but there he was struck and killed by a burst from a machinegun. By his intrepidity, great fighting skill, and supreme devotion to his responsibility for the well-being of his platoon, 1st Lt. Beaudoin single-handedly accomplished a mission that enabled a messenger to secure help which saved the stricken unit and made possible the decisive defeat of the German forces. Entered service at: Holyoke, Mass.[31]

EPILOGUE

We, the authors of this volume, have decided to leave the last word to a noble, clever veteran.

JOHN O'HARE, COMPANY E, 117TH INFANTRY REGIMENT

Reflections on Fifteen Minutes in a Small Rhineland Town: Experienced soldiers instinctively keep a running assessment of the danger level they face. My gauge stood at "low risk" late one afternoon in January or early February 1945.

We were in a small town inside the German border. The Rhine had not yet been crossed and Nazi propaganda promised a reoccupation of the area. Werewolf signs were painted on many walls warning the locals that anyone cooperating with the Allies would be killed.

The local German civilians seemed more war-weary than willing to be fooled again by a propaganda message from Dr. Goebbels. They were sullen but obedient and non-confrontational. They seemed resigned to their new circumstances and ready to make the most of the fact that their town had not been destroyed. The evidence was reassuring. Even the most modest old homes had deep, substantial cellars indicating an ingrained survival instinct and realism regarding their frontier exposure. They acted more like survivors than zealots. Several of the women were wearing silk stockings in the wooden shoes then popular in the Rhineland but everyone seemed to understand that the looting of other countries would not continue. Any thoughts of resistance were offset by the current anger of many residents whose bicycles had recently been stolen by retreating German soldiers.

Our part of the Western Front seemed quiet and half of the platoon was informally present in a local saloon, which was not functioning as anything but a large place to gather. The owner of the bar had been humiliated earlier when one of the soldiers found a large framed photo of Hitler hidden in a closet where it would have been convenient for rehanging in case Dr. Goebbels had been correct about a resurgent German offensive.

Private Blank was there (I don't remember his real name), and he was obviously drunk. He was normally very quiet and his one source of pride lay in the fact that he had been in the "Regular Army" before America began preparing for war.

Sergeant Stone (not his real name) was also there. He was not too bright and he was more like a cranky old woman than natural leader of men. He had been drafted early in the "preparedness period" and had gained sergeant-status in spite of his inadequacies. I noticed a circle of onlookers forming as Private Blank began unloading his grievances on Sergeant Stone. He said Stone was a prime example of how stupid draftees were being promoted and they were ruining the Army. His taunts became personal and bitter and he pointed his rifle at Stone's chest as his complaints became very heated. As Blank became more irrational, I began to maneuver into a position behind him to be able to disarm him and prevent a tragedy. He became aware of me, swung around, pointed the loaded rifle at me and clicked off the safety latch.

My mind flashed a very personal alarm, "Think fast, O'Hare. Now is the time to summon all the blarney you have inherited!"

I said, "Blank, I'm glad it is you who has that rifle pointed at me! I know you are Regular Army *and not one of those stupid draftees I see around here. There is one thing I know about* Regular Army *man, and that is the fact he would* never kill another American soldier."

Somehow this line of reasoning matched an idea firmly entrenched in Blank's mind. He reengaged the safety latch, lowered the rifle, and slowly handed it to one of the bystanders. No one had intervened on my behalf and the incident simply came to an end. Blank went to sleep, and Sergeant Stone remained inadequate. It was quiet again on our little part of the Western Front.[1]

UNITS OF THE 30TH INFANTRY DIVISION

COMMANDING GENERALS

Major General Henry D. Russell—September 1940–April 1942
Major General William H. Simpson—May 1942–July 1942
Major General Leland S. Hobbs—September 1942–September 1945

ORGANIZATION OF THE DIVISION

117th Infantry Regiment (Tennessee National Guard)
118th Infantry Regiment (South Carolina National Guard)—Relieved
    from Division 24 August 1942
119th Infantry Regiment (North Carolina National Guard)—Assigned
    to Division 1 September 1942
120th Infantry Regiment (North Carolina National Guard)
121st Infantry Regiment (Georgia National Guard)—Transferred to 8th
    Infantry Division 22 November 1941.
113th Field Artillery Battalion (155mm)
115th Field Artillery Battalion (75mm)—Transferred from Division 24
    August 1942.
118th Field Artillery Battalion (105mm)
197th Field Artillery Battalion (105mm)
230th Field Artillery Battalion (105mm)
30th Reconnaissance Troop (Mechanized)
105th Engineer Combat Battalion
105th Medical Battalion
30th Counter Intelligence Corp Detachment
Headquarters Special Troops
Headquarters Company, 30th Infantry Division
30th Military Police Platoon
730th Ordnance Light Maintenance Company
30th Quartermaster Company
30th Signal Company
743rd Tank Battalion
823rd Tank Destroyer Battalion

US ARMY ORGANIZATIONAL STRUCTURE

ORGANIZATIONAL STRUCTURE OF XIX CORPS US 1st ARMY

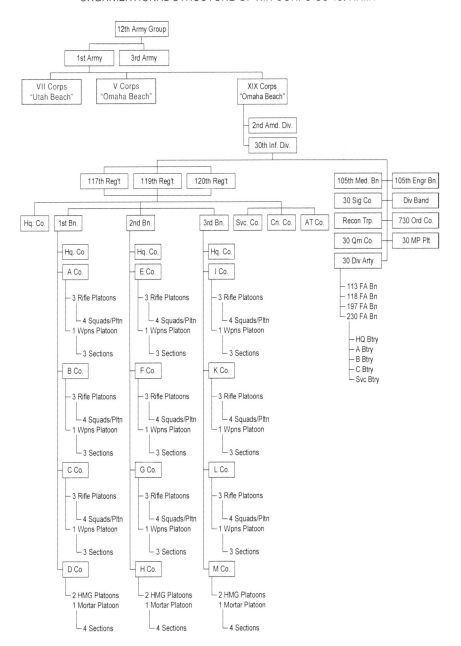

NOTES

INTRODUCTION

1. *Stars and Stripes,* "Sally's Sallies Suggest New Shoulder Patch for 30th Div." 7 January 1945, reproduced at http://www.oldhickory30th.com/REPORTS/FDRs%20SS%20article.pdf.
2. Headquarters Army Ground Forces, Army Ground Forces Fact Sheet, 1 March 1947. Record Group (RG) 407, Unit Records, file number 3 (Division #) – 0, National Archives and Records Administration (NARA), College Park, MD. Robert L. Hewitt, *Workhorse of the Western Front* (Washington, D.C.: Infantry Journal, 1946), is the source of the Presidential Units Citation (p. 282) and Purple Heart (p. 283) statistics.
3. S. L. A. Marshall letter, dated 16 March 1946, www.30thinfantry.org/marshall.shtml.

CHAPTER ONE

1. Harold Williams, interview and correspondence with author, 12 August 2014.
2. King Kenny, interview and correspondence with author, 25 August 2014.
3. Ed Middleton, interview with author, 15 August 2014.
4. Frank Denius, interview and correspondence with author, 23 April 2014.
5. William Gast, correspondence with author, 22 August 2014.
6. Frank Harper, unpublished memoir from the author's collection.
7. Middleton interview.
8. Denius interview and correspondence.
9. Marion Sanford and Jeff Rogers, *Old Hickory Recon: Memories of the 30th Infantry Division, 1943–1945* (Wetumpka, Ala.: Schweinhund, 2012); and Marion Sanford, correspondence with author via Jeff Rogers, 9 October 2014.
10. Kenny interview and correspondence.
11. Frank Towers, interview and correspondence with author, 18 April 2014.
12. Marvin Smith, "The Hedgerows: A Soldier's Memoir," http://www.oldhickory30th.com.
13. Frank Deegan, interview with author, 16 May 2014.
14. Sanford and Rogers, *Old Hickory Recon,* and Sanford correspondence.

15. Denius interview and correspondence.
16. George Schneider, "George Schneider, 120th Regiment, 30th Infantry Division," http://www.indianamilitary.org/30TH/Diary/GeorgeSchneider/GeorgeSchneider.htm.
17. Sanford and Rogers, *Old Hickory Recon,* and Sanford correspondence.
18. Williams interview and correspondence.
19. Towers interview and correspondence.
20. Gast correspondence.
21. Smith memoir.
22. Manfred Toon Thorn, notes provided by his wife, Hazel Toon Thorn, 2005, and telephone interview, November 2005.
23. Rudolf von Ribbentrop, interview with author; additional information from Rudolf von Ribbentrop's *Joachim von Ribbentrop: Mein Vater: Erlebnisse und Erinnerungen.* (Graz, Austria: Arles, 2008).
24. 230th Field Artillery Battalion, Action Against Enemy/After Action Report, dated 21 July 1944, NARA.
25. 30th Infantry Division, General Order (GO) 209.
26. 30th Infantry Division, GO 37.
27. 30th Infantry Division, GO 37.
28. 30th Infantry Division, GO 185.
29. 30th Infantry Division, GO 196.

CHAPTER TWO
1. Smith memoir.
2. Kenny interview.
3. Mark Schwendiman, personal notes provided to author by family.
4. Williams interview and correspondence.
5. Ibid.
6. John Nolan, interview and correspondence with the author, 21 April 2014.
7. Ernst Schmuck-Barkmann, interview with the author, 2003.
8. Richard Lacey interview and correspondence with author, 15 August 2014.
9. Schwendiman personal notes.
10. John O'Hare, interview and correspondence with author, 9 August 2014.
11. Charles W. McArthur. *Operations Analysis in the U.S. Army Eighth Air Force in World War II* (Providence, RI: American Mathematical Society, 1991).
12. Towers interview and correspondence.
13. Kenny interview.
14. Denius interview and correspondence.
15. Deegan interview.
16. Nolan interview and correspondence.
17. Smith memoir.

18. Denius interview and correspondence.

19. Hank Stairs, interview and correspondence with the author, 22 August 2014.

20. 30th Infantry Division Headquarters Company, After Action Report, 12 July 1944, NARA.

21. 823rd Tank Destroyer Battalion, After Action Report, 15 July 1944, NARA.

22. 30th Infantry Division, GO 20.

23. 30th Infantry Division, GO 25.

24. 30th Infantry Division, GO 37.

25. 30th Infantry Division, GO 61.

26. 30th Infantry Division, GO 60.

27. 30th Infantry Division, GO 195.

28. 30th Infantry Division, GO 25.

29. 30th Infantry Division, GO 196.

30. 30th Infantry Division, GO 195.

31. 30th Infantry Division, GO 20.

CHAPTER THREE

1. Matthew Cooper, *The German Army 1933–1945: Its Political and Military Failure* (Chelsea, Mich.: Scarborough House, 1990), 506.

2. Max Hastings, *Overlord: D-Day and the Battle for Normandy* (Westminster, Md.: Vintage, 2006), 277.

3. Schwendiman personal notes.

4. Ray Holmquist, interview with author, 16 September 2014.

5. O'Hare interview and correspondence.

6. Stairs interview and correspondence.

7. 120th Infantry Regiment, After Action Report, for the period 6–12 August 1944, dated 4 September 1944, NARA.

8. O'Hare interview and correspondence.

9. Rudolf von Ribbentrop, interview with author, and von Ribbentrop's, *Joachim von Ribbentrop.*

10. Bill Fitzgerald, interview with author, 16 September 2014.

11. Lacey interview and correspondence.

12. Sanford and Rogers, *Old Hickory Recon,* and Sanford correspondence.

13. Thorn, notes and telephone interview.

14. Kenny interview and correspondence.

15. Stairs interview and correspondence.

16. Gast correspondence.

17. Denius interview and correspondence.

18. O'Hare interview and correspondence.

19. James M. Lewis, "Repulse of the German Counterattack Aimed at Avranches, 7–11 August 1944. dated 25 August 1944. Reproduced at http://www.oldhick-

ory30th.com/30th%20artillery%20%20report%20repulse%20at%20Mortain.pdf.

20. Lacey interview and correspondence.

21. Kenny interview.

22. Stairs interview and correspondence.

23. Gunter Adam, *"Ich habe meine Pflicht erfüllt!": Ein Junker der Waffen-SS berichtet* ("I did my duty": Reports from a young man in the Waffen-SS). (Riesa, Germany: Nation & Wissen, 2012), 218.

24. Denius interview and correspondence.

25. 230th Field Artillery Battalion After Action Report, 3 October 1944, NARA.

26. 30th Infantry Division, GO 55.

27. 30th Infantry Division, GO 55.

28. 30th Infantry Division, GO 48.

29. 30th Infantry Division, GO 48.

30. Headquarters, 30th Infantry Division, Citation of Headquarters and Headquarters Company, dated 20 October 1945.

CHAPTER FOUR

1. O'Hare interview and correspondence.

2. Schneider interview with author, 13 September 2014.

3. Ibid.

4. Deegan interview.

5. Schwendiman personal notes.

6. Towers interview and correspondence.

7. Denius interview and correspondence.

8. Lacey interview and correspondence.

9. Nolan interview and correspondence.

10. Schneider memoir.

11. Sanford and Rogers, *Old Hickory Recon,* and Sanford correspondence.

12. Fitzgerald interview.

13. Francis Currey, interview, 16 October 2014.

CHAPTER FIVE

1. Heinz Günther Guderian, *From Normandy to the Ruhr: With the 116th Panzer Division in World War II* (Bedford, Penn.: Aberjona, 2001), 143 (original in city archive Aachen).

2. Schneider memoir.

3. August Gövert, interview; notes provided by Volker-Dederichs.

4. Waltraud Barth, interview with author, 19 March 2013.

5. Stairs interview and correspondence.

6. Ibid.

7. Williams interview and correspondence.

8. Nolan interview and correspondence.

9. Currey interview.

10. Stairs interview and correspondence.

11. Schwendiman personal notes.

12. David Knox, interview and correspondence with author, 16 September 2014.

13. Nolan interview and correspondence.

14. Victor Neiland, interview with author, 24 April 2015, and unpublished diary.

15. Lacey interview and correspondence.

16. Denius interview and correspondence.

17. Charles B. MacDonald, *The Siegfried Line Campaign* (Washington, D.C.: Center of Military History, 1993), 307, reproduced at http://www.history.army.mil/html/books/007/7-7-1/CMH_Pub_7-7-1.pdf.

18. Ibid., 315.

19. Williams interview and correspondence.

20. Charles Richardson, interview with author, 16 September 2014.

21. Hermann Wolz, personal notes provided by Robert Balsam (Berlin), 2009.

22. Schneider memoir.

23. Department of War, GO 48, 23 June 1945. Thanks to Frank Towers and his website, www.30thinfantry.org, for the text of the Medal of Honor citations.

24. Department of War, GO 24, 6 April 1945, www.30thinfantry.org,

25. 30th Infantry Division, GO 29.

26. Volker Dederichs personal archive

CHAPTER SIX

1. Schneider memoir.

2. Lacey interview and correspondence.

3. Stairs interview and correspondence.

4. Department of War, GO 95, 30 October 1945, www.30thinfantry.org,

CHAPTER SEVEN

1. Lacey interview and correspondence.

2. Towers interview and correspondence.

3. Sanford and Rogers, *Old Hickory Recon,* and Sanford correspondence.

4. Middleton interview.

5. Stairs interview and correspondence.

6. Currey interview.

7. Denius interview and correspondence.

8. Williams interview and correspondence.

9. Towers interview and correspondence.

10. Lacey interview and correspondence.

11. Stairs interview and correspondence.

12. Thorn interview.

13. 105th Medical Battalion, After Action Report, 2 January 1945, NARA.

14. Sanford and Rogers, *Old Hickory Recon,* and Sanford correspondence.

15. Letter from Edward Arn to the family of Mason Armstrong.

16. Stairs interview and correspondence.

17. Sanford and Rogers, *Old Hickory Recon,* and Sanford correspondence.

18. Nolan interview and correspondence.

19. Kenny interview.

20. 119th Infantry Regiment After Action Report, 2 January 1945, NARA.

21. Donald Strand, interview with author, 16 September 2014.

22. 7. Rudolf von Ribbentrop, interview with author, and von Ribbentrop's, *Joachim von Ribbentrop.*

23. 119th Infantry Regiment, After Action Report, 2 January 1945, NARA.

24. 120th Infantry Regiment, After Action Report, 3 January 1945, NARA.

25. Denius interview and correspondence.

26. Towers interview and correspondence.

27. Lacey interview and correspondence.

28. Currey interview.

29. Lacey interview and correspondence.

30. Currey interview.

31. 120th Infantry Regiment After Action Report, 3 January 1945, NARA.

32. Kenny interview.

33. Deegan interview.

34. Nolan interview and correspondence.

35. Schwendiman personal notes.

36. Department of War, GO 73, 30 August 1945, www.30thinfantry.org,

37. Department of War, GO 69, 17 August 1945, www.30thinfantry.org,

CHAPTER EIGHT

1. Kenny interview.

2. Nolan interview and correspondence.

3. 120th Infantry Regiment, After Action Report, 1 February 1945, NARA.

4. Lacey interview.

5. Neiland interview and diary.

6. Currey interview.

7. Neiland interview and diary.

8. Denius interview and correspondence.

CHAPTER NINE

1. Neiland interview and diary.

2. Stairs interview and correspondence.

3. 119th Infantry Regiment, After Action Report, 17 March 1945, NARA.

CHAPTER TEN

1. Stairs interview and correspondence.
2. O'Hare interview and correspondence.
3. Kenny interview.
4. Sanford and Rogers, *Old Hickory Recon,* and Sanford correspondence.
5. O'Hare interview and correspondence.
6. Stairs interview and correspondence.
7. Kenny interview.
8. Denius interview and correspondence.
9. 117th Infantry Regiment After Action Report, 28 March 1945, NARA.
10. 119th Infantry Regiment After Action Report, 24 March 1945, NARA.
11. 120th Infantry Regiment After Action Report, 25 March 1945, NARA.
12. Williams interview and correspondence.
13. Kenny interview.
14. Nolan interview and correspondence.
15. O'Hare interview and correspondence.
16. Nolan interview and correspondence.
17. Neiland interview and diary.
18. Towers interview and correspondence.
19. O'Hare interview and correspondence.
20. Kenny interview.
21. Neiland interview and diary.
22. Currey interview.
23. Williams interview and correspondence.
24. Stairs interview and correspondence.
25. Kenny interview.
26. Neiland interview and diary.
27. Currey interview.
28. Neiland interview and diary.
29. Kenny interview.
30. Nolan interview and correspondence.
31. Department of War, GO 9, 25 January 1946, www.30thinfantry.org,

EPILOGUE

1. O'Hare interview and correspondence.

BIBLIOGRAPHY

US DOCUMENTS

Department of the Army, Medal of Honor Citations, General Orders, April 1945–January 1946. National Archives, College Park, Md. (NARA)..

30th Infantry Division, General Orders, June 1944–May 1945. RG 407, NARA.

117th Infantry Regiment, After Action Reports, June 1944–May 1945, RG 407, NARA.

119th Infantry Regiment, After Action Reports, June 1944–May 1945, RG 407, NARA.

120th Infantry Regiment, After Action Reports, June 1944–May 1945, RG 407, NARA.

230th Field Artillery Battalion, After Action Reports, June 1944–May 1945, RG 407, NARA.

105th Engineer Combat Battalion, After Action Reports, June 1944–May 1945, RG 407, NARA.

743rd Tank Battalion, After Action Reports, June 1944–May 1945, RG 407, NARA.

823rd Tank Destroyer Battalion, After Action Reports, June 1944–May 1945, RG 407, NARA.

INTERVIEWS AND CORRESPONDENCE

Waltraud Barth, interview with author, 19 March 2013.

Francis Currey, Company K, 120th Infantry Regiment, interview with author, 16 October 2014.

Frank Deegan, Company D, 119th Infantry Regiment, interview with author, 16 May 2014.

Frank Denius, Battery C, 230th Field Artillery Battalion, interview and correspondence with author, 23 April 2014.

Bill Fitzgerald, Company E, 117th Infantry Regiment, interview with author, 16 September 2014.

William Gast, Company A, 743rd Tank Battalion, correspondence with author, 22 August 2014.

August Gövert, *116th Panzer Division "Windhund"* interview; notes provided by Volker-Dederichs.

Frank Harper, Company C, 743rd Tank Battalion, interview with author, 16 September 2014.

Knox Holder, Company M, 117th Infantry Regiment, interview with author, 16 September 2014.

Ray Holmquist, 120th Infantry Regiment, interview with author, 16 September 2014.

Henry Kaczowka, 117th Infantry Regiment, interview with author, 16 September 2014.

King Kenny, Reconnaissance Platoon, 823rd Tank Destroyer Battalion, interview and correspondence with author, 25 August 2014.

David Knox, 119th Infantry Regiment, interview with author, 16 September 2014.

Richard Lacey, Company M (Heavy Weapons), 120th Infantry Regiment, interview and correspondence with author, 15 August 2014.

S. L. A. Marshall, letter to Major General L. S. Hobbs, 16 March 1946, www.30th infantry.org/marshall.shtml.

Ed Middleton, 730th Ordnance Company, interview with author, 15 August 2014.

Victor Neiland, Company F, 117th Infantry Regiment, interview with author, 24 April 2015, and unpublished diary.

John Nolan, Company G, 119th Infantry Regiment, interview and correspondence with author, 21 April 2014.

John O'Hare, Company E, 117th Infantry Regiment, interview and correspondence with author, 9 August 2014.

Rudolf von Ribbentrop, interview with author, 8 October 2011.

Charles Richardson, 117th Infantry Regiment, interview with author, 16 September 2014.

Marion Sanford, 30th Cavalry Reconnaissance Troop (Mechanized), correspondence with author via Jeff Rogers, 9 October 2014.

Schmuck-Barkmann, Ernst, *4th Company, SS-Panzer Regiment 2,* interview, 2003.

George Schneider, Headquarters Company, 120th Infantry Regiment, interview with author, 13 September 2014.

Mark Schwendiman, Company I, 119th Infantry Regiment, personal notes provided to author by family.

Marvin Smith, Company K, 120th Infantry Regiment, "The Hedgerows: A Soldier's Memoir," http://www.oldhickory30th.com.

Hank Stairs, Headquarters Company, 117th Infantry Regiment, interview and correspondence with author, 22 August 2014.

Donald Strand, 119th Infantry Regiment, interview with author, interview with author, 16 September 2014.

Manfred Toon Thorn, *1st SS-Panzer Division "Leibstandarte Adolf Hitler,"* notes provided by his wife, Hazel Toon Thorn, 2005, and telephone interview, November 2005.

Frank Towers, Company M, 120th Infantry Regiment, interview and correspondence with author, 18 April 2014.

Harold Williams, 105th Engineer Combat Battalion, interview and correspondence with author, 12 August 2014.

Hermann Wolz, *Sturmgeschütz-Brigade 3,* personal notes provided by Robert Balsam (Berlin), 2009.

BOOKS AND ARTICLES

Adam, Günter. *9th SS-Panzer Division "Hohenstaufe," "Ich habe meine Pflicht erfüllt!": Ein Junker der Waffen-SS berichtet* ("I did my duty": Reports from a young man in the Waffen-SS). Riesa, Germany: Nation & Wissen, 2012.

Arn, Edward C. *Arn's War: Memoirs of a World War II Infantryman, 1940–1946.* Akron: University of Akron Press, 2005.

Atkinson, Rick. "Danger Zone." *World War II* (July/August 2013): 30–39.

Collins, Michael, and Martin King. *Voices of the Bulge: Untold Stories from Veterans of the Battle of the Bulge.* Minneapolis, Minn.: Zenith, 2011.

Cooke, David, and Wayne Evans. *Kampfgruppe Peiper at the Battle of the Bulge.* Mechanicsburg, Pa.: Stackpole, 2008.

Featherston, Alwyn. *Battle for Mortain: The 30th Infantry Division Saves the Breakout, August 7–12, 1944.* New York: Presidio, 1998.

Folkestad, William B. *The View from the Turret: The 743d Tank Battalion during World War II.* Shippensburg, Pa.: Burd Street, 1996.

Ford, Ken, and Howard Gerrard. *The Rhine Crossings, 1945.* New York: Osprey, 2007.

Harrison, Gordon A. *Cross-Channel Attack.* Washington: CMP, 1951.

Hewitt, Robert L. *Work Horse of the Western Front: The Story of the 30th Infantry Division.* Washington, D.C.: Infantry Journal, 1946.

Higgins, David R. *The Roer River Battles: Germany's Stand at the Westwall, 1944–45* Havertown, Pa.: Casemate, 2010.

Hymel, Kevin. "Strong Stand Atop Mortain," *WWII History* (July 2012): 48–55.

Lewis, James M. "Repulse of the German Counterattack Aimed at Avranches, 7–11 August 1944," dated 25 August 1944, reproduced at http://www.oldhickory30th.com/30th%20artillery%20%20report%20repulse%20at%20Mortain.pdf.

Charles B. MacDonald, *The Siegfried Line Campaign* (Washington, D.C.: Center of Military History, 1993), 307, reproduced at http://www.history.army.mil/html/books/007/7-7-1/CMH_Pub_7-7-1.pdf.

_____. *A Time for Trumpets: The Untold Story of the Battle of the Bulge.* New York: William Morrow, 1997.

McArthur, Charles W. *Operations Analysis in the U.S. Army Eighth Air Force in World War II.* Providence, RI: American Mathematical Society, 1991.

Mitcham, Samuel W. *The Siegfried Line.* Mechanicsburg, Pa.: Stackpole, 2009.

Pallud, Jean-Paul. *The Battle of the Bulge Then and Now.* London: Battle of Britain Prints International, 1984.

Parker, Danny. *Fatal Crossroads: The Untold Story of the Malmédy Massacre at the Battle of the Bulge.* New York: De Capo, 2011.

Reardon, Mark J. *Victory at Mortain: Stopping Hitler's Panzer Counteroffensive.* Lawrence: University Press of Kansas, 2002.

Ribbentrop , Rudolf von. *Joachim von Ribbentrop: Mein Vater: Erlebnisse und Erinnerungen.* Graz, Austria: Arles, 2008.

Rohrkamp, René. *Die "Schlacht um Aachen". Eine Rekonstruktion der militärischen Operationen im September/Oktober 1944* (The "Battle of Aachen": A Reconstruction of the military Operations in September/October 1944) (blog). http://www.freeaachen44.de/die-schlacht-um-aachen-1944.

Sanford, Marion, and Jeff Rogers, *Old Hickory Recon: Memories of the 30th Infantry Division, 1943–1945.* Wetumpka, Ala.: Schweinhund, 2012.

George Schneider, Headquarters Company, 120th Infantry Regiment, "George Schneider, 120th Regiment, 30th Infantry Division." http://www.indianamilitary.org/30TH/Diary/GeorgeSchneider/GeorgeSchneider.htm.

Stars and Stripes, "Sally's Sallies Suggest New Shoulder Patch for 30th Div., January 7, 1945.

Vannoy, Allyn R., and Jay Karamales. *Against the Panzers: United States Infantry versus German Tanks, 1944–1945.* Jefferson, N.C.: McFarland, 1996.

Weiss, Robert. *Fire Mission: The Siege at Mortain, Normandy, August 1944.* Shippensburg, Pa.: Burd Street, 2002.

Whiting, Charles. *Bloody Aachen.* Barnsley, U.K.: Leo Cooper, 1976.

Yeide, Harry. *Steel Victory.* New York: Presidio, 2003.

Zaloga, Steven. *Battle of the Ardennes 1944 (1) St. Vith and the Northern Shoulder.* New York: Osprey, 2002.

_____. *Operation Cobra 1944: Breakout from Normandy.* Westport, Conn.: Praeger, 2004.

Zaloga, Steven, and Steve Noon. *The Siegfried Line 1944–45: Battles on the German Frontier.* New York: Osprey, 2007.

UNIT HISTORIES

Adair, L. R., et al. W. H. Speer, R. Ivany, M. Q. Barbour, D. E. Taylor, F. E. Galati,

"The Battle of Mortain," Ft. Leavenworth, Kan.: Combat Studies Institute, USACGSC, 1983.

Ferriss, Franklin, "The German Offensive of 16 December: The Defeat of the 1st SS-Panzer Division, Adolf Hitler" 21 May 2001, NARA.

US Army, "Combat History of the 119th Infantry Regiment." World War Regimental Histories, Book 49. http://digicom.bpl.lib.me.us/ww_reg_his/49/.

_____. "On the way: a historical narrative of the Two-thirtieth Field Artillery Battalion, Thirtieth Infantry Division, 16 February 1942 to 8 May 1945." World War Regimental Histories, Book 136. http://digicom.bpl.lib.me.us/ww_reg_his/136/.

US Army, Wayne Robinson, and Norman E. Hamilton. "Move out, verify: the combat story of the 743rd Tank Battalion" (1945). World War Regimental Histories, Book 66. http://digicom.bpl.lib.me.us/ww_reg_his/66.

ONLINE SOURCES

www.30thinfantry.org (Frank Towers)
www.indianamilitary.org (Jim West)
www.oldhickory30th.com (Warren Watson)
teachinghistorymatters.com (Matt Rozell)

INDEX